Adventuring in Central America

The Sierra Club Adventure Travel Guides

Adventuring Along the Gulf of Mexico, by Donald G. Schueler

Adventuring Along the Southeast Coast, by John Bowen

Adventuring in Alaska, Completely revised and updated, by Peggy Wayburn

Adventuring in Arizona, by John Annerino

Adventuring in Australia, by Eric Hoffman

Adventuring in British Columbia, by Isabel Nanton and Mary Simpson

Adventuring in East Africa, by Allen Bechky

Adventuring in North Africa, by Scott Wayne

Adventuring in the Alps, by William E. Reifsnyder and Marylou Reifsnyder

Adventuring in the Andes, by Charles Frazier with Donald Secreast

Adventuring in the California Desert, by Lynne Foster

Adventuring in the Caribbean, by Carrol B. Fleming

Adventuring in Central America, by David Rains Wallace

Adventuring in the Chesapeake Bay Area, by John Bowen

Adventuring in Florida, by Allen de Hart

Adventuring in New Zealand, by Margaret Jefferies

Adventuring in the Pacific, by Susanna Margolis

Adventuring in the Rockies, Completely revised and updated, by Jeremy Schmidt

Adventuring in the San Francisco Bay Area, Completely revised and updated, by Peggy Wayburn

Trekking in Nepal, West Tibet, and Bhutan, by Hugh Swift

Trekking in Pakistan and India, by Hugh Swift

Walking Europe from Top to Bottom, by Susanna Margolis and Ginger Harmon

Adventuring in Central America

GUATEMALA
BELIZE
HONDURAS
EL SALVADOR
NICARAGUA
COSTA RICA
PANAMA

DAVID RAINS WALLACE

in association with The Wildlife Conservation Society,
the Caribbean Conservation Corporation,
and the Paseo Pantera Project

SIERRA CLUB BOOKS • SAN FRANCISCO

The Sierra Club, founded in 1892 by John Muir, has devoted itself to the study and protection of the earth's scenic and ecological resources—mountains, wetlands, woodlands, wild shores and rivers, deserts and plains. The publishing program of the Sierra Club offers books to the public as a nonprofit educational service in the hope that they may enlarge the public's understanding of the Club's basic concerns. The point of view expressed in each book, however, does not necessarily represent that of the Club. The Sierra Club has some sixty chapters coast to coast, in Canada, Hawaii, and Alaska. For information about how you may participate in its programs to preserve wilderness and the quality of life, please address inquiries to Sierra Club, 730 Polk Street, San Francisco, CA 94109.

LIBRARY OF CONGRESS CATALOGING-IN-PUBLICATION DATA
Wallace, David Rains, 1945–
    Adventuring in Central America : Guatemala, Belize, El Salvador, Honduras, Nicaragua, Costa Rica, Panama / David Rains Wallace.
        p. cm.
    Includes bibliographical references and index.
    ISBN 0-87156-473-4 (pbk.)
        1. Natural history—Central America—Guidebooks.
        2. Natural areas—Central America—Guidebooks.
        3. Central America—Guidebooks. I. Title.
    QH108.A1W35 1995
    508.72—dc20   95-1174

Production by Robin Rockey · Cover design by Bonnie Smetts · Book design by Amy Evans · Maps by Hilda Chen · Composition by Wilsted & Taylor

Printed in the United States of America on acid-free paper containing a minimum of 50% recovered waste paper of which at least 10% of the fiber content is post-consumer waste.

10 9 8 7 6 5 4 3 2 1

Contents

Acknowledgments

THIS BOOK WOULD not have been possible without generous help from many people. Chuck Carr, Kathleen Williams Jepson, and Jim Barborak of the Wildlife Conservation Society made a freelance writer's task unexpectedly pleasant in getting the project under way and keeping it on track. Susan Urstadt was helpful in making initial arrangements for the book's publication. David Carr and Eve Fewox of the Caribbean Conservation Corporation provided indispensable logistical help. John Tichenor and Kelly and Nate Bricker of World Heritage Travel Group provided much useful background material and information. For assistance and advice during research and travel, I wish to thank: Jorge Betancourt, Jim and Marguerite Bevis, Barry Bowen, Indra Candanedo, Jacinto Cedeño, Ralph Conley, Carlos Espinosa, Cecilio Estribi, Oscar Gibson, Peter Gore, Tom and Josie Harding, Carlos Hasbun, George Hassemann, Stanley Heckadon, Joe Kyle, Carlos Linares, Bruce and Carolyn Miller, Luis Moh, Kathy Moser, Balbo Mueller, Vicente Murphy, Eneida Palma, Stern Robinson, Ernesto Saqui, Tony Stocks, Nelbert Taylor, Lydia Waight, and Scott Wilbur. For reviewing the manuscript and offering many important corrections and additions, I'm grateful to: Juan Marco Alvarez, Mario Boza, Tom Divney, Maria José Gonzalez, Carlos Hasbun, Carolyn Miller, Vicente Murphy, Terry Pratt, Julieta Carrion de Samudio, Cindy Taft, and Alberto Vega.

Foreword

THIS BOOK, A PRODUCT of the Paseo Pantera project, is intended to be a service to conservation in Central America. Paseo Pantera is an effort to advance the status of wildland conservation in the Central American isthmus.

Two international conservation organizations, the Wildlife Conservation Society (WCS) and the Caribbean Conservation Corporation (CCC), are responsible for developing the Paseo Pantera project.

The Wildlife Conservation Society, since its founding in 1895 as the New York Zoological Society, has been saving wildlife and inspiring people to care about our natural heritage. Today, WCS conducts the world's leading international conservation program devoted to saving endangered species and ecosystems and manages the largest system of urban wildlife parks in the United States, including the world-famous Bronx Zoo. It has helped to establish more than 100 wildlife sanctuaries around the world. WCS manages over 270 field conservation projects in 50 countries, including those encompassed by Paseo Pantera.

The Caribbean Conservation Corporation is a Gainesville, Florida based nonprofit organization founded in 1959 and dedicated to the conservation and preservation of sea turtles and related coastal and marine wildlife through research, education, advocacy, and protection of natural areas. The CCC was founded on the pioneering work of sea turtle biologist Dr. Archie Carr, Jr. The famed Tortuguero National Park of Costa Rica, established in response to Dr. Carr's research, is a central component of the Paseo Pantera program and remains the location of a major CCC field station because the beaches of Tortuguero are the preeminent nesting grounds for green turtles in the Caribbean Basin.

Your interest in this book, and, particularly, your travel in Central America, will help the cause of the Paseo Pantera. Meanwhile, you may be assured that royalties from sales of this book will be dedicated by WCS and CCC to conservation in the region.

The protection and management of parks and reserves requires money. Money for staff; money for management plans; money for equipment and maintenance of facilities, including trails and visitor centers. Money is also vital to attend to people issues: inhabitants of the park or its perimeter, who may find themselves at odds with the park development process.

Conservationists don't have much money. We may have a lot of passion; we flare to self-righteousness about our cause—the cause of saving nature—and often we are even able to impress decision-makers with the merits of what we say. But, when asked how we might pay for the scale of conservation investment that we believe is needed, we find ourselves with few options to consider.

There are a very few options, and one of them is tourism: visitors to parks; visitors who pay fees and buy goods and services. The protected area is used in a money-earning, yet generally benign, way. The park becomes viable, especially in the frail economies of the Third World. Through tourism, conservation of wildlands earns more money for the countries of Belize and Costa Rica than any other sectors of their economies.

Tourism cannot become the sole source of support for parks. Other kinds of bolstering will always be needed, if only for the stability that such diversity might bring. But tourism yields a form of earned income, as opposed to philanthropy-dependent income; and nature tourism has the added benefit of educating the public and building support, or constituencies, for conservation.

We in the Paseo Pantera project were aware of this relationship. We also knew that the general public was unaware that in the narrow isthmus of Central America there is more of nature and culture to see, and ponder, and be moved by, than in any piece of geography of equivalent size in the world.

With this book, we hope to encourage travel in Central America. Through increased travel—call it nature tourism—we hope to improve the financial strength of parks and protected areas in Central America.

We hedged our bets by recruiting the best possible writer for the book: David Rains Wallace. What may appear as a travel guide at first glance is indeed a classic portrayal of the landscapes of Central America. We are in debt to David for the work he has done.

We negotiated with Sierra Club Books, believing that their "Adventure Travel" series was the ideal format, with the ideal traditions, to launch the English-language version of the book. For joining us in this unique publishing adventure, we are indebted to two bold editors of Sierra Club Books, Jon Beckmann and Jim Cohee.

The Paseo Pantera project was launched in 1990 by a consortium of the Wildlife Conservation Society and the Caribbean Conservation Corporation. Through a cooperative agreement with the United States Agency for International Development (USAID), we received funds to allow us to contribute to the conservation movement in Central America. Our project was based on the theme of restoring the Central American land bridge, the biotic corridor between North and South America that, in the early Pleistocene, allowed for an extraordinary exchange of plants and animals between the two continents. Among the early travelers was the progenitor of the puma, or, as we call it in Florida, the panther, *Felis concolor*, a beautiful cat that went on to occupy every continental country in the Western Hemisphere. Hence, the name, Paseo Pantera (Path of the Panther).

Restoring the Central American land bridge calls for helping existing parks in the region, and for introduction or support of numerous other strategies for improved land management. In December of 1994, at the Summit of the Americas, held in Miami, the seven republics of Central America and the United States signed the CONCAUSA treaty, pledging themselves to collaborate on sustainable development in the Central American region. The environment was well served by this treaty; protected area management was addressed directly. The nations of the region are committed to the Central American Biotic Corridor—the Paseo Pantera.

The Paseo Pantera project and this book were done in a spirit of goodwill among people and nations, enlightened to the interdependency of man and nature. We hope you will travel the Paseo Pantera, and by your travel be assured that you are tangibly fostering a new hope for harmony and understanding among human societies, and within the realms of nature.

Archie Carr, III
Wildlife Conservation Society
May 1995

Preface

CENTRAL AMERICA IS THE only active land bridge in the world today. It is the only place where overland migration of plants and animals between two very different continents is occurring on a large scale. This land bridge has existed for roughly three and a half million years, since an ocean strait that had separated South America and what is now western Panama became dry land. Formerly separated plants and animals quickly spread over this new land, causing a kind of biogeographical cross-fertilization between North and South America. North American organisms like oak trees and cats spread south and South American species like ceiba trees and armadillos spread north. More recently, humans used the land bridge to move into South America, and it has been a major zone of cultural as well as biological cross-fertilization as cultures from north and south have interacted here. Plant and animal species are still migrating north and south today, making the region a unique natural spectacle.

Like many geographical entities, Central America is a bit vague. The term "Central America" originally referred to the five nations that came into existence between Mexico and Colombia after the breakup of the Spanish Empire in 1821: Guatemala, El Salvador, Honduras, Nicaragua, and Costa Rica. Since then, two other nations have appeared: Panama (once a part of Colombia) and Belize (formerly British Honduras). This book thus deals with these seven countries, although parts of Mexico and Colombia also play a role in the land bridge. Mexico and Colombia are essentially North American and South American, however, with capitals far from the land bridge. Relevant natural areas within their borders will be referred to in the sections on Guatemala and Belize or on Panama.

Central America is a small region, with a land area a little smaller than France, and a population about half as large (i.e., around 26 million). An enormous amount of biological and cultural diversity is packed into what Chilean poet Pablo Neruda called "the sweet waist of America," however. With less than 1 percent of the earth's land area, Central America has about a tenth of its species, including many plants and animals found nowhere else. Northern species such as firs, alders, and ravens occur on mountains a few kilometers from tropical lowland rain forests full of monkeys and parrots. Roadrunners flit among cactuses in dry valleys overlooked by mist-covered peaks haunted by the legendary resplendent quetzal. Central America's human inhabitants are also diverse; contained within the seven nations are dozens of indigenous groups and languages with links to great ancient civilizations.

Central America is so diverse because it is a tropical region with high mountains, variable climates, and long coastlines on two oceans. This has created a range of habitats that is like a miniature of the continents to the north and south—from glaciated heaths on mountaintops, to moss-hung oak forests in highlands, to semideserts in interior valleys, to dry deciduous forest on the Pacific coast, to the second largest rain forest in the Americas along the Caribbean coast, to vast mangrove forests and the world's second-longest barrier coral reef. It also has created a landscape of seemingly inexhaustible beauty. Waterfall-festooned peaks soar above mile after mile of coastline. Whitewater rivers cascade from pine-forested plateaus to rain forest lowlands. "I regret," wrote nineteenth-century explorer John Lloyd Stephens, "that I cannot communicate to the reader the highest pleasure of my journey in Central America, that derived from the extraordinary beauty of scenery constantly changing." It's hard to find a dull landscape in Central America: a volcano or a beach or a jungle usually lies somewhere on the horizon. (Occasionally the landscape seems a bit *too* exciting: earthquakes and volcanic eruptions are common in the geologically young region.)

Central America's compactness, diversity, and beauty make it one of the world's best places for experiencing tropical wildlands and wildlife. Some of these wildlands are well known, such as Costa Rica's Corcovado National Park and Guatemala's Tikal National Park. But much of Central America's wilderness remains little visited by travelers, while some is almost unexplored. Honduras's Río Platáno Biosphere Reserve, for example, contains the remains of ancient cities about which very little is known. The Native Americans who now inhabit that area (and whose ancestors may have lived in the cities), the Pech and Tawahka peoples, were almost unknown until recently.

A century ago, Central America was mostly wildland, with scattered population centers in fertile volcanic highlands and along the Pacific coast. Rapid population growth and the spread of export crops such as coffee, bananas, and beef have greatly reduced wilderness and forest cover. Yet enough wildland remains to form a corridor of natural landscapes extending from Guatemala to Panama. This book is a guide to that corridor. It won't tell you about *every* natural area in Central America—Costa Rica alone has enough national parks and other preserves to fill several books—but it *will* tell you how to travel to and experience the wide range of ecosystems, wildlife, and cultures that has evolved since the Isthmus of Darien became dry land.

These wildlands can be experienced in a variety of ways. Some are vast and remote, and best approached expedition-style, with a guide and appropriate equipment. Some are accessible to self-guided backpackers, boaters, and other wilderness travelers. Some of these natural areas have comfortable resorts located in or near them. Some can be reached in day trips from small cities or towns, while others are only a bus or taxi ride away from big cities. All are different: from northwest Guatemala's pine-covered highlands, which seem like the Appalachians, to eastern Panama's lowlands, which pretty much *are* like the Amazon.

This book provides information on lodging, restaurants, transportation, and other support services related to visiting natural areas. It includes a range of options, from budget to upscale. The book is not meant to substitute for standard travel guides that cover all aspects of travel in the region (some of these are listed in the bibliography), but to complement them, along with other traditional sources of information such as tourism bureaus, airport information kiosks, and other travelers. The book *is* meant to supplement the information on wildlife, conservation organizations, and other environmental concerns available in standard guides. Sponsored by Paseo Pantera, a joint project of two conservation organizations, the Wildlife Conservation Society and the Caribbean Conservation Corporation, with partial funding by the United States Agency for International Development, the book is offered with the hope that it will encourage appreciation and active support of Central America's ecological riches as well as travel to them.

CHAPTER ONE

Exploring a Land Bridge:
The Past

THE GEOLOGICAL THEORY of plate tectonics has an explanation for why the Central American isthmus rose above the sea. Plate tectonics is based on the idea that the earth's crust is broken into a number of rigid, stony plates that move across the fluid mantle underneath. Plates form as mantle material wells up from great cracks in the crust called "spreading centers." The material then cools and moves away from the spreading centers at speeds of millimeters a year. Continents ride raftlike on the plates and thus change their geographical positions significantly over the vastness of geological time.

Geological and biological evidence suggest that North and South America were far apart several hundred million years ago and that North America was connected with Eurasia, while South America was joined with Africa. Then North and South America started moving toward each other, and eventually came close enough that "island arcs" began to form between them. Island arcs form as plates collide and one plate rides over the other, "subducting" it down into the mantle. Subduction pressure heats crust and mantle into molten magma, which erupts to the surface in volca-

noes. Central America's present active volcanoes are believed to result from subduction.

As island arcs formed and reformed between the two continents,
enough land rose above the sea that plants and animals could start
to move between them in a process called "island hopping," in
which winds or water currents carried seeds and other organic materials across straits. There may have been a continuous land bridge
during the "Dinosaur Age" about 70 million years ago, because
fossils of some North American dinosaurs and other animals have
been found in South America, and vice versa. That connection
didn't last, however, because subsequent fossils show that the two
continents evolved strikingly different faunas over the Tertiary era,
the "Age of Mammals." Horses, mastodons, dogs, cats, and deer
appeared in North America, creatures familiar in Eurasia and
Africa as well. South America, isolated from other continents,
produced a unique, strange fauna in which giant marsupials resembling dogs and cats preyed on giant placental animals similar to rhinos, horses, and other ungulates.

Animals are resourceful, however, and South America didn't remain completely isolated before the present land bridge. Fossils
show that monkeys and a group of rodents called caviomorphs arrived there in the Oligocene epoch some 35 million years ago. Unfortunately, we don't know if these animals came from North
America or Africa, since fossils or living animals somewhat like
them exist on both continents. Paleontologists probably will be ar-
guing about this for years (American paleontologists tend to favor
North American origins, while Old World paleontologists argue
for African origins). We can be fairly sure that racoonlike animals
that appeared in South America about eight million years ago came
from North America, because racoons are uniquely American.
Ground sloths from South America began appearing in North
America at about the same time.

The big rush, or, as paleontologists call it, "the Great American
Biotic Interchange," didn't begin until the Panamanian isthmus
formed, however. The details of that formation are perhaps even
more in doubt than are the origins of South American monkeys,

and certainly harder for the nonscientist to comprehend. Several crustal plates are thought to underlie the Panama region. The South American Plate apparently is moving in a northwestward direction, while the Caribbean and Nazca plates have been moving eastward. These movements are thought to have brought South America in line with an island arc formed by subduction of the Nazca and Cocos plates (the plate west of the Nazca Plate) under the Caribbean Plate. When subduction of the Nazca Plate under the Caribbean Plate ceased, a trench that had separated the island arc from the continent disappeared, and the relatively low-lying land of Darién arose.

The effects of this obscure geological event are clear. Fossils show that the mammal faunas of both continents changed dramatically after it. Large South American mammals mostly disappeared, and mastodons, horses, deer, camels, tapirs, dogs, and cats from North America took their place. A few large South American mammals persisted until the postglacial period, and a few of those—ground sloths and glyptodonts (which resembled giant armadillos)—became abundant in North America. South American porcupines, opossums, armadillos, monkeys, anteaters, and agoutis moved north, while North American mice, squirrels, weasels, and peccaries moved south.

Central America itself is a bit of a paradox in the Biotic Interchange, however, because very few of the fossils on which the story are based were found there. A mountainous or swampy, heavily forested region isn't best for fossil hunting. Pre–land bridge fossils dug from the banks of the Panama Canal and from the foot of Honduras's highest mountain, Mt. Celaque, show that mastodons, horses, dogs, rhinos, and other North American mammals lived there during the Miocene epoch about 10 million years ago. Post–land bridge fossils dug from the Guatemalan rain forest and Salvadoran dry forest show that ground sloths and glyptodonts had moved in by the Pleistocene epoch beginning two million years ago.

But those are about our only clear glimpses into Central America's deep past. Plants found with the Honduran fossils show that the climate was tropical then, but it would have been a basically

Agouti (*Dasyprocta punctata*). Photo by Kevin Schafer.

North American tropics, presumably without the South American monkeys and other organisms that moved in after the land bridge. Were there North American monkey counterparts that became extinct after South American monkeys invaded? And what lived in Central America before the Miocene epoch? Geologists believe that northern Central America from Guatemala to Nicaragua has been land at least since the Dinosaur Age (although they're not sure *where* it's been—possibly out in the Pacific Ocean). Startling surprises may be weathering out of jungle riverbanks.

Manioc and Maize, Gold and Jade

Humans are believed to have first crossed the land bridge about ten thousand years ago, but this is based on the age of human bones from South America. No early human fossils are known from Central America so far. The earliest archaeological finds, spear points used to hunt mastodons and ground sloths, show that by five thousand years ago Central America was already a cultural transition area. North American "Clovis" fluted points have been found as far south as Panama, while findings of South American "Magellan" fishtail points extend as far north as Costa Rica. Little more is known about the earliest, megafauna hunting people in Central America, although a project presently under way to survey rock shelters may turn up more clues. Presumably, they first entered the region from North America and were descended from people who crossed the Bering Land Bridge from Asia. The many physical and cultural similarities between North and South American indigenous people support this presumption, although much remains unclear (such as how agriculture was invented in the Americas independently from its invention in the Old World).

The first agriculture in Central America, beginning about five thousand years ago, may have come from South America. It was based on root and tree crops typical of Amazonian rain forest cultures. Manioc and pejibaye palm are two such crops still important in Central America. Like present-day Amazonians, ancient Central American farmers lived in small, shifting settlements and hunted and fished. Pottery from late in this period resembles South American earthenware.

About three thousand years ago, the effects of the domestication of maize and other seed crops in the Mexican highlands spread into Central America. These crops provide a more balanced diet than rain forest root crops, and larger, more permanent settlements developed around this time. Cultural traits typical of the Mexican civilizations of the Olmecs, and later of Teotihuacán, also spread south. In the highlands of Guatemala and El Salvador, the Maya developed city-states ruled from ceremonial complexes by priest-kings. These societies were highly competitive and hierarchical, with elites regulating trade, supervising large-scale communal farming, and leading warfare against rival states. Urban artisans produced a wide variety of ceremonial and luxury artifacts from materials provided through wide-ranging trade networks—jade and quetzal feathers from the highlands, cacao and parrot feathers from the lowlands. During the Mayan Classic Period from about two to one thousand years ago, large city-states based on conversion of wetlands to raised-bed agriculture spread through the swampy lowlands of the Petén, Belize, and northern Honduras. The largest of these was Tikal in the central Petén, which had a population estimated at 500,000.

We know about Mayan history because they left written records of royal reigns and conquests on stone stelae—carved slabs, or pillars. Less is known about the cultures to the south during the period from three to one thousand years ago. Excavations as far south as central Panama have shown that artifacts similar to those of Mexican cultures—jade ornaments, elaborate stone "metates" for grinding maize, ceremonial mace heads, flutes, rattles, and pottery—were increasingly common. Similar social organization may have prevailed, with warrior-priests leading small city-states, and populations may have been large. Central Panama sites of this period suggest a deforested environment.

Roughly a thousand years ago, Classic Maya organization collapsed, possibly from a combination of social turmoil, population growth, and environmental deterioration. Maya civilization withdrew from the Petén and Belize, back to the highlands and to the Yucatán Peninsula. A similar decline seems to have occurred in Maya-influenced cultures south to Panama, including withdrawal from lowlands to more easily defended uplands. At the same time, South American styles of houses, ceramics, and high-status artifacts proliferated. Gold replaced jade in amulets and other jewelry. Llama-like figurines and small vials possibly involved in chewing coca leaves appeared in Costa Rica; they may have been brought from Colombia in trade or through actual migration of Chibchan-speaking people. Stone buildings and monuments from this period in Costa Rica's Caribbean lowlands are very different from Mayan architecture. The north continued to have a strong influence, however. The expansion of the Toltec and Aztec empires of Central Mexico resulted in the spread of Nahuatl-speaking culture along the Pacific coast as far south as Costa Rica's Nicoya Peninsula. Nahuatl-speaking traders also established colonies along the Caribbean coast south to Costa Rica. The mysterious cities of the Honduran Mosquitia, which apparently reached their peak between eight hundred and six hundred years ago, may have been part of a cacao-trading network connected to the north. (The source of chocolate, cacao seeds were used as money by pre-Columbian cultures.)

The Conquest of Paradise

When Christopher Columbus reached the Honduran coast during his fourth voyage in 1502, he sought the opposite of a land bridge— a passage to India. He believed he'd found it and thought that Honduras was southern China. The populous, prosperous character of the land encouraged this belief; local people came in large numbers to trade with the newcomers, offering "fowls better than ours," as the Spaniards recorded. Columbus continued southward to Costa Rica and Panama, where large wooden houses, abundant wildlife, and many gold ornaments impressed him. When he reached Chiriquí Lagoon, a large bay in northwest Panama, he thought he'd found the passage to India, and he tried to start a colony. His men had begun extorting gold from the inhabitants, however, and the Indians drove him away.

Spain quickly realized that Central America offered the quickest route to the Pacific, and made it the hub of its empire. The size and wealth of indigenous cultures impressed the conquistadors. Balboa found a densely settled countryside in central Panama; a thousand Indians accompanied his 1513 "discovery" of the Pacific. When Gil González Dávila led an exploring party up the Pacific coast from Panama to Nicaragua in 1519, the Spaniards called the region around Lake Nicaragua "Mahomet's Paradise" because of its gardenlike pleasantness. The local "cacique," or chieftain, greeted them with gifts of gold. When Cortés's lieutenant, Pedro de Alvarado, invaded the Guatemalan highlands in 1524 with an army of Spaniards and Aztecs, his vanguard kept hurrying back to report that they had seen "yet another city as great as Mexico." According to historian Hubert Howe Bancroft, the Quiché Maya capital of Utatlán "vied with the city of the Aztec kings. . . . The palace was one of the most magnificent structures of Central America. It was built of hewn stone of various colors, mosaic in appearance, and its colossal dimensions and elegant and stately architectural form excited mingled awe and admiration."

Old-world diseases to which natives had little genetic resistance aided the Spanish conquest. Half the Caxchiquel Maya people in Guatemala had died in a smallpox epidemic before Alvarado invaded. Once in control of an area, the conquistadors enslaved the population and either put them to work at local mines and plantations or deported them for labor in Peru, Mexico, or the West Indies. Bartoloméo de las Casas, a Dominican priest who opposed these policies, estimated that four to five million people died in Guatemala alone during the first fifteen years of the conquest.

Spain soon exhausted Central America's wealth. Gold and silver deposits were small compared to Peru's, and exploitable land was limited to the highlands and Pacific coast. Spanish attempts to colonize the Caribbean ended in starvation, cannibalism, and defeat by natives, who never were conquered. A Mayan kingdom with a hereditary ruler named Can Ek (which probably meant "serpent-star") and a capital at Lake Petén Itzá persisted until 1697. Native rulers allied themselves with Dutch and British pirates to control the rain forests of the Mosquitia and Talamanca, and the Kuna defended the Darién region with blowpipes and poison darts. Pirates crossed the isthmus with native help and sacked Pacific cities from Chile to Mexico.

Except for the heavily traveled Panamanian isthmus, Central America remained largely isolated under the Spanish Empire. Although Indian slavery was abolished in the 1540s, peonage remained the main labor source of a hacienda system which was strongest in Guatemala but prevailed in arable areas south to central Panama. Colonization by Europeans was mainly limited to cities except in the poorest areas, like the Costa Rican Meseta Central, where the governor complained he would have starved if he hadn't grown food with his own hands. Isolation permitted indigenous cultures to persist, adapting social and religious traditions to the demands of church and government. Poverty and disease kept population low. When the Central American Federation formed from the colonies in 1823, it contained 100,000 whites, 900,000 Indians, and 450,000 mestizos. (No estimate is available for the population of African descent, who had either been brought to the colonies as slaves or had arrived in other ways, like the Zambos Miskitos, survivors of shipwrecks off the Nicaraguan coast, who mixed with local Indians.)

Filibusters and Bananas

The former colony of El Salvador temporarily proclaimed itself a part of the United States in 1821, as an alternative to the new Mexican empire of Agustín de Iturbide. By 1823, however, the five original nations of Central America had federated as the Provincias Unidas del Centro America. The federation fell prey to a series of complex struggles between urban liberals, who wanted to modernize the region and encourage European immigration, and an alliance of conservative landowners and indigenous groups who feared such changes. The conservatives' general, an illiterate mestizo named Rafael Carrera, proved more adept than the liberals', an educated white named Francisco Morazán, and the federation withered away, dying with Morazán's final defeat and execution in 1842.

Central America's isolation ended as the fast-growing mercantile empires of North America and Europe rushed to fill the vacuum left by Spain. The idea of a trans-isthmian canal had arisen as early as the sixteenth century, and schemes for building one proliferated as the technology to accomplish this emerged. The 1849 California Gold Rush greatly increased trans-isthmian traffic. Cornelius Vanderbilt opened a steamship and stagecoach line across southern Nicaragua (where the divide between oceans is only about a hundred meters above sea level, although the land is several hundred kilometers across) while John Lloyd Stephens, the American who had explored the Mayan city of Copán in Honduras, promoted a railroad across Panama. Yellow fever, malaria, and other diseases took hundreds of lives, including Stephens', during the four years required to build the roughly 50-mile railroad.

Canal schemes often were accompanied by grandiose ambitions of the kind that conservative Central Americans feared. Writers such as the English naturalist and miner Thomas Belt advocated mass colonization or annexation from North America or Europe.

In 1855, Nicaraguan liberals invited a U.S. lawyer and journalist turned adventurer named William Walker to help them against the conservatives. Walker and his mercenaries (called "filibusters") beat the conservatives, but then Walker proclaimed himself president of a new government in 1856 and turned many of his supporters against him by trying to reinstate slavery (which had been abolished throughout Central America in 1824). A coalition funded by Vanderbilt drove him out in 1857.

Commercial entrepreneurs had more success. What had been the most backward Central American province—Costa Rica—became the most progressive. It was the first Central American country to grow coffee, and by 1850 it was exporting large quantities to England via the Pacific port of Puntarenas. Construction of a railroad to the Caribbean by North American tycoon Minor Keith in 1890 increased coffee trade; such improvements in transportation also led to the banana industry, in which companies like United Fruit used West Indian labor to clear hundreds of square miles of rain forest for export crops. Exporting coffee and/or bananas, as well as sugar cane and cotton, became central to the other Central American countries' economies. Dependence on export agriculture typified Central American economies throughout the twentieth century, with a recent development being conversion of forest to pasture for low-grade beef, some of which was exported for pet food and for fast-food restaurants in the United States.

The Panama Canal was one of the great engineering achievements of modern times, and one of the horror stories. An 1879–89 French attempt to build a sea-level canal cost an estimated 22,000 lives, mostly from yellow fever and other diseases, before it went bankrupt. The United States succeeded in finishing the French ditch from 1904 to 1915, but first it had to engineer the secession of Panama from Colombia in 1903; eradicate yellow fever, malaria, and other diseases from the Canal Zone; and flood 164 square miles of the isthmus as part of a lock-and-dam canal system. Despite these Herculean measures, over 5,000 canal workers died from accidents, pneumonia, and other causes.

Like its paleontology, Central America's history has been paradoxical. Hispanic language and culture link the region to South

America, but North America has affected it greatly because of the Canal and other financial investments. The Canal Zone amounted to a state within a state until the 1977 treaty arranging transfer of sovereignty to Panama. U.S. Marines occupied Nicaragua from 1912 to 1933, and U.S. interests prompted varying degrees of intervention in other countries' politics. The Pan American Highway, which was hastily constructed during World War II to assure the Canal's security, has been a major factor in linking Central American nations to the north and to each other. The fact that the highway hasn't been extended south into Colombia reflects the north's present, but ultimately temporary, ascendancy in the ever-shifting "Great American Interchange."

CHAPTER TWO

Exploring a Land Bridge:
The Present

WHEN YOU FLY OVER Central America, you often can see two or three countries at once, sometimes two oceans. When you land, though, it doesn't seem quite such a small place. A turbulent geological past has resulted in an extremely varied and challenging terrain. It is a "bridge" only metaphorically, and plants, animals, and people have never moved across it as easily as evolution textbooks might suggest. Many plant and animal species have never gotten across it, or have only gotten partly across. It's a little as though two colorful parades have collided in a narrow alley, with the North American parade uniforms predominating up at the Guatemala end of the alley but thinning out down toward the Panama end, and the South American uniforms likewise predominating in Panama but thinning in Guatemala. For example, Panama has six monkey genera, Costa Rica four, Nicaragua and Honduras three, and Guatemala and Belize two. Nobody knows why some monkeys have spread farther north than others.

Rugged terrain was an important reason why Central America failed to federate successfully: the capitals were separated by barriers that were almost impassable in the 1820s and that remain formidable. To get to or from Costa Rica's gentle, temperate Meseta Central, for example, one must cross the glaciated Talamanca Massif and the 3,500-meter Cerro de la Muerte (the "Hill of Death") pass to the south; a range of active volcanoes to the north; or a series of rain forest–choked gorges to the east and west. Some of this land remains virtually unexplored, although modern highways cut through it.

Explorers' accounts are full of the hardships and privations of traveling distances that seem inconsequential nowadays. To cross the Isthmus of Panama in the 1540s, an Italian named Girolamo Benzoni walked fourteen days and found "we had accomplished little more than half the journey." An expedition of American soldiers who set out to cross the isthmus in 1854 under Lieutenant Isaac Strain fared even worse: they got lost, and several died from starvation. When they finally reached the other side after two months, Lieutenant Strain came out of the forest dressed in a blue flannel shirt, a Panama hat, and one boot, and weighing 75 pounds.

An Isthmian Climate

Explorers were often unprepared for the variations of climate they met. When Benzoni tried to travel north along Panama's Caribbean coast, high winds drove his ship to some small offshore islands for 72 days, "and in all this time, we did not see four hours of sunshine." When Perferan de Rivera, alcalde (mayor) of Nicaragua, crossed the Costa Rican cordillera in search of gold in 1571, the mountain cold so immobilized him that Indian porters had to carry him across high passes on their backs. Rivera established a town called Nombre de Jesus, "which must have presented a sad but curious spectacle—the people wandering about unclothed, for their clothes had rotted on their bodies during their peregrinations of more than two years through the virgin forests" (Ricardo Guardia, *History of the Discovery and Conquest of Costa Rica*).

Conditions have improved since the sixteenth century, but weather remains an important constraint on travelers in Central America. The region lies entirely within the tropics, from 18 degrees latitude in northern Guatemala to 7 degrees in Darién (about the same distance from the equator as southern Amazonia or southeast Asia). It thus lies entirely within the planet's equatorial rain forest belt, where rising air superheated by direct sunlight generally releases 200 cm or more of annual precipitation. Because Central America is so varied topographically, it doesn't rain that much everywhere (in some places it rains more), but "the rains" are something to keep in mind everywhere. Tropical rains like Central America's must be experienced to be understood. Often, they don't last long—a few hours in the afternoon or evening—but the amount of water released is impressive and sometimes seems to have been sent to earth by celestial firehoses instead of gravity.

On the Caribbean coast, where prevailing trade winds blow from east to west off the warm ocean, rains come throughout the year and may indeed continue almost uninterrupted for months, as Benzoni discovered. Annual peaks tend to come in December and January, when "northeasters" bring masses of wet air from the Atlantic. The Caribbean coast also gets hurricanes in the fall sometimes, and in the spring and summer precipitation increases as the sun passes overhead on its way to and from the Tropic of Cancer. It usually rains less from July to September, which is called "*veranillo*," or little summer. In general, though, some rain may fall anytime from Belize and the Guatemalan Petén to Darién.

Rainfall patterns in the mountainous interior and on the Pacific coast are more complicated, but also somewhat more predictable. There is generally a dry season during the winter months, when the sun lies over the southern hemisphere and less hot air is rising from land and ocean. The length of this dry season, however, varies from place to place. From Guatemala and El Salvador to northwest Costa Rica, the dry season generally lasts from December to May, and this area gets significantly less annual precipitation than the Caribbean, usually less than 175 cm a year. South from there, the winter dry season is shorter and less intense (except in west-central Panama), and some areas such as Costa Rica's Osa Peninsula get as much rain as the Caribbean. Inland, annual precipitation varies unpredictably according to the mountainous terrain. Ridges and slopes that face the trade winds may get almost continual precipitation. Some mountain areas have yet to be contour-mapped because clouds permanently hide them from aerial photography.

West-facing slopes and interior valleys, on the other hand, may lie in rain shadows and receive relatively little rain. Conditions vary abruptly: it's not unusual to stand in misty cloud forest and look out on a Pacific coastal plain where rivers are dry from months without rain. Central Americans call their dry season *"verano,"* summer, and their rainy season *"invierno,"* winter.

Temperatures are generally less of a constraint on travelers in Central America than rainfall. It gets hot, of course, but several factors make tropical heat less stressful than subtropical, or even "temperate" zone, heat. Tropical days aren't nearly as long as temperate zone summer days, so solar radiation has less time to accumulate. The summer solstice sun doesn't stay directly overhead for as long as it does in the subtropical zone near the Tropic of Cancer. Frequent rains also cool the air. Precautions definitely *should* be taken against going out in the midday sun (see health section), but Washington, D.C., in July is worse, on the whole.

You're as likely to suffer from cold as heat in Central America. Being drenched with rain in a stiff trade wind can be chilling even on the beach, and mean temperatures drop steadily as one climbs the mountains. I was glad to have a down sleeping bag at 1,500 meters in the Costa Rican mountains, although there were three monkey species living in the surrounding forest. Night frosts are common above 2,500 meters during the winter dry season in Costa Rica, although snow is virtually unknown even at its highest point, Cerro Chirripó, which bears the marks of Pleistocene glaciation. Central America's other small glaciated area, Altos Cuchumatánes in northwest Guatemala, is in a dry, interior range—there are no snow-covered peaks in the region. On the whole, Central America's temperatures are relatively comfortable. Nights and mornings are cool even in lowland rain forest, and so much of the lowlands are near coasts that there's often a sea breeze. Middle altitudes such as the Costa Rican Meseta or Guatemalan highlands have as near to perfect climates as anywhere—or did, before automobile pollution.

Winds can be surprisingly strong and persistent, particularly during the dry season. This can make camping difficult when you have to tie your tent to the ground to keep it from sailing away, and then come back from a hike to find that aluminum tent poles have been bent in half. Wind provides a convenient power source for sailing or windsurfing on lakes, however.

An Old, New Land

Central America's often turbulent geology is epitomized by the history of Guatemala's capital. Founded by Pedro de Alvarado in 1527, it was destroyed in 1541 by a flood and landslide resulting from an earthquake. Benzoni described this in his *History of the New World*: "Soon after midnight there began to arise from that mountain so great and so terrible a quantity of water, and with such an impetus and fury, as to precipitate rocks of incredible size, carrying along and destroying whatever it met with in its course, and there were heard in the air cries and lamentations and frightful noises." Another earthquake nearly destroyed a relocated and rebuilt capital at Antigua in 1751, and yet another completely destroyed it in 1773 "when it was left little more than a pile of rubbish in which the greater part of its 60,000 inhabitants lay entombed." The capital was again abandoned, and the city moved to its present location at Guatemala, or Guatemala City, which earthquakes nearly destroyed in 1917, then again in 1976.

As with the formation of the land bridge, the region's geological activity is attributed to the movements of crustal plates. With as many as six plates in its vicinity (the Pacific, North American, Cocos, Caribbean, South American, and Nazca), Central America is one of the most complicated and active tectonic areas on the planet. Subduction of the Cocos Plate under the North American and Caribbean plates is thought to have given rise to the chain of active volcanoes that extends along the Pacific coast from northwest Guatemala to northwest Panama. This subduction is also the cause of most of the more than ninety major earthquakes that have struck Central America since European colonization, as the land buckles and shifts along fault lines. Sideways movement between the North American and Caribbean plates along the huge Motagua Fault, which bisects Guatemala from east to west, is thought to have caused other major quakes such as the 1976 earthquake, mentioned above, which killed an estimated 22,868 people.

In terms of geologic time, Central America is really two lands, one old, one relatively new. Parts of Guatemala, Belize, El Salvador, Honduras, and northern Nicaragua have evidently been land for several hundred million years. Metamorphic and igneous rocks originally formed in the early Paleozoic era up to 500 million years ago underlie them, rocks of the same kind as those underlying continents. In the later Paleozoic and Mesozoic eras, thick layers of sedimentary rocks formed on this substrate. Since then, volcanic activity has deposited layers of lava, ash, and other materials. Southern Nicaragua, Costa Rica, and Panama, however, evidently lay underwater until roughly a hundred million years ago. Their "basement" rocks are oceanic crust similar to that of the Caribbean and Pacific. In the past sixty million years, tectonic activity, volcanic eruptions, and sedimentation have built up the present land area.

Overall, Central America has eight geological provinces: four highland ones and four lowland ones. The Northern Sierra province is an arc of steep ranges extending from Altos Cuchumatánes in Guatemala to the Cordillera Isabelia in northern Nicaragua. These mountains are made of ancient sedimentary, metamorphic, and igneous rocks that have been thrust up to their present heights in the past few million years by tectonic activity. This is the spine of the ancient continental part of Central America. Surrounding these mountains throughout most of central Nicaragua and Honduras, and extending into parts of Guatemala and El Salvador, is the Tertiary Volcanic Range and Plateau province, a complex of tablelands and volcanic peaks formed by the frequent eruptions of the past sixty million years.

To the west of the Sierras and volcanic plateaus is the Pacific Volcanic Chain province, a line of active volcanoes believed caused by the ongoing subduction of the Cocos Plate under the Caribbean Plate. This province extends from 3,946-meter Volcán Tajumulco in northwest Guatemala to 3,260-meter Volcán Barú in western Panama. This is certainly the most exciting province, since there are over forty active volcanoes. One of these, Volcán Cosigüina in Nicaragua, was responsible for the biggest known explosion in the western hemisphere when in 1835 it blew an estimated 6 cubic miles of debris into the air. Even when not erupting, volcanoes are the sites of smoking calderas, fumaroles, hot springs, and other interesting phenomena.

The other highland province is the Southern Sierra, which starts as low-altitude ranges on Nicaragua's Pacific coast. These mountains extend through Costa Rica to the Talamanca Massif, where they reach their highest point, then continue at lower altitudes through Panama to Colombia. Their highest point in Darién is 1,729-meter Cerro Tacarcuna near the Colombian border. The Southern Sierra consists of rocks formed no later than the Cretaceous period: ocean sediments and granite and volcanic rocks from tectonic activity. This province contains an unusual number of endemic plant and animal species because much of it was islands before the land bridge formed.

The Petén Lowland province covers northeast Guatemala and parts of Belize. This is a limestone plain formed when the area lay underwater during the Cretaceous period. Extending southward from the Petén is the Caribbean Coastal Plain province, which is narrow in Belize and northern Honduras, broadens in the Mosquitia region of eastern Honduras and Nicaragua, then narrows again in Costa Rica and Panama. It is essentially made up of sediments washed from the highlands in the past hundred million years or so, as is the Pacific Coastal Plain. The Pacific Plain is a flat, narrow corridor between ocean and volcanoes from Guatemala to Costa Rica (except for the Gulf of Fonseca between Nicaragua, Honduras, and El Salvador). The Costa Rican and Panamanian Pacific coasts (don't say "west coasts" because some of Panama's Pacific coast faces east) are broken by a number of bays, peninsulas, and islands.

The fourth lowland province is the Nicaraguan Trough or Depression, which marks the boundary between the old, continental land to the north and the younger land to the south. Extending from the mouth of the San Juan River on Nicaragua's southern border, the troughlike landform runs northwest to the Gulf of Fonseca. Like the highlands to the north and south, the depression is the result of tectonic activity, which has caused the land to subside. Drainage of surrounding streams into the center of the depression has created lakes Managua and Nicaragua, which amount to a small inland sea with interesting biological characteristics. About 500 kilometers long and 50 kilometers wide, the province is only about 50 meters above sea level.

Crustal plate movements also have shaped the geology of the sea bottoms on either side of Central America. Subduction of the Cocos Plate off the Pacific coast has created the deep Central American Trench, resulting in upwellings, strong offshore currents, strong tides, and other factors that foster large fish and seabird populations but inhibit coral reef formation. Much of the less tectonically active Caribbean coast is relatively shallow, creating the warm, clear waters that encourage reef corals.

Soils and Waters

Central America's curses have a way of being its blessings, and vice versa. Thus the crustal movements that cause earthquakes and erupting volcanoes have also created the region's agricultural wealth, because volcanic ash and lava are rich in mineral nutrients and make very fertile soil. This is why cities and farms cluster around active volcanoes and earthquake zones. Recently deposited alluvial soils on coastal plains can also be quite fertile. By contrast, the limestone soils of the Petén, the older alluvial soils of the Mosquitia and Darién, and the thin soils of igneous or metamorphic highlands have limited farming potential. Such areas contain most of the region's remaining wildlands.

Central America's copious rainfall causes high runoff rates. On the blessing side, this has created many beautiful rivers and sculpted many breathtaking canyons, gorges, and valleys. The most spectacular rivers are where the most rain falls, on the Caribbean slopes of the cordilleras. Costa Rican Caribbean slope rivers like the Pacuare and Reventazón are famous for whitewater rafting and kayaking, and rivers further north like Honduras's Plátano have great potential. On the curse side, soil erodes very quickly once forest cover is removed. One Costa Rican agricultural official has said that soil is his country's major export.

Because it is so narrow and mountainous, most of Central America's rivers are relatively short, dropping quickly from highland headwaters to coastal plain mouths. Highland streams are swift, rocky, and cool; lowland streams are warm and silty. Longer rivers run through the extensive lowlands: the Usumacinta and Río de la Pasión in the western Petén; the Patuca and Coco in the Mosquitia; the San Juan in the Nicaraguan Depression; and the Bayano and Chuncunaque in Darién. The Atrato River in Colombia just east of the Panamanian border runs through a depression which is the actual geological border between Central and South America.

Except for dammed reservoirs, most of Central America's lakes exist where water has accumulated in fault depressions, called "grabens," as with Lake Nicaragua. Honduras's Lake Yojoa and Guatemala's Lake Izabal are other examples. In the Petén, where groundwater dissolves limestone bedrock, lakes occur where surface rock has subsided, opening up sinkholes, or "cenotes." Because the bedrock is so porous, rainwater escapes underground, and the Petén has few surface streams.

Much of Central America's lowland is swampy. An expanse of sawgrass marsh and forest islands resembling the Florida Everglades covers the Laguna del Tigre region of the northeast Petén. Mangrove swamps cover river estuaries along both coasts. The Mosquitia and Darién both contain large expanses of swamp forest, which Hubert Howe Bancroft described as "dense with palm trees and matted with tropical undergrowth, through which flowed to the sea mountain streams, dammed in places with fallen trees, and covering the neighborhood with vast tracts of lagoon and marsh land."

Northerners and Southerners

Some paleontologists have attributed the replacement of large South American mammals by North American mammals (after the land bridge formed) to some kind of evolutionary superiority of North American organisms over South American ones. There may be some truth in this. It may be that mammals whose ancestors had evolved across large expanses of Africa and Asia as well as North America were somehow "more competitive" than those long isolated in one continent. But large mammals are only one small aspect of the land bridge story, an aspect that has received disproportionate attention because large mammals fossilize well (and make good museum displays). South American organisms have succeeded just as well in colonizing tropical parts of Central America as North American organisms have in colonizing temperate parts. Many temperate South American organisms live in Central America's highlands, and many tropical North American organisms live in its lowlands.

Pines and Ceibas

Central America's trees are a good example of the land bridge's biological complexity. Forest probably covered most of the region before humans arrived and began to burn and cut it. There are several thousand tree species. The majority of these species originate from South America and grow in the tropical forests of the lowlands and adjacent mid-elevations. Perhaps the most spectacular South American group is the ceiba family, or Bombacaceae, which grows in Africa also. It's often hard to identify tree species in tropical forests simply because there are so many, but ceiba family trees stand out through their enormous height and girth. *Ceiba pentandra,* the sacred tree of which Mayan stelae were stylized representations, may grow to over 7 meters in circumference and 50 meters in height. Also called "kapok" or "silk cotton" because of the commercially valuable fiber surrounding its seeds, *C. pentandra* grows throughout Central America at altitudes up to about 1,500 meters. Other large ceiba family species such as the barrel-trunked *barrigón* ("big-belly") and "*cuipo*" occur in the south. All these trees are deciduous, dropping their palmate leaves in the winter dry season when they produce their large white flowers. Large but blunt thorns often grow on their trunks and branches.

Two other very conspicuous South American families found in tropical forests are the Burseraceae and Bignoniaceae. Almost everybody notices *Bursera simaruba,* commonly called "gumbo-limbo" or "Indio desnudo" ("naked Indian" because of its coppery bark). A medium-sized tree with pinnate compound leaves, gumbo-limbo occurs throughout Central America and north to Florida. Like ceiba, it is deciduous. The Bignoniaceae is a large family that has spread into North America: catalpa and trumpet creeper belong to it. The genus *Tabebuia* includes a number of large trees with brilliant orange, pink, or yellow flowers that occur throughout Central America. Like catalpas, tabebuias have trumpet-shaped flowers and elongated, podlike fruits. They grow in wet and dry forest up to 1,500 meters, and are also planted as shade trees.

The Bignoniaceae family also includes a number of small trees with big fruits which apparently are indigenous to Central America, having evolved from ancestors that reached the region before the land bridge formed. The gourd trees of the genus *Crescentia* are common small trees which bear purple-brown flowers on their trunks (a largely tropical phenomenon called "cauliflory"—cacao also flowers this way). After pollination by bats, the flowers develop into gourdlike fruits resembling green or brown grapefruits. Horses relish the sweet, sticky pulp and spread the seeds. Such trees may have coevolved with the horses, rhinos, and mastodons that inhabited Central America 10 million years ago.

Tree families originating in North America are much less numerous in Central America, and grow mainly in the highlands. The pine family is perhaps the predominant one on mountains and plateaus from northwest Guatemala to northern Nicaragua. This family includes a species of fir, *Abies guatemalensis*, which grows on peaks from Guatemala to Honduras, as well as over a dozen species of pine (*Pinus*). For an unknown reason, the pine family doesn't extend south of northern Nicaragua, the border of "old" Central America. This is not because pines can't adapt to the tropics: one species, *Pinus caribaea*, covers huge areas of lowland savanna from the Petén to Nicaragua's Miskito coast. Also, transplanted pines thrive in Costa Rica and Panama, but natural populations are somehow too "conservative" to migrate south of the range they probably had before the isthmus closed.

Other North American families have proved more adaptable. The oak family has extended its range into Brazil since the land bridge formed, and oaks (*Quercus*) dominate misty cloud forests from Guatemala to the peaks of Darién. Central American oaks are evergreen, with serrated leaves—unlike most North American oaks—and they may be hard to recognize because of the mass of bromeliads, orchids, and other tropical epiphytes on their branches. A birch family genus, the alders (*Alnus*), has colonized highland riverbanks as far south as Bolivia. In Central America, alders may form large stands in logged or burned areas at altitudes of between 2,000 and 3,000 meters.

North American trees are not confined to highlands. A live oak species more or less identical to that of the southeastern U.S. has colonized Pacific lowlands south to Costa Rica. Willows line riverbeds in the Mosquitia and Darién. On the other hand, tree families that evolved in South America also grow in Central American highlands. *Drimys winteri,* a small tree sometimes used as a living fencepost in mountain pastures, occurs south to Patagonia and has close relatives in Australia and Asia. Its bark has been used to treat toothache, scurvy, and stomach ailments, while the structure of its wood suggests it is one of the most primitive angiosperms. Another very ancient genus, *Podocarpus,* a South American gymnosperm with broad evergreen leaves, has species in Central American highland and lowland forests. Some tree families like the laurels (*Lauraceae*) are so ubiquitous in Central American lowlands and highlands, and in the world at large, that it's hard to say where they originated. (A laurel genus, *Persea,* produces Central America's most famous fruit, the avocado.)

Cichlids, Salamanders, and Basilisks

Animal distribution in Central America is even more complicated and idiosyncratic than the plant life. For example, hardly any North American fish such as trout, bass, sunfish, perch, minnows, and bullheads were able to migrate to Central America. The habitat is suitable for them; they thrive when transplanted there. But the absence of any freshwater link through Mexico's deserts and mountains made migration impossible. Central American fish mainly belong to South American groups, the same groups that populate the Amazon and tropical fish aquariums. Virtually every lake and river has one or more species of cichlids—colorful perch or basslike fish that can often be seen guarding little schools of their young. The firemouth cichlid from Guatemala and the convict cichlid from Nicaragua and Costa Rica are sold in every aquarium store in the U.S. As one moves south, fish populations become increasingly distinctive as South American. Many streamlined, aggressive characids appear, the group that includes the Amazon's notorious piranha. Piranha don't live in Central American rivers, but small characids can curtail a river bath with their harmless but quite enthusiastic biting of dead cells off the epidermis. One common characid, the Mexican tetra, used to be popular in U.S. aquariums but was banned because it proved too adaptable to U.S. streams.

Some Central American stream fish come neither from north nor south, but from salt water, having moved up river mouths and adapted to freshwater. Shark, tarpon, and sawfish colonized Lake Nicaragua. Small, basically marine gobies and sleepers live in many streams. Of course, Central America has been a barrier rather than a bridge for most marine species. In the roughly 3.5 million years since the isthmus closed, significant differences have evolved between Caribbean and Pacific. There are many "sister species"— similar species that live in ocean waters on either side of the isthmus and that probably were a single species originally.

Amphibians and reptiles have been passing back and forth between the continents so long and in so many ways as to provide lifetimes of work for herpetologists. In many cases, North American groups have colonized the temperate highlands and South American species the tropical lowlands. The North American alligator, for example, does not appear in Central America's lowland swamps, which are occupied by tropical caimans and crocodiles (although the American crocodile, found throughout Central American lowlands, does live in Mexico and southern Florida). Frequent references to "alligators" in Central American travel lore are inaccurate.

Many typically South American snakes such as fer-de-lance, bushmaster, and boa constrictor don't live at higher elevations. The higher altitudes are occupied by snakes and lizards similar to what one might find in California, such as fence lizards and king snakes.

There are many exceptions to this, however. Rattlesnakes come from North America, but Central American rattlesnakes live in the savanna and dry forest of low or mid-elevations. One North American group has colonized both lowlands and highlands in Central America, and in a very striking way. In every other part of the world, the small, tailed amphibians commonly known as salamanders are confined to temperate regions. In Central America, for some reason, they have spread not only into the cool cloud forests of the highlands but also into the hot rain forests and dry forests of the lowlands. In the process, they have evolved over a hundred tropical species and some unique adaptations. Some species are skinny as worms and live underground; some have prehensile tails like monkeys and live in the trees. All belong to a single North American family, the Plethodontidae.

One of Central America's most interesting groups of reptiles probably evolved there, since Central America is the center of its geographical distribution. Basilisk lizards (genus *Basiliscus*) are good-sized brown or green lizards that have crests on their heads, backs, and tails and that often get up and run around on their hind legs like little dinosaurs. They are sometimes called Jesus Christ lizards because they can run, if not walk, on water: their webbed hind feet can carry them for considerable distances over the surfaces of streams or lakes in their dinosaur-like running posture. This is an amazing sight, and shouldn't be missed. Basilisks are fairly common throughout Central America below 1,500 meters, and also live in southern Mexico and northern South America.

Parrots, Trogons, and Ocellated Turkeys

If any single biological feature of Central America has attracted travelers, it is probably its birds. South America has the greatest diversity of birds in the world, and much of this has spilled over into Central America. With over 900 bird species between them, Panama and Costa Rica come close to Colombia's over 1,000 species. North America has far fewer bird species (650 north of Mexico) but many have spread into Central America or spend winters there. Many species also live mainly or only in Central America.

Lowland forest has the greatest bird diversity. Parrots probably are the most noticeable lowland birds because of their raucous noise, from the piercing honks of scarlet and great green macaws to the high-pitched chattering of parakeets and parrotlets. The long-billed toucans also are noisy, often sounding more like pigs or frogs than birds. Despite their brilliant colors, parrots and toucans blend in surprisingly well with the forest, and often stay high in the canopy. Less colorful birds of the forest floor may be easier to see up close. Tinamous—brown, grouselike birds—may fly up from the ground a few feet away, or simply stand there. The tinamou's plaintive, quavering whistle, usually heard at dusk, is one of the forest's most beautiful sounds.

Some tinamou species also live in highland forests, which are quieter than the lowlands, and often sound like the Appalachians because various species of thrushes sing. The trogons, a colorful bird family that probably evolved in North America and Asia when the climate was more tropical, live in Central American highlands as well as lowlands. Trogons are dove-sized blue or green birds with red, yellow, or orange breasts. The most famous trogon is the resplendent quetzal, so called because the male's long, curved tail feathers and iridescent green and scarlet plumage has led people to call it the Americas' most beautiful bird. The quetzal lives at elevations from 1,500 to 2,500 meters from southern Mexico to western Panama. Like parrots and toucans, quetzals blend into the canopy, but they can sometimes be located by their harsh "wek-wek" call. The sight of a quetzal flying with its long tail plumes streaming behind it is unforgettable.

Some typical North American birds have spread to the highlands and even the lowlands of northern Central America. Guatemalan or Honduran mountains can be almost like California, with Steller's jays, acorn woodpeckers, ravens, and band-tailed pigeons. In the Petén lowland lives a species of turkey, the ocellated turkey, which resembles its North American relatives except that the bare head and plumage of the male are iridescent blue. The male's call is also a kind of gurgling, bell-like sound rather than the gobbling of North American turkeys. South of the Petén, large turkey-like birds all belong to a family called the Cracidae, which includes chachalacas, guans, and curassows. Most species in this family live in South America today, but fossils suggest it may have originated in North America.

Monkeys and Other Mammals

The most commonly seen Central American mammals come from South America. Monkeys are noisy, curious, and diurnal, and inhabit all kinds of forest below 1,500 meters. The red spider monkey, as skinny and long-limbed as its name implies, lives everywhere except Darién, where the South American black spider monkey replaces it. Spider monkeys are rare in many places, however, because people like to eat them. Two species of howler monkeys, renowned for their lionlike roars, inhabit the region. Black and white capuchin or cebus monkeys, which live from Honduras southward, are the most intelligent Central American species and can be quite aggressive, making faces at intruders and even throwing things, including their own excrement. Small, greenish gold squirrel monkeys live in a few places in Costa Rica and Panama. Tiny black, white, and red tamarins are fairly common in Panama, which also has night monkeys, nocturnal and seldom seen.

Reddish, groundhog-sized South American rodents called agoutis or guatusos are common on forest floors everywhere. They have relatively long legs and hop about rather like small deer. Armadillos, opossums, and lesser anteaters, or tamanduas, are more nocturnal than agoutis but may be encountered in all kinds of woodlands. Like a great many South American mammals, monkeys, opossums, and tamanduas have prehensile tails which help them to move about in the trees. Tree sloths may be numerous in lowland forest from Honduras south, but are hard to spot because they move so slowly.

Tree squirrels have spread from North America across the land bridge, and live at every elevation. Cottontail rabbits are common in forest edge areas. Long-nosed, ring-tailed coatis are often abundant in the forest: one may encounter them in groups of twenty or more. Most large animals living in Central America today are descended from North American groups. Whitetail deer and collared peccaries are the most commonly seen. The most spectacular mammals—jaguars, pumas, ocelots, white-lipped peccaries, brocket deer, and tapirs (the largest Central American mammal, distantly related to horses)—are generally hard to see because they tend to have small populations and live in remote areas.

About half of all Central American mammal species are bats: they originate from both continents and are fantastically diverse. Large bat species are predators on birds, other bats, frogs, and even fish, which they catch by swooping over open water. Many feed on nectar and pollen and are important pollinators of night-blooming plants like ceibas. Vampire bats drink the blood of sleeping livestock after biting them with razor-sharp incisors. Tiny leaf bats spend days sleeping under banana or heliconia leaves.

Natural Habitats

Central America's diversity of landscape is bewildering. One ecological system, the Holdridge Life-Zone System, identifies twelve forest types in Costa Rica alone. In general, however, there are three kinds of forest corresponding to climate zones—lowland wet forest, lowland dry forest, and highland forest. Other natural habitats such as savannas and marshes are much less extensive than forest and often depend on factors like fire or human disturbance to maintain them.

Lowland Wet Forest

This is the classic "tropical rain forest" with most of the same plants and animals as Amazonia, although species richness declines northward from Darién. In undisturbed areas, it is a four-level forest, with huge "emergent" trees such as ceibas rising above a canopy of roughly 35-meter trees, which rise in turn over an understory of smaller trees and a shrub layer. Competition for space is intense, and many plants have evolved to live on other plants as "epiphytes," rooting themselves on the branches of trees. Small plants such as orchids, cacti, and bromeliads are the commonest epiphytes, but trees such as strangler fig and succulent-leaved clusias also are epiphytic. Often a tree's foliage is almost indistinguishable from the tangle of vines, lianas, aerial roots, and epiphyte leaves and stems covering it. Identifying trees by leaves is hard anyway, because the leaves of most rain forest trees appear similar. Fruits, flowers, bark color, taste, or smell are other ways to identify species.

Old-growth rain forest can be frustrating because much of its exciting life—flowers, birds, monkeys—stays high in the canopy. Places where visitors can get into the canopy by way of towers or other devices are increasing in Central America. Even without them, there's much to be seen with a little patience. The rain forest's most important animals, the ants, are everywhere. Leaf-cutter or *Atta* ants make broad, well-beaten paths along which they carry the leaves or flowers which they cut from plants, and which they use to grow their fungus food in huge underground nests. Sometimes columns of insect-eating army ants pass through, their presence indicated by flocks of antbirds which prey on the insects fleeing from them. There are dozens of antbird species, unique to Neotropical forests. (The "Neotropics" include tropical parts of Mexico and South America, as well as Central America.) Many other small animals frequent the shrub level, including manakins, chickadee-sized birds of several colorful species which make a variety of odd, startling sounds—like machine guns, snapping twigs, or Bronx cheers—as males perform mating displays. One white-breasted species looks and sounds like giant popcorn kernels popping as males display.

Wet lowland forest differs widely from locality to locality. Most has been burned or cut at some time by indigenous agriculture, particularly in the Mayan area. Large areas of Belize and eastern Honduras and Nicaragua that seem capable of supporting rain forest are covered instead with savanna, a vegetation of small trees such as palms and Caribbean pines interspersed with grasses and shrubs. The reasons for this are unclear, but soil infertility and fire may be among the causes.

Lowland Dry Forest

This type of forest grows along the Pacific coast or in valleys where marked dry seasons occur. During the summer rainy season it is lush green like rain forest, but during the winter many of the trees lose their leaves, and the forest appears gray and bare. Many tree species flower and fruit during the dry season, however, so it can be quite spectacular when masses of yellow- or orange-flowered tabebuias are blooming. The dry season is also a good time to see wildlife, since animals congregate around pools when most streams and rivers run dry. Many rain forest animals live in dry forest, which also has endemic species such as long-tailed, blue and white magpie jays and big gray *Ctenosaur* lizards. Coyotes have occupied dry forest areas south to central Panama.

Dry forest is shorter than rain forest, with a canopy at about 30 meters in old growth. Many dry forest tree species have rain forest counterparts, but there are generally fewer species. Epiphytes are much less prevalent. Tree-sized cactuses grow in dry forest, and many other plants have thorns or other defenses against browsing animals. One of the most interesting is the bull-horn acacia a small mimosa family tree with huge thorns which are inhabited by small but fierce red ants. The ants feed on nectar and protein-rich leaf structures from the acacia and defend it with their stinging bites from any animals that touch it.

Dry forest has largely been converted to cropland or pasture because its soil is more fertile and its climate healthier than the rain forest's. Less than 2 percent remains undisturbed, making it much more endangered than the "vanishing rain forest." Cut and burned dry forest reverts to savanna: grassland interspersed with small broadleaf evergreen trees and "coyol" palms. In particularly dry areas, such as Guatemala's Motagua Valley or Honduras's Comayagua Valley, dry forest and savanna may grade into a vegetation resembling desert, with large cactuses, prickly pears, agaves, and mimosa scrub.

Highland Forest

Highland forest occurs at varying altitudes according to latitude: above about 1,000 meters in Guatemala and Honduras; above about 1,500 meters in Costa Rica and Panama. Forests also differ at various altitudes. In northern Central America, forests of "ocote" pine and live oak cover the lower levels of volcanic plateaus. Above this, from 1,500 to 2,000 meters, is a moister forest of "pinabete" pine mixed with oaks, liquidambars (called sweet gums in the southeastern U.S., where they are common), and other hardwoods. Above this grows "cloud forest," which superficially appears more "tropical" than the forest just below because it gets more precipitation and thus has more epiphytes, ferns, and other lush plants. Cloud forest laurels and oaks reach massive size. Above cloud forest, other pine species predominate, along with fir, yew, and other cold climate plants.

In southern Central America, altitudinal transitions are less obvious because lush hardwoods predominate everywhere. Above 1,500 meters, however, oaks, laurels, alders, and a relatively small number of other species replace the hundreds of lowland forest species. As with the cloud forest farther north, this forest appears very tropical, with huge, epiphyte-festooned trees and tree ferns, begonias, and other "hothouse" plants in the understory. At higher elevations and on windswept ridges, trees become small and gnarled and grow over a dense understory of small bamboos, shrubs, mosses, and ferns. Bromeliads and orchids often grow on the ground, along with huge-leaved *Gunnera* plants, also called "poor man's umbrella."

Animal life tends to be quiet and sparse in cool highland forests, but many interesting species can be found, including the famous quetzal. The three-wattled bellbird is a white-headed, pigeon-sized brown cotinga whose mating call sounds as its name implies. It calls from March to June in the mountains from eastern Honduras to western Panama.

On high peaks such as the Costa Rican Talamancas and Guatemalan volcanoes, a semialpine shrub and herb vegetation grows, probably a relic of the ice age that ended about 15,000 years ago. In Costa Rica, this habitat is called "*páramo*" and resembles much larger Andean areas. In Guatemala, it is called "*zacatal*" and resembles larger areas in Mexico.

Aquatic Habitats

Marshes of rushes, sedges, and similar plants border lakes and freshwater lagoons in both highlands and lowlands. Wetlands are particularly common in the Caribbean lowlands, but occur throughout Central America, although many have been drained for farming. Egrets, herons, anhingas, and other waterbirds are common in wetlands. The most spectacular wading bird is the 5-foot-tall, black and white jabiru stork, a threatened species which still nests in a few parts of Central America. Another interesting species is the sun bittern, a heron-sized brown bird which gets its name from the surprising orange, cream, and black "sunburst" it displays when it opens its wings. Sun bitterns live mainly along forested rivers.

Central America's coastlines are intricate complexes of aquatic habitats. River estuaries usually contain salt marshes and mangrove swamps behind curving barrier beaches. Populations of multicolored crabs on beaches and adjacent swamps are striking—the ground sometimes seems covered with them—and are important to herons, hawks, raccoons, and other wildlife. Scarlet macaws and other parrots roost in mangroves. Among the few trees adapted to live in salt water, red, black, and white mangroves occur worldwide. Red mangrove grows directly on the water's edge on characteristic stilt roots; the black and white species grow further inland.

On the Caribbean coast, where offshore reefs buffer the surf, bays and lagoons contain flats of underwater turtle grass, an important habitat for sea turtles and manatees. Belize, Honduras's Bay Islands, and Nicaragua's Miskito Cays feature some of the world's finest coral reefs, and there are many smaller reefs to the south. There are hundreds of coral species: all are essentially colonies of polyps, small sea anemone–like coelenterates that live by trapping plankton with tentacles and also by absorbing food from symbiotic algae. Some species form reefs as the polyps secrete limy cases in which to live, and these "stony coral" colonies can reach fantastic sizes and shapes, such as those of brain, elkhorn, and star corals, three of the more common types.

Many corals live on the west coast, but few reefs form there because of the turbulent water conditions. Pacific waters tend to be rockier and murkier than the Caribbean. Tides can be quite dramatic—up to about 20 feet in the Bay of Panama—so exploring tidepools can be rewarding in some areas. Snorkeling can be good in bays and inlets, and some offshore islands have good reefs, such as Costa Rica's Isla de Cano and Isla del Coco and Panama's Islas Perlas. Both the Caribbean and Pacific coasts have some of the world's major sea turtle nesting beaches.

A Diversity of Humanity

Central America's population today is over twenty times what it was in 1820. There is now a majority of "mestizos," people of mixed European, Native American, and sometimes African or Asian ancestry, and minorities of pure Native American, European, African, and Asian descent. Racial prejudice exists, but it generally has not been systematic. Culturally, most Central Americans fall into the category of "ladino," a vague term which refers to Spanish-speaking, traditionally Catholic, rural or urban mestizos, but there is much regional variation. European ancestry predominates in Costa Rica's Valle Central and Mayan ancestry in northwest Guatemala. Ladino culture is a latecomer to Caribbean areas, where various native languages and English (brought by Afro-Antillean migrants, pirates, and entrepreneurs) predominated until the twentieth century and remain common.

The Indigenous Heritage

Although a small percentage of people are culturally Native Americans (usually referred to in Spanish as *indígenas*), native influence on ladino thinking, behavior, and local Spanish dialects is considerable, if inconspicuous. Identification with native ancestry is growing among ladinos, and historical native figures such as Lempira, who led the Lenca tribe in resisting the conquistadors in western Honduras in 1837, are revered. There is still much social discrimination against *indígenas,* however, and pressure to assimilate.

Remaining *indígena* cultures tend to be in remote areas and are given a variety of names, sometimes of dubious significance. Darién, for example, is often said to be inhabited by the Chocó people, but when I went there and met some natives, they told me they belonged to two groups, the Emberá and the Wounaan, who speak related but different languages. Similarly, when Peace Corps volunteers explored the Honduran Mosquitia in the early 1990s, they expected to find people of the Sumu tribe, but the people they met told them that their name was Tawahka, a group the Peace Corps people hadn't heard of. The Tawahka are a linguistic subgroup of the Sumu people of the Nicaraguan Mosquitia. (The Sumu call themselves the Mayangna.)

Linguistic studies have shown that, like everything else in Central America, indigenous cultures can be divided into a northern and a southern element. Almost all the languages known from Panama north to the Honduran Mosquitia are related to a group called Chibchan, which is centered in northern South America. Many languages known from Guatemala and El Salvador south to northwest Costa Rica, on the other hand, belong to a group centered in North America, Uto-Aztecan, which includes the languages of the Nahuatl-speaking peoples such as Pipils and Chorotegas.

The largest indigenous group is the highland Maya of Guatemala, over four million of whom still speak Caxchiquel, Quiché, or other dialects and follow somewhat Europeanized versions of their ancient lifeways. Most are small farmers or farm laborers. Small, scattered communities of lowland Maya live in the Petén and Belize, where they practice slash-and-burn farming (clearing forest, planting corn for a few years, then leaving plots to grow back to forest so the soil will be renewed), and they also hunt and fish.

Around 100,000 Miskito Indians live along the Caribbean coast of eastern Honduras and Nicaragua. The Miskito language is related to Chibchan, and resembles that of the Sumu people who live inland from the Miskitos. Today's Miskito culture is a blend of genes and language that has developed largely since Columbus. In the seventeenth century, there were about 1,000 Miskitos, and they lived symbiotically with the pirates who controlled the coast then. Every pirate ship hired several Miskito men to catch turtles and manatees for food. When not working on ships, men joined women in villages where they farmed, fished, and hunted for a living. A similar lifestyle has continued to the present, with men working as seamen, loggers, lobster divers, or on various development schemes of North American or European companies, while women maintain traditional village society.

A complex of native groups inhabits the mountains of southeast

Costa Rica and northwest Panama. These include the Bri-Bri, Cabecar, Boruca, Teribe, and Guaymí tribes. Missionaries and national governments have influenced groups living at lower levels of the mountains, but scattered villages in the interior are more traditional. The Guaymís are the most numerous, with a population of about 100,000. Originally confined to Chiriquí Province in Panama, in recent years they have spread to the Caribbean coast of Bocas del Toro and into Costa Rica.

The Kuna of eastern Panama are another numerous native group, with over 30,000 people. Until the mid-nineteenth century, the Kuna inhabited the interior of Darién, but afterward moved to Panama's northeast Caribbean coast and the adjacent San Blas Islands. There they adopted a way of life similar to the Miskitos', with men working on ships and other venues to supplement subsistence village life. The Emberá and Wounaan people moved from the Chocó region of Colombia into the areas the Kuna had vacated, and there lived by farming, hunting, and gathering.

A number of other indigenous groups still live in interior and Pacific regions, but their current status is not well known. About 5 percent of El Salvador's population consists of Nahuatl-speaking descendants of the Pipil tribe. Lencas live in the highlands along the Honduras–El Salvador border. Chortis live in highlands along the Honduras–Guatemala border. Xicaques live in the northcentral Honduran highlands. Pech and Tawahka live in the Honduran Mosquitia, usually inland from Miskito villages, and Sumu and Rama in the Nicaraguan Mosquitia. A few Guatusos, a very little-known group, live in northern Costa Rica.

Indigenous groups are becoming increasingly sophisticated and assertive in dealing with the outside world. The Miskito and Maya offered armed resistance to Nicaraguan and Guatemalan government policies in recent decades. Both sought greater cultural and regional autonomy. In Panama, Kuna lands form an autonomous province, or "*comarca*," administered by a tribal council which sends representatives to the national congress. In Costa Rica, a 1977 law granted reserves to indigenous groups, but there are problems with land use and ownership. Many groups are working to maintain or revive traditional cultural institutions.

The African Influence

African slaves or freedmen formed a part of the Spanish colonial population in Central America from an early date. This group largely has been assimilated into ladino society, but has influenced it considerably in the process, and some rural populations in places like Costa Rica's Nicoya Peninsula and southwest Nicaragua have a markedly African racial element. African cultural influence is greatest in those parts of the Caribbean where Spanish colonialism didn't prevail. In 1797, the British authorities on the island of St. Vincent north of Venezuela deported a people of mixed Carib Indian and African descent to Roatán, one of Honduras's Bay Islands.

These people subsequently colonized the coast from Belize to Honduras's Cape Gracias a Dios. Known as the Garífuna or Black Caribs, they live in small fishing villages and have many customs of African origin. The Garífuna language is related to the Carib language group of eastern South America rather than to the Chibchan group. Shipwrecked or runaway African slaves also formed part of the original Miskito population.

Many West Indians of African descent migrated to Central America in the late nineteenth and early twentieth centuries to work on banana plantations and other projects. Jamaica was the main country of origin. So many Jamaicans died working on the French attempt to build the Panama Canal (1879–89) that Jamaica outlawed immigration to Panama, and Barbados supplied most of the labor for the North American–built Canal (1904–15). People of West Indian descent live throughout Central America's Caribbean region now, and also in many inland cities and towns. Many or most are bilingual, speaking West-Indian English dialects as well as Spanish.

Europeans and Others

Spain continues to play an important cultural role in Central America, particularly through the Catholic church, the arts, and other professions. South America is a major influence on Panama and Costa Rica, but somewhat less so on other Central American countries, which tend to form a cultural "bloc" going back to the days when Guatemala and Nicaragua were Spain's main administrative centers between Mexico and Panama. The geological distinction between "old" northern Central America and "new" southern Central America holds true for culture as well.

Belize is the only non-Hispanic Central American country. Originally settled in the seventeenth century by British loggers from Jamaica, it remains predominantly English-speaking, with most of its population of mixed British and African ancestry (called "Creoles"). English also predominates on Honduras's Bay Islands, which were in British hands until the 1859 treaty by which England claimed Belize and relinquished other Central American claims. Bay Island and Belizean English are of the lilting Caribbean variety, whether spoken by blacks or whites.

Many other European nationalities have immigrated to Central America, particularly Irish, Germans, and Italians. Chinese first came to work on John Lloyd Stephens's trans-Panama railroad, and now live throughout the region. Lebanese and other Middle Eastern nationalities played a role as traders and peddlers in the nineteenth century, and remain important in business communities. Mennonites speaking a German dialect have immigrated to Belize in recent decades, and are mainly farmers.

Nature and Humans: Conserving the Land Bridge

Conservation of natural resources has probably been a problem in Central America since early hunters exterminated the mastodons, wild horses, ground sloths, and other megafauna. This could have changed vegetation greatly, since many plants such as the gourd trees mentioned above had been coevolving with large mammals. Archaeological evidence shows that human use did have considerable impact on land during prehistoric times. Bones of food animals from central Panama villages of some 3,000 years ago suggest that there was little old-growth forest in the vicinity then, since remains of forest animals such as tapirs and brocket deer were scarce. Evidence of deforestation and soil erosion from the Classic Maya period in presently forested areas of the Petén is considerable and has led archaeologists to suspect environmental problems as one cause of that civilization's downfall. Other areas such as the Mosquitia, Darién, and the cordilleras show less evidence of prehistoric human use, however, and probably were mainly forest. Spanish explorers referred frequently to large areas of apparently ancient forest.

Forest undoubtedly returned to many areas after the depopulation caused by the Spanish Conquest. Benzoni described many abandoned villages on his trip across the Isthmus of Panama. Iron tools and livestock facilitated forest destruction even with a much smaller population, however, and by the mid nineteenth century, ranching and farming had deforested much of the Pacific slope and interior valleys. In the twentieth century, deforestation has spread up the mountains and into the Caribbean area. Since 1950, Costa Rica has lost most of its Caribbean forest to colonization and cattle ranching. Much of Darién has been deforested since 1970. Deforestation has been slower in the Honduran Mosquitia and eastern Nicaragua, partly because of the Sandinista-Contra War, but pressures are growing there, too. The situation is similar in the Petén, where political turmoil has delayed colonization and development projects, but where pressure from population growth and economic needs is growing.

Deforestation and overexploitation endanger many wildlife species, particularly the spectacular ones like scarlet macaws. Once found almost regionwide, macaws have been decimated by the pet trade and now live only in the most remote or well-protected areas. Forest destruction also threatens less spectacular organisms of great potential economic value. Many of our most important foods and pharmaceuticals (including chocolate, vanilla, quinine, and of course maize) originated from Neotropical wildlands, and many others could be waiting to be discovered. Tropical hardwoods are also extremely valuable timber trees. Deforestation means destruction of over 100 million years of genetic evolution, yet much of the land now being deforested will not support even marginal human populations because of poor soil and other problems.

Central America's aquatic habitats also have suffered directly and indirectly from human activities. Siltation from soil erosion is killing coral reefs. Mangrove swamps have been extensively cut for firewood and cleared for shrimp farming. Destruction of reefs and mangroves affects the many fish and shellfish species that live and breed there. In general, all lucrative marine resources—sea turtles, manatees, shrimp, spiny lobsters, and fish—have been overexploited. Interior lakes, rivers, and wetlands also have been damaged by pollution, overfishing, siltation, and by the introduction of exotic species such as tilapia, rainbow trout, and black bass, which can harm native fish and other aquatic organisms.

Thoughtful Central Americans have deplored wanton forest and fishery destruction since colonial times, but governments have historically lacked the ability to protect wildlands. Game and forest fire laws went unenforced for lack of funds, as did various national park decrees, the so-called "paper parks." This began to change in the 1970s, when growth of an international conservation movement made "First World" funds available for tropical conservation, and Central American governments began establishing and funding conservation organizations. The growth of a lucrative tourist industry focused on wildlands and indigenous cultures—known as "ecotourism"—provided an economic incentive to protect land, although not enough tourism money has yet been applied to land protection.

Costa Rica established an effective national park system in the early 1970s and has placed over 10 percent of its territory in parks that protect examples of most ecosystems. Costa Rica has also created a national Institute of Biodiversity to coordinate the search for new foods, drugs, and other products from wildlands. Other countries have park or reserve systems, although less comprehensive and effective than Costa Rica's. Panama maintains sizable parks in its western mountains, in Darién, and around the Canal (which would be destroyed by siltation if the area were deforested). Belize has established large reserves and parks in its barrier reef and Maya Mountains. Nicaragua began a park system in the late 1970s, but the Sandinista and Contra wars delayed its implementation. Guatemala and Honduras both passed comprehensive park legislation in the late 1980s and have designated a number of parks and reserves, but still lack substantial administrative frameworks for protecting them. Heavily populated El Salvador has little wildland left, but has established a protected areas system. Unfortunately, enforcement of wildlife laws outside parks and reserves remains very limited throughout Central America.

Wildlife Corridors and Paseo Pantera

In general, no natural area in Central America is immune from poaching, deforestation, pollution, and other threats—if not from within its borders, then from adjacent areas. Biological studies have shown that protected areas steadily lose wildlife species after they become surrounded with towns and farmland. One way to avert this threat, however, is to connect various protected areas in "ecological corridors" which will allow wildlife to migrate back and forth. Because of its mountainous spine, corridorlike shape, and land bridge past, Central America seems a particularly suitable place for designing such corridors, both within and between countries. There are already a number of international protected areas, like La Amistad in the Talamanca Mountains of Costa Rica and Panama and Si-a-Paz between Nicaragua and Costa Rica.

Central American conservationists think that it might eventually be possible to establish a regionwide network of ecological corridors to allow species to continue to move between the continents as they have in the past. In 1990, the Wildlife Conservation Society (founded in 1895 as the New York Zoological Society) and the Caribbean Conservation Corporation began a joint project to encourage ecological corridors throughout Central America. Entitled Paseo Pantera, the "Path of the Panther," the project has been active in all seven countries of Central America and conducts field studies, public education, professional conservation training, and community and governmental planning to encourage a regional approach to conserving forest and aquatic habitats. **Contact:** Paseo Pantera's U.S. headquarters are at the Wildlife Conservation Society's Caribbean and Central American office, 4424 N. W. 13th St., Suite A-2, Gainesville, FL 32609. Phone: 904–371–1713; fax: 904–373–6443. In Central America, contact CCC-WCS, Apartado Postal 246–2050, San Pedro, Costa Rica. Phone: 506–224–9215; fax: 506–225–7516.

If the aspirations of Central American conservationists are realized, a protected corridor of primary or restored forest and other wildland habitats will eventually extend throughout the regions described in this book: from the limestone plain of the Petén, to the volcanoes and plateaus of the northern highlands, to the savannas and gallery forest of Belize and the Mosquitia, to the cordilleras of Costa Rica and western Panama, to the swamps of Darién. Within the corridor, wildlife will be able to ebb and flow across the isthmus as it has for millions of years, and Central America will remain a bridge of life.

CHAPTER THREE

Traveling to Central America

CENTRAL AMERICA IS PERHAPS the easiest and safest place in the world to experience a wide range of tropical nature, at least for North Americans. Caribbean islands may be closer and Hawaii safer, but they lack Central America's continental flora and fauna. Central America does have its share of tropical diseases and parasites and venomous animals, but these are generally less virulent than Asia's or Africa's. Central America is not only easy to get to but easy to get around in, without the enormous distances of South America. Instead of flying for a day from a capital to an outdoor destination, you can fly in an hour, or take a bus for a day. Central America also poses no great language or cultural barriers. The political and social turmoil for which the region has been in the news during recent decades is a cause for concern, but it poses little danger to the traveler except on an occasional, local basis, and such problems can be avoided. Crime is a greater problem for travelers, but it is mainly urban, and no worse than in U.S. cities.

On my first trip, through Guatemala and Belize in the early 1970s, I traveled by bus or hitchhiking, without shots or medical supplies, ate in markets or from vendors or whatever local people gave me, slept out in the forest without a tent or mosquito netting, and never got sick. The only precaution I took was to not drink the water, since I'd seen two companions fall by the wayside from doing so. In retrospect, this way of traveling was not wise. I've talked to people who've gotten malaria during such adventures (although not in Central America), and it sounds like a very disagreeable disease. My lucky trip does show how fears of the tropics can be exaggerated. With a few simple precautions, mishaps such as I courted can be prevented.

How You Go

On my first Central America trip, I simply went to the Mexican border and got on a bus south (small border towns like Calexico may be safer than big ones like Tijuana). This is an inexpensive way to go if you have the energy and time for the long haul through Mexico (and of course Mexico is interesting, too). There are many other ways, most of them easier. If you're going to spend much time in out-of-door pursuits you'll probably want to bring more equipment than I did (a small rucksack with a change of clothes and a jacket that doubled as a blanket), and such equipment could be unwieldy on a long bus trip. You'll also probably have less time than I did in those bygone hippie days, and you'll have more options, since tourism has grown considerably. In any case, some forethought as to the style in which you want to travel will be helpful.

Agency Tours

My second trip to Central America was a Sierra Club outing, a tour of the Costa Rican national parks, run by Costa Rica Expeditions, a major Costa Rican ecotourism agency. It was as rewarding and pleasurable as my first trip, though in completely different ways. I was able to experience much more wildlife and wildland in a shorter time, not only because a knowledgeable guide took my group right to the parks, but because I didn't have to worry about feeding and housing myself in the process. The trip's downsides weren't fear of malaria or "bandidos," but the more prosaic ones of group tensions (there was an "age gap" with older people wanting to go slower than the youngsters) and occasional dissatisfaction with food or lodging. I also would have liked to stay longer in the parks than the schedule allowed, but on the whole it was a very satisfactory answer to what I wanted at the time—a short, carefree nature vacation after a lengthy indoor job. It was, of course, a lot more expensive than my first trip.

Dozens of agencies schedule guided trips to Central America and offer not only park tours but whitewater rafting, visits to Indian villages, snorkeling or scuba diving, archaeological explorations, trekking, backpacking, serious birding, and various combinations of the above. You can start such a trip at home by contacting one of the agencies that advertise in the back pages of environmental or nature magazines such as *Sierra* and *Wildlife Conservation*. The agency will arrange for your trip to Central America as well as the in-country tour, which often will be coordinated with another, local agency (as with my Costa Rica trip). You also can arrange tours with local agencies after you arrive in-country, although you may run into scheduling problems at such short notice. There can be an advantage to this, however, in that you'll be able to size up the local agency before you commit to it. Agents in the U.S. sometimes don't pay enough attention to the services that local agencies offer their clients.

You don't necessarily have to hire an agency to run your life for your whole trip. In-country travel agents can handle your travel and/or lodging arrangements and leave the rest to you, for example, or you can go on a weekend or week-long expedition and then travel on your own for the rest of a trip.

A related option with agency tours is an increasing number of "eco-resorts," private nature preserves or resorts near public preserves which provide comfortable access to wildlands. Tour agencies often accommodate their tours at such resorts, and sometimes run them, but individuals can make their own arrangements to stay, and the resort may provide transportation from capitals, airports, or other points. Such resorts may be extremely expensive, though— especially the ones that cater to deep sea fishermen and scuba divers—but there are more modest ones too, sometimes with a conservationist or naturalist orientation. They also advertise in environmental and sporting magazines. Local English-language periodicals and brochures available at airports, hotels, and tour agencies also have ads for resorts.

Another possibility for those seeking a preplanned trip with a group is research expeditions in which the group helps scientists conduct field research in biology, ecology, anthropology, or archaeology. Research expeditions tend to be less expensive than agency tours and can provide an in-depth experience of biological stations or archaeological sites inaccessible to general tourists. They also entail hard work and somewhat spartan living conditions. **Contact:** Earthwatch, Box 403, 680 Mt. Auburn St., Watertown, MA 02272. Foundation for Field Research, Box 2010, Alpine, CA 91903. Smithsonian Odyssey, 1100 Jefferson Dr. SW, Washington, DC 20560. University Research Expeditions, University of California, Berkeley, CA 94720.

It is advisable to consult a few agencies and compare prices and services. The agency should be able to give you a clear picture of what the trip would consist of—not just the glowing descriptions of their handouts—and the quality of the guides and services in-country. Your satisfaction, and possibly your safety, will depend on the character of your guide, so try to get a good one. (**Note:** it is customary for tour groups to give substantial tips to guides and other trip personnel, an expense not mentioned in the brochures.) Another consideration in choosing tour agencies is their attitude toward the resources they use. Are they supportive of conservation, and if so, what do they do to support it? Will some of the money you pay them have a positive effect on wildlands and local people, as well as on U.S. bank accounts?

Going It Alone

In Central America, agency tours largely have operated in the most visited countries: Guatemala, Costa Rica, Belize, and to some extent Panama. If you want to get to the really remote places of the Mosquitia and Darién, as well as to many interesting corners of more populated but less visited places, you mainly have to organize your own access. Of course, you can go to the most visited places on your own, too; they're generally not hard to get to.

The main advantage to going it alone is that it's a lot cheaper, even when the economy of scale of the charter boat and/or plane rides included in many tours are factored into the equation. There's also a sense of accomplishment in finding your own way around, since you have to improvise and interact much more with the local people and environment. The downside, of course, is that finding your own way around can take a lot of time and effort, and can occasionally land you in a tight spot. You may, for example, have to spend days getting permission to visit some officially restricted area, like a park. You may get stranded in out-of-the-way places by bad weather or broken-down transportation. It's best to expect some delay, and allow for it in your schedule (of course, agency tours can get delayed too).

It may sometimes be advisable or necessary to hire your own guide after you arrive at the area you want to explore. Central American wildlands as yet have few of the maintained trails or designated campsites common to North American ones, and it's very easy to get lost. You may need to hire the guide's vehicle, boat, or pack animals or other means of transportation as well. This can be quite expensive, since guides have to pay a lot themselves for gasoline and other supplies in remote areas. Set a firm price at the beginning of a trip, and pay at the end (if the guide wants a 10 or 20 percent advance to pay for gas or similar expenses, that may be okay). Also find out details like whether the guide will provide food during the trip. Hiring a guide may seem like something out of a nineteenth-century adventure novel, but it's a business transaction like renting a hotel room. Try to get a guide who is recommended, either by someone who hired him before, or by some responsible authority. *Negotiate* for what you want—don't demand it. Backcountry people are independent-minded, and you don't want your guide quitting halfway through the trip. If you don't have confidence in a guide, don't hire him.

When to Go

The December-to-May *verano* (summer) is the high season for travel to Central American wildlands, for several reasons. It comes during the northern winter, when people want to get away. It's generally more convenient for traveling—even a modern highway can

be hard to travel on during rainy season downpours, and more remote areas become inaccessible because of high water, landslides,
and bad roads. Dry weather simply is more conducive to outdoor
activity for most people.

There are some good reasons to go during the *invierno* (winter),
if you don't mind some wetness and possible delays. High season
can be very crowded in popular places like Costa Rica; you may
find it hard to find accommodations without reservations in advance. Air fares and accommodations may be more expensive during high season, too. You may generally have a more relaxed and
pleasant visit if you avoid the crowded season. The beginning of
the rainy season in spring and early summer is also a very interesting time in natural areas because many animals breed then. The
roar of tropical frogs calling after the first rains flood their pools is
mind-boggling. There also may be some good weather during the
July-to-September *veranillo,* or "little summer," when rains abate
somewhat.

The Christmas and Easter holidays are the most crowded times
for traveling, since Central Americans also like to take their vaca-
tions then. There are many interesting festivals, and these can be
good times to visit if you have reservations. If you don't have reservations, they can be very inconvenient, because hotels are full and
many services may be suspended. Other local holidays can cause
popular beach destinations to be booked up.

Passports and Documents

A passport is usually required for entrance into Central American
countries. U.S. passports can be obtained by applying at authorized
post offices and federal courts. You will need to provide proof of
U.S. citizenship.

As of 1994, El Salvador was the only Central American country
that required a visa as well as a passport for U.S. travelers. When
you present your passport on entering each country, the immigration agent will stamp it with an entry date, which authorizes you
to stay in the country as a tourist for a certain amount of time, usually from 30 to 90 days. You'll also be given a card or slip of paper
with your entry date. *Hold on to this card, and make sure you have*

an entry stamp, because you will have a lot of trouble leaving the country if you lack either. Make sure you don't overstay your allotted time. Some countries, before they let you enter, require that you show a return ticket.

You are legally required to have your passport with you at all times, but often officials will be satisfied if you show them a photocopy of it. I keep several photocopies in various places in case my passport is lost or stolen: this will help in getting it replaced. It will also be easier to replace a passport if you have registered at your embassy or consulate in the country you're visiting.

Customs

Tourists' baggage is rarely searched thoroughly when entering Central American countries, except for the routine X-raying of hand luggage. It can happen, though, and illegal drugs, weapons, or other items will get you into a lot of trouble. If you make in-country flights, your baggage is more likely to be searched thoroughly, especially if you're going to remote areas. The likelihood of baggage searches is also fairly high when reentering the U.S., so you'll feel better if you declare anything you've acquired during your trip. As an "ecotourist," you should be careful to avoid acquiring leathers, furs, feathers, shells, corals, ivory, eggs, oils, or other materials that come from endangered parrots, sea turtles, wild cats, reptiles, coral reefs, or other organisms.

Money

U.S. dollars can be exchanged for local currency throughout Central America (in Panama, U.S. dollars are used as the local currency, but are called the "balboa"). Currencies other than U.S. dollars are much harder to exchange, and this goes for the currencies of other Central American nations, too. If you're going from country to country, or returning from your trip, try to spend all your local currency and retain dollars for the next part of your trip.

Carry traveler's checks, some in large denominations if you want to change them in banks or "casas de cambio," some in small for use in hotels, restaurants, etc. American Express and Visa are the most common and are easiest to exchange. You may have trouble cashing other kinds. Traveler's checks become progressively less useful the farther you get from cities, so before you go to wildlands, get all the cash you'll need. Even banks in small towns may balk at cashing checks. Make sure you keep your sales receipt for the checks and your record of check numbers in a safe, separate place. It may not be as easy to get lost or stolen checks replaced as in the U.S. Credit cards, chiefly Visa, American Express, and Master-Card, can be a big help even if you don't actually charge anything, since they establish your credit for things like renting cars. They can be used for the more expensive hotels, restaurants, and stores in cities. If all your cash and checks are lost or stolen, you may be able to get cash through a bank with your card.

Black market money operations range from the men who chant "Dólares, dólares" at you on the street to the backrooms of stores or restaurants. They're usually interested in currency, but may cash traveler's checks. They're usually illegal, but in varying degrees they are officially tolerated and offer better than official rates, although not necessarily a lot better. Find out about the current local market from fellow travelers or other sources before you think of using it. Counterfeit bills and quick-change artists are possibilities to watch for, too.

Physical Conditioning

It's common sense to be in good condition when you're traveling. This is especially true if you're visiting wildlands and participating in activities like hiking and snorkeling. The heat and humidity of lowlands, and the high-altitude, thin-air conditions of highlands, tend to multiply the stress of physical exercise. It's also important to maintain reserves of strength and energy for emergencies, because you'll need to be more self-reliant in Central America than at home. In general, there are no lifeguards at reefs or well-equipped search and rescue teams near wilderness areas to bail you out quickly if you get in trouble. If you go on your own, you're very likely to meet unexpected physical challenges—the best reef may be some distance offshore, or the place where the quetzals are may be several thousand feet up a steep trail.

An hour of brisk walking, running, bicycling, or swimming three times a week provides a minimum level of fitness. If you don't have a regular exercise program, you should start one as soon as possible before your trip.

Medical Preparation

You'll need to visit a doctor for various shots and prescriptions before your trip, and it's a good idea to get a general physical checkup, too. Your doctor can prescribe malaria prophylaxis tablets, which are highly recommended in most of Central America, except for the Costa Rican and Guatemalan highlands. The inexpensive chloroquine is adequate against malaria except in Darién, where chloroquine should be supplemented with Maloprim or Proguanil, or replaced with the much rarer and more expensive mefloquine. Mefloquine may cause dizziness and stomach upsets. Your doctor also can give you a gamma globulin shot as a prophylactic against infectious hepatitis. Gamma globulin only protects against one type of hepatitis, however, and it doesn't provide complete immunity. Careful sanitation practices, washing hands after bathroom use and before eating, are essential, as with other sanitation-related diseases such as typhoid and cholera. It can take up to six weeks to recover from the nausea, fever, and weakness of hepatitis.

Family doctors may have more difficulty providing other inoculations, since the ones recommended differ for each country and change with changing public health conditions. Some hospitals have adult inoculation centers that will tell you what shots are recommended at your destination(s) and can provide them at reasonable cost. Make sure your shots are recorded on an International Vaccination Card. It's best to start looking into getting your shots several months before your trip, because multiple shots are required for some inoculations. The common ones are:

Polio. A booster is recommended if you haven't had one since childhood.

Tetanus and Diphtheria. You need a booster every ten years.

Typhoid. Shots last three years, and there's an oral vaccine that lasts five. Both entail multiple doses. You may have a reaction to typhoid inoculation such as chills, fever, or nausea, so it's best to complete it a few weeks before your trip.

Yellow fever. Needed only in eastern Panama. Shots last ten years. Not recommended during pregnancy, for those who are allergic to eggs or who have immune-system deficiencies.

Cholera. Has broken out in Central America in recent years. A not very effective vaccine exists and lasts six months. Avoiding areas where cholera has been reported and using good sanitation practices are the best ways of preventing this possibly fatal disease.

Language

Although many Central Americans can speak English, Spanish is overwhelmingly the language of public discourse there, except for Belize. Even among the supposedly "English-speaking" people of the Caribbean, you will not hear much English spoken in stores or in the streets, and what you do hear you may have trouble understanding. So your visit will benefit greatly if you know some Spanish. It doesn't necessarily have to be a lot. A few hundred words will be enough to get you through most transactions. You'll have trouble at first understanding what people reply to your minivocabulary, but Central Americans tend to be patient about these things.

It would be well worth your while to take a conversational Spanish course at a local adult school or community college just before you go, so you won't forget everything. You can also try to teach yourself with books and tapes, although these are no substitute for actually conversing with others. The best way to learn is probably to take an in-country, intensive course where you have to speak only Spanish for weeks. There are many such courses advertised in travel magazines. Antigua, Guatemala, and San José, Costa Rica, are the language-study meccas.

Even if you have taken years of high school or college Spanish, you may have trouble understanding some Central Americans. The language varies regionally. Northern Central Americans generally sound more the way North Americans expect Spanish to sound. Southern Central Americans, Panamanians especially, may speak a Spanish that sounds more like some Indian dialect (to me, at least) than like a Romance language. But if you ask them to repeat a word a few times, it often turns out to be quite an ordinary one.

Courtesy plays an important role in Spanish, perhaps more than in English. You are more likely to get a helpful direction, for example, if you say *"Perdóneme, señor, puede decirme dónde está la terminal de bus?"* than if you simply say *"Dónde está la terminal de bus?"* This is especially true in rural areas, where lifestyles are more traditional, and with older people. If you approach such a person rudely, you're liable to have your manners corrected.

See language glossary for useful phrases and words.

Airlines

The major U.S. airlines provide regular flights to Central America, and all Central American countries have one or more international airlines. Budget flights and charters are common, although on them your chances of running into inconvenient delays tend to be higher. Central American airlines recently formed a partnership to provide special "Central America pass"–type fares that allow travelers to make multiple stopovers in the region.

Overbooking is a common problem, so you should be sure to reconfirm return reservations with your airline a week or two in advance of your return flight, *and* come to the airport a couple of hours before your departure time. This is especially important during the November-to-May "high season" in the most popular destinations—Costa Rica, Belize, and Guatemala.

Airlines generally allow two pieces of checked luggage. If you're checking backpacks or other strapped pieces, it's best to secure the straps so they won't be broken or lost during handling. Airlines tend to be pretty accommodating about carry-on luggage, although you shouldn't abuse the privilege by taking pieces too large for the overhead bins. It's advisable to carry on enough clothes and toiletries to get you through a night or two in the event your checked bags are delayed or lost. It will be helpful to keep a list of what's in your bags for replacement and insurance purposes.

Driving Overland

If you bring your own vehicle to Central America it will increase your access to wildlands, especially if it's of the sturdy, four-wheel-drive kind. It also will make it much easier to carry your own food, camping equipment, and other supplies. There are many difficulties involved, however. First, you will need to disconnect your catalytic converter after leaving the U.S., since unleaded gas may be unavailable. You will need to arrange for insurance. You will need to do a lot of paperwork when entering or leaving each country, and pay various fees and taxes. Your vehicle probably will be thoroughly searched at some point. In cities, at least, you will need to make sure that your vehicle is secure at all times, either by having somebody watch it or by keeping it locked in a garage or other enclosure (most hotels have such enclosures). You may encounter high costs and long delays if you have mechanical problems. Gas is more expensive and of much lower quality than in the U.S. You may have to pay imaginative traffic fines to enterprising policemen, and if you have an accident or otherwise run afoul of the law, you could be in for an expensive, lengthy encounter with the courts. And some of the best wildlands simply aren't accessible by road.

Cruises and Boats

Many tour cruises go to Central America and stop at various natural areas. Museums and other educational institutions sponsor some. Cruises generally have the advantages and disadvantages of agency tours in general. (Cruise ships have been known to cause pollution and other damage to coral reefs—by dragging anchors across them, for example. You might want to ask cruise companies what precautions they take against such damage.)

The days of cheap "tramp steamer" passenger service to tropical ports seem to be over, but there's still quite a lot of boat travel from the U.S. to Central America. Some freighters may still take passengers, although it's not likely to be cheap. Many North Americans take their own boats to Central America, an excellent way to experience the coastal environment, although with its own problems similar to those of bringing a vehicle, outlined above.

What to Take

The basic problems of travelers to wildlands is that of balancing capacity against weight. There are many useful things that can be packed, but if you pack too many you may have trouble moving.

It's also good to have some extra capacity in your luggage because food may be scarce in many wildlands, and you may want to carry a reserve of crackers, dried fruit, cheese, fruit juice, and other rations (you can get these in-country in local stores and markets). In some cases, you may have to carry food for several days.

Try to take durable, versatile luggage, something you can put on your back and walk with if necessary, or put on a horse (a small horse) or in a canoe. Outdoor stores sell special suitcases that can be converted into backpacks by unzipping compartments containing the straps. One of these has worked quite well for me. Make sure shoulder straps and waist belts are sturdy enough. Internal frame backpacks or rucksacks are also good, and may be cheaper, but the straps can get broken or lost in airline baggage and other situations. If you're going on agency tours or other trips where you won't need to carry your luggage much, duffel bags are best. Make sure your luggage is clearly marked with your name, address, and phone number. Also bring a day pack, fanny pack, or other small pack for use on day hikes. (*Watch out when wearing such packs in cities; they can attract thieves.*) My suitcase-backpack includes a zip-on day pack.

If you want to take larger items like tents, surfboards, kayaks, inflatable rafts, or bicycles, you can probably do so by paying an additional fee to your airline. Inquire before departure on costs and size limitations.

Clothing

Central Americans dress informally, but neatly and modestly, and it's best to approximate that standard in towns and cities. They generally don't wear shorts or other skimpy attire in public. In wildlands, dress for the climate. In the lowlands, some travelers spend most of their time in t-shirts, shorts, and sandals. When hiking in the forest, however, you may suffer less from sun, insects, and other stresses if you wear light trousers and a shirt. "Layered" clothing is good for insulating against heat as well as against cold. Baseball caps and UV-resistant sunglasses are good for keeping the sun out of your eyes. A light rain jacket and an umbrella can come in handy at any time on the Caribbean side. In the highlands you'll want sturdier clothes, a jacket, sweater, flannel shirt, and denim trousers or the equivalents, but remember that it can get quite hot during the day. Bring at least two pairs of pants and two shirts so you can change if you get wet. A bandanna or two may be useful as supplementary head covering, dust mask, neck warmer, etc. You'll feel better if you bring enough underwear and socks to change them often. They can be washed in hotel room sinks or in streams if you don't have time to do laundry. (Laundromats are uncommon in Central America, but hotel maids often will do laundry overnight for a fee.) You'll probably encounter plenty of swimming opportunities (hot springs are common in volcanic areas), so bring a bathing suit. Be advised that nude swimming and sunbathing are not practiced in public.

Light, easily cleaned and dried footwear is best for most Central American wildlands, since dampness is usually more of a problem than cold. I take a pair of tennis or running shoes for dirty situations—mud, dust, stream crossings, etc.—and a pair of leather walking shoes for clean areas. Bring plastic sacks to put dirty shoes in when traveling (and for many other uses—dirty clothes, etc.). A pair of flip-flops or velcro-strapped river sandals is useful if you're spending time at beaches or on whitewater trips. If you plan to do a lot of hiking or backpacking in the mountains, you may want to bring a pair of medium hiking boots. *Any footwear you take should be well broken-in.*

Basic Outdoor Equipment

A day pack is a good place to keep a standard kit of things you may need during hiking or other wildland travel. It may also come in handy in towns. A flashlight, for example, is as useful during not-uncommon power outages as in the backcountry. Bring a good but compact flashlight and plenty of batteries plus a spare bulb or two. Also bring one or more replacements in case you lose one, or in case you give one away (Central Americans have trouble getting good flashlights, so they make good gifts). Other standard items: water bottle (also purification tablets—iodine is the most effective kind), sunblock, jackknife, insect repellent, toilet paper, sunglasses (and/ or spare eyeglasses), Band-Aids, Pepto-Bismol tablets, aspirin, other medications, lip balm, maps, writing materials, nylon cord (for repairs, clotheslines, etc.), and a compass. A light pair of binoculars can usually fit in a day pack, still leaving room for lunches and spare sweaters or rain jackets, even small umbrellas.

More bulky items can be kept in your regular pack or duffel. You'll probably want to have more medical supplies: malaria pills, calamine lotion, tweezers, sterile gauze, Imodium or Lomotil for serious diarrhea or cramps, antihistamines for colds, tranquilizers and/or antibiotics if you have prescriptions for them and know how to administer them. Try to bring everything you think you'll need, because it may not be available in-country. Another useful health-related item is one of the small water-purification filter pumps sold in outdoor stores. Since tap water in many Central American places is not considered safe, these can be used in town as well as in the wild.

Camping Gear

The amount of camping supplies you take will depend on your trip, of course. Unless you have definite plans for lengthy camping expeditions, it's probably best not to burden yourself with too much equipment. Mosquito nets are recommended in the lowlands, although I've found them bulky to carry and not always needed. If you're sleeping outside, a small tent will suffice to keep insects off (I've even set up a tent in a mosquito-infested house—it takes just as long to set up a net). You'll probably be more comfortable with a tent and foam mat than with the traditional mosquito net and hammock. (When I stayed with Miskito families, they slept on foam mats and let me use the hammock.) A tent also will be useful for highland camping. Make sure you have a rain fly. A light sheet and a small towel can contribute greatly to your comfort. The sheet can serve as a sleeping bag liner in the highlands and may keep you warm enough by itself in lowland nights (though they can get surprisingly chilly). You'll be glad to have a sleeping bag above 2,000 to 3,000 feet. Remember that down loses its insulating power when wet, even though it's lighter and less bulky than synthetic fibers.

You may want to take a light stove and cookware if you plan to do a lot of backpacking or isolated camping. White gas or cartridges for stoves may be hard to find, and airlines don't allow taking gas on planes. A kerosene-burning stove would be best. If you want to use freeze-dried food, bring it with you.

Miscellaneous Items

It's possible to buy or rent some of the things you'll want in Central America: you just have to decide if the extra money this will cost is worth the reduced trouble of not having to pack them. Beach resorts often have snorkeling and scuba rentals, for example, although they may not always be open when you want. If you really want something, it's safest to bring it, or a substitute for it. A pair of swim goggles can provide a look at underwater reef or stream life almost as well as a snorkeling mask.

Large cities may have English bookstores selling country-related field guides and other nature material as well as paperback light reading. Prices are higher than in the U.S., but you might encounter something you wouldn't otherwise have thought of, and the people who run the stores can be interesting to chat with, especially if you buy one of their books. Light reading is worth the extra weight for sleepless nights when bites are itching or hours of waiting for buses to leave or for rain to stop. I bring secondhand paperbacks and give them away after I read them.

If you plan to take pictures, bring enough of the film you need to last the trip, the same goes for batteries. A lightweight, compact 35mm camera with a zoom/macro lens is easy to carry. Photoprocessing can be expensive; sending rolls home by mailer service is a possibility if you're taking a lot of pictures.

CHAPTER FOUR

Traveling Within Central America

NOVELTY IS THE MAJOR reason for traveling, and Central America offers a great deal of it, not only in its landscapes but in its people and cultures. I also find the region interesting for its natural and cultural similarities to North America. Some of these similarities are recent (and occasionally bizarre, as with finding that gruesome film, *The Silence of the Lambs,* playing on a satellite disk TV in a lunchroom in the little Honduran town of Santa Rosa de Copán). Other similarities are deep-rooted, as with the tendency to liberal-conservative political polarization that followed the breaks away from England and Spain. The result of this mixture of difference and similarity is that Central American places and people can seem quite familiar at one moment, and quite alien at the next. Even the rain forest can seem like an eastern woodland in August, with cicadas shrilling in the daytime, and katydids and fireflies at night, until the strange calls of tinamous or howler monkeys dispel the impression.

Both novelties and similarities have their downsides, too. Central America is much less affluent than North America or Europe, and many of its people live under conditions that seem primitive to visitors. Many Central Americans are justly proud of their independence and resourcefulness in leading lives that seem hard to North Americans, like the Miskitos I met who told me their lives are "*tranquilo*." Such tranquil lives are generally more ecologically sustainable than those of people living in the industrialized world. But there's no doubt that "underdevelopment" causes great suffering, particularly in the cities and countryside of the more heavily populated areas. The fact that Central America's affluent minority lives very much as does the First World can cause uncomfortable reflections.

Central Americans are forbearing about not imposing their problems on visitors, however. As a traveler, you are assumed to be well-to-do, and you probably are in comparison to most of the people you encounter, but you generally won't be treated less considerately than other Central Americans would be. A few people will try to take advantage of the "rich gringo" in various ways, but a surprising number will go out of their way to help the stranger. I've experienced more acts of helpfulness than attempts to take advantage.

Cultural Contacts

Ladino culture generally presents few pitfalls to the well-behaved foreign visitor. If you travel independently and inexpensively, you'll encounter your share of smelly markets, scrawny animals, curious children, and ramshackle sanitary arrangements. This can get depressing, but it won't be a big problem unless you're planning to spend a long time in some backcountry village. "Machismo" can cause difficulties ranging from idle harassment of attractive women to hair-raising traffic encounters. Disagreeing with men or questioning their veracity may provoke responses that seem out of proportion by Anglo standards. Machismo and alcohol are a particularly volatile combination, and you may encounter a drunk on the trail as well as in town. He may be carrying a machete, which probably isn't as threatening as it may seem, since the machete is the all-purpose tool of the backcountry. As with drunks everywhere, be polite and firm ("*correcto y decente*") about avoiding them.

There's a certain amount of resentment and prejudice toward U.S. citizens in some parts of Central America. (The word "gringo" isn't necessarily a manifestation of it, since the more correct term is the jaw-breaking *"estadounidense"* (literally "United States-ian"). "Gringo" may also apply to Canadians or Europeans. U.S. citizens should describe themselves as *"norteamericano"* rather than *"americano,"* since Central Americans also regard themselves as Americans. (Norteamericano also applies to Mexicans and Canadians.) The best way to deal with it is to be *"correcto y decente."* Occasionally such prejudices can cause dangers, as in Guatemala in 1994 when rumors that foreigners were stealing small children to get organs for transplants resulted in the severe beating of several U.S. women. One of the women was beaten because she was seen taking photos of children. Such rumors may crop up in other countries as well.

Beggars and "street people" are becoming almost as common in North America as in Latin America, so they probably won't come as a shock to most travelers. In large cities, especially, beggars are in even greater need than in the U.S., and there's more of a tradition of giving to them. In the country, begging may be simply a bad habit that some children get into from contact with tourists.

Cultural contacts become somewhat more complex with the indigenous or African-descended populations of more remote areas. Indigenous cultures are so diverse that it's hard to generalize, but Caribbean coast cultures probably are more comfortable about relating to strangers than others because they've had more contact with foreigners and have undergone less pressure from ladino culture. Miskitos seem quite casual and unimpressed about the arrival of a backpacker in one of their communities. The Kuna (in Panama) are more traditionalistic, but have their tourist industry organized to give them quite a lot of control over visitors. On the other hand, strangers arriving without a local guide or other "credentials" in a backcountry village of the Maya Highlands, Talamanca, or Darién are likely to be viewed with suspicion and fear.

Indigenous people (the Spanish word for Indian, *"indio,"* may have pejorative connotations) are also diverse in their retention of traditional beliefs and practices. Miskitos, for example, are mostly

Moravian Protestants. Traditional beliefs may still underlie apparently "western" lifestyles, however. Basic politeness and attention to people's responses are probably the best ways to avoid cultural gaffes. It's simply good manners to ask people if you can take their photographs, for example—whether or not they think that you might be trying to steal their souls by doing so.

Impacts of Tourism

Although it has been a major force behind protection of wildlands and indigenous cultures, tourism has also had its negative impacts, particularly in more heavily visited areas. Tourism has caused pressure for development of resorts or other facilities in areas better left natural, and in some cases it has caused wildlife to withdraw from heavily used trails. It has caused some resentment among local people who have had to accommodate the traffic without necessarily benefiting from it, and it has caused some less than desirable social changes in local cultures. Such impacts lower the quality of both the environment and the visitor's experience.

Visitors can help by behaving at least as well as they would in a national park back home, even though it may be a little harder to do so, given the stresses of the alien environment—and a little easier *not* to do so, given the scarcity of rangers, posted rules, and other restrictions. Littering, careless use of fire, wanton harm of plants or animals, or other destruction may be occurring around you, but that doesn't mean you should do it. If you see a guide, resort owner, or other ecotourism professional doing something that seems harmful, and you can let them know how you feel in a polite way, do so. Tour agencies or resource administrators may appreciate being informed of problems.

Surviving the City

Chances are you will spend some time in capitals or other large cities during your visit. Cities are good places to get acclimatized to a different culture, to gather information about in-country destinations, and to have some indoor R and R after a strenuous outdoor expedition. They also are good places, if you're not careful, to get robbed, sick, or otherwise handicapped in your travel plans.

Central American cities generally are no more hazardous than North American ones, but there are a few special problems. Tap water is unsafe in some countries. Electricity outages are frequent because of energy problems such as the silting of hydroelectric reservoirs that results from deforestation.

Your time of greatest vulnerability to such disasters is probably your arrival, burdened by luggage and dazed by travel, at an airport or bus station. The advantage of traveling light becomes clear at once, because if you can't carry everything you will have to hire somebody else to, and you will have to watch them. There is usually some inexpensive bus service from airports, but it may be worthwhile to take a cab. If you don't know what the fare should be, compare among a few cabbies to make sure you're not overcharged. (Beware of cabbies who rush in and grab your luggage before you call them: they're likely to overcharge.)

Hotels

It's best to arrive knowing of a hotel or other destination to tell the cabbie (see in-country sections, below, for recommended hotels). Cabbies can suggest hotels, but they may not be very good if they have to have cabbies touting for them. It's hard to make reservations at less expensive hotels. If the hotel you've chosen is full, see if you can get the desk clerk to help you find another one. If they do have a room, you may want to *ask to see it first,* and check for insecure locks or windows, broken toilets or air conditioners, lack of hot water, and other problems. Try to get a room in the back or on upper floors if possible, since streets can be incredibly noisy until late at night, especially if the hotel is near a bus station, nightclub, or other gathering place. You obviously can't stay in a room with a broken toilet, but don't be afraid to ask for another room if there are less obvious faults in the one you're shown.

There are many small hotels or guest houses (*casas de huéspedes*) where you can stay for less than $15 a night, often as little as $5. In big cities, they tend to be in out-of-the-way and sometimes scary neighborhoods, but in smaller towns they may be more conveniently located (and they may be the only hotels). Comfortable medium-priced rooms can be had for $15–30, and are usually conveniently located in large cities. Luxury hotels may approach U.S. prices.

Less expensive hotels, especially in the lowlands, may not have hot water. Those that do may have an electric shower head that heats the water just before it comes out. This may have a switch to turn it on: make sure you don't leave it on after your shower.

If you're planning an expedition during which you won't need all your luggage, you may be able to leave it at your hotel. Make sure they lock it up, and that it's clearly labeled.

Theft and Personal Safety

Checking valuables with hotel desks is the safest way of avoiding theft both in and out of hotels (make sure you get a receipt). For valuables you must carry, travel stores sell money belts and pouches that will reduce risk from pickpockets. Don't wear valuable jewelry on the street. Keep photocopies of your passport in several places so you'll be sure to have some proof that you have one. (You'll be asked to fill out your passport number on numerous forms, so keep a photocopy in your wallet or purse.)

On the street, keep your eyes open not only for theft, but for drivers who expect pedestrians to get out of their way fast. If somebody bumps into you or drops something near you, you may very well have encountered pickpockets, so hang on to your wallet. If you have a day pack, carry it on your side rather than your back: it may be emptied as if by magic otherwise. Slashing open packs or even pockets with a razor is a common technique. Walking through the streets with a bulky backpack may attract such techniques. Pay attention to the neighborhoods you're in if you're exploring or looking for an address. If the neighborhood looks as though you might get mugged in broad daylight, you might indeed. If you walk at night, avoid the areas around parks or bars. Night theft is the most to be avoided, because it may involve physical assault. You're less likely to be physically assaulted during the daytime thefts that occur on the street or in public transportation.

Cities, of course, aren't the only places where you may get robbed or cheated. Small, remote towns may be as villainous as the slummiest barrio. Beaches and campsites often develop robbery problems. I knew someone whose day pack was stolen out from under his head as he dozed on a beach in La Ceiba, Honduras. Local people probably fear the villains as much as you do, and, if you ask, they may be glad to warn you about where not to go.

Food / La Comida

Like everything in Central America, food changes as you move north to south. Guatemalan food is like southern Mexican, only perhaps cheaper—handmade tortillas, black beans, guacamole, tamales, plenty of fruits, herbs, and spices. It's essentially Mayan food, and the Maya are excellent gardeners and horticulturalists. El Salvador, Honduras, and Nicaragua also have essentially Meso-American cuisines based on corn, beans, and chiles, but with more of a "ranchero" style (and less indigenous), which largely means that fewer fruits, vegetables, herbs, and spices are used. This can be very good, but it also can be rather monotonous. Some country places still serve a *"comida corriente"* of tortillas, beans, white cheese, and fried plantains three times a day, just as when John Lloyd Stephens was exploring Mayan ruins in the 1840s. *"Tapados,"* meat and vegetables in bowls of clear broth, are usually appetizing and wholesome.

The Meso-American influence diminishes rapidly south of Guanacaste Province in Costa Rica. If you order a "taco" in Costa Rica's Valle Central, you may get something resembling an egg roll. In Panama, "tortillas" are bright yellow, deep-fried disks of corn dough. Traditional Costa Rican food is heavy on starches like potatoes, rice, pasta, and cassava, perhaps a reflection of their colonial poverty ("Ticos" still have a reputation for carrying large amounts of food with them wherever they go). One typical dish is the *"casado"* (which means "married" or, literally, "housed") in which potatoes, rice, pasta, and beans are served together with some meat and vegetables. This seems odd, but it can be quite good in a homey way. *"Gallo pinto"* ("painted rooster"), black beans and rice fried with onions, peppers, and coriander, is a common breakfast dish, and can also be quite good. Orange, cherry-sized pejibaye palm fruits cooked in oil are ubiquitous in street stalls, but are more of an acquired taste than the tasty heart-of-palm from the same tree.

The Caribbean coast has its own African-influenced cuisine, with much use of coconut for cooking and baking. Little coconut bread rolls sold in markets and bus stops make good snacks. Rice, beans, and cassava (called *"yuca"* in Central America, although it has no relation to the yucca of North American deserts) are staples, usually cooked more spicily than in the highlands. If you can find lightly pan-fried breadfruit, try it.

Fish and other seafoods are popular and good throughout Central America, although their quality is declining as overfishing and pollution increase. *"Corvina"* or sea bass with various sauces is a staple, as are *"camarones,"* shrimp. On the Caribbean, you may find interesting things like spicy conch fritters. Delicacies such as conch and spiny lobster are among the main victims of overfishing, however. *"Ceviche de pescado,"* raw fish cured in lime juice, is popular, as throughout Latin America. Raw seafood may have its dangers. Ceviche was implicated in the Peruvian cholera epidemic of the late 1980s, and raw shellfish may come from polluted water. Be especially wary of ceviche made from various types of bivalves, called *"piangues"* or *"chuchecas."*

When traveling through wildlands, I've often been offered wild fruits or fruit drinks by local people. These have not always been utterly delicious, but they've been tasty, nourishing, and safe. (Don't eat wild fruits at random, however; things like *"manzanillo"*—small, applelike fruits that grow from trees beside beaches—can be poisonous.) I've never been offered things like monkey, iguana, paca (a large rodent especially prized for its meat), guan, or sea turtle, although I have encountered paca (under the Belizean name of *"gibnut"*) and turtle in restaurants. My impression is that game is a market rarity in Central America, either because of scarcity or because people like to eat it themselves. Since it *is* scarce, if not threatened, this is a good thing.

Restaurants / Los Restaurantes

It's quite possible to travel through Central America eating mainly hamburgers (*"hamburguesas"*), steaks (*"bistec,"* *"carne asada"*), pizzas, fried chicken (*"pollo frito"*), and french fries (*"papas fritas"*). As in the U.S., such fast foods are liable to be on the greasy side. North American food chains are extremely popular in the larger Central American cities. Most towns have Chinese restaurants, which may be somewhat better than their North American counterparts.

The more expensive restaurants serve just about every kind of food, and cost about as much as North American counterparts. There are many medium-priced places serving mediocre food, and many cheap places serving lousy food, especially along highways. Food poisoning is a possibility in such places; if something smells or tastes unpleasant—like dirty socks or rancid fat—send it back. There are also many small, inexpensive restaurants (including vegetarian and health food restaurants) that serve wholesome, tasty food in pleasant surroundings. Look for these, especially in quiet backstreets of business or residential districts. Often such places offer a "*plato del día*" that provides a full meal at a very reasonable price.

Small, remote towns may not appear to *have* restaurants at first glance, but there's usually some corner where you can get a meal, if you ask around. The menu won't be large, but it may have some regional specialty, like the delicious, burrito-like concoction of flour tortillas, eggs, cheese, and peppers I got in a two-table place in Gracias, Honduras. Markets almost always have a number of stalls where you can get a bowl of soup or stew and some "*empanadas*," little pastry turnovers filled with meat or vegetables.

Drink / Las Bebidas

Although Central America is one of the world's great coffee producers, coffee drinking is rather plain there compared to the refinements of First World cities. This, of course, is because their best coffee is exported. There's "*café con leche*" with the hot milk in a separate container or added by the waiter, and "*café negro*," although a few restaurants have "*café expreso*" and the varieties thereof. Commonly served teas include chamomile ("*té manzanillo*") as well as regular tea.

Fresh fruit drinks made in blenders with ice and/or milk ("*batidos*," "*licuados*") are everywhere. I've always been a little nervous about drinking them because of warnings about ice and milk, but

I've drunk them anyway, so far without ill effects. They're hard to resist.

Wine is very expensive in Central America because it has to be imported. Local beers (*"cervezas"*) are cheap, and quite good. Locally produced hard liquors, usually distilled from sugarcane and going under names like *"cana brava,"* should be approached with caution. Some bars serve *"bocas"* or *"tapas,"* little dishes of hot food, often very good, along with each drink. The idea is to prevent alcohol overindulgence by adding food, although you can indulge in a lot of alcohol this way if you're not careful. If you do, have the management call you a taxi (*"Se puede llamarme un taxi, por favor?"*).

Camping Food

Cities and towns have large food stores (*"el super-mercado"*) or small (*"la bodega," "la pulpería"*) where you can buy things like canned tuna, cheese (*"queso"*), milk (*"leche"*), eggs (*"blanquillas"*—*"huevos"* refers to cooked eggs), bread (*"pan"*), cookies and crackers (*"galletas"*), rice and beans (*"arroz y frijoles"*), coffee and tea, etc. They'll probably have familiar U.S. brands, but local ones are much cheaper. They also have fruits and vegetables: common ones are carrots (*"zanahorias"*), cabbage (*"repollo"*), cooking plantain (*"plátano"*), potatoes (*"papas"*), onions (*"cebollas"*), garlic (*"ajo"*), tomatoes, hot or sweet peppers (*"chiles picantes o dulces"*), avocados (*"aguacates"*), mangoes, papayas, zapotes (large fruits from native trees), bananas, oranges (*"naranjas"*), and lemons.

Fruits and vegetables in outdoor markets usually are fresher, cheaper, and more varied than in stores. Markets also often have fresh breads, empanadas, and other foods you can take on the trail or to camp. Some extra caution is recommended with fruits, vegetables, or other uncooked foods. It's best to peel things yourself, and to cook things like cabbage. Fresh milk and cheese from markets may be unpasteurized.

If you camp you're not unlikely to find people living nearby. They may be glad to sell you some food or even whole meals as a way to pick up some cash. They may even offer you food or a meal for free. If they don't mention payment, offer it, and if it's refused, accept the gift in the spirit it's offered. You might want to offer a return gift. Of course, you can't count on such a food source, so try to have a day or two's worth of reserve food when you're in backcountry.

Personal Hygiene

Poor personal hygiene is one of the most common complaints about tourists by Central Americans, both urban and rural. "Ecotourists," particularly young ones, are the worst culprits. Don't expect a warm welcome if you breeze into a restaurant or hotel unwashed after a few days of backpacking or camping. Clean clothes and daily baths are very important, both for maintaining your own health and for maintaining good relations with local people. Don't let the frequent lack of hot shower facilities discourage you from bathing—there's almost always *someplace* to wash in, no matter how remote or seemingly primitive a place is, and the local people will be appreciative if you use it.

Tropical Hazards

Of course, Central America *is* "jungle country" and there are dangers you don't have to think about at home. Still, the biggest dangers are probably pretty much the same—injuries from car crashes or other accidents. An injury sustained in a rural or remote area is of course an extra problem. Limited health care services in much of the region can also make such injuries more threatening than they'd otherwise be.

Diseases and Internal Parasites

Many of the diseases threatening travelers in Central America can also be found at home—AIDS (called "SIDA" in Spanish), venereal infections, tuberculosis, tetanus, and influenza. There are a few diseases to watch out for in particular in Central American wildlands. They sound rather alarming, but most are preventable and/or treatable. In many cases, the body defeats the infection without symptoms or treatment.

Malaria is caused by parasitic protozoans that are spread to the blood of human hosts in the bites of female *Anopheles* mosquitoes.

The mosquitoes fly at night, and their bites can be avoided by wearing clothes and insect repellent when outside (although they may still bite) and by sleeping in screened enclosures (tents, houses with window screens, mosquito nets) and/or by using repellent sprays or coils. See previous chapter for details about prophylactic pills. If despite precautions you get bitten by a malaria-infected mosquito, the symptoms could appear as soon as eight days later, or as late as months or years. Symptoms include headache, fever, chills, and profuse sweating, and may subside, only to reappear later. Malaria is easier to treat early, so such symptoms after visiting lowlands shouldn't be ignored. Remember that taking the pills doesn't guarantee that you won't be infected. Fortunately, the most dangerous form of the disease, caused by a protozoan named *Plasmodium falciparum*, occurs only in eastern Panama.

A day-flying mosquito may carry **dengue fever,** a viral disease for which there is no preventive medicine. Symptoms include headache, fever, joint and muscle pains, and a rash which starts on the trunk and spreads to legs and arms. The disease usually runs its course in a week, but there may be serious complications.

Sand flies may carry **leishmaniasis,** a parasitic protozoan that causes unhealing sores of the skin. There is no preventive medicine and cures can be difficult. Covering the skin in areas where sand flies are biting is the best protection.

Yellow fever, confined to eastern Panama in Central America, is a mosquito-borne virus disease for which an effective vaccine exists (see previous chapter). If contracted, symptoms may progress rapidly from headache, fever, and vomiting to liver failure, coma, and death, although medical treatment to lower fever and reduce dehydration can be effective. Survivors acquire immunity, unlike with malaria. The same mosquito species can carry dengue and yellow fever.

Chagas's disease is a rare (in Central America) disease spread by assassin bugs called *"vinchucas,"* oval, brown insects with cone-shaped heads that live in palm trees or thatched huts in remote areas below about 3,000 feet. The bugs bite at night while victims are sleeping. The disease agent is a protozoan called a trypanosome. Symptoms include a hard swelling at the site of the bite after several days followed by fever, vomiting, and shortness of breath in the disease's acute form. There is also a chronic form in which the disease may cause slow deterioration of internal organs, especially the heart.

Various forms of bacterial disease generally called **typhus** can be spread by ticks, mites, or lice. Symptoms first resemble a bad cold, followed by fever, chills, swollen glands, and a rash. There may be a sore where the bite occurred.

Rabies is fairly common in Central America. It's one more reason to sleep within screens or tents, since vampire bats can spread it. The bats are very stealthy about approaching victims. If an animal bites you, try to get it tested. An effective rabies vaccine does exist.

Botflies are housefly-like insects whose larvae are parasitic on mammals. Female botflies lay their eggs on mosquitoes (after first catching the mosquitoes) and when such a mosquito bites an animal, the egg is deposited on the victim. After hatching, the grub or larva then burrows under the skin and feeds on the victim's tissues until it emerges to pupate. Botflies mainly parasitize wild mammals but larvae also are deposited on humans, particularly those spending much time in the rain forest. Symptoms include pimplelike swellings and needlelike pains as the larvae grow under the skin. The larvae require an airhole to breathe and can easily be killed by covering the hole with Vaseline and adhesive tape. They then must be squeezed out, which may not be so easy. They seem easier to squeeze out the smaller they are, so prompt attention to burning bumps is advisable. (It's also said they can be coaxed out by taping meat over their breathing holes, though I haven't tried this.) Larvae in scalp or hands may require minor surgery. Although unpleasant, botfly infestation isn't dangerous except in the case of secondary infection.

Diarrhea and Attendant Ills

Diarrhea usually is caused by the body's normal reaction to strange water, food, and other conditions. Usually Pepto-Bismol, plenty of (clean) liquids, and a day of rest will cure it. Stronger medicines like Lomotil should only be taken in "emergencies" (as when you need to ride the bus for a day) since they can cause problems themselves.

Diarrhea is the body's way of eliminating material it can't handle, and it's best not to interfere with it too much unless it's a symptom of disease. If diarrhea lasts more than a few days, or is accompanied by fever, vomiting, or pain, it may be a symptom of the following parasites, which can be diagnosed by getting a stool test. This can be done inexpensively in most Central American cities.

Giardia is a protozoan that lives in water, including cold, clear mountain streams. Symptoms may include bloating and gas, and may be intermittent. Medicine (not antibiotics, which don't work against protozoans) should be taken under a doctor's supervision.

Amoebic dysentery also is caused by a protozoan, and can become chronic. Symptoms may include blood or mucus in feces. Treatment is like that of giardiasis.

Parasitic roundworms or **flatworms** may be contracted through food and water, or through walking barefoot on contaminated soil.

Diarrhea may also be a symptom of the following diseases or poisons:

Bacillary dysentery is caused by bacteria, and may cause high fever, bloody feces, headaches, and vomiting. It is very contagious, but usually lasts no more than a week. It can be treated with antibiotics.

Diarrhea associated with tingling, itching, or numbness of the lips, hands, and feet six to eight hours after eating saltwater fish or shellfish may be a symptom of **dinoflagellate,** or **ciguatoxin, poisoning.** Reef fish such as barracuda, jack, and snappers may carry the toxin, especially in disturbed or polluted areas. If severe symptoms persist, seek medical help.

Cholera and **typhoid** are the most dangerous diseases of which diarrhea may be symptomatic. Cholera may cause fatal dehydration if not treated promptly. Typhoid, which has influenzalike early symptoms, can lead to pneumonia or other life-threatening complications.

Bothersome Animals and Plants

An important aspect of tropical biodiversity is the incredibly ingenious array of survival strategies organisms have evolved. But these ingenious strategies may be employed against you if you run afoul of them. A good, overall way to avoid doing so is to stay on trails or other established routes when in wildlands. If you do move off the trail, be careful where you step and what you touch. Even on trails, be careful when stepping over logs or other obstructions.

With very rare exceptions, the only dangerous large animal in Central America is the domestic dog, which can get nasty to hikers passing rural settlements. Usually it's enough to ignore dogs and pass on, but if they get too close, just picking up a potential throwing stone can be enough to keep them from getting carried away. Walking sticks are also reassuring in such situations. Other domestic animals such as pigs and bulls can also be dangerous.

Among the larger wild animals, the white-lipped peccary has a reputation for treeing hunters. It is the larger and darker of the two peccary species and travels in sizable herds. It survives only in remote forest areas, however, and you'll be unlikely to see one. Large crocodiles and caimans survive in a few remote or protected areas. Don't swim in such areas, and be watchful near the water's edge. I've never heard of a recent crocodile attack on a human in Central America, but the founder of California's wine industry, Agoston Haraszthy, is believed to have been eaten by a crocodile when traveling across Nicaragua after a European vine-collecting tour in the 1860s.

Snakes

You need to be more careful about small animals. A number of poisonous snake species live in Central America. The most dangerous is the fer-de-lance (*Bothrops asper*), also known as the "*terciopelo*" in Hispanic Central America and the "*tommigoff*" in Belize. Terciopelos are large (up to 8 feet), common, and aggressive snakes of wet forest up to 5,000 feet. They are pit vipers, like rattlesnakes, and have similar triangular heads. Terciopelos have velvety smooth skin (thus their name, which means "velvet" in Spanish), with dark brown diamond patterns over tan. Young ones have yellow tails. Another large but less commonly seen pit viper is the bushmaster (*Lachesis mutus*), or matabuey (ox-killer), which can reach a length of 12 feet, but is less aggressive than the terciopelo. Tropical rattlesnakes (*Crotalus durissus*), called "*cascabeles*," live in dry forest. A number of small pit viper species live in various habitats at all elevations. Some spend much of their time in branches of trees or shrubs, so be careful of head, arms, and hands when moving off trail as well as feet. The small red, yellow, and black coral snakes have even more potent venom than pit vipers, but their fangs are so small that they present little danger unless handled. There are some mildly poisonous snakes as well as the dangerous pit vipers and coral snakes. They lack the triangular head of the pit vipers. Nonpoisonous snakes also may bite. Such bites will show the marks of many small teeth instead of deep puncture wounds of viper fangs.

Chances are you'll see few snakes, and the ones you see will be nonpoisonous species. The only Central American bite I've even heard about firsthand was when a rattlesnake struck at a jogger. The fangs glanced harmlessly off the jogger's leg, but running through the forest in shorts isn't recommended. If you can see and avoid a snake, it presents no further danger to you unless you try to catch or kill it (although there may be another of the same species nearby, particularly in the mating season). Even if a snake bites you, in about a third of cases it will not inject venom. Partly because of this, the old treatments for snakebite such as applying tourniquets or incising the bite and trying to suck out the venom are no longer recommended. Getting the victim to a hospital or other medical facility for antivenin injections and other treatment is the first priority. It can help if you bring the snake in for identification, but you may be further endangering yourself and your companions by trying to capture it. (In recent years, outdoor stores have begun selling venom extractors, small pumps for removing venom or insect stings without incisions. As usual, there is some debate about their effectiveness, and they shouldn't be considered as a substitute for getting bite victims to the hospital.)

Insects and Others

Scorpions, tarantulas, centipedes, and other interesting but possibly venomous creatures are common. They are another reason for not wandering far off trails. They also move readily into houses and campsites, so exercise a little extra caution about where you sit and where you put your hands and feet when staying in forest quarters. The chances of a fatal or even dangerous bite from them are not large.

There are hundreds of native bee and wasp species in Central America, many of which can sting if molested, but none of which pose any particular danger except to those allergic to bee stings. There has been much concern recently about Africanized honey-bees, which have become established in Central America, mainly in dry forest areas. These can be extremely aggressive in response to perceived threats to their hives, and there have been several deaths from their attacks. If you come across a honeybee concentration or hear a loud buzzing from a tree or other location, move quietly but rapidly in the other direction. If the bees come after you, run, but watch where you're going. One victim tried to find shelter in a small cave, but that didn't stop the bees.

Ants also can deliver painful stings when they feel their nest or host plant is threatened. Large black ants called "*balas*" (bullets) are particularly to be avoided because of the quantity of formic acid they can inject. The red acacia ants are small, but have a painful bite. Army ants can bite, but tales of their leaving behind them the picked bones of large animals as they swarm through the forest are fictional.

To me, one of the most bothersome creatures is the chigger, a virtually invisible mite that takes a tiny sip of cell fluid from its victim before dropping off. Chiggers carry no dangerous diseases, but their bites trigger an immune system response that causes major itching. Since dozens of chiggers may bite, sleepless nights may result during which you feel like jumping up and down screaming. There are supposed to be many ways of evading chigger bites, such as sprinkling powdered sulfur on clothes, keeping pants tucked into socks, or spraying insect repellents. These may reduce bites, but, in my experience, none *stops* chiggers. You'll get bitten less if you avoid walking in pastures or off-trail. Calamine lotion or other preparations can relieve the itching. If you scratch the bites, they'll just itch more.

Ticks can carry disease, so check your skin and clothing for them regularly. They may be abundant or uncommon, depending on place and time. In Darién, tiny ticks dug themselves under my fingernails and toenails—very uncomfortable. Ticks that have attached themselves can be removed by first covering their mouthparts with Vaseline or some other substance that will make them loosen their grip, then pulling them off gently with tweezers, making sure not to leave the mouthparts in the skin.

Other insects may be locally bothersome, such as sandflies on beaches, or no-see-um gnats in wet forest. Conditions can vary surprisingly. No-see-ums were a torture during one visit to southwest Costa Rica's coastal rain forest. In the somewhat drier forest of the Nicoya Peninsula, there were so few biting insects we slept without screens. The mosquitoes were so bad in a dry forest in Guanacaste Province that I had to set up a tent in a house. Nothing I've experienced in Central America, however, was as bad as arctic or north woods mosquitoes and black flies.

Reef Animals

Generally, the same is true about bothersome animals in reefs as in rain forests. Large animals such as sharks, barracuda, or moray eels pose much less danger than small ones like stingrays, sea urchins, bristle worms, jellyfish, and even the corals themselves, which can give painful stings if you touch them. Be careful when walking on the bottom, because you may step on sea urchins or stingrays. The dead coral rock that makes up most of reefs can give nasty cuts if you fall. Stings can be treated with vinegar to deactivate the poisonous substance, and with calamine lotion to relieve irritation. Make sure to remove jellyfish stingers or sea urchin spines. Reef animal stings may cause allergic reactions similar to those associated with bee stings. If you feel faint or have trouble breathing after a sting, you may need medical help.

It's best not to touch *any* corals or other sessile animals in reefs, since you may damage them if they don't damage you. In the unlikely event a large shark or barracuda takes an interest in you, don't try to swim away in a panic, but keep facing the fish as you work your way to shore.

Plants

Poison ivy doesn't grow in Central America, but it has many relatives (in the family Anacardiaceae) that are poisonous to touch or eat, as well as others that are quite good to eat (like mangoes and cashews, although some people are allergic to green mangoes and cashews are poisonous if eaten raw). Black poisonwood (*Metopium browneii*), a tree-sized poison ivy relative of northern Central America, has virulently irritating black sap that often drips down its whitish trunk. Manzanillo, manchineel, or poison guava (*Hippomane mancinella*, also mentioned in the food section) is a member of the Euphorbia family: its milky sap is poisonous externally as well as internally, causing severe swelling, blistering, and temporary blindness. It is a small tree or shrub with alternate, oval leaves, yellow flower spikes, and small fruits shaped like crab apples. It mainly grows near beaches.

In general, be cautious about touching forest plants, because there are so many kinds, and so little is known about most of them. If you lose your footing and grab a stem or vine to steady yourself, you may find that it has thorns, or, worse, urticating spines or hairs that can inject poisons. These may cause long-lasting numbness or necrosis as well as temporarily acute pain (animals such as caterpillars and tarantulas also may have urticating spines). Touching plants may elicit attack from resident insects such as acacia ants, too.

Heat and Sun

You may feel dull and lethargic for some time after arriving in the lowlands. This is a natural reaction to unaccustomed heat and humidity, and it's best not to resist it. Take it easy, drink lots of cool, nonalcoholic drinks, and don't overdo snorkeling or walking expeditions. Keep your head covered. Strenuous activity when not acclimatized can lead with surprising speed to the dizziness, headaches, and abdominal upsets of heat exhaustion (not to mention bad sunburn—the direct rays of tropical sun have a quality all their own). In extreme cases, the flushed, dry skin, intense, throbbing headache, and mental confusion of heatstroke may ensue, and medical help should be sought.

Cold and Wet

Getting chilled can be just as much of a problem in lowlands as getting overheated. Temperatures may become quite cool during "northeaster" storms, and if you're out in the woods in one, you'll find it very difficult to stay dry. You also can get chilled very easily while snorkeling, at the same time you're getting sunburned.

Hypothermia—a dangerous lowering of core body temperature—can be a possibility in highlands, where wind, rain, and cold nights can make being outside very stressful, particularly if you're camping or backpacking. Symptoms include extreme fatigue, mental confusion, and shivering or numbness. Judgment can be impaired, a serious matter if you're trying to find your way. Keeping your head covered and changing into dry clothes will help you conserve body heat, and warm, sweet drinks help to generate more.

Getting to Wildlands

Central America has very few places like Yosemite or Yellowstone, where you can drive on a good road to the middle of a big wildland and stay in an extensive complex of resorts and campgrounds. This is partly because Central American countries haven't had the wealth to develop such large tourist facilities in their protected areas, and partly because they've been wise enough to foresee the problems of building virtual recreational cities in the heart of supposed wilderness. They have tried to keep tourist services in existing communities, where local people will profit from them. This does complicate logistics. Often you may need to use several modes of transport to reach your destination.

Bus

Bus is the way most Central Americans travel, and it is the cheapest and in some ways the easiest. Buses go just about everywhere there are roads, although they become scarce and irregular in remote areas. You can usually travel across most of a country for a few dollars. On the downside, buses tend to be crowded and uncomfortable (although there are deluxe buses on some routes), and some of the roads and drivers can be scary. Mechanical breakdowns are not uncommon (buses tend to be old—many are secondhand yellow schoolbuses from the United States), but personnel are conscientious about trying to keep things running.

Finding bus stations can be the biggest problem of bus travel. Sometimes all the buses serving a town use a single terminal, although it may be a mile or so out of town. Sometimes different terminals serve different routes; other times each bus company has its terminal in a different location. Such terminals may be well camouflaged: I once spent what seemed like hours going up and down a crowded market street in San José looking for a bus to Guanacaste. I would get intricate directions toward one end of the street from somebody, then other intricate directions toward the other end of the street from someone else. Especially if you have luggage, getting a cab to the bus station may be worth the expense. Usually you can just tell the driver you want to go to "*la estación de autobús para . . .*" and he'll know the way. If he doesn't, find another cab: you can spend a lot of time and money looking for things in cabs.

At the station, there may be a ticket office or you may need to buy your ticket from the driver or his assistant. Passengers usually line up where the bus parks—often there's a sign saying the destination. Buses often leave very early, at 5 A.M. while it's still dark. It's good to get there a while in advance to be sure to get a seat. They may let you ride standing, but that's not very comfortable or safe. There may be a luggage handler who'll take your bags and put them in a rack or compartment, or you may have to carry your luggage on the bus. Be careful of theft when standing in line. Don't leave carry-ons unattended while you buy food or visit the restroom.

Food and drink are seldom problems, because vendors crowd around at every station and sometimes ride the bus between stations selling soft drinks, rolls, fruit, ice cream, empanadas, and a kind of iced fruit jello in plastic bags. Buses also may stop at restaurants. I've never had any digestive problems from bus vendor food, but it's best to be cautious. Buses never have toilets, and toilets in bus stations may not be well maintained (they never have toilet paper).

Few buses in Central America go to parks or other wildlands. They go to adjacent towns, and you have to make your own way from there. You also may need to change buses several times to reach a remote destination, so allow plenty of time for bus travel.

Airplane

Central America has many small domestic airlines forming an indispensable travel network to remote areas, many of which have no road access. Although much more expensive than bus travel, they are quite reasonable: you can fly anywhere in most countries for less than $50 one-way. This is quite a popular way to travel, so you'll usually need reservations in advance. Local travel agencies can make reservations for you. Be sure to have two-way reservations when visiting remote areas, because it's easier to get into them than to get out. Bad weather can strand large numbers of people, and when the planes begin to fly again, those with reservations will have priority. Also make sure you know where your reservation flies *from*. The small airlines often use different airports than the large ones. You may get bumped from your seat if you show up late.

Small planes *do* have much worse safety records than jetliners, and Central America is a tricky region to fly in because of its mountains, trade winds, tropical rains, and often primitive runways. Taking off or landing in the lowlands may be one time you won't be entirely pleased with the majestic height of rain forest trees, as your plane speeds toward them with a full load of ranchers, nuns, medical missionaries, and tourists. On the other hand, flying in small planes gives an incomparable bird's-eye view of the landscape.

Boat

In general, traveling by boat is less reliable and relatively more expensive and time-consuming than by bus or plane. Large coastal vessels such as ferries are inexpensive but may have erratic schedules. Finding passage on private cargo or fishing ships is possible if you hang around docks, but even less reliable than scheduled ferries. Hiring a small boat is surprisingly costly because fuel for outboard motors is very expensive. You can spend as much to go a few dozen miles up a river as you would to fly halfway across the country. Boat travel also has its hazards from weather, mechanical failure, and collisions with reefs, bars, or snags.

Boat travel is simply the only way to get to many coastal and river locations, however, and it usually passes much interesting country—estuaries, swamps, and riverbanks. You can see a lot of birds, and sometimes other wildlife. Unless you have a good guide, you probably won't see things at great leisure, since the boatmen are there for the business, not the birds, and tend to whisk you along as fast as they can go. On upper reaches of rivers like the Plátano in Honduras, where outboards can't go, you will need to hire paddlers or polers as well as a boatman, and you'll probably encounter more wildlife because of the lesser accessibility.

Automobile

See the previous chapter (pages 52–53) for the advantages and disadvantages of bringing your own car to Central America. Similar pros and cons apply if you rent a car in-country. You'll have greatly enhanced mobility and carrying capacity, but you'll have to be very careful about accidents, road conditions, and theft. With a rental, of course, you won't have to worry about getting it home. Car rental costs are at least as high in Central America as in the U.S., and often much higher. There are many small companies, as well as the big U.S. firms, so you can probably find bargains if you shop around (check under *"alquiler de automóviles"* in phone books or other listings), but you get what you pay for—it won't be a bargain if you rent a piece of junk and it breaks down. As in the U.S., there will be various complicated rate packages and insurance arrangements by which you can save money if you understand them.

Rental companies are very meticulous about checking for damage when you return cars—not surprisingly, considering road conditions. They may have regulations against taking two-wheel-drive cars off paved roads, which will be an obstacle against using them to reach many, but not all, wildlands. You can get around this by renting a four-wheel-drive, which may not be that much more expensive, but which they also will check meticulously for minor damage on return.

Renting a car or jeep with a driver is another possibility. Most rural communities have some kind of backroads taxi service. Drivers can serve as guides as well as transportation, and costs tend to be reasonable (less than boat rental). Of course, after you reach your destination, if you want to spend the day hiking or birdwatching and still have the car there, you will have to pay the driver for his time. You may be able to save some money by having him come back and pick you up. If it's not too far, you might simply walk back to town after you've seen what you want. Local taxi drivers often are willing to provide this service. If there seem to be no taxis, ask at your hotel or at a bodega or cafe. The owner may close up shop and take you himself.

Hitchhiking

If you spend much time in the hinterland, you'll probably encounter situations in which there is simply no public transport to a particular place at a particular time. Since many Central Americans also find themselves in this situation, hitchhiking is a respectable occupation. You'll probably get a ride quickly, if there's any traffic on the road you want to take. Drivers may or may not expect to be paid for the ride, so you should ask. They'll usually name a reasonable figure. Hitchhike early in the day so that you won't find yourself on the road at night.

Of course, you can hitchhike where there is public transportation, and you should offer to pay in this situation too. It's easiest to hitch on the open road outside of towns. Trucks pick up hitchhikers, so a group of two, three, or even four may be able to get a ride. Central American hitchhiking carries the same dangers of encounters with criminals, intolerant lawmen, and accidents as in the U.S. When hitching by dirt roads, watch out for rocks thrown up by the wheels of passing trucks. Hitchhiking in areas of social unrest may lead to encounters with soldiers or other armed people. Women shouldn't hitchhike alone.

Other Travel Modes

Railroads are currently at a low ebb. Panama has let its transisthmian railroad deteriorate badly, although there are plans to reopen it. Costa Rica had a recreational "jungle train" from San José to the Caribbean until recently, but that is now partly closed. In some cases, small-gauge trains originally built for banana plantations have been adapted to provide access to wildlands.

A few Central Americans are cross-country bicyclists, and this is a possibility for visitors, too. Central American motorists aren't used to giving way to bicycles, however (for that matter, one might say they're barely used to giving way to other cars). Traffic on main, paved roads tends to be heavy and fast, and roads are narrow. Secondary roads tend to be dirt—dusty in the dry season, muddy in the wet. You'll have to watch your bike all the time it's not safely stashed in a hotel. In the lowlands, the heat and humidity will make cycling very thirsty work. In the highlands, secondary roads and tracks are quite likely to be too steep, rocky, and muddy even for trail bikes. On the other hand, Central America's "small scale" seems appropriate for bicycles. They probably have a future there, but pioneers need to be hardy and experienced.

Horses and their relatives still are a workaday mode of transport in the Central American "campo," so horseback-riding skills may come in very useful in getting to wildlands. Some tour agents feature special horseback trips. Even if you don't have horseback skills, guides may want you to ride rather than walk, since they will be riding. Use your own judgment on this; Central American horses are small and easygoing, in my limited experience. (My first horseback ride was an 11-mile trip up a Costa Rican volcano.) You can always dismount and walk over the scariest parts of the route (as I did). Even if you don't want to ride, hiring a horse or mule (and its owner) to carry baggage is an option. The steepness and poor condition of many Central American trails may take some of the pleasure out of carrying it yourself.

Things to Do

Cross-country skiing is out in Central America, but you can enjoy just about every other kind of nature-related recreation there. Facilities will generally be more limited than in the U.S., but that's not necessarily bad. In some of the less visited areas, you may find you have a national park to yourself (except for the people who live around it, and may be farming in it). In such cases, your presence is important as a living embodiment of the "ecotourism benefits" everybody talks about.

Urban Nature

You can learn a lot about what there is to see and do in a country by strolling through its museums, city parks, and other facilities. Archaeological museums tend to be quite good, as pre-Columbian culture is a source of pride. Natural history museums have lagged behind, and may contain rather gruesome arrays of badly stuffed specimens, but they are an expression of concern for the country's wildlife, and for that they deserve support. Expensive presentation isn't necessary for useful information. If I hadn't gone to a tiny "Museo de Fauna" at the University of Honduras in Tegucigalpa, I'd never have known about a major fossil site near a park I wanted to visit. Similarly, conditions at zoos may be depressing, but they're an expression of interest in wildlife, and perhaps the only chance that most Central Americans get to see much of it. Conservation agencies or organizations run zoos in some countries, and may run environmental education programs in connection with them. On Earth Day 1990, relatively few Costa Ricans attended the official ceremony presided over by President Oscar Arias, but the zoo in Parque Bolívar was crowded (as was the country's first Burger King). Facilities can be expected to improve to the extent that eco-tourism provides revenue.

City parks aren't extensive in most of Central America—usually a few squares of shrubs and trees downtown, and perhaps some acres of soccer fields and baseball diamonds on the outskirts. Tropical diversity has a way of populating even these small areas, however. I counted about a dozen species of songbirds, woodpeckers, parakeets, and other birds in downtown San José on my first day there, all completely new to me. Panama City is an exception, having a sizable forest, the Parque Natural Metropolitano, populated by monkeys, hawks, agoutis, and other creatures within a ten-minute cab ride from the hotel district. Most Central American capitals have interesting natural areas accessible by day-trip.

Day Hiking

Don't be fooled by old movies that show jungle explorers as miserable wrecks. Lowland tropical forest is a delightful habitat to hike in, full of light, color, and interest. You'll probably sweat a lot, and if you wear glasses they'll steam up, but a bandanna and some spec-spray will take care of that. In general, sun and insects won't be bothersome, since the forest canopy will shade you very effectively, and the kinds of insects that bite people will not have large, concentrated populations. (Because of competition, predation, and other factors that cause high tropical biodiversity, few species have large, concentrated populations in rain forest.) If you wear the right clothes and footwear and take plenty of water, you'll come back feeling better than when you left.

Highland hiking may be a bit more stressful than lowland because of steep and slippery trails, chilly or damp weather, and the effects of altitude, which can be emotional (anxiety, irritability) as well as physical (breathlessness, fatigue). (My Sierra Club outing almost came to blows as we were walking around on 11,000-foot Cerro de la Muerte.) In drier highlands such as the northern plateaus, the sun can be very stressful because pines and live oaks don't provide much shade. Sun is also stressful in the coastal plain and interior valleys of the dry forest zone in winter when the trees are bare.

One of the nice things about hiking in Central America is how often it is possible to walk through a number of habitats in a day—say, from the dry forest and savanna of a volcanic plateau, down to the evergreen gallery forest of a river bottom, to crocodile-haunted lagoons and mangrove swamps and turtle beaches. Or, conversely, one can go from the dry forest of a valley bottom up through gorges of pines and sweet gums, ravines of tree fern and laurels, to fir forest on high ridgetops.

Backpacking and Trekking

Backpacking in Central America would benefit from more extensive, better maintained trail systems than currently exist. There are a few places, such as Costa Rica's Chirripó National Park, where a backpacking tradition is firmly established, but opportunities for self-guided backpacking are still limited. Some tour agencies offer guided backpacking expeditions over extensive rain forest routes.

The Guatemalan highlands have potential for the kind of trekking with local porters that has become popular in the Andes and Nepal, with gorgeous scenery and a colorful indigenous culture. Unfortunately, the political situation has ruled this out so far.

There are established international walking routes through various roadless areas—the best known of these is that from Panama to Colombia through Darién. Such routes are commercial as much as recreational, however, and some of the commerce is illegal. Darién is increasingly being used by the drug trade, for example. Such routes certainly offer plenty of adventure in the good old sense of grueling hardship and danger, but whether they're the best way to experience nature is questionable.

Camping

Camping is less of a tradition in Central America than in the U.S., although some young, middle-class urban people do it. Of course, the average campesino family's daily life is like camping in some ways. Designated campsites as in the U.S. are still rather uncommon, although many national parks have them. Even if there isn't a designated campsite in a park, you may be able to arrange with rangers or caretakers to camp (in some parks, you can also arrange to stay at ranger stations).

Outside of parks, people may be willing to let you camp on their land, but you should always ask, and offer to pay. Even if a place seems empty and remote, there's likely to be somebody around who owns it in some way.

Snorkeling and Scuba Diving

Snorkeling opportunities range from the casual, as with exploring small reefs a few yards from coastal beaches, to the intense, as with the massive offshore reefs of the Belizean cayes or Honduran Bay Islands. The best coastal snorkeling is on the Caribbean side, because Pacific coast waters don't favor coral reefs, but a few offshore Pacific islands such as Panama's Pearl Islands and Costa Rica's Caño and Coco islands have coral reefs. Pacific coast snorkeling can still be worthwhile in sheltered bays. Snorkeling in rivers and lakes is another possibility because of the region's colorful tropical fish fauna. Be careful about swallowing fresh water, since it may harbor amoebas or other parasites.

Accommodations for snorkelers range from expensive resorts, to simple guest houses and hotels, to campgrounds and empty beaches. Central America largely has been spared the massive, high-rise resort development that has beset the Mexican coast, although pressures for this have been growing.

Scuba diving is the fastest growing form of recreation on the Caribbean coast, mainly in Belize and Honduras's Bay Islands. Many resorts and guides offer full-length courses in diving, as well as trips to diving locations.

Boating

Whitewater rafting is a thriving industry in Costa Rica, with numerous agencies running trips on Caribbean slope rivers. Agencies in Guatemala, Honduras, and Panama also offer whitewater trips. The quality of the agencies and guides offering such trips obviously is particularly important, since poor equipment, skills, or judgment on white water can be life-threatening. Agencies should provide such safety equipment as helmets and life jackets, as well as advice on how to take care of yourself if you fall in the water (for example, you should lie on your back in the water and face downstream, and try to go feetfirst so that you'll be able to fend off rocks).

Agencies also run rafting trips on lowland rivers such as the Usumacinta in the Petén, the Macal in Belize, and the Patuca in Honduras. Before the Nicaraguan civil war, the trip from Lake Nicaragua down the San Juan River was very popular, and has been revived in the past few years.

Sailing and sea-kayaking among the cays of the Caribbean coast and in the bays of the Pacific are increasingly popular. Many tour agencies run sailing or kayaking expeditions.

Birding and Wildlife Observation

A substantial proportion of ecotourists in Central America are birders, and with good reason, since the region has over a thousand resident and migratory species. Excellent field guides are available for Costa Rica and Panama (see Stiles and Skutch's *Birds of Costa Rica* and Ridgely's *Birds of Panama*). Peterson's *Mexican Birds* includes most northern Central American species. Tour agencies run a number of trips specifically for birding.

Field guides for mammals, reptiles and amphibians, or insects are less available as yet (even the bird guides are large and pricey). Given the large numbers of species, and the scarcity of scientific data on many of them, this isn't surprising. This is also true of trees and flowers, of which there are thousands, many still hard to identify. Natural history compendiums such as Janzen's *Costa Rican Natural History* can be hard to lug around, but are useful.

Observing animals in Central America is the same as elsewhere: you need to know the right place, season, and time to do so. Dawn and dusk are the times of greatest activity. The dry season is good for wildlife in Central America because many plants flower and fruit then, and animals time their highly active breeding seasons to coincide with high food availability. Wildlife also is more visible during the dry season because many trees, particularly on the Pacific side, lose their leaves at that time. There is much local variation, however. The time to see sea turtles mating en masse on Pacific beaches (events called *"arribadas"*—arrivals) is mostly in summer. In the tropics, one species or another is reproducing virtually year-round.

Central American countries are increasingly concerned about protecting their native species, for commercial as well as scientific reasons. All are signatories of the Convention on International Trade in Endangered Species of Wild Flora and Fauna (CITES), which strictly controls trade of sea turtles, black coral, orchids, and other organisms. Collecting and other "taking" of any species will generally require official permission, as will buying any live or dead wild specimen. Don't buy wild plants or animals from campesinos or local markets; you'll be encouraging their extinction if you do. (This doesn't apply, of course, to organisms raised specifically for legal sale, although you may still have trouble getting anything like that through U.S. Customs.)

Archaeology

The great restored cities at Tikal and Copán are world famous, and there are a number of smaller restored pre-Columbian (and post-Columbian) sites. Most are in the Maya area, but other parts of Central America also have rich archaeological resources such as the little-known stone ruins at Guayabo National Monument on Costa

Rica's Caribbean side. Some sites still have cultural significance to local indigenous people, such as the ruins of the Quiché Maya capital of Utatlán, destroyed by Pedro de Alvarado in 1524. There also are dozens of unrestored and unprotected sites scattered throughout wildlands, such as the mysterious "white cities" of the Mosquitia. If you stumble across one of these, don't dig or remove artifacts or buy them from local people. If you want to get actively involved in archaeology, Earthwatch and other cooperative research organizations usually have projects in Central America which welcome volunteer participation.

Mountaineering

Central American mountains aren't high enough for classic mountaineering, but there's plenty of rugged climbing. Many peaks are so remote, heavily forested, or otherwise inaccessible that they remain little explored, particularly in the eastern highlands of Nicaragua and Honduras and the Talamanca region of Costa Rica and Panama. Even the relatively low peaks of Darién and Belize's Maya Mountains have seldom been climbed, and offer real challenges. There is no snow and ice climbing in the region, although small regions of Costa Rica and Guatemala were glaciated during the Pleistocene. The active volcanoes that overlook the Pacific from Guatemala to northern Panama offer exciting, sometimes hazardous, climbing.

Caving

Central America has many caves, particularly in areas of limestone bedrock. Many have fascinating local lore attached to them, such as "The Cave of the Vampires," which paleontologists from Chicago's Field Museum of Natural History heard of while hunting fossils in Honduras. Blood was said to drip from the ceiling, but when the paleontologists visited it, the blood turned out to be water full of iron oxide. Caves are the haunts of large bat colonies, blind fish, salamanders, and other interesting creatures. At Barra Honda National Park, a deep cave complex in Costa Rica's Nicoya Peninsula, spelunkers also found pre-Columbian archaeological remains. Belize, Honduras, and Guatemala have enormous, incompletely explored limestone cave systems, some accessible to casual travelers. In the volcanic region, lava tubes lead hundreds of meters underground.

Surfing

Pacific coast beaches offer excellent surfing, particularly in El Salvador—which was a surfing mecca until the 1980s civil war and probably will become one again—and in Costa Rica. The Caribbean generally is too shallow and protected for big waves, but windsurfing is increasingly popular, and a good way to visit small offshore cayes and reefs. Windsurfing on freshwater bodies such as Lake Nicaragua and lakes Arenal and Cachi in Costa Rica is also growing in popularity.

Fishing

Fishing for tarpon, billfish, snook, and other saltwater gamefish is probably the oldest form of recreational tourism in Central America and continues to thrive. There is a wide range of options, from world-class resorts which provide crewed vessels for deep-sea forays to local guides for dory fishing. Since many gamefish such as tarpon swim up rivers, freshwater fishing is also popular, and some native freshwater fishes such as the large cichlids called "*guapotes*" are valued gamefish. Introduction of exotic gamefish such as black bass and trout, however, has often had negative effects on native aquatic wildlife. Further introductions shouldn't be encouraged, although in cases where "the damage has been done" there's no reason not to fish for exotics.

CHAPTER FIVE

Guatemala

A T THE NORTH END of Central America, Guatemala is a land of extremes. It has the highest mountains, the largest population, and some of the wildest country. It's perhaps best known as the nation central to the ancient culture of the Mayas. World famous for its ancient Mayan cities like Tikal, Guatemala remains a land of the Maya today. Over half of its nearly 10 million people speak one of twenty-two Mayan languages and otherwise live much as their pre-Columbian ancestors did. The populous, highly productive Mayan world made Guatemala the primary Spanish colony in Central America, and the Maya still distinguish Guatemala as a nation. Yet the Maya have never had an equal voice with ladino society in ruling the nation, and this inequality continues to be a source of conflict.

As might be expected, the influence of North American ecosystems is strongest in Guatemala, where the highlands have a temperate climate, and an oak and pine vegetation, somewhat like California's. Yet that influence is manifested in some unexpected ways. The temperate highlands in Guatemala are in the center of the country, while the vast tropical lowland forest of the Petén is in the north. Some of the Petén forest's characteristic inhabitants, moreover, are North American in ancestry rather than South American, relict reminders that there were uniquely North American tropical ecosystems before the land bridge formed. Today's Petén forest shows a strong South American influence like its southern neighbors, but a somewhat reduced diversity of southern species. Only spider and howler monkeys inhabit it, for example, compared to Panama's seven monkey species.

No ecosystem in Central America has been influenced by humans as much as Guatemala's. The Petén once supported a complex of Mayan city-states with at least hundreds of thousands of inhabitants, and the highlands perhaps had a population similar to today's when the conquistadors arrived. The fact that diverse highland and lowland forests have survived is encouraging, although the pre-Columbian Mayas did not have the livestock, chainsaws, bulldozers, and other forest killers of today. Forest has been disappearing rapidly in this century, caught between the demands of export agriculture and the needs of the rural poor. Political turmoil has made it hard for government or private groups to effectively address the problems of disappearing flora and fauna. A lot of fascinating wildland remains, however, and Guatemala's well-developed tourism industry helps to conserve it.

The Land of Many Trees

Guatemala is one of two countries in Central America underlain by the North American tectonic plate, which extends as far south as the Motagua Valley, a deep valley running from the Gulf of Honduras to just north of Guatemala City. This means that the Petén rain forest, the most "South American" part of Guatemala, is tectonically part of North America. The Caribbean Plate underlies western Guatemala, and is riding over the offshore Cocos Plate in the tectonic process called "subduction." The tremendous stresses that occur as the Cocos Plate is forced into the earth's crust cause the earthquakes, volcanic eruptions, and land uplift which make Guatemala (and the rest of Central America) such a dramatic place.

Guatemala has four geological provinces. The Pacific coastal plain is made up of sediments eroded from the volcanic highlands, and is up to 70 kilometers wide. Its shoreline is uninterrupted by bays or large estuaries, and there are no offshore reefs. East of the coastal plain is the Pacific Volcanic Belt, which extends from the

Mexican to the Salvadoran border, and includes three of Central America's most active volcanoes: Santa María, Fuego, and Pacaya. Fuego has erupted fifty times since 1524; a 1971 explosion deposited ash up to 160 kilometers west of the crater. Central America's highest mountain is 4,220-meter Volcán Tajumulco near the Mexican border. Because of volcanic soil's fertility, the valleys and calderas of this region are the most heavily populated parts of the country despite the dangers of eruptions and, more seriously, earthquakes. Very powerful earthquakes occur where the North American and Caribbean plates move against each other along the Motagua fault zone. A 1976 quake on this fault killed 22,868 people.

East of the Volcanic Belt is the Cordillera Central, a complex of mountain ranges made up of ancient continental material—Paleozoic and Mesozoic sedimentary or metamorphic rocks underlain by igneous rocks from the earth's crust and mantle. The westernmost range is the Sierra de los Cuchumatanes, which includes the highest nonvolcanic mountains of northern Central America. A rolling plateau called Altos Cuchumatanes, mainly above 3,000 meters, contains the only evidence of glaciation in Central America except for Costa Rica's Chirripó Range. Separated from the Cuchumatanes by the valleys of the Chixoy and Polochic rivers (part of the Motagua fault complex) are the Sierra de Chuacús, the mountains of Alta and Baja Verapaz, and the Sierra de las Minas, which rises abruptly north of the Motagua Valley. Scattered through the cordilleras are outcrops of peridotite and serpentine, rocks which originate in the earth's mantle and are brought to the surface by tectonic activity. Serpentine is the source of jade, a precious stone very important to pre-Columbian cultures.

North of the Cordillera Central is the Petén lowland, which encompasses about a third of Guatemala's 108,889 square kilometers, but only about one-fortieth of its people. The Petén is an eroded limestone plain, mostly below 200 meters in elevation on its western half, rising to hills of 300 meters on its eastern side and in the Sierra del Lacondón in the west. Although rainfall ranges between 1,000 and 2,000 millimeters, surface streams are scarce in much of the Petén because of the porous limestone bedrock. The northwest quarter, however, is mostly an enormous wetland, the Laguna del Tigre area, which has been called the largest freshwater wetland system in Central America. It is perhaps the wildest place in Central America north of the Mosquitia. Except for a few rivers in the east, most of the Petén drains northwest into the Usumacinta River and Gulf of Mexico.

Guatemala's Paleozoic and Mesozoic limestones have yielded fossils of marine invertebrates from those eras, but there are few fossils of land animals. Fossils from the Petén and Motagua Valley are of large Pleistocene mammals such as mastodons and ground sloths, which shows that the land bridge already existed at the time the animals lived (since ground sloths are South American). Entirely North American fossil faunas from before the land bridge have only been found farther south, in Honduras and Panama.

Guatemala's native flora and fauna are very diverse because of the many local climates produced by the mountains. It has about 1,500 vertebrate animal species, including 700 bird species, and an estimated 8,000 vascular plant species, including 700 trees. Almost all of it was forested: "Guatemala" means "land of many trees" in the Aztec language ("Iximche" in Mayan). The Pacific coastal plain, where rain almost never falls from November to April, has a narrow band of mangrove forest along the shore, evergreen forest along rivers, and tropical deciduous forest on uplands. On the western slope of the volcanic belt, where more rain falls, evergreen tropical forest replaces the deciduous forest. Above about 1,000 meters, tropical forest begins to be replaced by a montane forest of pine, oak, and other trees with temperate affinities such as madrone and hornbeam. Higher still on the volcano slopes is a lush cloud forest of oaks, laurels, pines, figs, and other moisture-loving species—a forest that seems, paradoxically, more "tropical" than the drier oak-pine woodlands below. More pine species and other even more northern plants, such as yew, fir, and alder, grow above the cloud forest. Above about 2,700 meters, the trees begin to get stunted, and stretches of alpine meadow vegetation appear, and above 3,000 meters, trees are scarce.

Most of the Central Cordillera is covered with pine-oak woodlands, with altitudinal zonation similar to that on the volcanoes.

The Guatemalan mountains are the southernmost extension of some North American plants like sugar maple and birch, and northern birds such as ravens are common. In interior valleys such as the western Motagua Valley, where overhanging mountains cause a "rain shadow," grows a desertlike vegetation of tall cereus cactus, yucca, acacia, and other thorny shrubs. East and north of the Cordillera, where elevations drop and the dry season is less pronounced, semievergreen tropical forest is intermixed with areas of savanna and marsh. The animals in the Petén forest are much the same as those of the Mosquitia, although some southern species such as sloths are absent.

Mayan civilization began within this complex of ecosystems, or similar ones of adjacent Mexico, but nobody knows just how. Squash and avocados may have been domesticated in the area as long as nine thousand years ago, and corn six thousand years ago. Since the wild ancestor of corn is a highland grass, this may indicate that settled farming life began in the highlands. Over three thousand years ago, an urban civilization appeared in the Mexican lowlands of Tabasco north of Guatemala. This civilization has been called "Olmec," but since the languages still spoken in that area are related to Mayan, the people may simply have been "proto-Mayans." By two thousand years ago, large cities had spread to the Guatemalan highlands, particularly one called Kaminalhuyu near Guatemala City. These cities were considerably influenced by Teotihuacán, the great city in the Mexican highlands.

About 1,700 years ago, a huge civilization which is called "Classic Maya" developed in the Petén lowlands. It depended economically on a sophisticated system of canals and reservoirs which irrigated raised-bed farmlands, and centered on ceremonial complexes ruled by hereditary priest-kings. The ruins of the complexes are scattered throughout the area and indicate that population was very dense. Recently deciphered glyphs on stelae and other ceremonial carvings indicate that the ruling dynasties competed fiercely with others for prestige and resources. Competition and environmental deterioration may have contributed to the rather sudden abandonment of the Petén cities 1,100 years ago. Forest reclaimed the Petén, although what grows there now probably differs significantly from the forest that was standing before the Mayan cities. City-states continued to flourish in the highlands and in the Yucatán Peninsula to the north of the Petén.

The Conquest

Highland Mayan civilization was still rich and powerful when Hernando Cortés's lieutenant, Pedro de Alvarado, invaded Guatemala in 1524. One tribe, the Quichés, who had immigrated from the north a few centuries before, had established an empire that covered most of the highlands and Pacific coast. The ruins of their capital, K'umarcaah (also called Utatlán), are near present-day Santa Cruz del Quiché. Although Alvarado had only a few hundred soldiers (Tlaxcalan mercenaries from Mexico as well as Spaniards), he was able to defeat the highland Maya by first allying himself with the rebel Caxchiquel tribe against the Quichés and their allies, and later turning on the Caxchiquels. (The highlands had also been devastated by the first smallpox epidemic in 1521.) Maya resistance continued in the hinterlands for many years—in the Verapaz mountains until Bartoloméo de las Casas pacified and evangelized them in 1539, and in the Petén, where the Itzá dynasty controlled the kingdom of Tayasal around Lake Petén Itzá, until 1697. But disease and persecution reduced their population by as much as five million people, according to Bartoloméo de las Casas, and they remained at the bottom of colonial society.

Guatemala was Spain's major colony in Central America, the administrative center or "*audiencia*" for the others. Its wealth was based on exploitation of Maya labor, first through slavery, then through debt peonage after Las Casas had slavery abolished. The English pirate William Dampier described Guatemala in the seventeenth century as "famous for many rich commodities that are produced thereabouts (some almost peculiar to this country) and yearly sent into Europe, especially four rich dyes, indigo, otta or anatta, silvester, and cochineel." (Cochineal, a red dye, was made from scale insects grown on the fruit of prickly pear cactuses.) The colony declined along with Spain in the eighteenth century. When the American archaeologist John Lloyd Stephens visited in the early 1800s, he found many large churches and towns more or less abandoned. "Coming upon them in a region of desolation, and by mountain paths which human hands had never attempted to improve," he wrote, "their colossal grandeur and costliness were startling, and gave evidence of a retrograding and expiring people."

The Autocratic Republic

Guatemala's large landholders didn't welcome independence from Spain in 1821, but Guatemala City became the capital of the Central American federation which arose in 1823 after a brief alliance with Mexico. It also became the focus for struggles between conservatives who wanted to maintain the old ways and liberals who wanted to modernize. Liberal dictator Francisco Morazán dominated the federation until overthrown by conservative dictator Rafael Carrera, who ruled Guatemala until 1865. Dictators or would-be dictators dominated politics thereafter, from Justo Barrios in 1873–85 to Jorge Ubico in 1931–44. Guatemala's economy was largely devoted to export agriculture—of bananas, cotton, and sugarcane in the Motagua Valley and Pacific coast, and of coffee in the highlands, where communal Mayan lands were appropriated and sold to European immigrants.

Government became more democratic under the presidencies of Juan Arévalo and Jacobo Arbenz in the late 1940s. By 1954, however, Arbenz's moves toward land redistribution ran afoul of the United Fruit Company, which (aided by the CIA) put another dictator, Castillo Armas, in power. A series of military strongmen dominated thereafter, and conducted a thirty-year civil war with leftist guerrillas. The economy grew rapidly in this period, but the growth didn't benefit the majority of the population, particularly in rural areas, where most arable land remained in the ownership of a small minority.

Crushed in the early 1970s, the guerrillas reemerged after the 1976 earthquake and began to enlist the support of the highland Mayas. In the early 1980s, many thousands of Mayas and other Guatemalans were killed, and perhaps a million were forced into exile. The U.S. cut off military aid because of atrocities. The situation improved after a return to civilian rule in 1985, although the army and guerrillas are still at odds. Poverty and unemployment remain prevalent, and government instability continues, although public opposition stopped an attempt to abolish Congress and suspend the constitution by then president Jorge Serrano in 1993. Congress elected a former human rights ombudsman, Ramiro de León Carpio, to replace Serrano.

The Fate of the Quetzal

Overpopulation and deforestation may have been problems for the ancient Maya, as is suggested by archaeological evidence of soil erosion, malnutrition, and, of course, abandonment of cities. Even in the highlands, where cities were smaller, the tradition that unauthorized killing of quetzals was punishable by death suggests wildlife may have become rare. (The quetzal had religious significance for the Maya, and is Guatemala's national bird.) Although highland forest probably increased after the Conquest because of depopulation, quetzals remained almost legendary, at least for western science. The Spanish Empire discouraged travelers, and those who came during early nationhood tended to be more interested in civilization, past and present, than in nature. The first scientific quetzal specimen wasn't obtained until the 1860s. The first quetzal life history study in Guatemala, by wildlife biologist Anne LaBastille, came in the 1960s.

By 1895, hunting and deforestation in the mountains of Verapaz had made the quetzal sufficiently rare that killing them was outlawed. Even if it had been enforced, this prohibition would not have stopped destruction of quetzal habitat (largely in cloud forest), which declined from an original 30,000 square kilometers to about 3,500 by 1960. Other forests suffered as well. The forests of the Pacific slope disappeared almost completely, converted to cotton, sugarcane, and coffee plantations. Landless poor from the highlands began to move into the Petén, burning forest to make cropland which often lasted only a few years before its fertility declined, leaving savanna fit only for poor grazing. A reforestation law was passed in 1935, but amounted to little more than planting of pine and eucalyptus trees.

Guatemala decreed some national parks in the 1950s, but as elsewhere in Latin America, created no institutions to maintain

them. The only national park that took hold was Tikal, more for
its famous Maya city than for the 576 square kilometers of forest
around it. In 1976, the University of San Carlos in Guatemala City
instituted a system of protected areas called Biotopos Universita-
rios. These included a "Biotopo del Quetzal" in the Verapaz mountains. The program struggled through the turbulent 1980s, but has
attained a measure of stability, with five areas. San Carlos University's Center for Conservation Studies (CECON) administers the
biotopos with cooperation from the Guatemalan Institutue of
Tourism. (See below for address.)

In 1989, the government passed a Protected Areas Law which
recognized previously declared protected areas in all categories (including biotopos) and listed forty-four areas under "special protection," pending study of their potential to be declared as parks or
other official categories. The law also established boundaries for
six existing reserves and created a National Council of Protected
Areas (CONAP). Reserves include a vast Maya Biosphere Reserve
in the northern Petén and "special protection areas" in the Sierra de
las Minas Biosphere Reserve and Altos Cuchumatanes mountains.
The Council of Protected Areas (CONAP) is at 6-28 Calle 3, Zona
1 (phone: 519-468, 29527). Management remained weak, however. In 1992, for example, satellite photos of the Sierra de las
Minas showed that illegal logging and land clearing had deforested
half the area in the previous decade. Overall, an estimated 60 percent of Guatemala's forest has been lost.

For information on the biotopos, contact the Centro de Estudios
Conservacionistas (CECON), 0-63 Ave. Reforma, Zona 10, Guatemala City (phone: 310-904). For information on visiting protected areas, contact: INGUAT, Ave. 7, 1-17, Zona 4 (Centro
Cívico), Guatemala City (phone: 311-333, 311-347); or CONAP,
6-28 Calle 3, Zona 1, Guatemala City (phone: 519-468). Other
governmental and private environmental organizations include:
Fundación Defensores de la Naturaleza, 20-21 Ave. las Américas,
Zona 14 (phone: 373-893, 370-319; fax: 682-648), a nongovernmental organization with property and management authority in

Sierra de las Minas, and Comisión Nacional del Medio Ambiente (CONAMA), 25-59 Ave. Pelapa, Zona 12 (phone: 761-026; fax: 760-055).

Guatemala City

This city is Guatemala's third capital, the first two having been destroyed by a volcanic eruption, a flood, and earthquakes in 1541 and 1773. Founded in 1776, the present city was leveled by an earthquake in 1917, and was severely damaged by the quake in 1976. Located on a plateau at about 1,500 meters, it has a pleasant climate with little temperature variation through the year. Rainy season storms, from April to October, are usually short and tend to come in the afternoon. Since the city is enclosed by mountains (and smoldering garbage dumps), smog can be a serious problem in the dry season.

With between one and two million inhabitants, Guatemala City has been divided into twenty-one zones, with Zona 1 around the city center at the north end. Streets are arranged in a grid pattern in each zone, with avenidas running north-south and calles running east-west. Addresses are by street number, usually with the number of the avenue or street first, followed by the house number (I've listed them in the North American way, however, with street numbers first). The city's heart is the Parque Central at Ave. 6 and calles 6-8, which has the cathedral and main government buildings. Guatemala City isn't famous for architecture, since most of its colonial buildings were destroyed by earthquakes. Many shops, hotels, restaurants, and other facilities are located in surrounding blocks.

Guatemalans generally are very kindly and polite people. The local underworld is extremely adept at exploiting the unwary traveler, however, and a vehicle left unguarded may be rifled in minutes. When I first arrived, it seemed as though every foreigner I met had just been robbed (although *I* hadn't). The usual cautions about being out at night apply.

Most parks and museums are located in the zones to the south of Zona 1. City buses are ramshackle and crowded, but cheap and frequent, running north and south on the avenidas. Buses stop running at 10:30 P.M. (when traffic lights also stop working) and are replaced by jitneys. Cabs may be hard to find outside of Zona 1, especially in residential areas. Average fares in town are $3–6, but they can be much more expensive. Cabs are unmetered, so agree on the fare before you get in or you'll be overcharged. Bargaining may be possible. Cabs generally don't circulate in search of passengers, but congregate at stands near major hotels.

Transportation

Visas aren't required for U.S. citizens and most other American and west European nationalities entering by air with passports. A tourist card valid for thirty days from entry date is issued, renewable for up to ninety days at the *"migración"* office in Guatemala City. In 1994, visas *were* required for U.S., U.K., Canadian, and Mexican citizens entering by land, and had to be obtained in advance. Check with travel agents or Guatemalan consulates for current requirements. There's a $5–12 airport departure tax, a $1 entry tax at land borders, and a $4 tourist tax on departure from land borders. Land border taxes may be hiked by corrupt officials. Airline overbooking is common, so reconfirm return flights a week in advance, and get to the airport early.

INTERNATIONAL AIRLINES: Guatemala's national airline, Aviateca, flies to Guatemala City via Los Angeles, Miami, New Orleans, Chicago, and Houston (phone: 800-327-9832). Continental flies via Houston (phone: 800-525-0280). American flies via Miami, Chicago, and Dallas (phone: 800-433-7300). Lacsa flies via San Francisco and Los Angeles (phone: 800-225-2272). United flies via San Francisco and Miami (phone: 800-241-6522).

DOMESTIC FLIGHTS: Five airlines have flights from a separate terminal at Aurora International Airport in Guatemala City to the town of Flores in the Petén. They are Aviateca, Aeroquetzal, Tikal Jet, Aerovias, and Tapsa. They have ticket offices at the airport, but it's easier to make reservations through a travel agency in the center of town. Flights are often overbooked, so arrive early. Other do-

mestic flights must be chartered. There are also small flights to Belize, Cancún (Mexico), and near Copán, Honduras.

La Aurora International Airport is 8 kilometers south of the city
center, in Zona 13. There is a tourist information desk next to the
immigration office, open 6 A.M.–9 P.M., also a Banco de Guatemala
exchange office. Taxi drivers try to keep fares to the city center inflated to about $8, although you may be able to bargain for less.
Buses with black numbers 5, 6, 20, and 83 run to the city center
from just outside the upper level every half hour. (As is generally
true in Central America, the airport closes at night.)

ROADS: Main highways in the highlands are generally paved and
in good repair. Side roads are gravel and may be in bad shape. The
highway to Flores in the Petén is very bad. Few buses run at night:
road travel after dark is considered dangerous throughout the
country, and particularly in remote areas. Armed robbery of buses
occurs, and travel agency vans or large chartered buses are pre-
ferred targets. Travelers are unlikely to be harmed if they offer no
resistance. There is guerrilla activity in the departments of El
Quiché, Huehuetenango, San Marcos, Petén, Escuintla, Suchite-
peque, and Sacatatepeque: army or occasionally guerrilla road-
blocks are possible. Guerrillas may charge travelers a "war tax."

BUSES: As with city buses, Guatemalan bus transport is rickety
and crowded, but abundant and cheap. There is a bus terminal
serving areas west of Guatemala and the Pacific coast at aves. 1 and
4 and calles 7 and 9 in Zona 4. Bus companies that go to the Caribbean and Petén are concentrated around aves. 8 and 9 and Calle
19 in Zona 1. You pay on the bus. Most buses leave early in the
morning and fill up quickly. More expensive, first-class buses leave
from various office locations (see area descriptions), and tickets can
be bought in advance. The INGUAT office (see below) has detailed
information on bus routes and schedules. Tica bus has service to El
Salvador, Nicaragua, Costa Rica, and Panama.

Hitchhiking is riskier than in other Central American countries.
As in other countries, it's polite to ask if the driver wants some payment for the lift. Bicycling on the Pan American Highway north of

Guatemala City is possible, if you're in good shape for steep roads and high elevations. Buses will carry bicycles on roofs for partial fare. It's possible to rent bikes, including mountain bikes, in larger towns.

CAR RENTALS: All the big companies have Guatemala City and airport offices, and there are many smaller, generally cheaper local ones, including Quetzal, Tikal, Tabarini (which has Toyota Land Cruisers), and Tally (which has Mitsubishi and Nissan pickups). A current driver's license and credit card are usually required. Make sure any damage on the vehicle has been recorded before you take it out, or you may be charged for it. Traffic away from cities is light. Gas stations may be few and far between away from main highways; INGUAT sells a map with gas station locations. After dark, bandits with vehicles may force cars off the road or block the road to rob travelers. Never leave a vehicle unguarded if you can help it.

TRAINS: Trains to Puerto Barrios on the Caribbean leave from the Guatemala City Terminal (Calle 18, aves. 9 and 10, Zona 1) at 7 A.M. Tues., Thurs., and Sat. The fare is a few dollars, but it takes almost 24 hours, much longer than a bus, and there is no dining car or other amenities. Trains also go to Tecun Uman on the Mexican border at 7:15 A.M. Tues. and Sat. Trains tend to be less crowded than buses.

U.S. Embassy

7-01 Avenida de la Reforma, Zona 10 (about 3 kilometers northeast of the airport) (phone: 311541-55 or 23115-41).

Health Advisory

Gastroenteric diseases and parasites are endemic. Beware of untreated water, milk, raw vegetables, peeled fruits, and street vendor food. Cholera is active, but not a threat to travelers' taking standard anti-diarrhea precautions (it might be best to avoid "ceviche," raw fish or shellfish cured in lime juice). Malaria is something to watch for at elevations below 1,500 meters, particularly in the Pacific lowlands along the Salvadoran border and in the north. The rainy season is when most cases occur. Chloroquine is an adequate prophylactic. Dengue fever is also present in lowlands. Altitude sickness is a possibility in the highlands.

HOSPITALS AND DOCTORS in Guatemala City: Hospital Herrera Llerandi, 8-71 Ave. 6, Zona 10, phone: 366-771/2/3/4/5. Coordinator, International Assn. for Medical Aid to Travelers: Rodolfo Herrera-Llerandi, M.D., phone: 324-444.

Hotels

There is a cluster of upmarket hotels in zones 9 and 10 toward the airport (The Camino Real, Avenida de la Reforma and Calle 14, is the classiest, with rooms a little over $100; phone: 334-633, fax: 374-313). The small Princess, 7-65 Calle 13, is less expensive; phone: 344-545; fax: 344-546.

The following are in Zona 1: The Ritz Continental, 10-13 Ave. 6 "A," has air-conditioned rooms with TV for about $50 single (phone: 81-671). The Pan American, 5-63 Calle 9, is comparable, with more old-fashioned character (pre–WW II) but noisy on street side (phone: 535-991). Posada Belén, "A" 10-30 Calle 13, is quiet, with courtyards and fountains, in the $30–40 range, owners speak English (phone: 29-226, 534-530, 513-478). Hotel Colonial, 14-19 Ave. 7a, is comparable, in a converted mansion (phone: 26-722), as is Hotel Centenario, 5-33 Calle 6 (near Parque Centenario) (phone: 80-381). Chalet Suizo, 6-82 Calle 14, is very popular (often full), with rooms with or without shower in the $10–20 range (phone: 513-786). Hogar del Turista, 10-43 Calle 11, is comparable (phone: 25-522), as are Mansión San Francisco, Ave. 6 and Calle 14 (phone: 251-2528); Hotel Excel, 15-12 Ave. 9a; and Hotel Capri, 15-63 Ave. 9a. Casa Real, next door to Hogar del Turista, has rooms without bath for under $10. Comparable are: Lessing House, 4-35 Calle 12 (rooms with shower for $15); Hernani, 6-56 Calle 15; Spring House, 12-65 Ave. 8; San Diego, 7-37 Calle 15; and CentroAmérica, 16-38 Ave. 9. Still cheaper: Fénix, 16-18 Ave. 7; Bilbao, Ave. 8 and Calle 15; Pensión Mesa, 10-17 Calle 10; San Angel, Calle 14 between aves. 9 and 10; Ajau, 15-62 Ave. 8. (Hotels tend to be full-up in peak season because of Guatemala's popularity, but reserving in advance may be hard except at the more expensive ones.)

Restaurants

Los Antojitos, 16-28 Calle 15, Zona 1; El Parador, Ave. 4 and Calle Montufar, Zona 9 (near Museo Popul Vuh); and Arrin Cuan, 3-27 Ave. 5, Zona 1, have good "*comida típica*" in the upper price range ($10–20 a meal). Guatemalan food is the most "Meso-American" in Central America, with chiles rellenos, tamales, guacamole, but is generally less "*picante*" than Mexican. There are many Italian places: Mediterraneo, 3-31 Ave. 7, Zona 9; Piccadilly, Ave. 6 and Calle 11, Zona 1; Bologna 6-20 Calle 10, Zona 1 (near Ritz Continental); and A Guy from Italy, 6-33 Calle 12 and 5-70 Ave. 5, Zona 1. Chinese restaurants are also common: Fu-Lu-Sho, 12-09 Ave. 6; Hai-Ba-Wan, 13-27 Ave. 7; Canton 14-20 Ave. 6 (all in Zona 1). Puerto Barrios, 10-65 Ave. 7, Zona 9, has seafood.

For vegetarians: Señor Sol, 11-32 Calle 5, Zona 1; Vegetariano 6-72 Calle 14, Zona 1; Comida de Vegetales (several places in Zona 1). For desserts and pastries: Pastelería Jensen, 0-53 Calle 14, Zona 1; Pastelería Lins, 6-12 Calle 11, Zona 1; Dixie Deli, aves. 6 and 7, Calle 12, Zona 1; Los Alpes, 1-09 Calle 10, Zona 10. There are many fast food places, and you can eat for about a dollar at "*comedores*" (dining rooms).

Communications

The main post office is at Ave. 7 and Calle 12, Zona 1. Hours are 8–7 weekdays and 8–3 Saturdays.

There is 24-hour national and international phone service at Empresa Guatemalteca de Telecomunicaciones (Guatel), 12-39 Ave. 7, Zona 1.

Money Exchange

The Guatemalan currency unit is the quetzal, which contains 100 centavos. High denomination quetzal notes (100's and 50's) may be hard to change. The exchange rate in 1994 was 5.55 quetzales to the U.S. dollar.

Banks change U.S. dollars at the going rate, and most will change traveler's checks. There are Banco de Guatemala offices at the main post office and the airport, and at Ave. 7 and Calle 22, Zona 1. American Express has agents at Clark Tours, Edificio el Triángulo, 6-53 Ave. 7A, Zona 4 (phone: 232-0213) and Banco del Café, 9-00 Ave. La Reforma, Zona 9, 9–4:30 weekdays (phone: 311-311, ext. 1113). Visa and American Express cards are widely accepted, Diners Club and Access MasterCard less so.

There is a legal street exchange for cash and checks at Ave. 7 and calles 12 and 14 near the post office. Dealers take a commission, and pickpockets may be hovering nearby. There is also an exchange at Le Point Shoe Shop, Calle 14 and aves. 4 and 5.

Tourist Information

Staff at the INGUAT office, 1-17 Ave. 7, Centro Cívico, Zona 4, are friendly and speak English, and have city and country maps, bus schedules, hotel listings, and information on major tourist attractions. They can answer general questions about nature reserves and direct you to other offices for answers to more specific questions (see above for address of CECON). Hours are 8:15–4:30 weekdays, 8–1 Saturdays (phone: 311-333/47).

Maps

INGUAT has city and country maps (see above). The Instituto Geográfico Nacional, 5-76 Ave. las Américas, Zona 13, has detailed topographic maps, although those of militarily sensitive areas may be hard to obtain (at least, they can be examined and hand-copied at the office). Hours are 8–4 weekdays. Hertz has a good city-country map.

National Geographic published a map of the Maya region and its nature reserves (including adjacent Honduras, El Salvador, Belize, and Mexico, as well as Guatemala) as a supplement to its October 1989 issue (page 424A).

Museums and Zoos

The national museums and zoo are concentrated in Parque Aurora in Zona 13 west of the airport. Bus 5 goes there from the city center.

The best of these is the National Museum of Archaeology and Anthropology on the west side of Parque Aurora. Displays cover Mayan culture from its beginnings to the present, with models showing ceremonial and daily life, and artifacts, past and present. There's a room of artifacts made from jade and other precious materials. Hours are 9–4 Tues.–Fri., 9–12 and 2–4 weekends. (The jade room is closed on weekends.) Admission is $.40.

The National Museum of Natural History is south of the archaeology museum. Displays are less imaginative than in the archaeology museum, consisting mostly of mounted specimens in glass cases (including a quetzal), but you can get some idea of Guatemalan flora, fauna, and geology. Hours are 9–4 weekdays; admission is free.

The National Museum of Modern Art is east of the archaeology museum. It has nineteenth- and twentieth-century work: a good insight into how modern Guatemalans see themselves and their land. Hours are 9–4 Tues.–Fri., 9–12 and 2–4 weekends. Admission is $.15.

La Aurora Zoo is at the north end of the park (Parque Aurora). It has recently been enlarged and renovated to allow more space for the animals and to keep up with the modern role of zoos as wildlife conservation centers as well as animal displays. There are no quetzals: the species is famous for dying promptly in captivity, which is one reason it is Guatemala's national bird—as a symbol of liberty. Phone: 720-885; fax: 715-286. Admission is $1.

There are good private museums along the tree-lined Avenida de la Reforma in Zona 10 between the city center and the airport. Bus 5 runs there.

Near the north end of the Ave. Reforma, at Calle 1, Zona 10, is the Botanical Garden of the University of San Carlos. Founded in 1922, the small garden has hundreds of labeled plant species. It's a good place to look for the odd warbler, tanager, or hummingbird. Hours are weekdays 8–12 and 2–6, and Saturdays 8:30–12:30. Admission is free.

Next door at 1-56 Calle Mariscal Cruz is the university's Natural History Museum, with not-very-recent mounted specimens. Hours are the same as the garden's.

Several blocks south, at Calle 8 and Ave. Reforma, is the Popol Vuh Museum of Archaeology. Named for the Popol Vuh, one of the three examples of Mayan literature that survived the Inquisition, the museum contains a copy of the document (a creation myth about the underworld adventures of divine twins) and an artifact collection, particularly of decorated funerary urns. It's on the sixth floor of 8-60 Ave. Reforma, an office building. Hours are 9–4:30 Mon.–Sat. Admission is $1.20.

Parque Minerva in Zona 2 north of the center features a giant relief map of the country built in 1904 during the twenty-two-year dictatorship of Manuel Cabrera, who also built temples throughout the country to Minerva, the Roman goddess of wisdom. The map's vertical relief is exaggerated, but it gives a sense of the country's topographic diversity. Hours are 8–5 daily. Buses 1, 45, and 46 run to the park, which is a couple of kilometers north of the central park on Ave. 6.

Bookstores and Libraries

The Popol Vuh Museum (see above) has a small bookstore with titles in natural history as well as archaeology. Gemini, 7-24 Ave. 6, Zona 9, and Liberaria Arnel, Ave. 9 and Calle 7, Zona 9, have books in English as well as Spanish. La Plazuela, 6-14 Calle 12, Zona 9, has used books. El Palacio de las Revistas, 10-14 Ave. 9, Zona 1, has some English magazines and newspapers. Vista Hermosa Bookshop, Zona 15, has books on natural history and archaeology, mostly in English.

The Biblioteca Nacional is on the west side of the Parque Centenario (which is across Ave. 6 from Parque Central). The Instituto Guatemalteco Americano, Ruta 1 and Via 4, Zona 4, has a library.

Excursions Around Guatemala City

The summits of the volcanoes surrounding Guatemala City are protected areas, and it may be possible to hike on some or all of them, depending on social and geological conditions. At least two, Fuego and Pacaya, have been active enough in recent years to pose danger, and armed robberies, assaults, rapes, and murders have occurred in the area since 1990. Find out the present situation before venturing on them. Most of the slopes are heavily cultivated, and wildlife is scarce, but there are plenty of interesting plants, birds, and small animals such as frogs and butterflies. Vegetation is a mixture of northern plants like boneset, a white-flowered herb common in North American meadows, and frangipani, a small tree with fragrant, trumpetlike white flowers which also grows in the South Pacific.

Strong shoes and warm clothes are required: lava rock can be very sharp, and temperatures on the summits very cold. Clouds often obscure the view. Take a hat and plenty of water, as sun, wind, and exertion are very dehydrating. Around craters, fumes can irritate lungs and eyes.

Volcán Pacaya south of Guatemala City is accessible by bus from the Zona 4 bus station. Buses leave at 7 A.M. to San Vincente de Pacaya. From there it is a 3-hour walk via the village of San Francisco to a TV tower on a ridge. From there it's another half hour to a plateau with views of the summit and of the cones of the other volcanoes (which are much higher) to the north. The last bus back to Guatemala City from San Vicente leaves at 4 P.M. If you want to stay longer, local people may offer overnight accommodation and guide service for a small fee, or there are tour companies in Antigua that offer guided trips (see below). Pacaya erupted in October 1994, ejecting ash clouds and lava flows that forced evacuation of three villages.

The best access to the other volcanoes is from Antigua, the former capital a few dozen kilometers southeast of Guatemala City. Most travelers prefer its quietness and charm, and with its many language programs it's an excellent place to study Spanish. Buses to Antigua leave frequently from two stops in Zona 1, Calle 18 and Ave. 4 and Calle 20 between aves. 2 and 3. Much of the city destroyed in the 1773 earthquake has been restored, and the remaining ruins, mainly convents and churches, are picturesque. It's a relaxing place, though not free of thieves and violent crime.

There are many hotels, likely to be crowded, especially in the dry season. The town is laid out in a grid pattern, with avenidas north of Parque Central labeled *"norte"* and those south labeled *"sur"*; calles west of Parque Central are labeled *"poniente"* and those east are labeled "*oriente*." Hotel Caso Santa Domingo, 28 Calle 3 Oriente, is in a seventeenth-century convent, with gardens and good restaurant, and rooms beginning at $115 (phone: 320-140; fax: 320-102). Antigua, Ave. 5 sur and Calle 8, is somewhat less and has a pool (phone: 320-288). Posada de Don Rodrigo, 17 Ave. 5 norte, is in a beautiful colonial house, with good food, in the $50–70 range (phone: 320-291). Aurora, 16 Calle 4 oriente, is $30–50, around a courtyard (phone: 320-217). Posada San Sebastián has two locations, 67 Ave. 7 norte and 4 Ave. 3 norte, for $20–40. El Descanso, 9 Ave. 5 norte, is $10–20 with bath.

There are many inexpensive posadas around the bus station: Posada Asjemenou, 31 Calle del Arco; Casa de Santa Lucia, 5 Alameda Sta Lucia; and Posada el Refugio, 28 Calle 4 poniente.

Restaurants are also abundant, and crowded. El Sereno, 30 Calle 6 poniente, and Welten, 21 Calle 4 oriente, serve expensive international food in garden atmospheres. Pastelería Doña Luisa, 12 Calle 4 oriente, is a meeting place with good breakfasts and snacks, and cable TV. Café Mistral across the street has moderate French food. Su Chow, Ave. 5 norte and Calle 1 poniente, Comedor Veracruz and Lina, in the market out Calle 4 poniente, and Martedino, Calle 4 west of Parque Central, are good and inexpensive. Sueños del Quetzal, 3 Ave. 5 norte, has vegetarian food.

There is an INGUAT office at the south side of Parque Central, open daily 8–6 (phone: 032-0763). Staff are friendly, speak English, and can tell you about present safety conditions on the volcanoes (although they're not infallible). Other sources of information for volcano tours: bulletin boards at Pastelería Doña Luisa and Sueños del Quetzal; Casa Andinista, 5 Calle 4 oriente; Club Chicag, 34 Ave. 6 norte; Quetzal Expeditions, 6 Alameda Santa Lucia; ICO's Expeditions, 2 Calle del Desengano; and Popeye Tours near the bus station. The standard price for a tour in 1993 was $15.

Volcán Agua, at 3,760 meters, is the easiest to climb, and has a football field in its crater. A bus leaves Antigua at 5 A.M. to the village of Santa María de Jesús, from which it's a 4–5 hour climb to the top, if you are fit and acclimated to the high altitude. If not, it might be better to take longer: agencies have overnight tours, and the volcano is said to be best under a full moon. Thomas Gage, an Englishman who lived in Antigua in the 1620s, called Agua "a goodly prospect to the sight, being almost all the year green, and filled with Indian milpas."

Acatenango, 3,976 meters, and Fuego, 3,763, are a double volcano, their craters connected by a ridge. The top of Fuego may not be accessible because of increased activity, but the crater is visible from the top of Acatenango. A trail up Acatenango begins at a place called La Soledad. To reach it from Antigua, take an early bus to Ciudad Vieja (the site of Guatemala's first capital, an interesting trip in its own right), and hitchhike to Finca Concepción Calderas, from which it's an hour's walk to La Soledad. (A bus to Finca Concepción Calderas leaves Antigua at 6:45 A.M., Saturdays.) Or take a bus to San Miguel Dueñas and hitch to La Soledad. A small plateau known as La Meseta or El Conejón is 3–4 hours up the trail. Climbers use this as a campsite (you'll want a warm sleeping bag if you camp). From there it's another 3–4 hours to the summit, where there is a shelter holding up to fifteen people. You may get spectacular views of flames from Pacaya and Fuego. If you want to spend another day, you can hike on the col to the slopes of Fuego. It's also possible to climb Fuego from the town of Alotenango east of Fuego, but the trail is very rough and partly through forest; you should have a guide, or be very experienced. Thomas Gage found Fuego "unpleasing and more dreadful to behold" than Agua, "For here were ashes for beauty, stones and flints for fruits and flowers, baldness for greenness, barrenness for fruitfulness. . . . Thus is Guatemala seated in the midst of a paradise on one side and a hell on the other."

The Highlands

"This is altiplano," said someone who had lived in Peru as we drove along the Pan American Highway south of Huehuetenango. The grassy tableland around us, punctuated with the occasional spindly eucalyptus, could very well have been in the Andes. Alder trees border streams in both places; water ouzels, or dippers, fly up- and downstream, or dive for insects in the icy water. Yet Guatemalan ouzels still have more in common with Alaskan than with Peruvian

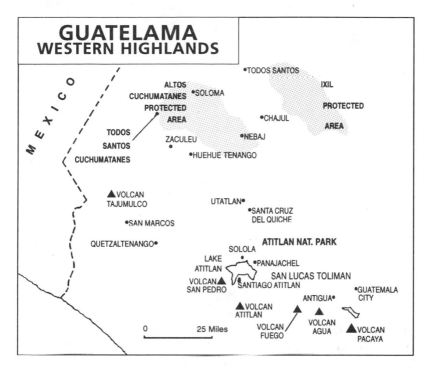

GUATELAMA
WESTERN HIGHLANDS

MEXICO

•TODOS SANTOS

ALTOS
CUCHUMATANES •SOLOMA
PROTECTED
AREA   •CHAJUL

IXIL

PROTECTED

AREA

TODOS
SANTOS   ZACULEU   •NEBAJ
CUCHUMATANES   •HUEHUE TENANGO

▲VOLCAN
TAJUMULCO   UTATLAN•
                    •SANTA CRUZ
•SAN MARCOS   DEL QUICHE

QUETZALTENANGO•   **ATITLAN NAT. PARK**
                    SOLOLA
LAKE   •
ATITLAN   •PANAJACHEL
VOLCAN▲   SAN LUCAS TOLIMAN
SAN PEDRO   SANTIAGO ATITLAN
                    ANTIGUA•   •GUATEMALA
▲VOLCAN   CITY
ATITLAN   ▲   ▲
0   25 Miles   VOLCAN   VOLCAN ▲VOLCAN
                    FUEGO   AGUA   PACAYA

ouzels: they're the same species, while the Peruvian ouzel is a South American species, with a white head instead of gray. The small plants of Guatemala's high moors—lupine, Indian paintbrush, penstemon—also have more relatives in Alaska than in Peru.

Colorfully dressed shepherds and little black or white sheep grazing on the slopes might also have been in Peru. As centers of ancient, heavily populated highland cultures (65 percent of Guatemalans live above 1,000 meters on 30 percent of the land), the Andes and the Cuchumatanes have a lot in common. Yet again there are differences. The Maya speak a language more closely related to that of the Penutian-speaking Nez Perce of Montana than to the Quechua of the Andes. And Maya culture as a whole is perhaps less specialized to cold highland environments than is the Quechua.

Another difference between the Andes and Guatemala's "*zacatal*" (a Nahuatl word for alpine grassland) is that trekking has never caught on in Guatemala as in the Andes. This is perhaps partly because Guatemala lacks the still-glaciated peaks that rise above the altiplano, and certainly because political violence has made it difficult in recent years. Still, there is a great potential for hiking in the many foot trails that lead through the countryside. The political situation remains tense, however, and you shouldn't try to walk in an area (or even visit it) without learning current conditions. Officials may not always be the best sources to ask, since they may downplay dangers for fear of reducing tourist revenues. The U.S. Embassy security office is usually up to date on problems.

The great geological age and varied terrain of Guatemala's highlands have resulted in high levels of biodiversity and endemic species. For example, herpetologists identified fifteen species of plethodontid salamanders (the mainly temperate zone amphibians that have spread into the neotropics—see chapter 2) in a transect ranging from sea level to 4,000 meters in the 1970s. Many of these occur nowhere else. Deforestation threatens this diversity: when the scientists who conducted the salamander study returned to their study site in 1980, they found that pasture had replaced forest below 2,700 meters. Since most of the salmanders lived in trees or other forest features, few salamanders remained.

Lake Atitlán

Overlooked by 3,000-meter volcanoes, this roughly 30-by-10-kilometer lake is generally agreed to be one of the most beautiful in the world, and its basin has been declared a national park. The lake is over 300 meters deep and has no surface outlet, the water draining to springs on Pacific watersheds through deep fissures. Visitors are enchanted by the way the lake water continually changes color, from deep blue to green, even to purple at twilight. Ethnic costumes of the Caxchiquel and Tzutuhil Maya villagers around the lake are among the most striking and colorful in the country. Volcanic soils around the lake are very fertile, and the upper slopes of the volcanoes still support a lush forest of oak, magnolia, and pine.

Unfortunately, Atitlán is being "loved to death." Tourism and second-home development on its shores have caused sewage and chemical pollution, and the expanding farm population has pushed the forest farther up the slopes, with resultant soil erosion also polluting the lake. Asociación Amigos del Lago de Atitlán, 14-76 Ave. 14, Zona 10, Guatemala City, is working to protect the lake (phone: 374-886).

The fate of the Atitlán giant grebe, or "poc," is symbolic of the lake's plight. Named as a species in 1929, the giant grebe was a chicken-sized, flightless relative of the common pied-billed grebe. Somehow, it evolved only on Lake Atitlán. There were two hundred pocs in 1929, feeding on small fish and crabs and building huge nests in lakeshore rush beds. In 1958, the Panajachel Hotel Association and Pan American Airways introduced largemouth bass and other North American fish into the lake, and these promptly ate up much of the grebes' small fish and crab food source. (Local Maya fishermen also had depended on the native fish and crabs.) Poc numbers dropped by more than half, to a level where biologist Anne LaBastille feared the population couldn't maintain itself. She convinced the government to establish a poc reserve, and poc numbers returned to two hundred in the early 1970s as the situation stabilized.

Two unforeseen disasters destroyed this stability, however. The 1976 earthquake changed the lake's drainage and lowered its level, which combined with lakeside development to destroy much of the poc's rush bed nesting and shelter habitat. Any measures that might have ameliorated this were prevented by the political violence of later years, during which the poc reserve warden was murdered. By the mid 1980s, poc numbers had declined to the extent that recovery was judged impossible, and it was declared extinct, although a few large grebes, increasingly hard to distinguish from still common pied-billed grebes (and possibly interbreeding with them), may still be seen. The poc reserve on the lake's south shore still exists, and you can camp there.

The Rebuli bus company, 1-34 Calle 21, Zona 1, has hourly service to Panajachel, the main town on the lake, from its terminal at Calle 1 and Ave. 3, Zona 9, in Guatemala City. Fare is about $2 and the ride takes three hours. From Antigua, minibuses leave from the Ramada Hotel at 8:30 A.M. Tuesday, Thursday, and Sunday to the Hotel del Lago in Panajachel, or you can take a Chimaltenango bus to the Pan American Highway and flag down any bus labeled Panajachel or the neighboring town of Solola.

Panajachel is also called "*Gringotenango*" because resident and visiting foreigners are so common. Hotels and restaurants are also common, although they may get crowded on weekends and holidays. The Hotel del Lago on the lake is very expensive, but good for meetings and breakfasts, and the pool can be used by nonresidents for $2. Cacique Inn near the lake has a pool and gardens in the $60 range (phone: 621-205). The Playa Linda near the public beach is $40–50 (phone: 621-159). Rancho Grande Inn, Calle Rancho Grande, is comparable (phone: 621-554). Closer to town, the Fonda del Sol on Calle Principal is in the $10–20 range (phone: 621-162), with a good restaurant (open to nonresidents). Mayan Palace, also on Calle Principal, is comparable. Posada de Doña Carmen and Cabana Country Club, both on Ave. Rancho Grande, are under $10. Most places have hot showers, but water may not be available all day, and may cost extra at cheaper hotels. Rental houses may be available, starting at about $125 a month. There are also designated campsites.

La Laguna on Calle Principal has good food in a garden setting. Also on Calle Principal, Rancho Mercado Deli/Restaurant has homemade bread and a lending library as well as good sandwiches and hot meals. The Last Resort on Calle 14 de Feberero, halfway between downtown and the lake, has good, inexpensive food and is a meeting place. Casa Cakchiquel next door has very good, somewhat expensive dinners and lunches. Blue Bird near the market has good vegetarian food.

INGUAT has an office on the Calle Principal, open Wed.–Sun. 8–12 and 2–6, Mon. 8–12, closed Tues. They have timetables for buses and boats to other places on the lake.

Roads or trails go most of the way around the lake, and it's possible to walk around it in 4 or 5 days, camping or staying in Maya villages. Walking alone around the lake is not recommended, especially for women, and guerrilla and counterinsurgency activity are possibilities. Except for cliffs, most of the lakeshore is farm fields or homes. To reach forest, you need to climb high on the volcano slopes. The summits of Volcán Tolimán (3,158 meters) and Volcán Atitlán (3,535 meters) are accessible from the town of San Lucas Tolimán on the southeast lakeshore (the lake is at about 1,500 meters). A trail from the south end of the town leads to a ridge (called Los Planes) between the two summits from which trails lead south to V. Atitlán and north to V. Tolimán. The trails are heavily used by local people and hard to follow, clouds often obscure higher altitudes, and either climb will probably take more than a day. No maps are available; it would be best to hire a guide in San Lucas. Ask at the municipal office there. Volcán San Pedro southwest of the lake can be climbed on a day trip (3–4 hours up), but its trails also are hard to follow, so getting a guide is advisable. You can do this in San Pedro la Laguna on the lakeshore north of the volcano.

There are buses from Panajachel to San Lucas daily at 6:30 A.M. and 4 P.M.—it takes an hour. Buses serve other lakeside communities, but the roads (and the buses) are not in particularly good shape. The easiest way to get around the lake is by the boats that leave frequently from Panajachel, either on scheduled trips or by hire. When the lake is rough from wind, as it often is around midday, it may be dangerous for small boats. When hiring boats, watch out for overcharging, or raising prices in mid-journey. Standard rate for a two-way fare is about $3.

Boats to San Pedro la Laguna leave about every 2 hours from near the public beach at the end of Ave. Rancho Grande in Panajachel. There are also frequent boats, mainly in the morning, from this site to the town of Santiago Atitlán on the lake's south side. You also can go to Santiago Atitlán on the mail boat, which leaves from the end of Calle Principal. If you go out on the mail boat, it will be more convenient to come back on one of the more frequent other boats, so don't buy a return trip ticket. Santiago de Atitlán is famous for its embroidered fabrics, and residents probably will offer to sell you some. This is also one of the towns that revere Maximón, a mysterious deity whose attributes include dark glasses and a cigar. Maximón has been associated with Christian figures such as St. Simon and Judas, with pre-Columbian Maya gods, and with historical figures including Pedro de Alvarado and an unidentified

Maya shaman of the Conquest period. His wooden image is kept in the houses of the local "*cofradía*," a religious fraternity.

The poc reserve is on the lakeshore a few kilometers northeast of Santiago Atitlán. There are guards on duty, and it's a nice place to experience a bit of the remaining natural lakeshore. The lake has eighteen native fish species, and many water bird species are still present. Bring food and water if you want to camp. You can get there by canoe for less than $1, or walk on the road to San Lucas Toliman (but you'll need to get directions about where to turn off the road for the reserve).

There is a quetzal reserve in the forest 7 kilometers south of Santiago Atitlán. Another species that may survive in the vicinity, even more endangered than the quetzal, is the horned guan, a black and white, turkey-sized bird which has a startling, bright red "horn" on its head and bright red feet. It lives in forests between 2,000 and 3,000 meters, and is thought to survive on only a few volcanoes of highland Guatemala and Chiapas, and in the Sierra de las Minas. A road to the reserve goes left from the road to San Pedro after you pass the Posada de Santiago, a resort run by North Americans, with cabins for $30–50 a night, a restaurant, and boat trips on the lake. It's located 2 kilometers from Santiago Atitlán (phone: 962-7158).

K'umarkaah

This ruin of the Quiché Maya capital, burned by Alvarado in 1524, is not very impressive as an archaeological site (its stones were plundered for newer buildings), but it has living significance. Maya shamans called "day keepers" still use it for rituals. It's also in a lovely spot, a pine grove a few kilometers west of the town of Santa Cruz del Quiché. Tunnels (smelling of the incense day keepers burn during rituals) lead beneath the ruined pyramids and plaza. The tunnels may have been burial crypts, ritual chambers, or secret passages to other sites—nobody is sure. John Lloyd Stephens wrote: "Under one of the buildings was an opening which the Indians called a cave, and by which they said one could reach Mexico in an hour. . . . The Padre told us that thirty years before, when he first saw it, the palace was entire to the garden. He was then fresh from the palaces of Spain, and it seemed as if he were again among them." A small museum on the site includes a model of what the city may have looked like.

To reach the site, walk west along Calle 10 from the bus station at Santa Cruz del Quiché. The road leads through cornfields for about an hour to the pine grove. Bring a flashlight to use in the tunnels: they're quite long, and there are deep pits off some side tunnels. Hours are 7–6 daily, admission is $.60. Buses from Guatemala City to Santa Cruz del Quiché leave frequently from Calle 10 and Ave. 1 at the Zona 4 bus station. The trip takes about 5 hours. There are also frequent buses from Chichicastenango, the main tourist town of the highlands, 30 minutes. In Santa Cruz del Quiché, the Posada Calle Real, 7-36 Ave. 2, has hot showers and a good restaurant for less than $10. Hospedaje Hermano Pedro and Hotel San Pascual (0-43 Calle 7) are comparable. There is a market on Thurs. and Sunday. The town is at 2,000 meters, so nights can be cold.

Volcán Tajumulco

At 4,220 meters, this inactive volcano is the highest peak in Central America. Its upper slopes have grassland *zacatal* like Altos Cuchumatanes. The forests of the lower slopes are believed to contain the largest remaining population of horned guans (see above). The peak is remote and untouristed. Access is from Quetzaltenango (also called Xela), the main city of western Guatemala. From Guatemala City, Lineas Americas, 18-74 Ave. 2, Zona 1, and Transportes Galgos, 19-44 Ave. 7, Zona 1, have daily, early morning buses. Pensión Bonifaz, 10-50 Calle 4 northeast of the parque central, is a good hotel in the $60 range, with central heating, hot water (the town is at 2,335 meters and has a cool climate) and a good restaurant (phone: 612-279). Modelo, 2-31 Ave. 14 A, Zona 1, is good in the $20–30 range (phone: 612-529). Río Azul, 12-15 Calle 2, has rooms with bath for $10–20. Casa Kaehler, 3-33 Ave. 13, is good for around $10 (612-091).

Utz'Hua, Calle 3 and Ave. 12, has good Guatemalan food. Royal Paris, 3-05 Ave. 16, Zona 3, near Parque Juarez four blocks north of center, is a small French restaurant, not too expensive. La Gondola, Ave. 10 between calles 5 and 6, has inexpensive Italian food. Shanghai, near the center at 12-22 Calle 4, has good Chinese food.

Xela was destroyed by nearby Volcán Santa María in 1902, so it lacks authentic old buildings, although the modern ones look fairly old. It has a good Natural History Museum on the south side of the parque central, open weekdays 9–6 and Sat. 8–4, and a contemporary Guatemalan Art Museum at Ave. 12 and Calle 7. The Tourism Office is next to the Natural History Museum, open weekdays 9–12 and 2:30–5. You can ask them about Tajumulco and other volcanoes and hiking places.

To get to Tajumulco, you follow the highway west from Xela another 50 kilometers to the town of San Marcos (buses leave from Xela at noon) where you turn north on a secondary road that leads to San Sebastián and Tacana. At the top of a pass several kilometers beyond San Marcos, turn left off the main road to begin the climb, which takes 5 hours. Again, find out about the present safety situation before you try this.

Sierra de los Cuchumatanes

This region of high tablelands and deep gorges north of the volcanic belt is a block of Paleozoic limestones and underlying continental rocks uplifted by the tectonic stresses that produced the volcanoes. The highest part, the Altos Cuchumatanes north of Huehuetenango, must have borne a miniature ice cap during the last glaciation. Meandering ridges in its high valleys (Llanos de San Miguel) are moraines—piles of rock and soil accumulated as glaciers flowed, and left piled up after they melted. This was only discovered in 1968: the landscape is not obviously glacial like that of the Chirripó Range in Costa Rica, with its cirques and tarns. Instead of forming on the north sides of high peaks and carving deep narrow U-shaped valleys, as at Yosemite, the Cuchumatanes glaciers must have formed more as those in the eastern U.S. did, with unmelted snow accumulating on the rolling plateau until the weight made the compressed ice start flowing.

The high Cuchumatanes don't look very glacial now. The broad valleys seem quite dry, with only small streams and a vegetation of low grass and herbs, agaves, and scattered, stunted pines. The apparent dryness is partly due to the porous limestone bedrock, which absorbs surface water, and perhaps partly to sheep grazing. Rainfall patterns are similar to the rest of the highlands, with a winter dry season. Morning frosts are frequent, but snow is a rare event, if it occurs at all.

There are two large protected areas in the region, one covering most of the Altos Cuchumatanes, one in the lower "Ixil Triangle" to the east. Unfortunately, both areas suffered a great deal of violence during the 1980s, and neither is considered entirely safe today, so protection has been more theoretical than actual. Deforestation and soil erosion are serious problems on the steep slopes surrounding the high tablelands. Botanists would expect to find unusual plants on areas of serpentine bedrock, but not much information exists. Large wildlife is scarce, although there are pumas, deer, and other mammals. Many of the birds are what you'd expect on the California coast: ravens, Steller's jays, horned larks, meadowlarks, bluebirds, bushtits, and kinglets, although the meadowlarks and bluebirds are of the eastern instead of the western species.

The local capital, Huehuetenango, is a 5-hour bus ride from Guatemala City. The fare is less than $5. Companies serving the route: Rapidos Zaculeu, 11-42 Calle 9, Zona 1, leaving at 6 A.M. and 3 P.M. (their Huehuetenango address is 5-25 Ave. 3); Los Halcones, 15-27 Ave. 7, Zona 1, leaving at 7 A.M. and 2 P.M. (3-63 Ave. 7 in Huehuetenango). The Huehuetenango bus terminal is a couple of kilometers southeast of town; yellow city buses run to the parque central. The Hotel Zaculeu, 1-14 Ave. 5, Zona 1, a half block northwest of the parque central, has rooms in the $20–50 range. Less expensive are: Río Lindo, 0-20 Ave. 3, east of the parque central, with electric showers; Hotel Mary, 3-52 Calle 2, just northeast of the parque central; Gran Hotel Shinula, Calle 4 between aves. 2 and 3. If you're driving, El Prado at the entrance of town is similarly priced. Cheaper are: Maya, 3-55 Ave 3; Central, 1-33 Ave. 5; El Viajero, 5-20 Calle 2.

Las Brasas at Ave. 4 and Calle 2 has Chinese food and steaks. Rincon Hogareño, 7-21 Ave. 6, Pizza Hogareña, Ave. 6 between calles 4 and 5, and La Fonda de Don Juan, 5-35 Calle 2, have Italian food. Jardin, Ave. 6 and Calle 4, and Ebony, Ave. 5 and Calle 2, are good and inexpensive. Local banks will cash traveler's checks, but only Banco de Guatemala, 5-07 Calle 4, will cash Mexican pesos, if you're coming from that direction. There's a tourism office on Calle 2 opposite Hospedaje el Viajero.

The ruins of Zacaleu, the capital of the local Mam Maya nation until Alvarado arrived, are located on a river bluff about 5 kilometers north of Hueheutenango. Buses run there from Hotel Maya. An excavated ball court, pyramid, and other structures have been reconstructed, although without the bright colors with which the originals probably were painted. There's a good view of the Altos Cuchumatanes to the north. John Lloyd Stephens wrote of seeing the bones of "a colossal animal, supposed to be a mastodon" in a riverbank near "GueGuetenango." "The bank was perpendicular, about thirty feet high, and the animal had been buried in an upright position. . . . The impression of the whole animal, from twenty-five to thirty feet long, was distinctly visible."

There are no towns on the high plateau of the Altos Cuchumatanes, but buses run from Huehuetenango to towns on its northern and eastern slopes. The main road, unpaved, runs over 100 kilometers north to the towns of San Mateo Ixatan and Barillas, where the highlands begin to drop into the Petén. The town of Soloma on the north edge of the Altos, about a 4-hour bus ride from Huehuetenango, has hotels, including the Río Lindo, $10–20, with hot water. The bus leaves Huehuetenango at 2 A.M. and you need to get your name on a list of passengers. You board the bus when your name is called: if you didn't arrive early enough, you have to wait another day. Buses leave San Mateo Ixatan to return to Huehuetenango at 5 A.M. and 1:30 P.M. If you want to take a day hike on the high plateau, you could get off the bus at a spot that looks interesting, then return to the road to wait for the return bus. Of course, the return bus may not run, or may not have room for you. Don't try a day hike without asking at least the tourist office and possibly the local police. (If they say it's all right, ask the bus conductor if he thinks it's a good idea.) Army, rural guard, and possibly guerrilla units may be active in the area. There are no facilities, except a "*mirador*" (scenic viewpoint) where the road reaches the plateau.

Todos Santos Cuchumatán is a famous Mam Maya town east of the plateau (famous for its eye-catching costumes and for its Nov. 1 festival featuring horse races; there's also a language school where you can learn Mam Maya as well as Spanish—Proyecto Lingüístico de Español a block from the square). Buses from Huehuetenango leave at 4 and 11 A.M. and return at 5:30 and 11:30 A.M. and 1 P.M. Buses are most crowded Mondays and Fridays. The trip takes 4 hours, and also goes part way over the high plateau before dropping into the valley where Todos Santos is located (2,481 meters). There are a couple of cheap hotels (La Paz, Olguitas) and a comedor (Katy), not hard to find. Trails lead into the countryside. One that starts on the hill above the main square leads over a ridge into another valley where the village of San Juan Atitán is located, about 5 hours away (without overnight facilities).

The Ixil Triangle

This eastern part of the Cuchumatanes isn't as high and wild as Altos Cuchumatanes, but is equally scenic. Many villages in this area were destroyed and the people relocated during the 1980s. Access is not via Huehuetenango but via Santa Cruz del Quiché (see above), from which two or three buses a day leave between 7 and 11 A.M. to Nebaj, the main town in the Ixil. The Ixil Hotel near the entrance of Nebaj is in the $6 range. Hospedajes Esperanza, Las Tres Hermanas, and Las Clavellinas are less. Comedores Olimpia Moreno and Las Delicias near the square are good. The surrounding hills are good for hiking. A waterfall is located on the river east of town: follow the road to the town of Chajul for 20 minutes, then turn left on a track before you get to a bridge and follow the river another half hour or so.

Alta and Baja Verapaz

The mountains of Alta and Baja Verapaz east of the Cuchumatanes are also formed of uplifted crustal blocks, but aren't as high, mostly under 2,000 meters. Being closer to the Caribbean, they get a lot of rain, which has carved the limestone bedrock of the northern part, Alta Verapaz, into steep, cone-shaped "karst" topography. There are extensive limestone caverns near the village of Lanquin to the east of the main town of Cobán. These mountains were less heavily settled than the western highlands when Alvarado arrived, and many Maya fled here to join the local Rabinal tribe in resisting the conquistadors. Bartoloméo de las Casas pacified the area by sending Maya-speaking missionaries in 1537–39, which is when the region got its name, "true peace." In the nineteenth century, the region became the center of the coffee industry, with German and other European immigrants establishing large *"fincas."* Much of the rain forest and cloud forest that formerly grew here has thus been cleared.

The only easily accessible protected area in the region is the Biotopo del Quetzal Mario Dary, 4 kilometers south of the village of Purulha at km 163 of the Guatemala City–Cobán highway. You can get there from Guatemala City by taking a Cobán bus and asking to be let out at the biotopo. Transportes Escobar–Monja Blanca, 15-16 Ave. 8, Zona 1, has hourly buses from 4 A.M. to 5 P.M. It's about 3 hours to the biotopo. To leave the reserve, you'll need to flag a bus on the road.

You can camp for free at the biotopo (you should arrange this with the CECON office in Guatemala City, 0-63 Ave. Reforma, Zona 10), but you'll need a good tent: it's likely to be very wet and buggy. Outdoor cooking facilities, showers, and toilets are provided. You can get meals at the Hospedaje Los Ranchos a short walk north on the road from the biotopo entrance. The Hospedaje also has bunkhouses with showers and toilets where you can lay out your sleeping bag for around $6 a night. Four kilometers south of the biotopo is the Posada Montaña del Quetzal, a comfortable resort with a garden, pool, and restaurant in the $30–40 a night range. Phone 351-805 in Guatemala City for reservations, which are advisable, especially on weekends. In Purulha there's a comedor, San Antonio, and the local drugstore rents rooms.

The biotopo is named for Mario Dary, a San Carlos University professor (and later rector) who was largely responsible for the program. Unknown assassins murdered him in 1981. It is open from 8–4 daily, free, although donations are welcome. There's a small visitor center and ranger station at the head of two trails: one 2 kilometers long and the other 8 kilometers. Chances of seeing quet-

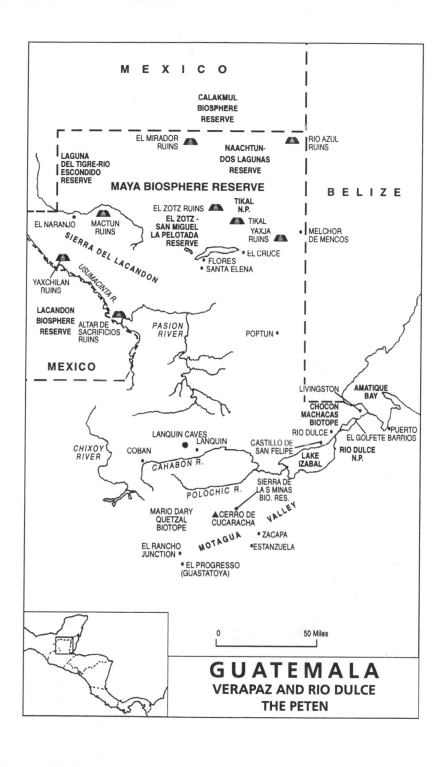

MEXICO

CALAKMUL
BIOSPHERE
RESERVE

EL MIRADOR
RUINS

NAACHTUN-
DOS LAGUNAS
RESERVE

RIO AZUL
RUINS

LAGUNA
DEL TIGRE-RIO
ESCONDIDO
RESERVE

MAYA BIOSPHERE RESERVE

BELIZE

EL ZOTZ RUINS

TIKAL
N.P.

EL NARANJO

MACTUN
RUINS

EL ZOTZ -
SAN MIGUEL
LA PELOTADA
RESERVE

TIKAL
YAXJA
RUINS

MELCHOR
DE MENCOS

SIERRA DEL LACANDON

EL CRUCE

FLORES
SANTA ELENA

YAXCHILAN
RUINS

USUMACINTA R.

LACANDON
BIOSPHERE
RESERVE

ALTAR DE
SACRIFICIOS
RUINS

PASION
RIVER

POPTUN

MEXICO

LIVINGSTON

AMATIQUE
BAY

CHOCON
MACHACAS
BIOTOPE

RIO DULCE

CASTILLO DE
SAN FELIPE

EL GOLFETE

PUERTO
BARRIOS

CHIXOY
RIVER

LANQUIN CAVES

COBAN

LANQUIN

CAHABON R.

LAKE
IZABAL

RIO DULCE
N.P.

POLOCHIC R.

SIERRA DE
LA S MINAS
BIO. RES.

MARIO DARY
QUETZAL
BIOTOPE

CERRO DE
CUCARACHA

VALLEY

EL RANCHO
JUNCTION

MOTAGUA

ZACAPA

ESTANZUELA

EL PROGRESSO
(GUASTATOYA)

0   50 Miles

GUATEMALA
VERAPAZ AND RIO DULCE
THE PETEN

zals are best during the March–May breeding season, and if you spend several days in the area, going out each morning and evening, when they're most active. (They're seen at the Hospedaje Los Ranchos and Posada del Quetzal as well as the biotopo.) The reserve is not really big enough to have a substantial quetzal population, because the birds need to make fairly long altitudinal migrations to find feeding and breeding habitat. Quetzals do nest near the biotopo road and in the Posada del Quetzal. Even if quetzals evade you, there's a good chance of seeing monkeys, emerald toucanets, and other wildlife among the huge fig and oak trees, epiphytic orchids and philodendrons, and begonias and bromeliads of the cloud forest.

River Trips in Verapaz

The Río Cahabón, which runs from Alta Verapaz into Lake Izabal, is considered Guatemala's best whitewater river, with Class III and IV rapids, waterfalls, caves, and hot springs. The nearby Río Candelaria, a tributary of the Chixoy, has underground stretches navigable by boat. Maya Expeditions, 16-52 Ave. 3, Zona 10, Guatemala City (phone: 683-010/562-551/374-666) offers trips on these rivers, as well as the Usumacinta and Pasión in the Petén (see below).

Sierra de las Minas

This roughly 200,000-hectare biosphere reserve north of the Motagua Valley contains the largest remaining area of contiguous cloud forest in northern Central America. The rapidity with which it was being deforested in the 1980s led The Nature Conservancy to include the reserve in its "Parks in Peril" program. The reserve is now being managed by a Guatemalan NGO (nongovernmental organization), Defensores de la Naturaleza, with buffer zones of sustainable development surrounding the core cloud forest zone. Studies of quetzal migration are under way to make sure enough land on the lower slopes is being protected for when quetzals move downhill after the breeding season.

The reserve is an area of dramatic contrasts. Like the other highland ranges, the Sierra de las Minas is a large block uplifted by faulting activity (the Motagua fault separating the North American and Caribbean plates is just south of it). Since the Motagua Valley is only a few hundred meters above sea level, the Sierra's peaks (the highest is 2,992-meter Cerro la Cucaracha) look dizzyingly high. It is composed of metamorphic and plutonic rocks, and contains precious metal deposits which led to its name, the Sierra of the Mines. There are also large marble quarries. The lush cloud forests on its upper slopes contrast sharply with areas of serpentine bedrock where short grass and scattered conifers grow, and with inland lower slopes where conditions are desertlike. Fourteen species of pines occur in the reserve. Wildlife is more abundant than in the more heavily settled western highlands, and includes jaguars, tapirs, and horned guans. An estimated 70 percent of Guatemala's native species live in the reserve. The biosphere reserve is also the principal water source for the Motagua Valley to the south, which gets less than 500 mm of rainfall a year.

The main highway from Guatemala City to the Caribbean runs through the Motagua Valley, whose cactuses and dry heat can be a nice change after the chilly highlands. Desert fauna like roadrunners and Mexican beaded lizards live here. Second-class buses to Puerto Barrios on the Caribbean leave frequently from the Zona 1 terminal at Calle 18 and Ave. 9, and Litegua, 7-66 Calle 15, Zona 1, has first-class buses hourly. Either should be willing to let you off in the valley, although you should ask first. There are hotels in the valley: Hotel Guastatoya, about $10 a night for a room with bath, swimming pool, restaurant, at El Progreso at the west end of the Sierra; Motel Longarone, $30–50 for air-conditioned bungalows with pool at Km 126 on the Atlantic Highway; Hotel Atlántico, $10–20 near Longarone; and Hotel Wong, $10 with bath at 12-35 Calle 3 in the town of Zacapa at the east end of the Sierra a few kilometers south of the highway.

The little town of Estanzuela just north of Zacapa has a museum housing the skeletons of large Pleistocene mammals which were unearthed in the vicinity, including a ground sloth, a glyptodont (a kind of giant armadillo), a mastodon, and a horse. The arid conditions in the valley make it much better fossil-hunting territory than most of Central America. The museum is open 9–5 weekdays; admission is free.

Getting into the cloud forest of the Sierra isn't easy. Roads require 4wd (four-wheel drive) and are impassable in the rainy season. There is a hospedaje at Los Albores, the finca of Don Carlos Mendez, the sector ranger. There are spare bedrooms in the upper story of the house. The finca is located on a 4wd road 2 hours north of the El Rancho junction on the Guatemala–Puerto Barrios Road. There are trailheads into the cloud forest 20 minutes' drive above the finca at some radio towers. To stay there, you need to make arrangements in advance with Fundación Defensores de la Naturaleza, 20-21 Ave. las Américas, Zona 14, Guatemala City (phone: 373-893/370-319; fax: 682-648).

There's also access into the western end of the Sierra via the town of Chilasco on the road between the El Rancho junction and the quetzal biotopo. Defensores de la Naturaleza has an office a block from the central square at Chilasco where you can ask for directions. Again, 4wd will be needed. There's also a Defensores office in Salamá, in the valley of San Jeronimo.

Lake Izabal and the Río Dulce

As you travel northeast along the Motagua Valley past the Sierra de las Minas, you experience one of the more startling natural transitions in a land of startling transitions. Cactus-covered hills and bottomlands begin to support palm trees and banana fields, and by the time you reach the foot of the valley you're in lush forest. It's like going from Arizona to Amazonia in a hundred kilometers. If you cross the hills north of the valley, it's even more like Amazonia, since the forest encloses a large expanse of freshwater lake and marsh. This is Lake Izabal, which, like the larger Nicaraguan lakes to the south, was formed by land subsidence on a fault line. Like the Nicaraguan lakes, Izabal drains into the Caribbean by a river, the Río Dulce, which widens into the smaller lake of El Golfete.

When John Lloyd Stephens went up the Río Dulce in 1839, he called it "a fairy scene of Titan land, combining exquisite beauty with colossal grandeur. . . . On each side, rising perpendicularly from three to four hundred feet was a wall of living green. Trees grew from the water's edge, with dense, unbroken foliage, to the top; not a spot of barrenness was to be seen; and on both sides, from the tops of the highest trees, long tendrils descended to the water, as if to drink and carry life to the trunks that bore them." The area has not changed much since then: the Río Dulce from Lake Izabal to the Caribbean has been declared a national park, and on El Golfete's northern shore is located the Chocón-Machacas Biotopo, a refuge for manatees and mangrove swamps administered by CECON (see above for Guatemala City address). The 7,200-hectare biotopo has a boat jetty with a visitor center and nature trails through the forest. There also are "boat trails" through the area's swampy lagoons. The swampy mouth of the Polochic River at Lake Izabal's west end is one of the forty-four "special protection" areas in the 1989 law which may eventually become units of the conservation system.

Río Dulce is worth visiting for its own sake, and also makes an excellent rest stop on the grueling bus journey to the Petén. There are two ways to get there: you can simply get off a Petén-bound bus at Río Dulce (also called Fronteras, or El Relleno), where the highway crosses the river, or go to Puerto Barrios on the Caribbean, from which boats go to the Garífuna town of Lívingston. From there you can hire boats upriver, which will take you back to the Petén Highway at Río Dulce. Second-class buses to Puerto Barrios and the Petén leave Guatemala City from the area around Calle 19, and aves. 8 and 9, Zona 1. Litegua, 7-66 Calle 15, has hourly first-class buses to Puerto Barrios (phone 27-578).

At Río Dulce–El Relleno, which is 34 kilometers from the La Ruidosa turnoff of the Atlantic Highway, there are cheap hospedajes by the bridge (Marilu, $10); and resort hotels are scattered up and down the river. Turicentro Marimonte is near the road on the river's south bank and has accommodations in the $50 range, restaurant, and pool (phone: 047-8585: reservations needed on weekends), also a camping area for $5. Several kilometers upstream, near the Castillo de San Felipe, a restored seventeenth-century fort built as a defense against pirates, are Izabal Tropical, with accommodations in the $25 range (phone: 047-8115), and

Hotel Don Humberto, $10. Downstream from Río Dulce–El Relleno are: Catamaran in the $40 range (phone: 364-450) and Del Río in the $50 range (phone: 310-016 in Guatemala City). Good restaurants at Río Dulce are Bar Hotel California, Olimar, and Comedor El Quetzal. There's a restaurant at San Felipe.

There are many different kinds of boat rentals at Río Dulce, mostly under the bridge. The going rate for a morning trip downriver to Lívingston (with a stop at the biotopo) for up to eight people is $50, but you're unlikely to see much in so short a time. The best way to see wildlife would be to find a knowledgeable and patient boatman who'll take you out for a day or two. (Manatee sightings are unlikely.) You'll need to ask around for this, and probably do some bargaining.

In Puerto Barrios, El Reformador, Calle 16 and Ave. 7 (phone: 481-533) is a good hotel in the $25 range. The Hotel del Norte, Calle 7 and Ave. 2, is also good and clean (phone: 480-087). Less are: Español, Calle 13 between aves. 5 and 6 (phone: 480-738); Europea, Ave. 8 between calles 8 and 9; and Caribena, Ave. 4 between calles 10 and 11. Lívingston is about 20 kilometers east of Puerto Barrios on the mouth of the Río Dulce. Scheduled launches leave the municipal dock at Barrios for the one-and-a-half-hour trip to Lívingston several times a day (probably midmorning and midafternoon, but ask around). The fare is very cheap. Tickets are sold on the boat (arrive an hour early to be sure of a seat) and at the ALM shipping office at Ave. 1 between calles 11 and 12. You can also hire boats, but they'll be much more expensive than the scheduled trips.

Lívingston was founded by the Garífuna in the early nineteenth century with, Stephens wrote, "that eye for the picturesque and beautiful in natural scenery which distinguishes the Indian everywhere. . . . Their leaf-thatched huts were ranged along the bank, shaded by groves of plantain and coconut trees. . . . It was a soft and sunny scene, speaking peace and freedom." The town retains a strong Afro-Caribbean atmosphere, with a modern, reggae accent, and is popular with young travelers. It's not really much of a beach resort: what beach there is isn't too clean, and there have been robberies. About 6 kilometers northwest along the shore from

Lívingston is a river swimming place called Los Siete Altares, with pools and waterfalls, located along a path inland from where the small river enters Amatique Bay. Just before this is a hotel, El Chiringuito, with a restaurant and bungalows.

In Lívingston, Tucan Dugu is a luxury resort on the water, with pool, restaurant, and bar in the $60 range (phone: 0-481-572/588 or 321-259 in Guatemala City). Casa Rosada, 800 meters to the left of the dock, has thatched cottages for $10–20. Caribe is nearer the dock, with rooms in the $10 range. Río Dulce, Lugar Africano, and Flamingo, all in the $10–20 range, are located along the main street. Restaurants include El Malecón, near the docks, El Jaguar on the main street, La Cueva across from the church, Margoth, and La Cabana.

Mail boats go from Lívingston to Río Dulce–El Relleno in the mornings twice a week—check locally for exact times. This is inexpensive, but doesn't give you much opportunity to experience the biotopo. Hiring a small motorboat or "*cayuco*" probably is the best way to do that. You'll need to shop around carefully to get a good guide. About halfway between Lívingston and El Golfete, a hot spring flows up from the riverbed at the base of a cliff. You can swim in this off your boat: there's no landing spot. The biotopo is 12 kilometers upriver. Via Real Travel Center, Calle 7 oriente, Antigua, has charters to offshore cays (phone: 032-3228).

The Petén

John Lloyd Stephens met a priest in the highlands who told him that, as a young man, he had climbed to a mountaintop from which "he looked over an immense plain extending to Yucatán and the Gulf of Mexico, and saw at a great distance a large city spread over a great space, and with turrets of white glistening in the sun." Stephens felt "a craving desire to reach the mysterious city. . . . One look at that city was worth ten years of everyday life." Stephens's "craving desire" has been felt by so many since that "the city in the jungle" has become as much a movie and adventure novel archetype as a real phenomenon. There are no living Mayan cities hidden away in the real Petén (and almost certainly weren't in Stephens's day), yet it still manages to surpass the movie version with its real forest and the mysteries of its dead cities, many of which remain unstudied.

Although it seems flat compared to the highlands, most of the Petén has a rolling topography. Its limestone bedrock was formed when the area lay under water during the Oligocene epoch some 30 million years ago. It has been uplifted since then by the same tectonic forces that have uplifted the highlands, but little is known of its terrestrial past: the only land fossils are of mastodons, ground sloths, bison, and other animals of the fairly recent Pleistocene epoch. The limestone bedrock gives the land an odd character. There are few streams, but water accumulates in low-lying areas called "*bajos*" during the rainy season. The Maya depended on small depressions called "*aguadas*" to hold water during the dry season.

Rainfall in the Petén is not very heavy compared to the Mosquitia farther south, and rain seldom falls from December through April. The forest is thus not true rain forest, with its tremendous growth of epiphytes. Old growth is very impressive, however, with ceibas, zapotes (genus *Manilkara*), mahoganies, ramóns (*Brosimum*), and Spanish cedars (*Cedrela*) sometimes reaching heights of 50 meters in the "high forest" of better-drained areas. In bajos the forest is lower and thicker, with *Sabal* and *Chrysophila* palms, or stands of logwood (*Haematoxylon*), a small tree from which a commercial dye used to be extracted. Extraction of "chicle" sap, the basis of chewing gum, from zapote trees remains a commercial industry. Some parts of the Petén have pine savanna, grassland, or marsh instead of forest. Farm field borders, presumably from Maya times, are still visible from the air in some of these areas.

Although parrots, toucans, and spider and howler monkeys live in the Petén forest, visitors will encounter more northerly animals too. The most spectacular of these is the ocellated turkey, a deep blue bird about two-thirds as large as the wild turkey found in the U.S. Fossils in the LaBrea tarpits in Los Angeles show that turkeys apparently identical to the ocellated turkey lived north to California in the Pleistocene epoch and shared habitat with now extinct mastodons and ground sloths. Today, it is confined to the Petén, Belize, and Yucatán, a relic of a largely vanished North American tropics. Threatened in unprotected areas, the turkeys (called "*pa-*

Ocellated turkey (*Agriocharis ocellata*). Photo by Carolyn Miller.

vos ocellados" in Spanish) are quite common and tame in Tikal National Park, where you can see and hear males displaying during the spring breeding season. They strut about with tail spread like ordinary turkeys, but make very different sounds. Other resident birds that reach their southernmost distribution here are cardinals and black-and-blue jays. Dozens of North American migrant songbird and waterbird species come to the Petén during the winter. On the other hand, many of the most spectacular animals typical of the rain forests to the south—tapirs, jaguars, king vultures, jabiru storks, great curassows—live in the Petén.

The town of Flores, on an island in Lake Petén Itzá, is the Petén's capital. The lake's story is also an archetype. It was the site of Tayasal, a city founded in the thirteenth century by the Itzá, a Maya dynasty fleeing the fall of Chichen Itzá in Yucatán. Tayasal was so remote that, although Cortés passed through on an expedition to Honduras in 1524 (leaving behind a horse, which the Itzá tried to feed on flowers and meat, then deified after its death), the Spanish didn't conquer it until 1697. The Englishman Thomas Gage, who participated in one of many attempts to conquer the Petén and its

rumored treasure in the two centuries before 1697, got only fever
and dysentery before his party was attacked and repulsed by
"about a thousand Indians . . . which uproar and affrightment
added sweat and fear to my fever." An earlier expedition, in 1623,
ended as sacrifices to the Mayan gods. When the Spanish finally
captured Tayasal, they found it covered with pyramids, plazas, and
stelae (which they destroyed). Tayasal's ruins, little more than low
mounds, are on a peninsula just north of Flores. Today, Flores is a
picturesque, colonial-looking town across a causeway from the
larger, more modern town of Santa Elena, and a good starting
point for trips to Tikal and other parts of the Maya Biosphere
Reserve.

The easy way to get to Flores is to fly from Guatemala City. Aviateca, Aerovias, Aeroquetzal, Tikal Jet, and Tapsa have daily flights
at 7 or 8 A.M. (including weekends) from La Aurora to Santa Elena
airport. Flights are in the $100–150 range, round-trip. Passports or
other identity documents are needed. An INGUAT information office is open from 8 to 5. There are rental vehicles at Santa Elena
airport, which is about a kilometer east of the causeway between
Santa Elena and Flores.

The hard way to get to Flores, and it can be very hard, is by road
from Río Dulce, dust in the dry season, and mud or water in the
wet. Deforestation is proceeding rapidly in the Petén south of Flores, so it's not even a very scenic trip. It takes around 14 hours from
Guatemala City under good conditions, but can be over 24 in
bad. Army checkpoints are common (be sure to carry passport or
other I.D.), and holdups not unknown. Second-class buses to Flores leave from the area around Calle 19 and aves. 8 and 9, Zona 1,
Guatemala City. First-class companies include: Maya Express,
9-36 Calle 17, Zona 1, which has daily nonstop buses at 4, 6, and
8 P.M. (returning from Santa Elena at 4, 7, and 8 A.M.); and Fuente
del Norte, 8-46 Calle 17, Zona 1, which has early morning and evening buses. Fares range from $10–20 one-way.

The bus trip will be easier if you stop over a day or two along the
way, though you'll need to make sure your bus will let you do so
without paying full fare. The Lake Izabal–Río Dulce area is a good
stopover (see above). Another is the Finca Ixobel, an inexpensive

resort 3 kilometers south of the town of Poptun about halfway between Río Dulce and Flores. The finca has a good restaurant,
rooms, cabins, and camping facilities, as well as horse rentals, a library, and guides for forest hikes. The resort also runs a restaurant
and hospedaje near the bus station in the town of Poptun.

Accommodations abound in the Flores area, although many
may be booked up with package tours. There also have been some
problems with flooding on shore properties in recent years because
the lake level has been rising from unusually heavy rains.

Some restaurants around Flores may have game on the menu:
"*venado*" (deer), "*pavo silvestre*" (wild turkey or other large game
birds such as curassow, guan, or chachalaca), "*tepiscuintle*" (paca,
a large rodent), and "*cusuco*" (armadillo). Since at least tepiscuintle and pavo are dwindling through much of their range, it's probably not a good thing to encourage market hunting of them.
They're under enough pressure from subsistence hunters. There
have been schemes to raise tepiscuintles commercially, but so far it
hasn't been feasible. (You might ask restauranteurs where their
game comes from.)

In Flores itself, the Casona de las Islas on the lake is in the $60
range, with restaurant and bar (phone: 500-675). Also on the lake
is Hotel Savanna, in the $25 range including some meals. Petén
(phone 501-392) is in the $15 range. Tucan is small, by the lake,
with a garden restaurant, in the $10 range. Gran Jaguar, El Faisan,
and La Jungla are good restaurants. In Santa Elena, Del Patio Tikal
has air-conditioned rooms with color TV in the $50 range (phone:
501-229; fax in Guatemala City: 237-4313). Maya Internacional
has a striking lakeside setting, in the $30 range (phone: 501-276;
fax: 500-032). Costa del Sol near the bus station is in the $25 range
(phone: 501-336). Jade near the causeway to Flores is in the $5
range. Leo Fu Lo and Don Quijote, both on the lake, are comparable. El Lago Azul and El Rodeo are good restaurants.

There are also hotels along the lake on the paved road between
Flores and Tikal. The Villa Maya, in the $80 range, is on a lagoon
about 10 kilometers east of Santa Elena, with restaurant, pools,
and tennis courts (phone: 501-276; fax: 500-032). The priciest hotel is El Camino Real, located at El Remate on the east shore of the

lake. It's in the $130 range, with cable TV and is run by the Camino Real in Guatemala City (see above: reservations should be made there—phone: 334-633).

Lake Petén Itzá is a beautiful lake, with clear turquoise water over a white sand bottom, although urban growth and deforestation have caused some pollution in recent years. You can swim and watch cichlids and turtles. There are 24 fish species in the lake. At the causeway, you can rent dugout canoes for a few dollars, or hire a boat for a lake tour for about $10. There's a "tourism park" with a small zoo at Petencito east of Flores.

Farther away, on the lake's east side, is the Biotopo Cerro Cahui, a 650-hectare preserve for monkeys, Morelet's crocodiles (a small crocodile that lives in Yucatán and the Petén), and other forest and lakeshore wildlife. Like the quetzal biotopo, it's administered by the University of San Carlos. Nature trails are open daily 7–5. You can get there by boat or by road via El Remate. Buses or minibuses going to Tikal will drop you off. It's a 3-kilometer walk west along the lake to the biotopo entrance (although the lakeside road is sometimes flooded). At the entrance is the Parador Ecologico el Gringo Perdido, an ecoresort with cabins in the $20 range and campsites for a few dollars. There's a small restaurant, boat rental, and horse rentals, and guides for forest hikes (phone: 363-683 in Guatemala City; fax: 538-761).

There is a limestone cave system called Las Grutas de Actun-Can an hour's walk south from Santa Elena. You follow the causeway through town to where the road forks before a small hill, then turn left, then right. A "*dueño*" (proprietor) will turn on the lights for a small admission fee. There are stalactites and other formations.

Tikal National Park and World Heritage Site

This is *the* "city in the jungle," the restored ruins of the major Classic Maya metropolis surrounded by the longest-protected forest in Guatemala. Along with Barro Colorado Island in Panama, it is the longest-protected area in Central America, and wildlife is correspondingly common and even tame. Ocellated turkeys, gray foxes, agoutis, spider monkeys, toucans, and parrots are frequently seen. Howler monkeys, which suffered greatly from a yellow fever epidemic in the 1960s, are recovering. The Asociación de Rescate y Conservación de Vida Silvestre has a wildlife rehabilitation facility near the Villa Maya Hotel (phone: 050-0566). An ambitious new initiative of Paseo Pantera and Guatemalan conservation organizations is working to improve trails, exhibits, and other park facilities.

The scarcity of surface water facilitates wildlife observation because animals concentrate around available water, such as the old Maya aguadas around the park ruins. Another advantage to wildlife watching at Tikal is that the forest is *not* rain forest, which swallows everything up in its soaring profusion. I've never had such a good look at the buffooneries of keel-billed toucans and blue-crowned parrots as in the trees around the Tikal campsite. (Toucans seem to like teasing parrots.) Being able to observe the forest canopy from the tops of the pyramids is yet another advantage you don't get in places like Darién or the Mosquitia. Temple IV is 64 meters high, the tallest pre-Columbian building in the Americas.

Humans began settling in the area at least 2,700 years ago, attracted by local supplies of flint and relatively dry terrain. Two thousand years ago, Tikal was a well-developed trade and ceremonial center whose dynastic rulers steadily expanded its power and influence, perhaps partly by introducing new military tactics from Mexico. At its peak, between 1,500 and 1,100 years ago, Tikal covered some 30 square kilometers, with 3,000 buildings in its core area, and a population which may have been about 100,000.

Much has been learned about Tikal's history in recent decades by interpretation of inscriptions found there and in neighboring cities. The inscriptions, which commemorate important acts of rulers, indicate that the city of Caracol about 80 kilometers to the southeast (now part of Belize) conquered Tikal and ruled it between about 1,450 and 1,300 years ago, but that a ruler named Ah-Cacao ("Lord Chocolate") restored its dominance, which lasted until the general collapse of Petén cities about 1,100 years ago. (Ah-Cacao's tomb in Temple I has been excavated, and some of his grave ornaments are on display at the park museum.) The ruins at Tikal today are a composite of structures from the thousand years of its existence, since the Maya periodically rebuilt new ceremonial centers on top of older ones. The most impressive structures such as temples I–V were built in the final two centuries.

Tikal's ruins were first discovered by a Guatemalan government expedition in 1848. Early explorers such as the Swiss Gustav Bernoulli found carved wooden door lintels still intact, although the buildings were so covered with soil and vegetation as to seem as much like natural hills as manmade structures. Scientific excavation began in the late nineteenth century, and continues today under direction of the Instituto de Antropología y Historia. One recent discovery has been a network of tunnels beneath the southwest part of the ruins (called El Mundo Perdido).

Excavated and partially restored ruins in the park cover a couple of square kilometers of plazas, causeways, acropolises, ball courts, and steeply pyramidal temples. Like the ancient Greek cities, Tikal must have been a rather gaudy place when alive: paint traces indicate many of the structures were bright red. Today the limestone is weathered a bone white that seems appropriately ghostly, especially in the evening. Dusk and early morning are among the best times to experience the ruins, which are open from 6 A.M. to 5:30 P.M. (It may be possible to get special permission to visit the ruins on moonlit nights, by applying at the "Inspectoria" building on the path to the ruins.) The ruins are too extensive and elaborate to describe adequately here: if you want to explore them in detail, you'll do best to hire a guide (ask at hotels and the Inspectoria) or get a copy of William R. Coe's *Tikal: A Handbook of the Ancient Maya Ruins*.

The ruins and public facilities at Tikal are in the center of the park, at the end of the 65-kilometer paved road from Santa Elena. There's a $6 admission fee, payable at the entrance to the park, good for one day. Accommodations in the park are limited, and many visitors stay around Flores and make day trips to the park. A 6 A.M. minibus from Santa Elena arrives at the park at 7 and returns to Santa Elena at 3 or 4 P.M. You can make reservations on it at travel agencies in Flores and Santa Elena. There will probably be other vans going in the morning. If you do want to stay at Tikal, you should reserve a room or camping space as soon as you arrive. In the high season (Nov.–May) it's best to reserve in advance, though this isn't easy because of poor communications. You can make reservations with a travel agent, or write the hotels care of Tikal N.P., El Petén, Guatemala, but there are no guarantees.

The three hotels at Tikal are all in the $20–50 range. The Jaguar Inn across from the museum has English-speaking staff and will rent tents for use in its campground as well as rooms in rustic bungalows, with or without board. It has electricity from 6 P.M. to 10 P.M. You may be able to make reservations by phoning 760-294 in Guatemala City. The Posada de la Selva (Jungle Lodge) off the path to the ruins is the largest hotel, with thirty-five rooms, some with bath and fan. Electricity is from 6 P.M. to 10:30 P.M. Reservations may be made at 18-01 Calle 29, Zona 12, Guatemala City (phone: 768-775) although this requires a one-night advance payment and the "reservation" may not be held. The Tikal Inn near the airstrip includes breakfast and dinner in the room fee, and has a dozen rooms and a few bungalows.

There's a public campsite near the airstrip, with a dozen or so tent and hammock spaces and a toilet and shower, although water may not always be available. There's a $6-per-night fee. (Campsite use may soon be restricted to organized school groups.) I slept at the campground (a site now occupied by the Tikal Inn) without net or tent in March 1971, and the only discomfort I recall was the night chill. The Petén's population has tripled since then, however, and the chances of getting malaria from the odd mosquito bite have probably increased proportionately. Vampire bats also have increased because of the growing cattle population, and they may carry rabies.

As well as the hotel restaurants, there are several comedores across from the visitor center, and there's a more expensive restaurant at the visitor center. The visitor center has a scale model of the ruins and a collection of sculptures and stelae, as well as rest rooms and a gift shop. There's a small post office next door. North from the visitor center is the Sylvanus G. Morely Museum, with exhibits on artifacts from the ruins and history of the excavations, and a replica of Ah-Cacao's tomb. It's open weekdays 9–5, weekends 9–4, admission $2. A gift shop has handicrafts and books, including William R. Coe's *Tikal,* mentioned above.

The Maya Biosphere Reserve

Tikal is part of this roughly 1.3-million-hectare reserve, which was established on the entire Petén above the 17th parallel in 1990. The reserve adjoins the Calakmul Biosphere Reserve in southern Yucatán and the Río Bravo Reserve and Aguas Turbias National Park in Belize to form one of the largest continuous protected areas in Meso-America. A number of parks and biotopos have been established to serve as core conservation areas within the reserve boundaries, while the rest is to be devoted to buffer zones and controlled extraction of forest products. CONAP is being assisted by U.S. AID and private conservation organizations in developing a management plan for the area, but its remoteness and the presence of guerrillas, drug smugglers, archaeological site looters, wildlife poachers, and loggers make this difficult. U.S. AID has estimated that most of the reserve's primary forests will be gone by 2010 if present trends continue. CONAP (the National Council of Protected Areas) has a branch office in San Benito, the town adjacent to Santa Elena in the Petén (phone: 050-0178; fax: 050-0137). Another organization, ProPetén, funded by the U.S. organization Conservation International, is working to encourage sustainable development in buffer zones. They have an office in Flores (phone: 510-370). The Wildlife Conservation Society has an ongoing research project on wildlife populations in the region.

Uaxactún

If you want to take an overnight hike into the forest around Tikal, the 25-kilometer road to this ruin and Kekchi Maya village makes a good day's walk. (As elsewhere, walking off-trail can easily get you lost.) There's not much traffic, and you may get a look at one or two of the shier creatures that tend to shun the heavily visited Tikal ruins—ocelot, margay, jaguarundi, or possibly even tapir or jaguar. Bring plenty of water and insect repellent. There were no hotels or restaurants in the village as of 1994, but you can camp near the ruin or perhaps stay with a local family. Ask at the tienda, which sells soft drinks, etc. Buses may run from Tikal to Uaxactún in the dry season, or you can arrange for a guided tour with the

Posada de la Selva in Tikal. A recently formed local guides coop-erative will offer local tours and longer forest treks.

The ruins are located around a now disused airport, where there's a guard station. A wooden tower west of the airport pro-vides an overview of the former city, which may be the oldest in the Petén. The remains of a thatch-and-post temple believed to be 4,000 years old were found at the base of one structure. Tikal con-quered Uaxactún around 1,650 years ago, which is perhaps why the structures there are less impressive, although restoration has not been as extensive, and early excavations (some with dynamite) caused some destruction. More recent excavations in the area have uncovered traces of extensive soil erosion that evidently occurred when the land was denuded by the high populations of Classic times.

Biotopo el Zotz–San Miguel la Pelotada

This biotopo has been created along the west side of Tikal National Park. It contains a small ruin 30 kilometers from Uaxactún by dirt road. You can camp at the ruin, but there are no services. From El Zotz, the road continues another 20 kilometers to the village of San Miguel, which is another 20 kilometers north of Flores. So it would be possible to make a loop trip, either by foot or vehicle, starting in Flores and returning via Tikal, Uaxactún and El Zotz.

Biotopo Naachtún–Dos Lagunas

This extremely remote biotopo was created as a breeding refuge for jaguars and other large forest species. Much of it is swamp. The only settlement in the area is the village of Dos Lagunas, located about 50 kilometers northeast of Uaxactún on a road passable only by 4wd vehicles in the dry season. A biological research station is located there, but there are no facilities for travelers. Thirty kilo-meters past Dos Lagunas on an even worse road is the roughly 400-hectare Maya site of Río Azul, noted for the murals which have been unearthed in its tombs. One of the temples is 41 meters high. Ongoing excavations are being carried out in the dry season.

Getting to this area requires 2–3 days by 4wd and about 5 by foot or horseback, a regular expedition. You may need permission from local and archaeological authorities to do so. Check with the INGUAT office at the Santa Elena airport, or ask at travel agencies. Servicios Turísticos del Petén, 7-78 Ave. 2, Zona 10, Guatemala City, also operates the Hotel Maya Internacional in Santa Elena.

Biotopo Laguna del Tigre–Río Escondido

The western third of the Maya biosphere reserve is covered by a complex of sawgrass marshes, small lakes, mudflats, and seasonally flooded forests in the watershed of the San Pedro River (which eventually runs into the Usumacinta). It is probably the largest inland wetland system in Central America. This little-explored area contains healthy populations of jabiru storks, Morelet's crocodiles, and other threatened wetland species. It also may contain poachers, drug smugglers, and guerrillas, so a trip here should not be approached lightly. Access is via the town of El Naranjo on the San Pedro River, 160 kilometers from Flores. Buses leave Santa Elena daily at 5 A.M. and 12:30 P.M. The Posada San Pedro has basic rooms for a few dollars. It also is connected with Servicios Turísticos del Petén and the Hotel Maya Internacional in Santa Elena (see above), so you can check with them about the possibilities of making the trip up the San Pedro to the Maya ruin of Mactún. Two hours above Mactún, the river becomes unnavigable by motorboat, but the Chocop River can be ascended by dugout canoe. There is oil exploration going on around El Naranjo, and there is a large army base, so you shouldn't try to travel off established routes (it's a border crossing for Mexico with boats going down the San Pedro to La Palma) without an experienced guide and official permission.

The Usumacinta and Pasión Rivers

Week-long raft trips on these slow-moving lowland rivers are among the best ways of experiencing the Petén forest. The rivers pass a number of important Maya sites, including Altar de los Sacrificios, Yaxchilan, and Piedras Negras, and the Usumacinta is bordered by the Sierra del Lacandón National Park on the Guatemala side for much of its length. Many adventure tour companies in the U.S. offer raft trips. Locally, river trips as well as walking, birding, and archaeological expeditions are offered by Maya Expeditions (see Verapaz section); Servicios Turísticos del Petén (see Maya Biosphere Reserve); Izabal Adventure Tours, 14-44 Ave. 7, Zona 9, Guatemala City (phone: 340-323; fax: 340-341); Aventuras sin Limites, 9-30 Ave. 11, Zona 1, Guatemala City (phone: 28-452; fax: 947-293), and 8-15 Calle 4, Santa Elena (phone: 505-196); and Expedición Panamundo, 14-75 Ave. 6, Zona 9, Guatemala City (phone: 317-621/317-588; fax: 317-565).

Yaxhá

This archaeological reserve on the southeast edge of the Maya Biosphere Reserve is another good way to experience the Petén forest. The Yaxhá ruin, almost as large as Tikal, is on a lake accessible by dirt road from the highway between El Cruce on Lake Petén Itzá and the town of Melchor de Mencos on the border with Belize. The distance from the highway is about 12 kilometers. There's also a 30-kilometer trail to Yaxhá from Tikal. Yaxhá is a Classic Maya ruin, although it shows more influence from Teotihuacán than other Petén sites. On an island in the lake are the ruins of a small city, called Topoxte, which was occupied after the Classic Period, between eight hundred and six hundred years ago.

There's a small resort on the lake near the Yaxhá ruins that has rooms, a restaurant, and camping space. It has fishing, boating, and horseback expeditions to more remote sites.

CHAPTER SIX

Belize

BELIZE EXTENDS FARTHER north than any other Central American nation, although its lowland climate is warmer than the highlands of neighboring Guatemala. Belize also has northern cultural affinities that make it unique in the region: it is the only former British colony, and English remains the official language, although most Belizeans speak Creole (an Afro-English dialect), Spanish, or Maya as their first language. Belize is unusual in other ways. Although slightly larger than El Salvador, it has somewhat over 200,000 people, making it the least populous country in the region. So far, its highly diverse population (which includes Afro-British Creoles, Ladinos, Mayas, Garífunas, and Mennonites) has managed to live without major conflicts, although the economy is fragile, and many Belizeans have emigrated to the U.S.

Because of its small population, Belize has a high percentage of wildlands and healthy wildlife populations. Habitats are diverse, ranging from the largest barrier reef in the Western Hemisphere on the east to pine-forested peaks on the west, and from subtropical hardwood forest in the north to rain forest in the south. About 70 percent remains forested. Belize also has an abundance of Maya archaeological sites, many still unexplored. Since independence in 1981, the government and private conservation groups have created an outstanding protected areas system that encompasses 35 percent of national territory.

Belize is a highly desirable destination for nature-oriented travelers, and tourism growth has been explosive in the past decade. The annual number of visitors (about 250,000) presently exceeds the nation's population. Tourism has encouraged conservation, but also has begun to stress Belize's social fabric, with increased crime, property value inflation, and other problems. Public services such as buses remain limited, and tourism is largely upmarket, with many expensive resorts, although budget travelers can also find plenty of places to stay. Accommodations tend to be heavily booked during the December–April high season, and reservations are recommended (they're easy to make by phone and are usually reliable).

The Muddy River Country

One explanation of Belize's unusual name is that it derives from a Maya word for muddy water, *Belix*. When you fly along the coast, the name seems appropriate, because land and water are hard to distinguish in a maze of lagoons, winding streams, marshes, and mangrove swamps. Explorer John Lloyd Stephens compared Belize City to Venice, while zoologist Ivan T. Sanderson wrote of "pancake shaped islands" which "seemed to float toward us, then pause, and finally drift away aft."

Lying at the fringe of continental Central America, Belize is an ambiguous land. Its interior limestone hills were sea bottom during the Paleozoic and Mesozoic eras, yet its offshore coral reefs were dry land when the Pleistocene glaciation lowered sea level a few million years ago. Only the granitic plutons at the roots of the Maya Mountains in southern Belize are true continental bedrock, and there is doubt whether they are related to the highlands of Guatemala and Honduras. They may be a "suspect terrane," a minicontinent created by the collision of crustal plates 250 million years ago and existing as an island until tectonic movements pushed it into the rising Central American landmass. Unlike Honduras or Panama, Belize has not yielded fossils showing it was connected to

North America as much as 10 million years ago (although this doesn't prove that it wasn't, either).

Whatever its distant past, present-day Belize has evolved ecosystems similar to those of its neighbors. Northern Belize is a limestone plain covered with a dense but relatively short hardwood forest like Yucatán's, while central and southern Belize are a mosaic of pine savanna, highland forest, and tall rain forest like that of Guatemala and Honduras. Belize's proximity to the Caribbean and its generally low relief mean that annual rainfall is high throughout the country, although the south has significantly more rain, and a shorter winter dry season, than the north. Nonforested habitats such as savanna or scrubland are caused by fire, hurricanes, or seasonal flooding rather than water scarcity. Hurricanes can be severe, stripping trees (and buildings) from large areas. Many small lakes and lagoons occur in the north and along the coast.

Because Belize is mostly lowland, its fauna and flora are more "tropical" than those of the Guatemalan and Honduran highlands. Monkeys, parrots, tapirs, and jaguars live throughout the country, and tropical trees such as ceiba, cecropia, and cohune palm predominate. Yet many organisms of northern origin also live in the lowlands. Ocellated turkeys and gray foxes are typical animals in Belizean forests, and acorn woodpeckers, meadowlarks, and live oaks share the pine savannas with parrots and palm trees. In winter, Belizean forests and wetlands fill up with North American migrant songbirds and water birds. On the Maya Mountains are small areas of ocote pine and other highland species, relics of the glacial period.

Early hunter-gatherers entered Belize at least 7,500 years ago, but little has been learned about them from the scattered spearheads and campsites they left. The oldest human settlement in Belize, located at Cuello near Orange Walk, has been dated to around 3,000 years ago. It is believed to be one of the earliest Maya sites. Maya civilization was well established in Belize by 2,000 years ago, with cities such as Lamanai regulating trade from the coast. During the Classic Period, from 1,700 to 1,100 years ago, the Maya focus moved inland to large city-states based on sophisticated raised bed agriculture. Most of these were located in the Guatemalan Petén, but Caracol, on the Vaca Plateau in east-central Belize, rivaled Tikal. Other Classic sites in Belize include Xunantunich, Altun Ha, La Milpa, and Lúbaantun.

The Classic cities were largely abandoned by a thousand years ago, but Maya civilization continued in coastal sites such as Lamanai and Santa Rita, whose remains lie near Corozal in northern Belize. That city remained rich and powerful when conquistador Alfonso Dávila captured it in 1513, and its inhabitants eventually drove the Spanish out. Spanish attempts to found missions at Lamanai and other communities also were repulsed by the Maya as late as 1640. The Maya cities couldn't maintain their populations against old-world diseases, however, and all were abandoned by 1700, although small groups of Mopan Maya remained.

Pirates and Loggers

Belize's reefs and swamps had little attraction for the Spanish, and English-speaking mariners who prowled the Caribbean gradually occupied them. By the late 1600s, they had established several settlements which preyed on Spanish shipping. They also supported themselves by cutting first logwood (a small tree whose heartwood was used for inks and dyes) and later mahogany. Settlers imported African slaves, who soon overwhelmingly outnumbered whites. Spain failed to dislodge the settlements, and signed treaties with Britain in the 1700s which allowed the "Bay Colony" to remain in return for guarantees against piracy. The colony repulsed a last Spanish takeover attempt at St. George's Caye in 1798, and Britain rejected Guatemalan and Mexican claims to the area, formally declaring it the Colony of British Honduras in 1840.

Britain's policy toward its new colony was one of benign neglect. Slavery was abolished, but former slaves were barred from receiving Crown land grants. Logging remained the chief industry, but didn't produce enough revenue or employment to bring prosperity. Population grew slowly, partly by immigration from neighboring countries—of Garífuna moving north from Honduras, then of Yucatec Maya fleeing the Caste Wars in Mexico and Kekchi Maya fleeing forced labor in Guatemala. By the 1930s, the colony's stagnation had prompted Belizeans to call for independence, while

Guatemala renewed territorial claims. The independence movement became influential enough in the 1950s to gain universal suffrage and home rule, and Britain agreed to independence in 1961.

Guatemala's claims complicated the independence process: the British army had to continue defending the border even after full independence in 1981 because of invasion threats. The Guatemalan government finally recognized Belizean sovereignty in 1992, and the British army was being replaced by a Belizean Defense Force in 1994, although some border disputes continued. With a small tax base and large trade deficit, the new government faces a challenge in maintaining political and economic stability. Unemployment remains high, and illegal immigration of Guatemalans and Salvadorans stresses social services. Foreign aid, remittances from expatriates, and illegal drug trafficking make up a large percentage of Belize's income. Belizeans enjoy a relatively high standard of living compared to their neighbors, however, with improving health services and sanitation, universal education, and a literacy rate over 80 percent. They have so far been spared the bloody class conflicts of more populous countries.

The Tapir and the Toucan

Although still mostly forest, Belize has been thoroughly logged: few large mahoganies or other premium hardwoods remain. Britain established large forest reserves during colonial times, which didn't exclude logging, but most logging was selective, allowing forest to regenerate. It also established a few Crown Reserves where natural areas were preserved, such as Half Moon Caye, set aside in 1929 to protect a red-footed booby colony. In 1969, the Belize Audubon Society began promoting conservation as a foreign chapter of the U.S. National Audubon Society, and became independent in 1973.

A Wildlife Protection Bill and a National Parks Bill were among the first legislation the new government passed in 1981. The tapir (or mountain cow) and keel-billed toucan (or billbird) were named the national animals, and a number of parks, wildlife sanctuaries, natural monuments, and nature reserves were designated through the 1980s. The government lacked funds to manage all the reserves, however, so the Belize Audubon Society took on part of this responsibility, and now manages eight reserves. Their headquarters is at 12 Fort Street, P.O. Box 1001, Belize City (phone: 2-35004/34987/34988; fax: 2-34985/78562). Other organizations managing privately owned reserves include the Community Baboon Sanctuary, Bermudian Landing, Belize District (phone: 2-44405/77369), and Programme for Belize, 1 King Street, Belize City (phone: 2-75616; fax: 2-75635). The Belize Center for Environmental Studies has a reference library on reserves and other environmental matters: 55 Eve Street, P.O. Box 666, Belize City (phone: 2-45545; fax: 2-31997). The U.S. Peace Corps is active in conservation: P.O. Box 487, 35 Gabourel Lane (phone: 2-31771). (See text for other organizations.)

The 1990s have seen a deepening of the Belizean government's commitment to conservation, with substantial increases of protected areas, including three areas—the Cockscomb Jaguar Sanctuary, Bladen Nature Reserve, and Chiquibul National Park—comprising over 80,000 acres. A Conservation Unit of the Forestry Department eventually will manage many government-owned reserves. The Forestry Department is at Forestry Drive, Belmopan (phone: 8-23629). For the present, Belize depends largely on domestic and international conservation organizations to support its park systems. There is hope that tourism, approaching agriculture as a source of income, will provide more funds for park management in the future through a Protected Areas Conservation Trust, which would return tourism revenue to park administration. Admission to most reserves is free at present (but voluntary contributions are appreciated). The government also manages many Maya sites, for which a $1.50 entrance fee is charged (Belize Department of Archaeology, Belmopan; phone: 8-22106; fax: 8-23345).

Belize City and Belmopan

With about a third of the nation's people, Belize City is the metropolis, and was the capital until a 1961 hurricane prompted the government to move 50 miles inland to Belmopan. Only the government has moved, and Belmopan remains an isolated compound of official buildings and civil servants' housing in farmland. If you have business there, a day trip from Belize City may be best: accommodations in Belmopan are limited.

Belize City began as a pirate camp on the Belize River's swampy estuary in the 1700s, and has retained a raffish atmosphere, with smelly canals and tumbledown frame buildings. When I first passed through, in 1971, it was like being in a John Huston movie (*Beat the Devil*, to be precise). Things have gotten more tense, largely because of crack cocaine and other drugs, but there's still an enjoyably colorful ambience if you stay out of dangerous areas and avoid persistent conmen. Even the conmen can be interesting, although letting them engage you in conversation will almost invariably cost money. Many tourists simply bypass Belize City, getting local flights to reef or forest resorts at the airport, but if you want to get acquainted with Belize as a nation, you should spend a little time there.

The center of town is the Swing Bridge over Haulover Creek, which is swung open to let ships pass on the creek at 6 A.M. and 5:30 P.M. The post office and tourist office are on Front Street just north of the bridge. Banks and other commerce are located mainly around Regent and Albert streets on the south side of the bridge. At the south end of Regent Street is the 1812 Anglican cathedral, where the kings of the Mosquitia were crowned. Many inexpensive small hotels, restaurants, and shops are located on the blocks along Queen Street north of the bridge. A concentration of upmarket hotels, embassies, and parks is at the tip of the peninsula southeast of Queen Street, between Marine Parade and Fort Street.

Belize City has public buses, but they're crowded, with complicated routes, and you can walk across the city center described above in a half hour or so. Taxis are inexpensive, and are recommended at night or in the daytime if you're carrying luggage or other encumbrances. Driving conditions are bad, and guarded parking lots are recommended.

Transportation

Visas aren't required for U.S. citizens and most other American, European, and British Commonwealth nationalities entering with a passport, return ticket, and sufficient funds. Visitors are allowed

30 days in the country, which may be renewed every 30 days for a period of 6 months by paying a small fee at the Immigration Office in Belize City (115 Barrack Road). Overland travelers may be turned back at the discretion of border guards if they appear indigent or otherwise undesirable.

There is a $10 airport departure tax, and a $1.25 security screening charge. Airline overbooking is common, so reconfirm and get to the airport 2 hours in advance of return flight.

INTERNATIONAL AIRLINES: American Airlines flies to Belize City via San Francisco and Miami (phone: 800-433-7300). Taca International flies via San Francisco, Miami, Houston, and New Orleans (800-535-8780). Continental flies via Houston (800-525-0280). United flies via Miami (800-222-8333).

DOMESTIC FLIGHTS: Several small airlines and charter services fly out of Belize City's Municipal Airport, located on Barracks Rd. just north of town, about $3–5 by taxi. Some domestic flights also originate at the international airport (see next paragraph). Island Air has daily flights to San Pedro, Caye Caulker, and Caye Chapel; also charters, General Delivery, San Pedro. Phone: 2-62180/2-62435; fax: 2-62192. Tropic Air has daily flights to most Belizean airports and to Flores in Guatemala, also charters, P.O. Box 20, San Pedro. Phone: 2-62012; fax: 2-62338; U.S. 800-422-3435. Maya Airways has daily flights to Belizean airports and charters, Box 458, 6 Fort Street, Belize City. Phone: 2-7215/2-62611; fax: 2-30585; U.S. 800-552-3419. Javier's Flying Service has charters and Mon.–Wed.–Fri. flights to Gallon Jug. Phone: 2-45332; fax: 2-32731.

Phillip Goldson International Airport is 16 kilometers west of Belize City off the Northern Highway. Taxi fare is about $15, and shuttle buses for $5 leave six times daily. There is a Bank of Belize money exchange desk at the exit to the arrivals area. The airport is small but new and well maintained.

ROADS: The Western Highway from Belize City to Belmopan and San Ignacio and the Northern Highway from Belize City to Orange Walk and Corozal are paved and well maintained. Other roads are gravel or, worse, asphalt in varying stages of deterioration. Driving on them is slow and dusty in the dry season, and may become impossible in the wet if there is flooding. Traffic is generally light on highways, and crime is not a problem, but watch out for pedestrians and bicyclists.

BUSES: Several bus companies have service from Belize City to major towns. Their stations are clustered near the intersection of Orange and Collett Canal streets a few blocks north of the Swing Bridge (not a good area to be in at night). Batty Bus, 54 E. Collett Canal (phone: 2-72025) goes north and west, to Orange Walk, Belmopan, San Ignancio, etc. Venus Bus, Magazine Rd. and Vernon St. (2-73354) goes north. Novelo's, W. Collett Canal (2-77372), goes west. Z-Line has buses to Dangriga and Punta Gorda, leaving from the same location as Venus (2-73937). Fares are inexpensive, but buses are old and make frequent stops, except for expresses. Most reserves and resorts are some distance off bus routes: tour companies provide shuttle bus service to resorts.

Many Belizeans hitchhike, and hitchhiking visitors will have to compete with them for the few available rides. Paying for rides doesn't seem to be a common practice.

CAR RENTALS: Visitors who plan much travel between reserves often rent vehicles, which is expensive because poor road conditions make high-clearance, 4wd rentals the norm (even though 4wd isn't really needed that much in the dry season). Companies usually give unlimited mileage, but expect to pay (with taxes) over $80 a day for a small vehicle and over $100 for a large one, plus any damage caused by the ubiquitous potholes. Reservations should be made well in advance, and aren't always reliable. Budget, 771 Bella Vista near airport (phone: 2-32435; fax: 2-30237). Avis, 50 Vernon Street (phone: 2-78637). Crystal, Mile 1.5 Northern Highway (phone: 2-31600; fax: 2-31900). National, Intl. Airport (phone: 2-31586; fax: 2-52272). Ace, 12 N. Front St. (phone: 2-31650; fax: 2-31586).

BOATS: Tour and passenger boats are the main ways of getting to cayes, reefs, and wetland reserves. Conmen may offer nonexistent trips, tell you that scheduled boats aren't running, or impersonate known guides: always pay for boat rides at the *end* of the trip. (See area descriptions, below, for boat details.)

U.S. Embassy

P.O. Box 286, 29 Gabourel Lane, Belize City (phone: 2-77161/62; fax: 2-30802). Consulate is around the corner on Hutson St. Hours: 8–5 weekdays.

Health Advisory

Water supply in Belize City and other large towns is chlorinated, but travelers may want to stick to bottled or treated water for drinking. Malaria is present throughout the country below 400 meters, although there is no risk in Belize City. Visitors spending time in the countryside should use malaria prophylaxis: chloroquine is adequate. There is limited risk of dengue fever, and cholera. Botflies seem more common in Belize than other Central American countries, perhaps because of sizable wild mammal populations.

HOSPITALS AND DOCTORS in Belize City: Belize City Hospital has 75 beds. Manuel Lizama, M.D., 13 Handyside (phone: 2-45138). Manuel Cabrera, M.D. (phone: 2-44368).

Note for scuba divers: A decompression chamber is located in San Pedro, Ambergris Caye.

Hotels

IN BELMOPAN: Belmopan Convention Hotel, 2 Bliss Parade (phone: 8-22130) is expensive, with swimming pool. Mid-priced are the Bullfrog, 23/25 Half Moon Ave. (phone: 8-22111) and Circle A, 35/37 (phone: 8-22296). El Rey Inn, 23 Moho St. (phone: 8-23438) is in the $20–30 range.

IN BELIZE CITY: Radisson Fort George, 2 Marine Parade, P.O. Box 321 (phone: 2-77440; fax: 2-73820) is $125–200 with pool, etc. Chateau Caribbean, 6 Marine Parade (phone: 2-30800) is in the $100 range, in a handsome older building on the water, with a good bar and restaurant (opens 6 A.M. for breakfast). Glenthorne

Manor, 27 Barracks Rd., P.O. Box 1278 (phone: 2-44212) has rooms with breakfast for $60–85 (less in summer). Fort Street Guesthouse, 4 Fort St., P.O. Box 3 (phone: 2-30116; fax: 2-78808), has six rooms for $45–60, with an excellent restaurant. Mopan Hotel, 55 Regent St. (phone: 2-73356; fax: 2-75383) has rooms with bath for $25–48 (also part-time bar restaurant and tour agency). Also midpriced are: El Centro, 4 Bishop St., Box 122 (phone: 2-72413; fax: 2-74553); Belize Guest House, 2 Hutson St. (phone: 2-77569); Bakadeer Inn, 74 Cleghorn (phone: 2-31286; fax: 2-31963). Freddie's Guest House, 86 Eve St. (phone: 2-44396) has three comfortable, secure rooms with bath for $20–25, good location (across from Belize Environmental Center). In same price range are: Sea Side Guest House, 3 Prince St., serves breakfast and has tour connections (phone: 2-78339); North Front Street Guest House, 124 N. Front St. (phone: 2-77595); Eyre Street Guest House, 7 Eyre St. (phone: 2-77724). Mira Rio, 59 North Front St. (phone: 2-44248) and Marin Travel Lodge, 6 Craig St. (phone: 2-45166) are less.

Restaurants

BELMOPAN: The Caladium next to the market is moderately priced. The Bullfrog Inn and El Rey Hotel have restaurants.

BELIZE CITY: Fort Street Guest House has nice atmosphere: opens for dinner at 6, Belizean and continental food (phone: 2-45638). GG's Cafe and Patio, 2-3 King St. off Regent has good Belizean dishes, nice patio, very clean, open for breakfast (phone: 2-74378). Mom's Triangle Inn, 11 Handyside St., is popular for breakfast and lunch and is also a travelers' information center (phone: 2-45523). Pearl's Pizza at 13 Handyside next door has good Italian food. Macy's, 18 Bishop St., has Belizean and Creole dishes (phone: 2-73419). Golden Dragon, Queen St., has good Chinese food (phone: 2-72817).

(Note: Belizean restaurants may serve wild game such as gibnut—the Creole word for paca, a large rodent—and sea turtle. The legality of this is unclear—sea turtles at least are protected except during a June–August season—and market hunting doesn't benefit wild populations. Lobsters are in open season from July 14 to March 15, and the conch open season is Sept. 30 to July 1. Visitors who order lobster or conch in restaurants during closed season will be contributing to overfishing, since the closed season protects their breeding time.)

Communications

The post office is at Queen and North Front streets across from the Swing Bridge, open 8–12 A.M. and 1–5 P.M.

Belizean Telecommunications Ltd., 1 Church St. (near park), has telegraph, telephone, telex, and fax services, open 8–9 Mon.–Sat., 8–noon Sunday.

Money Exchange

The Belizean currency unit is the Belizean dollar, which contains 100 cents. The exchange rate in 1994 was two Belizean dollars to the U.S. dollar.

Banks change traveler's checks for a commission, and have facilities to advance cash on Visa cards. Hours are 8–1 Mon.–Thurs. and 3–6 Friday. There's an American Express agent at Global Travel, 41 Albert St. (phone: 2-77185/77363).

Belizean restaurants, hotels, tour agencies, etc., commonly accept U.S. dollars and traveler's checks, although checks much higher than the charge may not be accepted, or a commission may be charged to exchange them.

Tourist Information

The Belize Tourist Board, 83 North Front St., P.O. Box 325, has a Belize City map, bus schedule, list of hotels and prices, reserve brochures, guide and tour agency listings, and archaeological site descriptions. Phone: 2-77213/73255; fax: 2-77490. Hours are 8–12 and 1–5 Mon.–Thurs., 8–4:30 Fri. The Belize Tourism Industry Association, 99 Albert St., Box 69, has brochures on resorts, tour agencies, etc. Phone: 2-75717; fax: 2-78007.

Maps

The survey office above the post office sells 1:250,000 contour maps for $10; country maps for $2. Hours are 8:30–12, 1–4. The Belize Tourist Bureau across North Front St. has good country maps for $3.

Museums and Zoos

The Baron Bliss Institute, 1 Bliss Parade, has Mayan artifacts and art and culture exhibits (phone: 2-77267).

The Belize Zoo and Tropical Education Center, Mile 30 Western Highway, P.O. Box 1787, Belize City, is the best zoo in Central America, and also has a small ecology museum and bookshop. Begun in 1983 with seventeen animals that had been collected to make a nature film, the zoo now has over two dozen mammal, bird, reptile, and fish species on 1,700 acres of land. Species include king vultures, tapirs, jaguars, ocelots, peccaries, macaws, parrots, and crocodiles. Animals are kept in large enclosures full of native plants and surrounded by electric fencing and other unobtrusive restraints; some animals may be hard to see at first, so allow yourself plenty of time. The zoo is active in captive breeding, conservation, and environmental education. It has no phone but can be contacted by radio from its Belize City office above Mom's Triangle Inn, 11 Handyside St. Its location, 30 miles west of Belize City, is clearly marked: Venus and Batty buses run past, and taxis can be hired for about $60 round-trip. Hours are 9:30–4 daily except Christmas and Good Friday. Admission is $5 for non-Belizeans. There's no restaurant at the zoo, but there is a small refreshment stand at the parking lot. Because of the rural setting, it's a good idea to bring insect repellent and a hat and suntan lotion.

The Mayan Artifact Vault at the Department of Archaeology in Belmopan can be visited by appointment (two days in advance) from 1:30–4:30 Mon., Wed., Fri. (phone: 8-22106; fax: 8-23345).

Bookstores and Libraries

The Baron Bliss Institute, 1 Bliss Parade, has a public library (phone: 2-77267). (Baron Henry Bliss was an English yachtsman who left a two-million-dollar trust fund to Belize in 1926.) The Be-

Black howler monkey (*Alouatta pigra*). Photo by Kevin Schafer.

lize Bookshop on Regent St. across from the Mopan Hotel has a good selection of books, including natural history titles. The Belize Audubon Society sells natural history books and posters at its office on Fort St. Angelus Press, 10 Queen St., has maps and office supplies as well as books. Go Graphics, 23 Regent St., has books, art, and gifts.

Excursions Around Belize City and Belmopan

The Community Baboon Sanctuary encompasses about 4,664 hectares of private land along the Belize River an hour's drive northwest of Belize City (take the Northern Highway to Mile 15, then turn left to Bermudian Landing). Landowners in eight Creole villages are cooperating to protect a population of black howler monkeys ("baboons" in Creole), a species that occurs only in Belize, Yucatán, and the Petén, and that is threatened by habitat loss, hunting, and disease. (The howler monkeys in the rest of Central America are another species, the golden mantled howler.) The sanctuary was begun in the mid 1980s with the help of biologist Robert Horwich, and the howler population has grown large enough to allow transplantation of some monkeys to areas where the species has been extirpated by hunting or disease (howlers fall victim to yellow fever). The monkeys are quite easy to see along the sanctuary trails, and other animals are common, including 200 bird species. The Belize Audubon Society, 12 Fort St., helps to manage the sanctuary, and can provide information on local buses that go there, starting at noon from Belize City and returning at 6 the next morning. Visitors are required to check in at the headquarters at Bermudian Landing, where licensed guides can be hired at $2.50 an hour or $20 a day. In addition to the sanctuary trails, canoe trips along the Belize River are available. There is a good small museum at the headquarters, and a guidebook is available for purchase. You can camp on the headquarters grounds for a few dollars a night, and bed and breakfast accommodations can be arranged at headquarters or with Belize Audubon.

Altun Ha is one of the more thoroughly excavated and restored Maya sites in Belize, located an hour's drive from Belize City on a short spur road off the old Northern Highway. A famous jade ceremonial mask found at the site is Belize's national symbol: it can be viewed at the Archaeology Vault in Belmopan (see above). The jade may have come from Guatemala's Sierra de las Minas. There are thirteen structures arranged around two plazas: two of the structures are over 20 meters tall. The site, named "stone water" in Maya after a nearby reservoir site, was occupied from 3,000 to 1,100 years ago as a trading and ceremonial center. Several square kilometers of woodland and swamp surround the site, good for birding. Admission is $1.50. There is no overnight accommodation or food service, and no regular public transportation.

Guanacaste National Park is a roughly 20-hectare parcel of woodland located at the turn-off to Belmopan on the Western Highway. Originally a Crown Reserve, the park centers on a large guanacaste or tubroos tree (*Enterolobium cyclocarpum*) which has escaped logging because of its spreading form. A self-guiding trail introduces visitors to other tree species such as mahogany and quamwood. Many birds, iguanas, and small mammals such as agoutis, armadillos, and jaguarundis live in the park, and may be encountered along the trails, or viewed from lookout sites along the Belize River. A visitor center contains natural history exhibits. The park is about 30 kilometers west of the Belize Zoo, and would make a good complement to a zoo trip. It is 3 kilometers from Belmopan: Belize City–Belmopan buses go right past it. (Be advised, however, that there were robberies and rapes by gangs in the park in 1993 and '94.)

Another natural area near the Belize Zoo is Monkey Bay Wildlife Sanctuary, located at Mile 31 on the Western Highway. The area includes a government reserve and a privately owned sanctuary which is carrying on research, environmental education, and land restoration. The sanctuary includes pine savanna, gallery forest, and freshwater marshes. Admission is free: camping is permitted for a small fee. Visitor accommodations are planned. P.O. Box 187, Belmopan, or contact the Belize Center for Environmental Studies (see above).

All the above sites can be reached with a non-4wd vehicle.

The Reefs and Cayes

The Belize barrier reef and associated cayes (small islands) and atolls (shallow lagoons ringed with cayes and reefs) occupy an offshore area almost as large as the country itself. It is the largest reef complex in the Western Hemisphere, and is surpassed in size only by Australia's Great Barrier Reef. The area is an underwater continuation of the limestone topography of the mainland, a series of ridges dissected by ancient stream channels and pitted with sinkholes where underground erosion has caused the surface to subside. Much of it probably was dry land during the Ice Age, but where forests once grew, fantastic gardens of dozens of coral species now cover submerged ridgelines, and hundreds of brilliantly colored fish species hover. Manatees and sea turtles feed in turtle grass beds on sand flats around the cayes, while many seabird species nest in the safety of caye woodlands. Although most of the area is shallow, fault fissures thousands of meters deep run through it, inhabited by

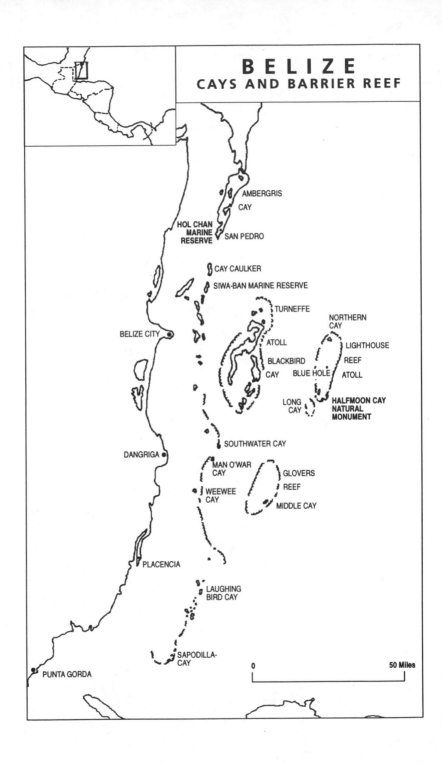

BELIZE
CAYS AND BARRIER REEF

AMBERGRIS CAY

HOL CHAN MARINE RESERVE

SAN PEDRO

CAY CAULKER

SIWA-BAN MARINE RESERVE

TURNEFFE

NORTHERN CAY

BELIZE CITY

ATOLL

LIGHTHOUSE REEF

BLACKBIRD CAY

BLUE HOLE

ATOLL

LONG CAY

HALFMOON CAY NATURAL MONUMENT

SOUTHWATER CAY

DANGRIGA

MAN O'WAR CAY

GLOVERS REEF

WEEWEE CAY

MIDDLE CAY

PLACENCIA

LAUGHING BIRD CAY

SAPODILLA-CAY

0   50 Miles

PUNTA GORDA

the streamlined fish of the deep ocean. Caves underlie the limestone, and some connect with mainland rivers, as evidenced by the appearance of ocean fish such as snappers and tarpon in inland cave streams.

Protecting this extraordinary resource is of global importance: the United Nations has proposed it as a World Heritage Site. The Belizean government has established several reserves, but the Belize Center for Environmental Studies has identified a number of critical habitat sites still in need of protection. Pressure from tourism, commercial fishing, and shipping is growing, and there is evidence of overuse of existing reserves. The Belize Audubon Society recently decided, for example, to close Half Moon Caye Natural Monument to overnight camping because the number of visitors has grown so much.

Hol Chan Marine Reserve

This 1,215-hectare area of reef, seagrass beds, and mangroves at the tip of Ambergris Caye on Belize's northern shore is the nation's first underwater reserve, established in 1987. By encompassing a transect from mangroves and seagrass shallows to deeper waters offshore from the barrier reef, the reserve protects spawning and feeding areas necessary to reef species as well as the coral gardens and mature fish populations of the reef itself. This holistic approach has served as a model for other marine reserves. The three zones—reef, seagrass, and mangrove—are marked by buoys.

Because of its proximity to the tourism mecca of San Pedro, Hol Chan is the most visited of marine reserves. Snorkeling centers on a channel through the barrier reef ("*Hol Chan*" means "little channel" in Maya) where underwater scenery and fish populations are outstanding. Crowds of snorkeling boats visit the area in high season, but this doesn't seem to bother some fish. Large groupers and schools of snappers actually take up position beneath boats when they arrive. (This is in response to being fed from the boats, which is not good for the fish.) Channel walls are lined with spectacular growths of elkhorn, brain, starlet, and sheet corals while bright purple sea fans wave in the currents. Chances of seeing spiny lobsters and green moray eels lurking in small caves among the coral masses are good, and harmless rays and nurse sharks prowl the seagrass beds. Reef fish are bewilderingly diverse—over five hundred species have been identified. Barracuda are present, but fire corals and sea urchins are the main things to avoid. Swimmers should also beware of strong currents in the channel during outgoing tides. Because of the high visitation, swimmers should take special care not to touch or stand on live coral. A guard boat is on duty at the channel during the day and collects a $1.50 entrance fee.

Scuba diving mainly takes place in deeper waters offshore from the reef, and both day and night diving are popular. Only certified divers can use scuba equipment in the reserve. Another diving site is the Boca Ciega, a sinkhole underlain by caves and freshwater springs in the seagrass zone. Special clearance from the reserve manager is required for diving in the Boca Ciega caves. Reserve headquarters is located in San Pedro, across from the town hall on Barrier Reef Drive, the main street.

Getting to the reserve from San Pedro is easy: dive boat agencies and gear rental shops line the main street, and you can arrange a trip in a few minutes of shopping around. Slow-moving glass-bottom boats generally are the least expensive: they provide a view of the seagrass beds inshore of the reef and the deeper waters offshore, as well as an opportunity for an hour or so of guided snorkeling. Guides are a big help in drawing attention to concealed animals and showing places where shallow snorkel dives are safe. Faster boats are also available for those who want to snorkel longer (an hour is plenty of time if you're just arriving—the sun is very powerful). Most trips are from 9 A.M. to noon, or 2 to 5 P.M. The common rate for a round-trip was $15 in 1994. Trip arrangements can also be made through many hotels. A rather bewildering variety of scuba certification course packages is available: it would be advisable to talk to several agencies before you decide.

Getting to San Pedro is also easy. Island Air, Maya Airways, and Tropic Air have daily flights from Belize City for under $20 one-way. San Pedro Airport is a 5-minute walk south of downtown. Boats leave from the Swing Bridge, the Texaco Station on Crossover Creek a little way inland from the Swing Bridge, and from the Bellevue Hotel pier on Baron Bliss Promenade. The trip takes about an hour and a half and should cost around $10 one-way. You can take the boat out and a plane to return, or vice versa.

Finding a hotel room in San Pedro may not be easy if you arrive without a reservation in high season, although there are many places. Upmarket resorts abound, and even budget rooms aren't cheap. Ramon's Village Resort just south of the airport is an outstanding full-service diving resort in the $100–200 range, with private dock, beach, swimming pool, restaurant, and 61 rooms (phone: 2-62071/62213; fax: 2-62214; in U.S. phone: 601-491-1990; fax: 601-425-2411). Victoria House, 3 kilometers south of town, is another upmarket, full-service resort, P.O. Box 22, San Pedro (phone: 2-62067; fax:2-62429; U.S. phone: 800-247-5159). A less expensive downtown full-service resort is the Holiday Hotel, with rooms and apartments ranging from $74 to $160, P.O. Box 1140, Belize City (phone: 2-62014/62103; fax: 2-62295). Rubie's Hotel has beachfront rooms at a quiet location downtown (near south end of Barrier Reef Drive) for $26–37 (phone: 2-62063/2434). La Joya del Caribe, just outside of town, is comparable (phone: 2-62360; fax: 2-62316). Martha's Hotel has large, plain rooms in a rambling old building for $23–30, and is not too close to the discotheques on the beach (phone: 2-62052; fax: 2-62589).

The Lagoon Restaurant on Pescador Drive has continental dinners at about $10 an entree. A block south is Elvi's, with seafood and Belizean dishes for lunch and dinner—popular and nice atmosphere (a live tree inside). A block north of the Lagoon is Ambergris Delight, inexpensive and popular. Celi's next to the Holiday Hotel serves breakfast at 7 A.M. Casa de Cafe next to the Belize Bank has coffee and deserts. Rubie's Hotel has a small cafe for lunches and pastries.

The north end of Ambergris Caye has been identified as a critical habitat area, with hardwood forests, freshwater ponds, mangroves, and smaller cayes supporting bird rookeries and turtle beaches. Tour agencies offer birding and snorkeling tours. Flamingos are sometimes seen.

Lighthouse Reef and Half Moon Caye

Lighthouse Reef is one of three coral atolls in the Belizean reef system, and lies at its eastern edge about 70 kilometers from the mainland. Belizean atolls are unusual in that they have formed on fault-controlled limestone ridges rather than on extinct volcanoes, as is common with Pacific atolls. Within Lighthouse Reef atoll's shallow lagoon is Blue Hole, a limestone sinkhole 300 meters across and 150 meters deep. Jacques Cousteau explored it in 1971. There are stalactites and stalagmites in caves at its bottom, indicating that it was a dry-land, freshwater environment during the Ice Age. Outside the atoll's enclosing reefs, sheer walls descend from coral gardens at 10–15 meters to depths of over 1,000 meters. The blue and turquoise colors of the water are extraordinarily brilliant, and the corals are clearly visible even at the 10–15 meter depth.

Half Moon Caye at the atoll's south end was declared a Natural Monument in 1982. The 18.2-hectare island, made up of sand formed from coral, seashells, and calcareous algae, supports a breeding colony of 4,000 red-footed boobies in the dense woodland of orange-flowered ziricote trees, figs, and gumbo-limbos on its western half (the trees can grow because of nutrients from the birds' droppings—the island's east half is sparsely covered with coconut palms). The boobies on the island are unusual in that most have white plumage, whereas most of the species has brown plumage. Magnificent frigatebirds also nest here: during the winter nesting season, the treetops are literally covered with birds, a sight visible from an observation tower. Ninety-eight other bird species occur here, and common iguanas, somewhat smaller lizards called wish willys, and an endemic small anole lizard also inhabit the island. Loggerhead and hawksbill turtles nest on beaches.

Lighthouse Reef trips are among the main attractions at San Pedro, and tour agencies' offerings range from several days on overnight, on-board motorboats or sailboats to single-day diving and snorkeling trips. There are also trips for birders. Camping on Half Moon Caye was the recommended way to go, but the Belize Audubon Society planned to close the caye to overnight camping in 1994. Live-aboard boats, the remaining alternative for overnight trips, charge $150–250 per day. Day trips range from $100 for snorkelers to $150 for divers. Day trips are hurried, particularly on Half Moon Caye, but offer opportunities to experience the Blue Hole and the walls off Long Caye. Facilities and services on trips may not be all that was promised. A day trip I took didn't have a promised shower, and the toilet wouldn't flush. Crew attitudes to-

Boulder brain coral and sea fans. Photo by Julie Robinson.

ward safety were more casual than on Hol Chan trips. The trip was still well worth it, though. It's easy to arrange trips after you arrive in San Pedro: you also can arrange them as part of a hotel reservation, but you may want to talk to the agency yourself before buying. There is an upmarket fishing and diving resort at Northern Two Caye on Lighthouse Reef: Lighthouse Reef Resort, Box 26, Belize City (phone: 2-31205; U.S. 800-423-3114).

Turneffe

Between San Pedro and Lighthouse Reef is Turneffe, another atoll ringed with coral islets and mangrove flats. Northern Lagoon and Soldier Caye there have been listed as critical habitat: conch, lobster, manatee, turtles, and crocodiles live in the lagoon, and roseate terns and white-crowned pigeons nest on the cayes. Raccoons and boa constrictors also are present. There are several resorts on Turneffe. Blackbird Caye Resort on a 1,600-hectare caye has an ecological orientation, and is used by researchers and conservation organizations such as the Oceanic Society. Texas A&M University

has a research station on the caye. For resort reservations: 81 West
Collet Canal St., P.O. Box 1315, Belize City (phone: 2-77670/
30882; fax: 2-73092; in U.S. phone: 713-658-1142). Also Turneffe
Flats, 56 Eve St., Belize City (phone: 2-30116/45634); Turneffe Islands Lodge, P.O. Box 480, Belize City (phone: 2-2231; in U.S.
800-338-8149).

Siwa-Ban Nature Reserve

This reserve at the south end of Caye Caulker, the caye just south
of Ambergris Caye, had not actually been designated by the government in 1994, but it's strongly supported by conservationists
(including the U.S.–based Siwa-Ban Foundation, 143 Anderson St.,
San Francisco, CA). It has been designated as critical habitat for
wildlife of littoral forest, mangrove, seagrass flat, and barrier reef,
particularly for crocodiles and for the black catbird, a species that
lives only in scattered locations of Belize, the Petén, and Yucatán.
("Siwa-ban" is the bird's local name.) The reserve will be modeled
after Hol Chan to encompass a transect from the cocoplum and
seagrape woodland and mangrove forest on the caye to the seagrass
flats and barrier reef. Access to the reserve land is limited to an unmarked path at present, and mosquitoes appear almost unlimited,
but black catbirds are fairly easy to see, and delightful to listen to.

Caye Caulker is Belize's second-largest reef resort, with excellent
snorkeling and diving at the barrier reef close offshore. It is quieter
and cheaper than San Pedro, and attracts a younger, more bohe-
mian clientele. Fish populations at its reef seem somewhat less
abundant than at Hol Chan, but visitor populations are also much
less abundant, allowing for a more dispersed and relaxed experience. A channel partway through the reef near the island's south
end has spectacular corals and large parrotfish, butterflyfish, an-
gelfish, and triggerfish. You can also swim and snorkel from the island in a "cut" north of town that was formed by Hurricane Hattie
in 1961. Watch for crocodiles there. As at San Pedro, snorkel boats
go out for a few hours in mornings and afternoons, and average
about $15 per trip. Guides tend to be less professional, and you'll
be more or less responsible for your own safety. You can go to Hol

Chan and Lighthouse Reef from Caulker, but it's easier to go from San Pedro.

Many San Pedro boats stop at Caulker along the way, including the ones that leave from Swing Bridge. Belize–Caulker fare is about $6. Beware of swindlers. Island Air and Sky Bird (phone: 2-32596) have daily flights to Caye Caulker Airport, a short walk from town.

Caye Caulker accommodations are as likely to be booked in high season as at San Pedro. The Tropical Paradise at the south end of the beach road has rooms and cabins for $40–60, with a good restaurant and snorkeling boats, P.O. Box 1206, Belize City (phone: 2-22124; fax: 2-22225). Vega's Far Inn about halfway between the main dock and the Tropical Paradise has double rooms for $45, also camping on nice beachside grounds (phone: 2-22142). Shirley's Guest House at the south end of town is comparable (phone: 2-22145). Marin's Hotel is in the $30 range, and also offers reef trips (phone: 2-244307). The Sandy Lane Hotel a block off the main street is in the $20 range (phone: 2-22217).

Tropical Paradise and Marin's have good seafood. Melvin's specializes in lobster. There are many small places selling burritos, cakes, pastries, fruit drinks, coffee, etc.

Glover's Reef Marine Reserve

Glover's Reef is Belize's other coral atoll, the most remote and seldom visited. It has been described as having the richest biology of any Caribbean atoll. Located about 100 kilometers southeast of Belize City, it is an oval ring of reefs and cayes rising from 1,000-meter-deep waters and surrounding a deep lagoon. In 1990, the Wildlife Conservation Society bought 6-hectare Middle Caye, the most ecologically significant caye in the atoll, and is conducting research and working in cooperation with the Belizean government to establish a reserve with the assistance of U.S.-AID and the United Nations Development Program (U.N.D.P.). Recent studies have concentrated on analysis of coral cover and density of conch and lobster populations. (Conch and lobster are the species most threatened by overfishing on the barrier reef.)

Live-aboard dive boats make trips to Glover's Reef from San Pedro, and you could arrange a trip from there if you have time. There is an upmarket fishing and diving resort, the Manta Reef Resort, on Southwest Caye, which offers minimum one-week packages including transportation from Belize City, P.O. Box 215, 3 Eyre St., Belize City (phone: 2-31895/2-3767; fax: 2-322764; in U.S. 800-342-0053). Glover's Atoll Resort on Long Caye is inexpensive and basic (cold water, no electricity or indoor plumbing), and also offers packages with transportation included, P.O. Box 563, Belize City (phone: 8-22149). Glover's Atoll Resort is associated with a guest house at Sittee River Village on the coast south of Dangriga: transportation from there to the reef is by boat (phone: 8-22149/22505).

South Water Caye

A large area around this caye at the outer edge of the barrier reef 40 kilometers offshore from Dangriga has been identified as critical habitat. Coral Caye Conservation Ltd., an English organization, is conducting reef management studies. The Smithsonian Institution has had a research station on nearby Carrie Bow Caye since 1977. To the north, Man o' War Caye is an important rookery for frigatebirds and other species.

Blue Marlin Lodge is an upmarket diving resort on South Water Caye, P.O. Box 21, Dangriga (phone: 5-22243; fax: 5-22296). They can provide trips to Glover's Reef. Leslie Cottages is a small, moderately priced snorkeling and boating resort (phone: 5-22004; fax: 5-23152; in U.S. 800-548-5843). Pelican Beach Resort, a $50–80 range resort on the coast just north of Dangriga, owns land on South Water Caye and offers transportation and accommodation there and to other reef locations, P.O. Box 14, Dangriga (phone: 5-22044/22541; fax: 5-22570).

Laughing Bird Caye National Park

This small caye southeast of Placencia was designated a national park in 1991 to protect the rookery of laughing gulls and other seabirds for which it is named. Tourism had begun to stress the birds, and nests had become increasingly rare by 1990, so overnight visits to the caye have been prohibited. The moderately priced Paradise Vacation Hotel in Placencia arranges boat trips to this area (phone: 6-23118/23179).

Sapodilla Cayes

This group of small cayes lies at the southern tip of the barrier reef about 30 kilometers east of Punta Gorda, almost as close to the Guatemalan shore as to the Belizean. It has been designated as critical habitat, and is the subject of a long-term reef study, but is seldom visited. Steep coral walls lie offshore, offering good diving opportunities. Nature's Way Guest House (phone: 7-22119) and the Toledo Visitors Information Center (phone: 7-22470), both in Punta Gorda, can arrange trips.

The Coastal Plain

Belize's coast is low and swampy. In the northern half of the country it is very broad, rising gradually to low limestone hills and plateaus in the west. In the southern half it is narrow, rising abruptly to the Maya Mountains. The coast was once lined with mangrove and littoral forest, although much of this has been cleared. Saltwater lagoons are common, and are critical habitat for Belize's estimated 300 to 700 manatees, whose population is thought to be stable or growing. Inland from shore and lagoons, a variety of vegetation types grow according to soil and climate.

In the Corozal District of the far north, where rainfall (averaging 150 centimeters a year) and limestone plain topography resemble those of Yucatán, a subtropical hardwood forest grows, including northern species such as persimmon and bayberry. Like Yucatán, this area has few streams, although surface flooding is common during the rainy season. In the Belize District (and in the eastern parts of the Orange Walk and Cayo districts) the plain rises almost imperceptibly in a series of north/south–trending sandy ridges. A savanna of Caribbean pine, small hardwoods such as live oak and nancite, and palmettos grows on much of these ridges, interspersed with a hardwood forest of such species as bay cedar and cecropia along streams. Freshwater ponds and lagoons occur in depressions between the ridges. These support luxuriant underwater and marsh

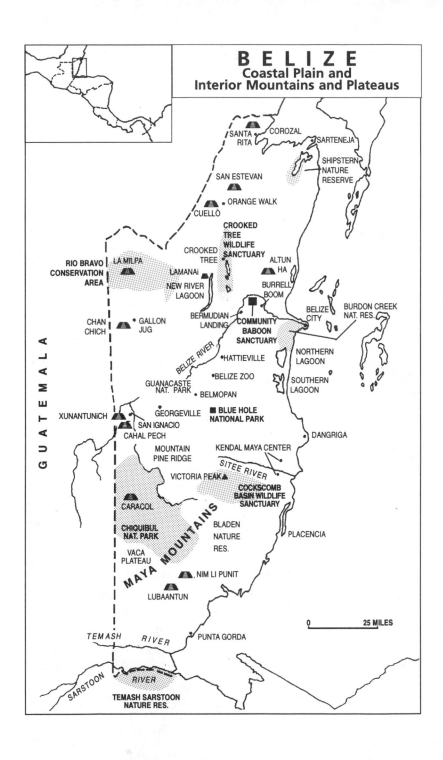

BELIZE
Coastal Plain and
Interior Mountains and Plateaus

SANTA RITA
COROZAL
SARTENEJA
SHIPSTERN NATURE RESERVE
SAN ESTEVAN
ORANGE WALK
CUELLO
CROOKED TREE WILDLIFE SANCTUARY
CROOKED TREE
ALTUN HA
RIO BRAVO CONSERVATION AREA
LA MILPA
LAMANAI
NEW RIVER LAGOON
BURRELL BOOM
BERMUDIAN LANDING
COMMUNITY BABOON SANCTUARY
BELIZE CITY
BURDON CREEK NAT. RES.
CHAN CHICH
GALLON JUG
BELIZE RIVER
HATTIEVILLE
NORTHERN LAGOON
GUANACASTE NAT. PARK
BELIZE ZOO
SOUTHERN LAGOON
BELMOPAN
XUNANTUNICH
GEORGEVILLE
BLUE HOLE NATIONAL PARK
SAN IGNACIO
CAHAL PECH
DANGRIGA
MOUNTAIN PINE RIDGE
KENDAL MAYA CENTER
SITEE RIVER
VICTORIA PEAK
COCKSCOMB BASIN WILDLIFE SANCTUARY
CARACOL
CHIQUIBUL NAT. PARK
BLADEN NATURE RES.
PLACENCIA
VACA PLATEAU
MAYA MOUNTAINS
NIM LI PUNIT
LUBAANTUN
TEMASH RIVER
PUNTA GORDA
0   25 MILES
SARSTOON RIVER
TEMASH SARSTOON NATURE RES.

G U A T E M A L A

plants in the rainy season, and large waterbird and fish populations, but may dry up in April and May. Low swamps of freshwater
mangrove, logwood, and other small trees surround them. Along
larger streams and in other areas where soil is unusually fertile, impressive forests of cohune palms and large hardwoods such as hog
plum, gumbo-limbo, and tubroos grow.

The mosaic of pine savanna and swamp hardwoods continues
into the Stann Creek and Toledo districts of the south, but rainfall
there is significantly higher than in northern Belize (averaging 400
centimeters a year in the Toledo District). A high-canopy, multi-
layered rain forest like that of Honduras's north coast thus occurs
in some areas. Because of its large, relatively undisturbed forests,
southern Belize has some spectacular species, such as scarlet macaws, which aren't found in the north.

Shipstern Nature Reserve

Shipstern is a privately owned, 9,000-hectare reserve near the town
of Sarteneja on the coastal plain's northeast tip. A 13,000-hectare
no-hunting area around Sarteneja buffers the reserve. It is the only
Belizean protected area containing hardwood forest like that of Yucatán, with typical species such as the brilliant blue Yucatán jay,
black catbird, yellow-lored parrot, and white-winged dove. A botanical trail leads through the forest near reserve headquarters,
with labeled specimens (both scientific and local, usually Mayan,
names) of dozens of species such as warriewood, negrito, zapote,
and pochote. Hurricane Janet blew down much of this forest in
1955, but the new trees are already quite large. A small springfed
pool along the trail is one of the few year-round water sources in
the area, and is a good place to look for wildlife. The reserve also
contains large areas of saline lagoon and mangrove forest which
support manatees, Morelet's crocodiles, and an important breeding colony of wood storks. Extensive pine savannas lie between the
hardwood forest and the lagoons. Tapirs, jaguars, brocket deer,
and other large mammals are present, though seldom seen. Howler
monkeys were present before the hurricane, and may be reintroduced. Although the reserve seems semiarid at times, at least sixty

reptile and amphibian species occur, and frog and toad choruses in the rainy season are spectacular.

Another interesting feature is the butterfly breeding center at reserve headquarters. In large net enclosures where the butterflies are raised, visitors can walk among the eggs, larvae, pupae, and flying adults of beautiful native butterflies such as zebra, jaguar, and postman heliconians, cattle hearts, giant swallowtails, morphos, and crackers. It's a spectacular sight. The butterflies originally were raised to produce pupae for sale to European "butterfly houses," but when I was there in 1994 this had been discontinued because of difficulties with getting paid, and the butterflies were released to replenish wild populations.

Reserve headquarters is on the road from Orange Walk to Sarteneja via San Estevan and Chunox. It's about an hour's drive from Orange Walk. Hours are 9–12 and 1–4. A $12.50 entrance fee includes a guided tour of the butterfly center and the botanical trail. Guided tours of primitive and semiprimitive trails leading into the savanna are also available by appointment. Mosquitoes are abundant even in the dry season. Nonguided visitors are restricted to the botanical trail. The reserve is managed by the International Tropical Conservation Foundation, P.O. Box 1694, Belize City or Box 31, CH-2074 Marin-Ne, Switzerland.

There are no visitor accommodations at the reserve. Orange Walk has several hotels, including the D-Star Victoria (formerly Baron's) just south of downtown on the Belize Road, which has air-conditioned rooms for $35–50, and with fan for $22–25, P.O. Box 74, Orange Walk (phone 3-22518; fax: 3-22847). Mi Amor on the Belize Road a little farther north (phone: 3-22031) and Jane's, 2 Baker St. (phone: 3-22473), are less. The Diner, west of the hospital north of town, and Lee's Chinese Restaurant, just west of the plaza, are the best restaurants in town. Juanita's, west of the Belize Road just past the Shell Station, is good for Mexican breakfasts.

In Sarteneja, 5 kilometers north of reserve headquarters, Diani's Hotel on the shore has inexpensive rooms and a restaurant. There are daily Sarteneja buses from Belize City via Orange Walk, leaving from the Venus Company station (see Transportation) at midday. Sarteneja was a Maya city until 1700, and was reestablished by Yucatec Maya refugees from the Caste Wars in the nineteenth century.

Lamanai Archaeological Reserve

This reserve lies in a forested area on the New River Lagoon about 30 kilometers southeast of Orange Walk. Lamanai was apparently the city's original name in Maya: it means "submerged crocodile." Visiting the ruins by boat up the New River is a popular way of combining archaeology with birding along the river. The ruins, still mainly covered by forest, spread over about 400 hectares. The main plaza and surrounding structures, including a pyramid over 30 meters tall, have been excavated and restored. The ruins also include the remains of chapels built by Spanish missionaries in unsuccessful attempts to convert the still-inhabited city between 1544 and 1700. A small museum displays artifacts found on the site, including vases, carvings, and tools.

Hotels and tour agencies in Orange Walk arrange day boat trips to the ruins: it takes about an hour and a half to get there. Tour operators include: MayaWorld Safaris, Box 997, Belize City (phone: 2-31063); Jungle River Tours, Box 95, 20 Lovers Lane, Orange Walk (phone: 3-22293); and Godoy and Sons, 4 Trial Farm, Orange Walk (phone: 3-22969). The reserve can also be reached by taking a taxi or car on the dirt road up the New River to the towns of Guinea Grass or Shipyard and hiring a boat from there. The ruins are also accessible in the dry season by a 4wd track from the town of San Felipe, about 25 kilometers to the northwest. There's an upmarket resort at Indian Church a short walk from the ruins: Lamanai Outpost Lodge, with thatched cabins with hot water baths, fans, and electricity in the $70–90 range, Box 63, Orange Walk (phone/fax: 2-33578). They have a variety of tour packages.

Crooked Tree Wildlife Sanctuary

Founded in 1984, this 6,500-hectare reserve encompasses a network of freshwater lagoons, swamps, and streams where thousands of migratory waterbirds nest and feed during the dry season.

It is famous for protecting the largest nesting population of jabiru storks in Central America. The white, black, and red storks are the biggest flying birds in the Western Hemisphere, with a 10- to 12-foot wingspan. They nest in the pine savannas around the lagoons beginning in November, feeding their nestlings on the abundant fish, snakes, and frogs of the lagoons. The sanctuary also contains large populations of a number of other sensitive species—roseate spoonbills, wood storks, sun grebes, Everglades or snail kites, limpkins, boat-billed herons, chestnut-bellied herons, bare-throated tiger herons, black-collared hawks, black-bellied whistling ducks, and muscovy ducks—and great numbers of commoner species such as least grebes, olivaceous cormorants, coots, jacanas, gallinules, kingfishers, great blue and little blue herons, snowy and American egrets, and ospreys, not to mention the hundreds of land bird species. When I was there, local guides showed me not only a jabiru with two young on a nest, but a limpkin sitting on a nest, and a jacana nest consisting of four speckled eggs on a floating clump of waterweed. I'd never seen so many snail kites and boat-billed herons.

The lagoons fluctuate in size, expanding in the rainy season until the village of Crooked Tree "gets smaller," as the guides say. Fish populations reach huge numbers, then are concentrated as the lagoons shrink in the dry season, providing food for Morelet's crocodiles, otters, turtles, and people as well as birds. Black howler monkeys, iguanas, coatis, and other land animals live in the forest along streams such as Black Creek.

Accessible only by boat a few years ago, Crooked Tree village is now easily reached via a 5-kilometer road and causeway west from the Northern Highway. Most northbound buses will stop at the well-marked turnoff. Reserve headquarters is on the right just after you cross the lagoon causeway, and visitors are required to stop and register there. There's no admission fee, but contributions are appreciated. The warden will tell you about possibilities for trips, and guides are usually on hand with their boats. The standard rate for 4-hour trips was $70 when I was there in 1994—boats can accommodate three or maybe four people as well as the guide. I found it a good deal: the guides were well informed and enthusiastic. When the lagoon dries up in May, guided trips shift to horseback.

Another feature at Crooked Tree is the Maya ruin of Chau Hix, a small city that was occupied from late Classic Maya to Spanish times. A test excavation yielded glass bottles mixed with painted potsherds. Still forest-covered, the site was due to be excavated beginning in 1995. A troop of spider monkeys occupied it when I was there, and yellow-headed savanna vultures circled overhead.

Crooked Tree is a quiet Creole village famous for its May Cashew Festival celebrating the harvest of local trees, many of which are over a century old. There are several modest resorts: staying there reminded me of Florida in the 1950s. The Paradise Inn on the lagoon north of town has comfortable thatched cabins with hot water and fans for about $35, and a good, simple restaurant in which a yellow-throated warbler flew about, eating crumbs. The owners have a ranch on the lagoon and offer guide services. Phone: 2-52535; fax: 2-5253; U.S. 718-498-2221. The Crooked Tree Lodge closer to town is cheaper and more rustic, while the Birds Eye View Lodge on the lagoon south of town is a bit more expensive for rooms (TV is available), and also offers tours, 91 North Front St., P.O. Box 700, Belize City. Phone: 2-77593; fax: 2-77594; U.S. 718-845-0749. Bed and breakfast rooms are also available in town: ask at the Belize Audubon Society or reserve headquarters.

Burdon Creek Nature Reserve

Established in 1992, this 2,429-hectare reserve just west of Belize City is a mangrove and wetland complex important to aquatic life, and to the city's environmental quality, since it acts as a buffer to flooding. Development and pollution threaten the reserve: in 1994 there was a display on its problems in the government office above the post office. It's not much of a tourist attraction at present, although boat trips there can be arranged in Belize City.

Gales Point Community Manatee Sanctuary

South of Burdon Creek, Northern Lagoon and Southern Lagoon are extremely important critical habitat for manatees, because they are the largest breeding ground in the Caribbean for the shy sea mammals. Distantly related to elephants, manatees evolved in Africa and South America and spread as far north as Florida. They can reach 4 meters in length and 900 kilograms (220 pounds) in weight. Their meat is very tasty because of their plant diet, and, along with green sea turtles, they were a staple of pirate diets. They are now officially protected almost everywhere because their populations have fallen so low.

The warm lagoons provide ideal habitat for manatees, and the government has declared a Manatee Special Development Area there. Particularly important are freshwater springs which flow into the bottom of Southern Lagoon, since manatees appear to like drinking fresh water, and congregate there. The lagoons are important to many other species as well. Small islands such as Bird Island in Northern Lagoon provide breeding habitat for white ibis, boat-billed herons and other waterbirds, while mangroves are nurseries for shrimp, fish, and other seafood.

In 1992, the village of Gales Point at the south end of Southern Lagoon established a community sanctuary for conservation-oriented tourism in the area. Local residents provide guide service and bed and breakfast accommodations to visitors. Guides know the "breathing holes" where the manatees congregate. You can arrange for accommodations by calling the Gales Point Community Progressive Cooperative at 5-22087. There's also an upmarket resort, the Gales Point Manatee Lodge, Box 170, Belmopan (phone: 8-23321; fax: 8-23334). Gales Point is accessible either by a 25-kilometer dirt road from Dangriga, or by boat from Belize City via Burdon Creek. Tour agencies in Belize City offer trips there. Scheduled boats go from Blackline Marina, Mile 2 Northern Highway (phone: 2-44145).

Visitors to the manatee sanctuary can also find accommodations at Dangriga, a few hours' drive from Belize City via the Manatee Highway which cuts south from the Western Highway at La Democracia just past the Belize Zoo. Dangriga is the main Garífuna town in Belize. The Pelican Beach Resort outside of town offers tours of the sanctuary and other local attractions (phone: 5-22044; see Reefs and Cayes section). The Bonefish Hotel on the beach next to the park in town also offers tours, and has rooms for $35–60 and a good restaurant, P.O. Box 21, 15 Mahogany St., Dangriga (phone: 5-22165; fax: 5-22296). The Hub Guesthouse just west of the second bridge as you drive downtown has comfortable rooms with bath and fan for about $12, 573 South Riverside (phone: 5-22397).

Possum Point Biological Station

This small private reserve is on the Sittee River between Dangriga and Placencia. The reserve owners also lease Wee Wee Caye (named for the leafcutter ants, called wee wee ants in Creole, which live there), about 12 kilometers to the east, for marine biology research. There are trails on the 16-hectare reserve, and trips up the Sittee River are available. Accommodations are limited (bungalows with separate toilets and showers) and by reservation only (phone: 5-22006). The station also operates the Bocatura Bank Campground on the river.

Nim Li Punit Archaeological Reserve

Uncovered by oil workers in 1971, this Late Classic Maya site has yielded unusually large carved stelae (commemorating rulers), including one 9 meters tall. The site's name means "big hat" in Maya, and refers to a headdress shown on one stela. It was looted before excavation began in 1983, but a royal tomb was discovered in 1986. A number of structures are arranged around two plazas. Some are strangely elongated: one is a meter high but 70 meters long. The site may have been mainly ceremonial in function, but this is uncertain. Nim Li Punit is located about a kilometer northeast of the Southern Highway (Mile 75) near the village of Indian Creek. The signed trailhead is near Whitney's Grocery Store. Punta Gorda is 35 kilometers to the south. There is no public transportation to the site, but Z-Line buses will stop there.

Lúbaantun Archaeological Reserve

This is the largest Maya site in southern Belize, consisting of five plazas surrounded by eleven structures reaching heights of 15 meters. An absence of ceremonial stelae at the site suggests that it may have been linked to nearby Nim Li Punit. Lúbaantun, which means "place of fallen rocks," was a Late Classic community, possibly a center for cacao growing. Excavations began in 1926, and many artifacts were removed to England and the U.S., including a famous "crystal skull," exquisitely carved from a single block of transparent rock crystal. The skull's significance is unknown. Lúbaantun is located at the edge of the coastal plain inland from Punta Gorda, about a kilometer and a half from the Maya village of San Pedro Columbia. There are a resident caretaker, rest rooms, and a picnic area, but no other facilities. Accommodations are available at San Pedro and nearby San Antonio (see below).

Temash-Sarstoon Nature Reserve

This 16,900-hectare reserve on the Sarstoon and Temash rivers in Belize's southeast tip is the least disturbed wildland on the coastal plain. It contains primary black mangrove forest, with individual trees over 30 meters tall, and primary rain forest of sapodilla, Santa Maria and other hardwoods. There are eleven vegetation types in the reserve. Wildlife includes the large animals found in the rest of the country, and possibly white-faced capuchin monkeys, giant anteaters, and other species whose rain forest range has a northern limit here.

Access to the reserve is by boat from Punta Gorda, Belize's southernmost main town, a long day's drive from Belize City on the bumpy, dusty Southern Highway. Z-Line has daily bus service, and Maya and Tropic airlines have daily flights (see the Transportation section, above). There is no road access to Punta Gorda from Guatemala, but there is a passenger ferry from Puerto Barrios running twice a week. Tickets are available in Punta Gorda at Godoy's, 24 Middle St. (phone: 7-2065).

Nature's Way Guest House offers guided boat trips to the Temash-Sarstoon reserve and also to Sapodilla Cayes: Box 75, 65 Front St., Punta Gorda (phone: 7-22119). The Guest House has rooms with shared bath for around $15. The Toledo Visitors Information Center near the main pier also arranges tours and boat charters, P.O. Box 73 (phone: 7-22470). It takes a day to travel from Punta Gorda to the Temash River mouth and go upstream about halfway to the Guatemalan border, and trip prices will be commensurate with the time spent. It also may be possible to walk inland from the Maya village of Crique Sarco about halfway up the river to the isolated village of Dolores near the Guatemalan border. This would require several days.

The Traveller's Inn above the bus depot has rooms in the $50–80 range and a restaurant (phone: 7-22568). Moderately priced accommodations in Punta Gorda include: St. Charles Inn, 23 King St. (phone: 7-22149), and G&G's Inn, 49 Main Middle St. (phone: 7-22086). Garífuna and Kekchi Maya villages in the vicinity also have guest houses or bed and breakfast facilities. Nature's Way Guest House and Toledo Visitors Information Center can help in making arrangements to stay in villages.

Interior Plateaus and Mountains

Belize's western half is largely uninhabited except for road corridors and scattered towns and villages, and is almost all forest. North of the Western Highway is a rolling limestone plateau, rising gently to 200-meter escarpments near the Guatemalan border. Erosion of the limestone has created a "karst" topography of steeply conical little hills and seasonally flooded sinkholes. Streams are relatively small and sluggish. South of the Western Highway, the Maya Mountains rise steeply in a series of granitic and metamorphic ridges interspersed with limestone plateaus. Karst topography here is even more dramatic than in the north, particularly in the foothills bordering the coastal plain, where improbably steep limestone cones soar above the savanna, perhaps the inspiration for Maya pyramids. Many streams head on the peaks and plateaus, then drop into the lowlands in some of the most spectacular waterfalls in Central America. Streams and gravity have also carved vast cave systems into the limestone plateaus.

Except for peripheral farming communities such as the Mennonite towns around Blue Creek in the far north and the citrus and cacao plantations around the Hummingbird Highway, the land is owned in large blocks, mainly by the government but also by a few private concerns. Most is being managed as wildland, for selective logging, chicle collecting, adventure tourism, and other relatively low-impact activities. Pressure on wildlife is light, so chances of seeing spectacular species such as tapir, jaguar, puma, brocket deer, and white-lipped peccary are as good as anywhere in Central America (although there are no guarantees). Scarlet macaws still inhabit the Maya Mountains, and populations of large game birds such as ocellated turkeys, crested guans, and great curassows are locally abundant. The region also contains two of Belize's largest Maya sites, the huge metropolis of Caracol on the Vaca Plateau to the south, and the sprawling, largely unexplored complex of La Milpa in the north. Many recently discovered sites have yet to be explored, and others doubtless remain undiscovered.

Río Bravo Conservation Area

This 61,500-hectare reserve takes up much of Belize's northeast corner. It is owned by the Programme for Belize, a nonprofit organization created in 1988 to manage the land in an economically and environmentally sustainable way. Management is to be funded through appropriate agricultural development, low-impact tourism, and limited logging and other forest industries, with the goal of preserving the land's present high levels of environmental quality and diversity. Biologists have counted 200 tree species, 110 orchid species, 400 bird species, and 80 bat species in the area.

The Río Bravo Research Station in the northwest part of the reserve has accommodations and educational facilities for 36 visitors. These include cabanas with private bath for $80 per person a day and dormitories with shared baths for $65 a day: both include three meals and two guided excursions. Excursions include trail walks, visits to La Milpa Maya site, and visits to surrounding villages. Field and evening lectures on various topics can be arranged on arrival. Transportation from Belize City is available for $125 round-trip for up to four people. Day visits to the station are $20, and include a two-hour guided tour. The station is accessible by road via Orange Walk and Blue Creek, but roads are rough and may be impassable except in the dry season. Contact Programme for Belize, P.O. Box 749, Belize City (phone: 2-75616; fax: 2-75635).

Gallon Jug

This 52,632-hectare area is the Río Bravo Conservation Area's southern neighbor, and is being managed in a similar, coordinated way by its owner, Belizean entrepreneur Barry Bowen. The property is named for a logging town which existed there in the early twentieth century, but which had reverted to forest by the time Bowen bought it. Bowen has developed about 800 hectares around the abandoned town site for agriculture, and is managing the rest to preserve its ecological and archaeological values. One of his strategies for doing so is to use tourism to protect forest and archaeological sites from poachers and looters. When he heard that a large Maya complex in deep forest near Gallon Jug was being looted, Bowen located it and arranged for a California couple, Tom and Josie Harding, to develop a resort there.

The resort, named Chan Chich ("little bird" in Maya) after a nearby creek, opened in 1988, and has since won the Wilderness Retreat of the Year award for 1992 and other distinctions. Situated in the plaza of the Maya site and surrounded by forest-covered temples, it seems to attract wildlife. Every evening, a large flock of ocellated turkeys struts about the grounds, and parrots and toucans congregate noisily in the trees above the twelve cabanas. A photographic survey of the 12-kilometer trail system by Wildlife Conservation Society biologists Bruce and Carolyn Miller has determined that the trails are regularly used not only by guests but by ocelots, jaguars, and pumas. (Their photos, taken by automatic cameras, are on display in the lodge.) When I was there, I missed a jaguar sighting by perhaps a minute. Lodge visitors also have access to a number of other natural areas and Maya sites at Gallon Jug, including Laguna Seca, a lake and wetland overlooked by a completely untouched plaza and temple complex. Trained guides can show visitors features such as an ornate hawk eagle nest. Canoe and horseback rentals are available. For those who want to learn about the two hundred tree species and other ecological lore, a self-guiding trail booklet and map by the Millers is available for $10.

The cabanas and lodge at Chan Chich are made of local hard-woods and thatch, but have screens, electricity, and hot water. The restaurant is very good, and the atmosphere is convivial. You'll need to make reservations well in advance: P.O. Box 37, Belize City (phone: 2-75634; fax: 2-76961). In the U.S., P.O. Box 1088, Vine-yard Haven, MA 02568 (phone: 800-343-8009; fax: 508-693-6311). Gallon Jug is accessible in the dry season by road either by the Iguana Creek Bridge Road, which branches off from the West-ern Highway near Belmopan, or by a road that continues south from Blue Creek and the Río Bravo Conservation Area. Most vis-itors fly in from Belize City. Javier's Flying Service has charters, and in 1994 began regular Mon., Wed., Fri. flights for $96 round-trip (phone: 2-45332). A day trip that includes lunch and a guided tour of Chan Chich is available from Javier's. There are plans to develop another resort on the escarpment west of Gallon Jug, which offers a breathtaking overlook from which king vultures, white hawks, and even an occasional crested eagle can be seen.

Xunantunich Archaeological Reserve

This is one of the most scenic Maya sites in Belize, with a 45-meter-tall temple, "El Castillo," on a limestone ridge overlooking the Guatemalan border. It is also one of the most accessible, located a few kilometers from the Western Highway, and was the first public archaeological site in the country, opened in 1954. It has been ex-cavated since 1894, with the result that many artifacts have been lost from the country and some archaeological evidence has been destroyed, but recent restorations have recreated some of the tem-ple friezes and other features. Visitors can climb to the "roof comb" at the top of El Castillo and get a striking view of the countryside. It faces another, smaller tower across a large plaza, and must have given an overwhelming impression of power and majesty to Maya who went there for ceremonial or political reasons.

Xunantunich is thought to have been occupied throughout the Classic Period, and to have been abandoned about 1,150 years ago. There is evidence of earthquake damage from about that time, but the site has not been as systematically excavated as others, so rel-atively little is known about its history. Extensive other structures, probably living quarters for high-ranking Maya and their servants, extend around the towers. Young forest covers much of the area. The lower slopes of El Castillo are covered with begonias and other flowers. There is a picnic area, rest rooms, and drinking water at the site, but no other facilities. The site is about 10 minutes' drive west of the town of San Ignacio. A hand-cranked ferry takes you across the Mopan River, then a steep road leads another kilometer and a half to the site.

Cahal Pech

Another Maya site on the Western Highway just west of San Ignacio, Cahal Pech, gives an insight into the less grandiose side of Maya life. The site is believed to have been the "country seat" of a Maya noble family, rather like an English castle, and includes family tombs, a small plaza and temple, and living and sleeping quarters. A tunnel leading to the back of the complex is believed to have led to a "garbage chute" for servants to remove waste material. When excavated, the garbage dump yielded evidence of elite diets—remains of roast venison and chocolate beverages. There is also evidence that the site continued to be occupied after the general collapse of the Late Classic Period, perhaps by impoverished descendants of the nobles, who may have moved from room to room as the once palatial quarters filled with bat dung and rubble and finally became uninhabitable. Cahal Pech is located in a patch of forest on a hill overlooking San Ignacio. There is a small museum, and a concessionaire sells snacks just outside the ruins. There's good birding in the trees around the site.

El Pilar Archaeological Reserve for Maya Flora and Fauna

About 10 kilometers northeast of San Ignacio on the Guatemalan border, this site was the area's main Maya administrative center from 2,300 to 1,300 years ago, and covers over 40 hectares with plazas, temples, and palaces. The site is largely unexcavated and will be developed to emphasize the Maya's relationship with their natural environment. (Zoologist Ivan Sanderson has written that the Maya had one of the most precise and extensive vocabularies for naming animals and plants that he has ever encountered.) Local farmers, many of Mayan descent, will be involved in managing the forest lands within the reserve, with the goal of preserving traditional knowledge and establishing sustainable use of forest resources. Ecotourism and educational facilities are planned.

The reserve is accessible by an all-weather road from San Ignacio via the village of Bullet Tree Falls on the Belize River. A community group in the village, Amigos de El Pilar, is coordinating with the reserve. There were no public facilities as of 1994. For information, contact the BRASS/El Pilar Project, MesoAmerican Research Center, University of California, Santa Barbara, CA 93106-2150 (phone: 805-893-8191; fax: 893-2790).

San Ignacio and Environs

The San Ignacio area has the largest inland concentration of resorts in Belize. Since this is a farming area, chances of seeing spectacular wildlife are not as good as in more remote places, but birding, canoeing, and other activities are excellent. Chaa Creek Cottages was one of the first resorts in the area: it's located on a 134-hectare reserve on the Macal River about 20 minutes from San Ignacio. It features canoeing and rafting on the river (excellent for watching birds, cichlids, and iguanas), nature trails, horseback riding, a blue morpho butterfly breeding center, and tours to Tikal, Mountain Pine Ridge, and Chiquibul National Park. The adobe and thatched cottages are $80–140. Transportation from Belize City is $125 for one to four persons. P.O. Box 53, San Ignacio, Cayo (phone: 9-22037; fax: 9-22501).

Right next to Chaa Creek is the Pantí Medicinal Trail on the grounds of Ix Chel Farm, a facility dedicated to the preservation of Maya herbalist medicine. The trail through the forest identifies the medicinal uses of dozens of native plants such as jackass bitters, a sunflower family herb used to treat malaria and diabetes, and negrito, a tree whose bark was until the nineteenth century the main remedy for dysentery. The trail is based on the knowledge of Don Eligio Pantí, a Belizean Mayan healer, and also includes a reconstruction of a traditional Maya healing house completely made from local materials. Ix Chel Farm is working with the New York

Botanical Garden's Institute of Ethnobotany in researching new drug sources. Self-guided tour is $5; $7.50 per person with guide. Ix Chel Farm, General Delivery, San Ignacio (phone: 9-23310), or contact through the Belize Center for Environmental Studies (see above).

Also on the Macal River near Chaa Creek are Du Plooy's, comparable in price with lodge and rooms in a small forest reserve (phone: 8-23180; fax: 9-22057), and Black Rock, more basic, with thatched tents, solar-powered electricity: P.O. Box 48, San Ignacio, Cayo (phone: 9-22341; fax: 9-23449). All three resorts are accessible via a dirt road that turns south off the Western Highway 9 kilometers west of San Ignacio. A little past that turnoff is the entrance to Nabitunich Cottages within sight of Xunantunich, with birding, canoeing, horseback riding, and camping. Contact Benque Viejo Post Office, Cayo (phone: 9-32309; fax: 9-32096).

In San Ignacio, the Hotel San Ignacio on the Western Highway just north of downtown is in the $38–75 range, with a pool and a good restaurant (phone: 9-22034). The Hotel Venus has rooms with bath and fan for $20–30, 29 Burns Ave., while the nearby Jaguar, 19 Burns Ave., is somewhat less for rooms with shared bath, and the even closer Central, 24 Burns Ave., is even less. The Serendib Restaurant, 27 Burns Ave., has good curries, and Eva's Bar, 22 Burns Ave., has inexpensive local dishes and pastries. The Belize Tourism Industry Association (BTIA) has an information office on Burns Ave.

About a kilometer east of San Ignacio, on the dirt road that branches south from the Western Highway toward the village of San Antonio, is Maya Mountain Lodge, P.O. Box 46, San Ignacio, Cayo (phone: 9-22164; fax: 9-22029). The lodge has cottages and rooms for $40–70, with or without private bath, and offers tours to Tikal, Caracol, Mountain Pine Ridge, and other destinations, and canoe, mountain bike, and horseback trips. It includes a nature trail with guided or self-guided walks available, a reference library, and facilities for classes and conferences. Another 10 kilometers south on this road, in the Yucatec Maya village of San Antonio, is the Tanah Mayan Art Museum run by the Garcia sisters, nieces of Don Eligio Pantí, who began doing traditional Maya carving in local slate in 1985. The museum holds impressive examples of the sisters' work and a variety of Maya artifacts. Locally carved slate statuettes and jewelry are for sale. There's a $3 admission fee to the museum. The small Chichan Ka Lodge, c/o San Antonio Village, P.O. Box 75, San Ignacio, Cayo, has rooms for $12–15, and offers local food and tours. The Pacbitun ruins near San Antonio, occupied from 3,000 to 1,100 years ago, contain a number of temples, some 20 meters in height.

Slate Creek Preserve

This private preserve has been established by agreement of landowners along Miles 6 through 10 of the Mountain Pine Ridge Road, which runs south from Georgeville on the Western Highway to the Mountain Pine Ridge Forest Reserve. Slate Creek is located on the karst landscape that lies at the foot of granitic Mountain Pine Ridge, and supports lush broadleaf forest. The preserve, still in the formative stage, contains a core forest area and buffer zones where sustainable farming and other economic activities will be carried out in voluntary compliance with a land use management plan. The preserve is working with Guatemalan and Salvadoran refugees in the neighboring village of Siete Millas to reduce pressure on forested land by developing sustainable farming practices and alternative income sources. The preserve is funded by donations, notably by wildlife artist Robert Bateman and his wife Birgit.

Accommodations at Slate Creek are available at Mountain Equestrian Trails, a roughly 120-hectare resort owned by preserve founders Jim and Marguerite Bevis. Operating since 1986, MET offers a wide variety of activities, and is located close to Mountain Pine Ridge Forest Reserve. Cabanas are $70–90, with a good restaurant and a relaxed atmosphere. Horseback riding on 90 kilometers of trails in the area is a major theme, and vehicle tours to Mountain Pine Ridge, Caracol, and other destinations are available (horseback trips to Caracol have been discontinued since upgrading of the road). On a separate part of the property is Chiclero Trails, a tent camp with outdoor cooking for about $35 per person a night. Four-night packages and rain forest workshops are available, and scientific and educational groups are especially welcome.

MET is associated with a wilderness adventure company, The Divide Ltd., which has a base camp in the Chiquibul area, and offers raft trips down the Macal River where scarlet macaw flocks and swimming tapirs are a regular sight. The Divide has served as expedition outfitter for the Wildlife Conservation Society, the Belize Audubon Society, and The Nature Conservancy, and can provide extended treks through the little explored Maya Mountains. MET is at Mile 8, Mountain Pine Ridge Rd., Central Farm Post Office, Cayo (phone: 8-23180/22149; fax: 8-23235). The Divide is at the same address, phone/fax: 9-23452.

Society Hall Nature Reserve

This 2,729-hectare reserve was created in 1986 to protect the rich broadleaf forest between Roaring Creek and Upper Barton Creek in the foothills of Mountain Pine Ridge. The forest, over 30 meters tall in moist valleys, grows on karst topography. The area forms a wildlife habitat corridor with Slate Creek Preserve. The Belize Audubon Society manages it as an educational and scientific reserve: there are no tourist facilities. Contact Belize Audubon for more information.

Mountain Pine Ridge Forest Reserve

This 59,000-hectare forest reserve encompasses one of the three main granitic areas in the Maya Mountains. The granite is exposed along a dramatic fault escarpment, with 300-meter cliffs overlooking the coastal plain. The rolling plateau on top of the escarpment has different flora and fauna than the surrounding karst lowlands. Fifty years ago it was largely Caribbean pine savanna, maintained by regular fires. Today, because of fire suppression by foresters, it is a sunny forest of Caribbean pine with an undergrowth of hardwoods such as oaks and miconias. Savanna herbs, such as a tall grass called dumb cane and a lacy fern called tiger bush, still cover much of the ground. Many streams run through the area, and a lusher vegetation including tree ferns and a South American gymnosperm, *Podocarpus* (locally called cypress), grow along them. Stream fauna is quite different from that of lowland streams. An endemic frog whose large tadpoles hold on to rocks with suckerlike mouths is common. The diverse large cichlids of lowland streams seem absent, and small live-bearers appear to be the only fish even in sizable streams such as Tiger Creek. The Río On Pools on the road between the reserve entrance and its headquarters at Augustine are fine swimming holes.

With its ancient gymnosperms and cycads, and its streamside bogs of carnivorous sundew and bladderwort plants, Mountain Pine Ridge has a "lost world" quality. The king vultures that frequent the escarpment are just about as majestic and bizarre as pterodactyls, with their white and black plumage and brilliantly colored heads. It's possible to see as many as a dozen individuals resting on the rocks at the top of 300-meter waterfalls. Occasionally one will take off and circle upward until it is out of sight, perhaps gliding off to feed in Guatemala or even Mexico. The reserve is also the main nesting area in Belize for the beautiful and rare orange-breasted falcon.

South and west of the granitic escarpment, past the reserve headquarters at Augustine, the land descends to the limestone Vaca Plateau, which supports tropical hardwood forest. There are several small caves along the road. A nature trail leads from the parking lot at these caves to the Río Frio Cave, where the river has carved a cavern over a kilometer long through a limestone hill. It's possible to walk through it if the river isn't too high; there are limestone formations and bats. (The road also passes Río Frio Cave farther on.)

The entrance to the forest reserve is accessible by the dirt roads from Georgeville and San Ignacio. A warden opens a gate to let you in: there's no admission fee. Reserve roads are fairly well marked, but bumpy, and may quickly become dangerous in wet weather. Watch out for logging trucks, and start with a full gas tank. There's no public transportation to the ridge, but many hotels and agencies offer minivan tours.

Hidden Valley Inn is on a private, 7,287-hectare reserve at the north end of the escarpment. The reserve encompasses some of the best scenery in the area, including a number of waterfalls. The inn is in a secluded, attractively landscaped location on top of the escarpment. Bed and breakfast in private cottages is $77.50–$137.50. Meals are in a comfortable, spacious lodge with a small library. Transportation from Belize City, San Ignacio, and other locations is available, and there are a number of tour packages including trips to Tikal and Caracol and boat expeditions on the Macal. Also on the reserve is the Hidden Valley Institute for Environmental Studies for investigating the area's little understood ecology. The institute is located at Hidden Valley Falls, the most famous waterfall in the reserve, and includes accommodations for researchers and a small natural history museum. Hidden Valley Inn, P.O. Box 170, Belmopan (phone: 8-23320; fax: 8-23334. In U.S. 904-222-2333; 800-334-7942). There are several other resorts in the area, and it also may be possible to rent a house in Augustine from the Forestry Department.

Chiquibul National Park

Established in 1991, this is Belize's largest national park, 107,649 hectares in extent. It is bordered by forest reserves to the north, east, and south, and by the Guatemalan border to the west, and its wilderness quality is thus very well buffered (although there have been problems with incursions from Guatemala). It includes the southern part of the Vaca Plateau, and the eastern slopes of the Maya Mountains, an area that has been unbroken forest since the Classic Maya abandoned it a thousand years ago, although there has been selective logging. In the late 1980s, Wildlife Conservation Society biologists Bruce and Carolyn Miller conducted a survey of the area, and found it one of the last places in Central America with a breeding population of a bird species that appears very near extinction—the keel-billed motmot.

The motmots (named for the "mot mot" call of one species) are a bird family that apparently evolved in Central America and tropical North America. With deep blue, green, and cinnamon plumage and characteristic "racket-shaped" tails, they are among the most striking neotropical birds. The keel-billed motmot originally lived in moist Caribbean slope forests from Mexico to Costa Rica, but most of its habitat has been destroyed, and there are almost no recent records of nesting pairs except in Chiquibul (there's also one pair in Slate Creek Preserve). The park may thus be the species' only chance of survival, and Belize's conservation community joined with the Millers in lobbying for it. The park also protects the main breeding population of scarlet macaws in Belize, as well as untold other species. Most of it remains unexplored.

The Chiquibul Cavern System within the park is thought to be the largest in Central America, although nobody knows how big it really is. The three largest caves so far explored total 32 kilometers in length. A chamber of one cave is the largest cave room in the Western Hemisphere, and the second largest in the world. Carved by underground streams, the caves have yielded new species of insects and crustaceans, as well as many artifacts left by the Maya when they used the caves for ceremonies. Because of their archaeological features, and because of the danger of flooding from sudden storms, the caves can be entered only with government permission.

The park is accessible via the road from Augustine to Caracol, but there are no public facilities as yet. Local resorts run guided trips from base camps in the area (see above).

Caracol Archaeological Reserve

Caracol is Belize's largest Maya site: it covered at least 14,250 hectares of the Vaca Plateau with structures and causeways during its peak about 1,500 years ago. Its population may have been almost 200,000. Its core of temples, plazas, ball courts, and other elite structures has more than twice as many buildings as Tikal's core. Yet it is located in such a remote area that, although loggers discovered it in the 1930s, it was thought to be a minor site until the mid 1980s. Discoveries since then include an altar stone with a hieroglyphic record of the conquest of Tikal by a Caracol leader, Lord Water, in the year 562 A.D. Caracol is believed to have dominated Tikal and other neighboring states for the next two centuries before declining for little understood reasons.

Caracol's core is 1,295 hectares in extent, and encompasses five plazas and many temples, one of which is higher than El Castillo at Xunantunich. Many unlooted tombs have been excavated in the past decade, and the information they provide will greatly enhance our knowledge of Maya history. Excavations are still under way, and most of the ruins still lie under heavy forest, with many trees 40 meters tall.

Named with the Spanish word for snail (the reason for the name is unclear), Caracol is located within Chiquibul National Park. Permission to visit must be obtained from the Department of Archaeology in Belmopan and from the Forestry Department in Augustine. Forestry Department permission will depend on whether conditions on the 45 kilometers of road between Augustine and the ruins are judged safe. Although the road has been upgraded, it can deteriorate rapidly during wet weather. There are no overnight accommodations at the ruins, and camping is not permitted. Visitors are advised to bring drinking water, since there are few streams on the plateau, and a local reservoir provides only enough water for site workers. Workmen at the site may be hired as guides if they have time, but are mainly Spanish-speaking. For the present, going on a tour from one of the local resorts is probably the best way to visit Caracol.

Blue Hole National Park

Located in the northern foothills of Mountain Pine Ridge, this 243-hectare park is easily accessible via the Hummingbird Highway. It's at Mile 13.9 south of Belmopan. A warden is on duty beside the road when the park is open (there have been problems with thefts from cars). Hours are 8–4. Concrete steps descend a short distance to the park's main attraction, a deep pool where an underground tributary of the Caves Branch River suddenly rises above ground, runs downhill for a few meters, then disappears into the limestone again. Big black band cichlids and mountain mullets and smaller Mexican tetras and tricolor cichlids live in the pool, and the warden told me that tarpon and snappers from the sea appear in larger pools downstream. You can swim in the hole, although this will scare the fish underground. Climbing on the sinkhole walls above the pool is prohibited.

About a kilometer farther north on the Hummingbird Highway is the head of a short trail leading to St. Herman's Cave, a rather spectacular cavern (although by Belizean standards not unusual) which can be followed over a kilometer underground along the same stream that rises at Blue Hole. You'll need a flashlight for this, of course, and you should definitely bring a spare, as it gets very dark indeed away from the entrance, and the going is not easy. There's no clear trail, and the riverbank is steep and slippery. You must notify the warden at Blue Hole before you enter the cave. Big bats and little brown swallows roost among the surreal limestone formations of the yawning cave entrance. A suitable lair for the Lords of Xibalba, the underworld Mayan deities of death. Mayan pots, spears, and torches have been found. A nature trail leading from Blue Hole to St. Herman's Cave was closed when I was there.

Farther south on the Hummingbird Highway, at St. Margaret's Village, is the turnoff to Five Blues Lake National Park, a 358-hectare park centering on a 3-hectare cenote named for the several hues of blue that can be seen in its waters. The cenote is over 66 meters deep. Steep, forested hills and swamp surround the lake. There is a small island, named for its profusion of orchids, which can be reached by wading over a ledge. Indian Creek, which has its source in the lake, has a small cave network. There are trails and a picnic area, but no other services.

Caves Branch Adventures has a camp on a private estate in this area, with tent, bunkhouse, and cabana accommodations from $5–20 for one person. They offer cave explorations, inner tubing through river caves, guided forest walks, and expeditions to Maya sites. Contact Adventure Tours Belize, Box 332, Belize City (phone: 2-33903; fax: 2-33966).

Cockscomb Basin Wildlife Sanctuary

When I passed through Belize in 1971, I heard it was famous for its abundance of jaguars. Scientific studies have supported this reputation. In 1982, the Belize Audubon Society asked the Wildlife Conservation Society to assess jaguar abundance in the country. Biologist Alan Rabinowitz found the highest density in the Cockscomb Basin, an area of thin granitic soils and heavy rainfall on the east side of Belize's highest mountain, 1,120-meter Victoria Peak. The area was never occupied by the Maya because of its poor soils, and a logging town at Quam Bank had been abandoned by the 1970s. The basin was judged suitable to be the world's first jaguar sanctuary. It was declared a forest reserve in 1984, and about 250 hectares were set aside as a jaguar preserve in 1986. In 1990, the sanctuary was enlarged to encompass 41,457 hectares.

An estimated twenty-five to thirty jaguars live within the sanctuary, the highest density of the species yet recorded. Studies have indicated that up to 90 percent of their diet consists of armadillos, although the species generally prefers to eat larger animals such as peccary, brocket deer, and paca. (Belizean jaguars are relatively small.) Belize's other cat species, the puma, ocelot, margay, and jaguarundi, also inhabit the sanctuary, as well as tayra, otter, coati, kinkajou, brocket deer, tapir, white-lipped and collared peccary, paca, and anteater. Monkeys were extirpated from the basin by yellow fever epidemics in the 1960s, but in 1992 a number of black howler troops were reintroduced from the Community Baboon Sanctuary with sponsorship of the Wildlife Conservation Society. There are presently eight to ten troops of from five to seven living in the Cockscomb, and they are usually visible along the trails. Over 290 bird species have been recorded, including scarlet macaw and great curassow.

The Belize Audubon Society manages the reserve, and maintains excellent public facilities. A well-marked and maintained trail system over 13 kilometers in extent leads through a variety of habitats, including abandoned "milpas," kaway swamps, cohune palm stands, and forested slopes. Outlying trails lead to steep bluffs and waterfalls—and to the wrecked plane in which Rabinowitz almost lost his life while studying the area. There is a self-guided nature trail booklet available at the visitor center which helps to identify trees and other natural features. There's also a small museum on the sanctuary's geology, history, and ecology in the visitor center. It includes an account of the first ascent of Victoria Peak (visible from the center) by colonial Governor Goldsworthy in 1888. Wardens can give a slide show about the sanctuary for groups of ten people or more; the fee is $25. They also lead groups on day or night hikes. Wardens aren't available to guide individual visitors, however. There are only four wardens for the entire sanctuary.

There's a camping area with fireplaces for cooking available at $1.50 per person a night. Camping is on a first-come, first-served basis. Campers should have good tents, as the insects are abundant. There are also cabins equipped with bunk beds, linen, cooking utensils, and kitchen facilities for $6 per person a night. Visitors have to bring all their own food, and are advised to bring drinking water too, as the supply at the sanctuary is limited. (Campers are not allowed to use cabin facilities.)

The reserve is increasingly popular, with 6,000 visitors in 1993, so those wishing to use the cabins should make reservations in advance. Tour groups and school groups usually book up the cabins during the tourist season, so individuals or small groups would do better to visit in the off-season if they want to use the cabins. The best way to reserve cabin space is by contacting the sanctuary directly: Ernesto Saqui, Director, Cockscomb Basin Wildlife Sanctuary, P.O. Box 90, Dangriga, Belize. Mr. Saqui advises reserving at least three weeks in advance during the tourist season, three days in advance in the off-season. There is no phone, but the sanctuary can be reached by radio from Pelican Beach Resort, Dangriga (5-22044). You can also try to reserve space through the Belize Audubon office in Belize City (see above).

The sanctuary is a two-hour drive from Dangriga on the Southern Highway, so a day trip from there is quite feasible. (See Coastal Plain section, above, for Dangriga accommodations.) There are two stream fordings on the 10-kilometer track from the highway at Maya Center just past the Kendall Bridge to the sanctuary visitor center. These are passable by non-4wd vehicles in the dry season (I watched a heavily loaded minivan wallow through), but the track may flood out during storms. You can take a Z-Line bus to Maya Center and walk or hire a ride from there. Visitors are required to stop and register in Maya Center (a Maya village that was originally located in the basin) before proceeding to the visitor center.

Bladen Branch Nature Reserve

Established in 1990, this reserve protects 37,247 hectares of forest along the Bladen Branch of the Monkey River in the southern Maya Mountains. Elevations range from 200 meters along the lower branch to 1,000 meters on Richardson Peak, Belize's second highest mountain. Several forest types occur in the reserve, from lowland rain forest in the valley to cloud forest on the peaks. A 1987 expedition by the Manomet Bird Observatory and Missouri Botanical Garden found a number of Maya sites and identified ninety tree species and hundreds of bird species, including two, the magnificent hummingbird and Audubon's oriole, never before found in Belize. All the large animals known from the Cockscomb Basin are likely to occur in Bladen as well. In 1993, a number of large Maya sites were discovered along the Monkey River near the Bladen Reserve.

The Bladen Reserve is managed by the Belize Audubon Society as a scientific and educational reserve, and is limited to biologists, archaeologists, and other qualified researchers. Access is by permission from Belize Audubon and government officials only, although low-impact tourism may be allowed in the future. There is a possibility that the Bladen Reserve will eventually be linked to the Cockscomb Basin Jaguar Sanctuary and Chiquibul National Park to form a Maya Mountains Biosphere Reserve, which would be a major step toward securing the area's wilderness quality.

CHAPTER SEVEN

Honduras

HONDURAS IS THE wild card of Central American nations. Although it is the second largest, after Nicaragua, with an area of 112,088 square kilometers, its population (5.3 million in 1991) is similar to El Salvador's. Much of the country is rugged plateaus punctuated with forested peaks, while the eastern fifth is largely uninhabited savanna and swamp. Perhaps because of this ruggedness, pre-Columbian cultures didn't reach the degree of urbanization here that they did in the north and west (the great Maya center of Copán is just within the Honduran border). Honduras's position since the Conquest generally has been less prominent than Guatemala's or Nicaragua's: nineteenth-century American traveler William Wells called it "a hermit's cell compared with the other Central American states." This obscurity hasn't been altogether a disadvantage. If Honduras has enjoyed less wealth and power than its neighbors (it was long considered the poorest Central American country), it also has suffered less violence and oppression.

A good deal of wildland has persisted in Honduras's rugged territory. Mountain ranges rising above the populated valleys of the volcanic plateau still support old-growth conifer and hardwood forest. Heavy tropical forest still covers much of the massive peaks of the north coast and the humid lowlands of the Mosquitia. Some fine mangrove forests and coral reefs line the shore. Honduras has designated a number of these areas as parks and reserves since 1980, and although it has not had the money to provide much in the way of administrative or visitor facilities, many of the areas are fairly easily accessible via trails or waterways. You certainly won't feel overcrowded in Honduran parks: I seldom met other travelers during a 1992 visit.

Land of the Deeps

Honduras's name is thought to have originated during Columbus's fourth voyage, when he made his first Central American landfall on its north coast. "*Hondura*" means "depth" in Spanish, so the name may have referred to the deep water off the north coast. Alternatively, Columbus's ships had great difficulty getting around Cape Gracias a Dios because of the offshore currents and winds, and he may have complained of the "*ondas duras,*" or "hard waves," which impeded his progress. The name is appropriate anyway: the country is full of deep canyons and gorges.

Three major mountain ranges run from southeast to northwest across Honduras. The northern cordillera, which follows the north coast, is part of the original continental crust which underlies Guatemala and Mexico. It continues offshore, where three of its peaks and ridges emerge from the Caribbean to form the Bay Islands. The central cordillera, which cuts the eastern province of Olancho off from the sea, is composed of uplifted Mesozoic sediments. The southern cordillera, which runs along the Nicaraguan border, is composed of metamorphosed Paleozoic sediments. At the country's eastern tip, the mountains dip down into the Mosquitia, a subsidence zone where an estimated 3,000 to 6,000 meters of sediment have been deposited in the past 100 million years.

A zone of faults cuts across Honduras from north to south, forming a chain of deep valleys that extends from the mouth of the Ulúa River on the Gulf of Honduras, to the Gulf of Fonseca. The zone includes Lake Yojoa, formed as a result of faulting activity. The Ulúa, Comayagua, and Choluteca valleys in this region have historically contained the main population concentrations in the country. Southwest of the fault zone is a high volcanic plateau punctuated with peaks which are the remains of long-extinct volcanoes. The active volcanic belt of the Pacific coast reaches Honduras only where it borders the Gulf of Fonseca, and the few volcanoes there are not currently active.

Honduras's steep topography causes a lot of climatic variation. Most rainfall comes on the trade winds from the Caribbean, so seaward-facing slopes are drenched with some of the highest precipitation in Central America, while interior valleys have semidesert conditions. There is a marked dry season from October to May in the south and west, while the north and east get almost year-round rain. Areas above a thousand meters' elevation have a temperate climate that gets cool at night and in the winter months. The lowlands around the Gulf of Fonseca, on the other hand, are said to be the hottest places in Central America.

Fauna and flora change markedly from place to place according to local climate. Extraordinarily dense rain forest covers the seaward slopes of the northern cordillera, and this rain forest extends inland along river valleys and in the Mosquitia. As mountaintops bar wet Caribbean winds, a variety of drier vegetations cover the lowlands. In the ranching valleys of Olancho and in parts of the Mosquitia are savannas—grassland dotted with acacias or Caribbean pines. In the eroded valleys of the fault zone, conditions can be desertlike, a scrub of small trees interspersed with yucca and cardon and opuntia cactuses. Remnants of the dry deciduous forest that once covered the Pacific lowlands grow in southwestern valleys. As elevation increases, a series of vegetation zones ensues, from sunny ocote pine woodland at 1,000 meters, to a denser forest of pinabete pine at 1,500 meters, to cloud forest at 2,000 meters, to northern pine and fir forest at 2,500 meters.

Natural diversity led to cultural diversity as humans occupied Honduras, first as hunter-gatherers, then as farmers. Existing evidence suggests that the earliest form of farming was the root crop kind that originated in South America. Indigenous peoples of Honduras's Caribbean, the Miskitos, Pech, and Tawahka, speak Chibchan-related languages similar to those further south. Later the cultivation of maize spread from the north and came to predominate in central and western Honduras. Honduras remained peripheral to the great northern empires, however. The city-state of

Copán was the southernmost extent of the Classic Maya urbanization which reached its zenith from about two to one thousand years ago. The Uto-Aztecan–speaking Pipil and Chorotega peoples who occupied western Honduras appear to have been as much refugees from the empires of central and southern Mexico as representatives of them. A major urbanization evidently occurred in the Honduran Mosquitia during the five hundred years before Columbus, but very little is known about it as yet because the extensive ruins in the area haven't been excavated. It's possible that the Aztecs and related cultures "developed" the area as a source of cacao, a commodity that they used as money as well as a luxury beverage.

Throughout the Mayan and Aztec periods, mountainous central Honduras was dominated by the Lencas, a people about whom little is known, although they still exist in sizable numbers (their population is estimated at 50,000). It is said they are a South American group much influenced by the Maya, but Lenca painted pottery resembles neither that of the Maya nor the pottery of the peoples to the south. The Lenca language is thought to be related to the Chibchan language group. Other indigenous groups that still exist are the Xicaques of the north coast mountains, whose language is related to others spoken in northwest Mexico and California, and the Chortis near the Guatemalan border, who speak a Maya dialect.

The Tail End of Conquest

Honduras was "the end of the line" for conquistadors exploring Central America from north and south. (Columbus made no attempt to colonize it during his 1502 voyage.) In 1524, three separate expeditions arrived there: one led by Gil González Dávila from Panama, one led by Cristobal de Olid from Cuba, and one led by Francisco de las Casas from Mexico. Olid tried to take control, and Dávila and las Casas beheaded him. In 1525, Hernan Cortés, who had dispatched the Olid and las Casas expeditions, led a large expedition overland from Mexico. He managed to assert his authority over the squabbling factions in Trujillo, the Spanish capital on the north coast, but suffered great losses, and returned to Mexico the next year, having found no rich cities to conquer.

Diego López de Salcedo was appointed governor in 1526. His

policies, which included deporting large numbers of Indians to slavery in the West Indies, soon brought native revolts and renewed squabbling among the Spaniards. In 1532, Cortés's lieutenant, Pedro de Alvarado, was designated to take control of the foundering colony. He established a gold and silver mining industry in the mountains of western Honduras, and founded several towns, including Gracias and San Pedro Sula. In 1537, Alvarado's successor established the capital at Comayagua, where it would remain throughout the colonial period. That same year, the Lenca posed the most serious challenge to the Conquest when they revolted under the leadership of a chief named Lempira. The revolt, based in an impenetrable fortress in the mountains above Gracias, successfully resisted the Spanish until 1538, when Lempira was killed (treacherously, after the Spanish had declared a truce).

Mining remained the main Honduran industry for most of the colonial period, and its "boom and bust" cycles conditioned the economy. First Indian, then African, slaves were used to work the mines. Gold and silver strikes around Gracias and Comayagua brought prosperity in the 1540s and 50s, and Honduras briefly was granted an "*audiencia,*" a regional legislative center, but the mines played out in the 1560s. Silver strikes around Tegucigalpa (now the capital) revived the economy in the 1570s, but only for another decade or so. The colony functioned as a subsistence farming society for most of the seventeenth and eighteenth centuries, although some cattle were exported from the savannas of Olancho and Yoro. In 1700, only Comayagua and Tegucigalpa had more than a hundred Spanish inhabitants. British pirates allied with the Miskitos to control most of the Caribbean coast, establishing settlements on the mainland and the Bay Islands.

A Tumultuous Nationhood

Economics didn't change significantly after Spain was expelled in 1821, but politics became much more complex as a bewildering succession of factions and rulers struggled for control. Honduras was first part of the Empire of Mexico, then of the Central American Federation, before it declared nationhood in 1838. Its constitution has been rewritten seventeen times since 1821, and there have been three hundred revolts, civil wars, and changes of government, sometimes engineered from neighboring Guatemala or Nicaragua. Honduras didn't gain control over the Bay Islands and Mosquitia from Britain until 1859. Its border with Nicaragua wasn't resolved until 1960. Its border with El Salvador was resolved in a 1993 World Court decision.

In the latter half of the nineteenth century, Honduras was drawn into the export economy that affected the rest of Central America. Gold, silver, and timber were the main exports until the 1890s, when the Vaccaro brothers of New Orleans began shipping bananas grown on Honduras's north coast to the United States. Within a decade, Honduras was the leading banana exporter in the world: the trade was controlled by large U.S. companies and these became major players in Honduran politics as well as economics. For many years, the Cuyamel Fruit Company, which owned land around Tela, financed and manipulated the Liberal party as part of its competition with United Fruit, based around La Ceiba. In turn, United Fruit financed and manipulated the National party. The U.S. government was drawn into Honduran politics in the wake of its financial interests: marines occupied the country temporarily in 1912.

Banana companies provided facilities for their employees, but the country remained largely undeveloped otherwise. Railroad schemes failed, leaving Honduras with a much larger national debt than its yearly revenues. A road from Tegucigalpa to the north coast wasn't completed until the 1950s. One result of the lack of development was rather positive, however. Since its only large export industry was the U.S.–controlled banana industry, Honduras did not acquire a large landholding class as in Guatemala and El Salvador. Much land remained in government ownership. Honduras has to some degree avoided the extremely violent conflicts over land ownership that have beset its neighbors (although a small percentage of the population still owns a large percentage of the land, and the majority lives in poverty, with an unemployment rate of over 40 percent).

When the banana industry slumped during the Great Depression in the 1930s, leading to widespread unemployment and unrest, a military dictatorship under General Tiburcio Carías Andino ruled the country for sixteen years. The army remained a major political force, and military coups overthrew the government in 1956, 1963, 1978, and 1984. A 1954 agreement with the U.S. gave Honduras military aid in return for access to raw materials.

Military events have continued to predominate in Honduras's history. In 1969 it fought a short but bloody war with El Salvador over the issue of illegal Salvadoran immigration. Throughout the 1980s, Nicaragua's and El Salvador's guerrilla wars raged along Honduras's borders, causing large influxes of refugees and other social problems. Large amounts of U.S. aid directed against the Sandinista government in Nicaragua and the FMLN guerrillas in El Salvador led to political controversy and to fiscal corruption in the Honduran army. The army was involved in a number of scandals concerning human rights abuses and drug trafficking as well as corruption in the 1990s. The 1986, '90, and '94 elections proceeded peacefully, however.

The Russia of Central America

Honduras's vast pine forests have been compared to the Russian taiga in their remoteness and inaccessibility, and scientists were slow to visit the area. William Wells, an American mining engineer who visited in the 1850s, found "inexpressibly sad" the "dreary solitudes" of the "deep pine forests, silent but for the murmur of the breeze in their tops." Wells also found deer "so abundant . . . that it is usual to travel with a gun slung across the shoulders." He thought that the scenery of Olancho "exceeded anything I had ever seen, both for softness of outline and splendor of coloring . . . a prairie, varied with broad undulations, and covered with deep grass and flowers . . . an ocean of gold and green undulating in the purple tints of sunlight!" Biologist Archie Carr, who lived in Honduras in the 1950s, wrote that the cloud forests of its high valleys "surpass in stateliness anything in my experiences."

Honduras has suffered considerable deforestation (over half of its original forest cover) largely because of expanding agriculture and ranching. Logging has been heavy in recent decades. Commercial forests have been cut faster than they can regenerate, and degraded through widespread fires in the pinelands. Subsistence farming is also a major cause of forest destruction. Much land in the heavily populated south and west has been permanently degraded by soil erosion, which has driven many small farmers into the eastern rain forest region, where soils are even less fitted for permanent agriculture. Mining and export agriculture also have caused serious pollution with heavy metals, pesticides, and other toxic substances. Illegal exploitation of wildlands and wildlife has been part of the corruption that has plagued the government. Although it is not yet as crowded as El Salvador or Guatemala, Honduras has one of the highest population growth rates in the Western Hemisphere.

Environmental concerns came relatively late to Honduras, which is understandable considering its economic problems. In the 1950s, protecting the La Tigra cloud forest, which supplies the drinking water for Tegucigalpa, became an issue, and the area was declared a national park in 1980. That same year, the Río Plátano Biosphere Reserve was designated, the first such reserve in Central America. In 1986, a group of ecologists and conservationists, the Asociación Hondureño de Ecología, published a report on the country's natural areas which listed the remaining cloud forests as well as reefs, islands, wetlands, dry forests, and rain forests. The national congress used the report as the basis of a 1987 law establishing thirty-seven new protected areas. Honduras presently has over a hundred protected areas, including fifteen national parks: over 7 percent of land is under a protected category.

The government didn't establish a functional system for administering the areas, however. The park system recently was placed under the national forestry service, COHDEFOR, which lacks the resources to protect all the new parks. Most of them still don't have on-site management, and farmers and ranchers have invaded many. To some extent, the U.S. Peace Corps (which had its largest mission in the world in Honduras in the 1980s) assumed the role of Honduras's "park service," putting many volunteers to work on park development and community relations. The Peace Corps' Tegucigalpa office is on the Ave. República de Chile a half block uphill from the Hotel Honduras Maya. It has a library of natural resource information.

Presently, COHDEFOR's Wildlife and Wildlands Department

retains overall responsibility for protected areas. COHDEFOR's main office is in San Pedro Sula at Ave. 10 and Calle 4 North (phone: 53-4959). It increasingly delegates day-to-day management to nongovernmental organizations or local governments, however. There are over eighty-seven NGOs. MOPAWI is concerned with protecting natural and cultural resources in the Mosquitia. Its address is Aptdo. 2175, Tegucigalpa, D.C. (phone: 37-7210; fax: 504-37-2864). Its Tegucigalpa office is on an unnamed street off the Ave. Gutenberg a half block north of the Hotel Granada, Barrio Guanacaste. The Fundación Cuero y Salado (FUCSA) administers the Cuero y Salado Wildlife Refuge on the coast east of La Ceiba, where it has an office: mailing address–Apdo. 122, La Ceiba (phone: 43-0032/0204/2971; fax: 43-0329/1391). In 1992, the office was on Ave. 1 east of Ave. Atlantida, but apparently it has moved to Edificio Reyes, No. 5 (second floor), Calle San Isidro, by Carrion's Dept. Store.

Despite their economic problems (or perhaps to some degree because of them), Hondurans have a growing environmental awareness. When I met some farmers who were planting a bean field on the edge of one park, they were aware of the dangers of deforestation and soil erosion, even though it was land scarcity that had driven them into the park. They said they planned to convert to tree crops eventually. In 1992, public opinion forced the government to back away from an agreement with a U.S. corporation, Stone Container, which would have resulted in widespread clearcutting for pulpwood in the Mosquitia. In 1994, environmentalists, fishermen, and indigenous people formed a coalition to oppose a huge oil refinery proposed for Puerto Castilla on the Caribbean near Trujillo. Financed by Arab investors, the refinery was planned to replace U.S. refineries closed because they were unable to meet federal Clean Air Act requirements.

Tegucigalpa

Although it didn't become the capital until 1880, Tegucigalpa retains more of an old-fashioned quality than much older capitals. This is partly because it is outside earthquake and volcano zones, and so it hasn't been destroyed, and partly because the city of San Pedro Sula to the north has become Honduras's commercial and financial center. Tegucigalpa still is the largest city, with a population of about 800,000. Tegucigalpa's natural setting is also rather constraining: it's at about 900 meters in elevation in a narrow valley surrounded by peaks. The canyon of the Choluteca River cuts through the valley and separates the original small settlements of Comayagüela and Tegucigalpa which coalesced to form the present city.

One effect of these constraints on Tegucigalpa's growth has been to make it a fairly pleasant place for travelers. The highland site provides a mainly temperate climate, with cool nights. It seldom rains from December through April. Although some facilities such as the national university have moved to the suburbs, the city remains unusually compact and thus easy to get around in. You can walk across most of the "tourist" parts in an hour or so. Public buildings are in fairly good shape, and street crime is not prevalent in the downtown (although more so in the less affluent Comayagüela area). The downtown is also fairly clean, and although there are crowds, they aren't dense or turbulent enough to be stressful. Of course, all this is marred by air pollution, not only from cars and industry but from the terribly polluted streams that run through the city and diffuse bad smells to nearby blocks.

Downtown Tegucigalpa is laid out in a very irregular grid pattern, with *"avenidas"* running east-west and *"calles"* north-south. A central avenue, called the Peatonal, is a pedestrian walkway with shops and street vendors. It passes the Parque Central, a large plaza which contains the national cathedral. The Avenida Miguel de Cervantes at the south end of town continues across a tributary of the Río Choluteca and becomes the Avenida República de Chile, which runs through the hilly, upscale Colonia Palmira, where many restaurants, shopping centers, and cinemas are located. Several bridges lead south across the Choluteca to the Comayagüela district, but walking there is considered less safe than in Tegucigalpa, particularly at night. Outside this core area, things become much more spread out, with roaring thoroughfares leading to various suburban facilities. Frequent and inexpensive city buses run to the outskirts from the north and south sides of the central plaza and other stops. The tourism kiosk on the north side of the plaza has schedule information.

Transportation

Travelers with passports from the U.S., Canada, Australia, New Zealand, Japan, and West European countries don't need visas for a 30-day stay. Extensions of 30 days, for up to 6 months, are easy to obtain at immigration offices in major cities. Proof of vaccination is required from travelers arriving within 6 days from areas infected with yellow fever or cholera. A ticket out of the country is required for entry, and travelers entering by land may be required to show proof of adequate funds. A $12.00 departure tax is payable at the airport.

INTERNATIONAL AIRLINES: American Airlines (800-433-7300) and El Salvador's Taca Airlines (800-535-8780) fly to Tegucigalpa via Miami. Continental (800-525-0280) flies via Houston. Costa Rica's Lacsa Airlines (800-225-2272) flies via Los Angeles and New Orleans.

DOMESTIC FLIGHTS: Sosa, Sami, and Isleña airlines have flights from Tocontín Airport to San Pedro Sula, La Ceiba, the Bay Islands, and the Mosquitia.

The national airport, Tocontín, is located 6.5 kilometers south of town along the narrow, frequently congested Carretara del Sur. It is an old, small airport, and is being superseded by the newer one at San Pedro Sula. Nos. 1 and 11 Loarque buses leave Tocontín Airport every 20 minutes from the left-hand side of the parking lot. Fare is about $.05. Buses for the airport leave from Ave. 4 between calles 6 and 7 in Comayagüela, and from opposite the Cine Palace in downtown Tegucigalpa. Taxi fare to or from the airport should be about $3.00.

ROADS: About 12 percent of Honduran roads are paved, generally the ones linking the larger cities. Stretches of even these roads may be in an ongoing state of rebuilding. Most unpaved roads are passable in all weather, however, and bus service is available on most roads, although it becomes less frequent and comfortable the more remote the area. Taxis are unmetered, so find out what the fare is before you hire a cab; if it seems high, you may be able to bargain. Hitchhiking is easy: ask if the driver wants to be paid.

The U.S. State Department advises that road travel between Nicaragua and Honduras, even on major highways, is potentially dangerous, and that travelers can expect a lengthy and meticulous search of vehicles and belongings at all crossings. The Honduras–El Salvador border is also classified as an area of instability.

BUSES: Tica Bus provides international bus service to other Central American capitals, leaving from the Condesa Inn, Ave. 7, Calle 12, Comayagüela, daily at 9 A.M. Advance booking is recommended. Most domestic bus lines also have terminals in Comayagüela.

CAR RENTAL: National, Budget, Avis, Hertz, and Molinari have rental offices in the Hotel Honduras Maya, Ave. República de Chile. Hertz has an office at Tocontín Airport. Local and international driving licenses are accepted. As elsewhere, leaving a car unprotected for any length of time, particularly in cities, is likely to lead to theft.

TRAIN: A single passenger ferrobus runs between San Pedro Sula and Puerto Cortés. A narrow-gauge railway originally built by Standard Fruit to service one of its plantations now provides access to Cuerro y Salado Wildlife Refuge on the north coast: see that section, below, for details.

U.S. Embassy

Avenida La Paz, APO AA 34022 (phone: 32-3120; fax: 32-0027). The embassy is located at the north end of Colonia Palmira. "San Felipe" buses from the north side of the Parque Central in downtown Tegucigalpa stop there.

Health Advisory

Cholera is active, and appropriate precautions should be taken. Malaria risk occurs year-round, mostly in coastal lowlands below

500-meters elevation and along the Nicaraguan border. Chloro-quine remains the drug of choice for prophylaxis. Risk of rabies is considered higher than in other Central American countries, and preexposure rabies vaccination is an option for travelers spending more than a month in the country. Tap water generally is not safe to drink unless boiled or otherwise treated: this is true for Tegu-cigalpa and other large cities as well as smaller towns. Dysentery and stomach parasites are common.

HOSPITALS: Hospital Esuela, Tegucigalpa (phone: 32-2322), is a government hospital with 400 beds; Hospital Leonardo Martinez, San Pedro Sula (phone: 32-2322), has 286 beds. Policlínica and Viera are private hospitals.

Hotels

The Hotel Honduras Maya (phone 32-3191) is very expensive ($121 single) but its restaurant is excellent for breakfasts, meetings, etc. Next door, the Hotel Plaza San Martin on the Plaza San Martin in Colonia Palmira is somewhat less expensive. Downtown, the Plaza Hotel on Ave. Paz Barahona across from the post office is an-other upscale hotel (phone: 37-0182). A midpriced hotel is the Ist-mania at Ave. 5 between calles 7–8 (phone: 37-1638). The most highly recommended inexpensive hotel is the Nuevo Boston, Ave. Jerez No. 321 (between calles Morelos and El Telegrapho) with rooms from $6.59 to $9.00 (phone: 37-9411). The Excelsior, Ave. Cervantes 515 (just past the bridge leading to Colonia Palmira) has clean, quiet rooms if you don't mind the smell from the nearby river (phone: 37-2638). The Granada, Ave. Gutenberg 1401, Barrio Guanacaste, and its annex a block and a half away, offer good rooms from $6.25 to $7.10, mostly with hot water (phone: 37-2318). There are many inexpensive hotels in Comayagüela, con-venient to the bus stations. The Condesa Inn, Ave. 7, Calle 12, is the Tica Bus departure point. The San Pedro at Ave. 6 between calles 8 and 9 is also near bus stations. The Centenario, Ave. 6, calles 9–10, is a little more than most places in the area, about the same as the Nuevo Boston, but is recommended (phone: 37-1050) and has a safe parking lot.

Restaurants

The best restaurant serving Honduran food is El Patio, which has two locations: downtown near the Parque Central on Ave. Dolores half a block from the Peatonal, and in Colonia Palmira on the Boulevard Morazán. José y Pepe's on Ave. República de Panama has excellent Mexican food. The Hungry Fisherman, Ave. República de Chile 209, Colonia Palmira, has good seafood. Alondra, near the Hotel Maya, has gourmet food at reasonable prices. Less expensive, and my favorite place in Tegucigalpa, is Café Allegro, Ave. República de Chile 360, Colonia Palmira (phone: 32-8122), which has excellent, imaginative pastas (including a very good one made with peanut sauce) and a very friendly, even homey atmosphere. It also has good coffee and desserts, books and magazines for sale, and information on ecotourist destinations such as parks and reefs. It's the place to go if you want to meet Peace Corps volunteers or others active in conservation (volunteers stay in rooms above the restaurant when they're in Tegucigalpa). Downtown, Marbella at Calle 6 between aves. 3–4 has good breakfasts, and Al Natural, Calle Hipolito Matute and Ave. Miguel de Cervantes, has vegetarian dishes (also meat) and fruit drinks in a garden atmosphere that includes tiny gecko lizards on the walls (service was a bit slow). There are a number of Chinese restaurants, including La Gran Muralla in Barrio Guanacaste and On-Lock on Blvd. Morazán, generally quite good. There are three Pizza Huts, one near the Parque Central with a good salad bar. Dunkin Donuts and Burger Kings are also popular. La Terraza de Don Pepe on Calle La Fuente two blocks west of the Parque Central has a band playing in the evenings.

Communications

The main post office is at Ave. Miguel de Cervantes and Calle Morelos, four blocks west of the Parque Central.

Hondutel, Calle 5 and Ave. 4, has phone, fax, and telegraph service, and is open 24 hours.

Money Exchange

Honduran currency is the lempira, which comprises 100 centavos. In 1994, the international rate of exchange was around eight lempiras to the U.S. dollar.

Many banks (Lloyds, Banco Atlantida, Banco de Honduras, Banco de Ahorro Hondureño) change traveler's checks into lempiras for a commission. Banking hours are 9–3, weekdays. American Express has an agent office at Mundirama Travel Agency, Edif. Ciisa, Ave. República de Panama, Colonia Palmira. MasterCard, American Express, Diners Club, and Visa credit cards are accepted. Traveler's checks and credit cards are hard to use away from cities.

There are money changers in front of the Plaza Hotel across from the post office, and on the Peatonal around the Parque Central. These may provide better rates than banks, but it may be necessary to bargain.

Tourist Information

The Instituto Hondureño de Turismo has an information office at Tocontín Airport, and a booth at the northwest corner of the Parque Central. Their main office is at Edificio Europa, Ave. Ramón E. Cruz and Calle República de Mexico above Lloyds Bank, Colonia Palmira (phone: 22-2124/6618). Hours are 7:30–3:30. They also have offices at San Pedro Sula, Ocotepeque, Copán, and Roatán.

Maps

The Instituto Geografico Nacional publishes the most up-to-date tourist maps of Honduras and Tegucigalpa, available at a few dollars each, also sectional topographical maps on a scale of 1:50,000, geological maps, and regional maps. Their office is in Comayagüela at Ave. 3 and Calle 14 (Aptdo. 20706, Comayagüela, D.C.), open 7:30–3:30 weekdays. Paperwork for buying from them involves selecting the map and getting an invoice at their office, taking it to window 21 at the Palacio del Distrito Central in downtown Tegucigalpa to pay, then returning to the IGN office to pick up the map. The Hotel Honduras Maya bookshop may sell the institute's 1:100,000 map, which shows many dirt roads unmarked elsewhere, and is useful for bicycling and hiking. Hotels, bookshops, and souvenir shops also sell maps. A new map showing national parks was published in 1994.

Museums and Zoos

The Museo Nacional Villa Roy has exhibits on Honduran archaeology and indigenous cultures, and is developing exhibits on post-independence history. It is located on a hill at the northwest end of Tegucigalpa's downtown. Follow the Peatonal west to the Calle Morelos, then turn north (right) and walk six long blocks. The museum is up a drive to the right, in a large blue house that once belonged to former President Julio Lozano Díaz. Hours are 8:30–3:30 Wed.–Sun. There is a small restaurant. The offices and library of the Honduran Institute of Anthropology and History are also located here. A few blocks away on Ave. Las Delicias is Parque la Concordia, with reproductions of Mayan ruins and a view of the city.

A small zoo with mostly native animals is located on El Picacho, a peak north of the city. It's open Thurs.– Sun., $.25 admission. (A resident describes the zoo as "old-style, very depressing.") There are buses to the United Nations Park on the summit on Sundays, leaving from Farmacia Santa Bárbara behind the Los Dolores Church (Ave. Máximo Jerez and Calle los Dolores). Taxi fare from that point on other days should be $2–3.

A small Museo de Fauna is located in the Life Science building at the National University. The university is interesting: a collection of impressive high-rises on a windswept plain east of the city. The Life Science building is toward the back, at the edge of a ravine on the slope of which native plants are being grown. The museum is in a room above the central courtyard: you may have to ask the "*dueño*" (proprietor) to open it for you. It has Pliocene and Pleistocene fossils and exhibits on living fauna, also a small library.

Bookstores and Libraries

Book Village, Centro Comercial los Castaños, Blvd. Morazán (phone: 33-4858), has books in English for sale or trade and U.S.

magazines. The Hotel Honduras Maya and the Café Allegro also have English books and magazines.

Editorial Guaymuras, 1055 Ave. Miguel de Cervantes, has books in Spanish, including books on Central America and Honduras.

The Instituto Hondureño de Cultura Interamericana, Calle Real de Comayagüela, has an English library and schedules cultural events (phone: 37-7539). The libraries at the Peace Corps office and the Honduran Institute of Anthropology and Archaeology (see above) are available to visitors: most material is in Spanish.

Excursions Around Tegucigalpa

Honduras's first national park, La Tigra, is a few dozen kilometers' drive from Tegucigalpa, although it's not possible to do a day trip there unless you have a vehicle because of limited bus service. Most of the park's cloud forest and pine forest is second-growth, having been cut to provide timbers and fuel for the many mines in the area, but the 7,482-hectare park still has plenty of beautiful vegetation and some wildlife. Pumas, ocelots, quetzals, and many other bird species live there. The park is over a thousand meters higher than Tegucigalpa (its highest point is the summit of El Picacho, at 2,270 meters), and temperatures can drop to near-freezing at night. Trails are steep, and may be slippery and unstable because of the continually damp conditions in the cloud forest.

There are two entrances to the park, both with visitor centers. The closest to Tegucigalpa is the La Tigra visitor center above the town of Jutiapa 24 kilometers from Tegucigalpa. A bus goes to Jutiapa via El Hatillo daily at 1 P.M., leaving from behind El Dolores Church (Ave. Máximo Jerez and Calle los Dolores), and returns to the city at 4 P.M. The visitor center is several kilometers past the end of the bus line. You may be able to stay overnight at the visitor center if you bring your own food and bedding.

The other entrance, the most visited, is El Rosario visitor center in the abandoned mining town of that name 4 kilometers above the town of San Juancito, 35 kilometers from Tegucigalpa. To get to San Juancito, a bus leaves daily from the San Pablo Market (located at the northeast edge of Tegucigalpa) at 10 A.M. (weekends at 8

A.M.) and passes through the Valle de Angeles. There is a small hotel, Hospedaje Don Jacinto, in San Juancito, and there are plans for more tourism developments at the former mining town. The climb to the visitor center is steep. Visitors can stay overnight on a first-come, first-served basis at El Rosario. Bring food and bedding.

An old road connects El Rosario with La Tigra, making it possible to hike across the park between the two visitor centers. Check at the centers for present trail conditions.

The Lake Yojoa Region

Although the zone of fault valleys that runs south from the Ulua River Valley to the Gulf of Fonseca is Honduras's most populated area, it still has some beautiful wildlands. The center of these is 22-kilometer-long Lake Yojoa. The lake is in a graben at about 700 meters in elevation, 75 kilometers south of San Pedro Sula and 124 kilometers northwest of Tegucigalpa. Because of its relative proximity to the humid coast, lush tropical vegetation grows around the lake, while the mountains that loom around it have old-growth cloud forest and conifer forest. Although national parks have been designated on these mountains, they are little explored, and rather difficult of access.

The roughly 10-kilometer-wide lake is natural, fed largely by underground runoff from surrounding peaks, and draining into nearby streams via subterranean springs. Early in this century, it was surrounded by rain forest and inhabited by large crocodiles. Since then, much of the surrounding land has been cleared for agriculture, the lake's level has been raised by a dam, and a canal has been built to supply hydroelectric power. Agricultural runoff has caused some eutrophication of the lake, and heavy metals drainage from a nearby mine at El Mochito has also caused pollution. Introduction of largemouth bass from North America and tilapia from Africa has changed the lake's aquatic fauna. Despite these problems, the lake is still very beautiful, with cool green wetlands of sedges and rushes inhabited by a wide variety of waterbirds (two hundred bird species have been observed in the vicinity). Thirty percent of the lake has been set aside as a nature reserve, and tropical forest still grows along much of its banks. Much of the lake is

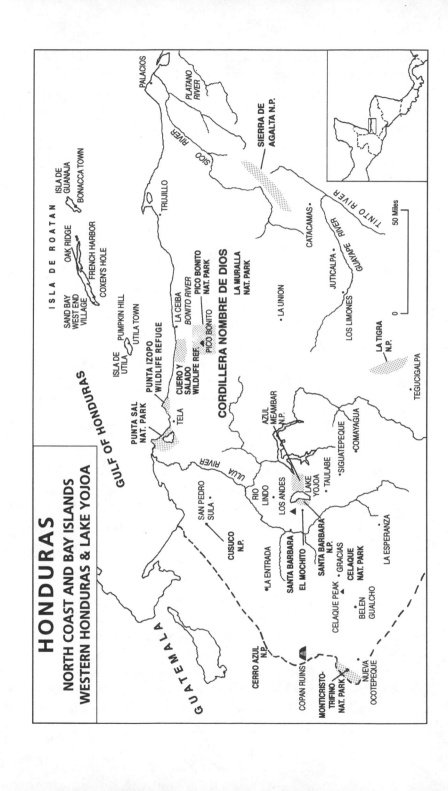

bordered with orange-blossomed *Symphonia* trees, a common waterside genus in Central America.

Lake Yojoa is easily accessible by the main road between Tegucigalpa and San Pedro Sula. It's three hours from Tegucigalpa, and any bus to San Pedro Sula will stop at the lake. Buses leave frequently from a number of stations: the corner of Calle 9 and Ave. 6, Comayagüela (El Rey, 37-1462); Calle 12, aves. 7 and 8, Comayagüela (Saenz, 37-6521); calles 13 and 14, Ave. 11, Comayagüela (Hedman Alas, 37-7143); Calle 12, aves. 6 and 7 (Norteños, 37-0706). From San Pedro Sula: El Rey, calles 5 and 6, Ave. 7; Saenz, Calle 9 sur, aves. 9 and 10; Hedman Alas, Calle 3, aves. 7 and 8 norte.

Probably the best place to stay at Lake Yojoa from a naturalist's viewpoint is the Motel Agua Azul, which is at the north end of the lake about 3 kilometers west of the main road on the road to Peña Blanca. There is a sign for the motel at the turnoff. You can wait at a restaurant across from the turnoff for occasional buses that run past the motel, or hitchhike. The motel management is active in a foundation for lake conservation, Ecolago, and its grounds and surrounding areas are a nature preserve, although the motel's main clients so far have been bass fishermen, many from the U.S. armed forces. Birding is good around the motel's cabins, which straggle up a wooded hill. Tropical species such as motmots mix with temperate ones. You can rent a rowboat and row through a marshy wetland populated by jacanas, gallinules, herons, and Everglades kites to a forested island with a large population of chachalacas (who make their presence known at dawn with a chorus of "chachalaca"), as well as toucans and parrots. The lake is often turbid with algae, but when it clears you can see many cichlid species, particularly around the motel dock, where the fish breed among the rocks. There may be some crocodiles still hiding in the wetlands, although I didn't see any. Frogs make loud "bu-bu-bu-bu" calls around the lake at night.

Fees are about $9 per night for a single and $16 for a double room, with simple and aged but comfortable furnishings and private baths with hot showers. There are also six-bed cottages for $25 a night. There's a restaurant specializing in lake-caught fish

with a veranda overlooking the lake. It may get crowded on weekends. The phone is 57-0955 or 52-7125, in San Pedro Sula, Apdo.
1031. When I was there in 1992, the owner was planning to start
running overnight horseback tours into the nearby national parks.
Bass fishermen can rent boats with or without guides: some of the
biggest largemouth bass ever caught came from the lake.

At the south end of the lake, near the main road, is Restaurante
y Balneario Los Remos, which has 19 rooms for about $7 single.
They also rent boats, and the restaurant has a beautiful view of the
lake from the balcony. There are many inexpensive comedores
around the lake specializing in bass.

Taulabe Caverns

Much of the bedrock around Lake Yojoa is limestone, in which
groundwater has carved extensive caverns. One of these is located
near the Tegucigalpa–San Pedro Sula Road 12 kilometers south of
Lake Yojoa, a mile north of the town of Taulabe. The 400-meter
cavern has stalactites, stalagmites, and other structures formed by
the deposition of dissolved calcium carbonate as water drips from
the cave ceiling. Some of Honduras's one hundred bat species live
in the cave. The cave is open daily, and has guides and illumination.

Pulhapanzák Waterfall

A spectacular waterfall is located about 11 kilometers north of
Peña Blanca, the town northwest of the lake. The area is a private
park, and there is a small admissions charge. The waterfall is over
25 meters high and 12 meters wide. Pools at its base provide excellent swimming. You can get there by taking the San Pedro Sula
bus that passes through Peña Blanca on its way to El Mochito and
asking the driver to let you off at Pulhapanzák village. The waterfall is about a kilometer from the village. There are some unexcavated ruins in the vicinity. The waterfall is on the Río Lindo. It may
get crowded on weekends.

Santa Bárbara National Park

About 3,000 hectares of the extremely steep limestone ridge west
of Lake Yojoa has been designated as a national park, including the

2,736-meter peak which is Honduras's second highest point. The forest in this area is remarkable in that northern and southern tree species are mixed together to an unusual degree. Paul H. Allen, who climbed the range in 1951, wrote: "Tracts of broadleaf woodland are to be found in close proximity to stands of pine and oak, and perhaps might be compared to a giant projection both in size and relief of the Florida Everglades, with each hill and depression a sort of gargantuan 'hammock' which may support either a basically North American or South American flora, the margins of which may be separated from one another by only a few yards." After climbing the cliffs that surround the summit, Allen found a forest of fir, yew, cypress, and pine, with an understory of oak, ragwort, blueberry, lobelia, and other northern plants, relics of the glacial age.

Cerro Santa Bárbara is no easier to climb today than it was in 1951: there's no trail to its cliff-ringed summit. A number of trails lead to its lower slopes, but they're not well marked and, because heavily used by local people, tend to be muddy and confusing. One way to reach the park is via the mountain village of Los Andes between Peña Blanca and El Mochito. A COHDEFOR *"guardabosque"* (forest ranger) and possibly a Peace Corps volunteer are stationed in the village, and may be able to guide you up the trail to the park. Check with the Peace Corps office in Tegucigalpa. You can take an El Mochito bus at Peña Blanca and ask the driver to let you off at the turnoff to Los Andes. From there it's a steep two-hour's walk (with plenty of time to rest) to the village. It's a typical backcountry village, friendly but very poor, with no public facilities: you'll have to improvise. Views of Lake Yojoa and the surrounding mountains are spectacular.

You can hike from the village to the center of the park and back in a single day, on a trail that eventually leads across the park to the town of Santa Bárbara in the valley to the west. After a very steep and slippery climb, first through bean and corn fields, then through dense second-growth, the trail levels off into a limestone plateau covered in heavy old-growth cloud forest. The ground is often hidden by several feet of vines and other plants. Peccaries, quetzals, trogons, guans, and other wildlife live in the forest, but are hard to see because of its density, and because of almost omnipresent mist. The limestone bedrock erodes so quickly that the ground is pitted with sinkholes, and there's a spectacular rock shelter just north of the trail at one point. A very weird landscape. Paul H. Allen wrote: "Some of the largest trees were found to be perched on limestone blocks 5–8 feet in height, which would seem to indicate that the apparently solid stone is actually almost as soluble as rock salt, and that the trees, probably in no instance more than a century or two old, may have begun life when the tops of these pedestals were on the level of, or below, the soil."

Another trail leads from El Mochito at the southwest side of the lake and intersects with the one from Los Andes just before the park, but neither trail is easy to follow.

You can also enter the park from Santa Bárbara, accessible by bus from Tegucigalpa at 6 A.M. Tuesdays, Thursdays, and Saturdays on Transportes Junqueños from Calle 12, Ave. 8, Comayagüela. Santa Bárbara is a small, pleasant city that specializes in handicrafts like hats, baskets, and rugs. There are caves and hot springs near it. The Boarding House Moderno at Barrio Arriba (phone: 64-2203) has rooms with hot showers for about $7. Try Doña Ana's comedor for meals, near the Cruz Roja office. The Asociación Ecológica Corazón Verde, Apdo. 28, Santa Bárbara, may have information about the trail into the park.

Azul Meámbar National Park

This 2,000-hectare park protecting pine and cloud forests in the mountains east of Lake Yojoa is even more remote and little known than Santa Bárbara. For this reason, more wildlife is believed to survive there, including quetzals and pumas on the higher slopes, and jaguars and monkeys on the lower. The park has no visitor facilities or maintained trails. For more information, contact COHDEFOR or the Project de Desarrollo Río Yure, San Isidro, Cortés, Apdo. 1149, Tegucigalpa. The NGO Aldeas Globales is in charge of park management (phone: 32-8287; fax: 31-4328).

Cusuco National Park

This 25-square-kilometer park northeast of San Pedro Sula is about 30 kilometers north of the town of Cofradia on the road between

San Pedro Sula and Copán. The gravel road is passable all year by 4wd vehicles. The park protects cloud forest with large quetzal populations. There are interpretive trails, and a visitor center was under construction in 1994. Contact the Fundación Ecológica Hector Pastor in San Pedro Sula (phone: 53-3397; fax: 53-0175).

The North Coast

This is the classic "banana country," and much land is still in banana cultivation, but it's *not* the stereotyped, sweltering "tropical hellhole." In fact, Honduras's north coast is one of the most scenic parts of Central America, and provides some of the most varied and interesting outdoor opportunities. Rain forest—covered mountains rise so dramatically from the Caribbean that you wonder why this area hasn't attracted more photographers. Perhaps one reason is that much of these mountains remains trackless. Pico Bonito National Park just south of La Ceiba contains the highest peak on the north coast, which has seldom been climbed (more because of the density of its vegetation than of height or steepness). The Bay Islands a few dozen kilometers offshore have become one of the most popular destinations for snorkelers and scuba divers in Central America, and have a wide range of facilities, from luxury resorts to budget hotels. The coast itself has some fine wildlife refuges, with manatees and crocodiles living among old-growth mangrove forest, as well as some very pleasant seaside towns, with good beaches and the colorful influence of Garífuna culture.

The small city of La Ceiba about midway along the coast has become the area's tourism hub. Its airport provides access to the Bay Islands (as well as to the Mosquitia), and some important protected areas are nearby. Developed as a banana port, La Ceiba has been superseded to some extent by Puerto Cortés to the east, so it is free of the heavy pollution of a big industrial port. It's a typical Caribbean city, noisy and untidy, but friendly. Carnaval, on the third week of May, is a big event, with dancing in the streets. The downtown is compact, with most hotels and restaurants near the Ave. San Isidro, which runs southward from the beach eight blocks to the central plaza. The Ave. de la República on the other side of the plaza runs out to the pier. The best beaches are east of town, across a bridge on Calle 1, at Barrio la Isla and toward the mouth of the

Río Cangrejal. (Watch out for theft on beaches.) A Honduran Tourism Institute (IHT) office is on the waterfront at Calle 1 and Ave. San Isidro, next to the municipal library: they also have a kiosk at the central plaza.

You can fly to La Ceiba from Tocontín Airport in Tegucigalpa for less than $20 on Isleña and other airlines. Getting tickets through local travel agents is easiest. You can also fly directly to La Ceiba from Miami and New Orleans. La Ceiba's airport, Golosón, is about 10 kilometers out of town. Baggage is likely to be searched when you arrive. Taxis to downtown just outside the airport cost about $2, but you can get a cheaper taxi or a bus if you walk out to the main road, about 200 meters. Direct bus service to La Ceiba from Tegucigalpa (otherwise you have to go to San Pedro Sula and change) is via the coastal town of Tela on Traliasa aves. 7 and 8, Calle 10, Comayagüela, and Mi Esperanza, Calle 6, Ave. 23, Comayagüela. Fare is about $5. From San Pedro Sula, buses to Tela and La Ceiba leave hourly from Ave. 2 norte and calles 1 and 2. The La Ceiba bus station is west of town along the Boulevard 15 de Septiembre. A taxi should be about $.40, or you can get a city bus there at the plaza.

The Hotel Colonial on Ave. 14 de Julio between calles 6 and 7 (phone: 34-1953; fax: 43-1955) has air-conditioned rooms with cable TV in the $20–30 range, with a pool and restaurant. The Hotel Iberia on Ave. San Isidro and Calle 5 has large air-conditioned rooms around a courtyard at $10–20 (phone: 43-0410); it's a nice quiet place, but don't try the restaurant. Italia, near the Hotel Colonial, is comparable. On the beach, the Hotel Partenon Beach at Calle 1 and Ave. Dionisio Herrera (phone: 43-0404) is comparable to the Colonial. There are several budget places near the beach, including the Amsterdam, 2001 on Calle 1 and Ave. Miguel Paz Barahona, four blocks east of the bridge, and the Hotel La Isla at Calle 4 and Ave. Pedro Nunó.

The cafe of La Ceiba's most expensive hotel (Gran Hotel París) is good for breakfast and lunch. It's called Le Petit Café and is at the north end of the plaza. Ricardo's on Ave. 14 de Julio near the cathedral has good, expensive food in a garden setting. The Palace on Calle 9 between aves. San Isidro and 14 de Julio is a good, mid-

priced, Chinese restaurant—try the noodle soups. The Pizzeria Ita-
liana on Ave. de la República a block from the plaza has nice atmosphere and good pizza. For Honduran food, La Carreta on Calle
4, Ave. 2, has an open-air setting. Paty's at Ave. 14 de Julio between
calles 6 and 7 has juices, milkshakes, etc.

Pico Bonito National Park

This park, over 50,000 hectares, encompasses the central part of
the massive Nombre de Dios cordillera lying between La Ceiba and
the Aguan River to the south. Its highest point is Pico Bonito, at
2,443 meters, visible southeast of La Ceiba (but it's said to take
nine days of climbing to *get* there). From La Ceiba you can also see
the massive waterfalls that cascade down the the peak's slopes.
Habitats in the park range from very wet rain forest on lower seaward slopes, to cloud and pine forest at higher elevations, to semidesert in the rain shadow of the peaks on the southern side. Cloud
forest starts at about 1,800 meters: there are three large cloud forest areas in the park.

Pico Bonito probably has the largest concentration of endangered species of any Honduran protected area. These include the
three native monkey species (howler, spider, and capuchin), jaguars, tapirs, brocket deer, and quetzals. Even from a distance, it's
not hard to see why this should be: the park is a veritable natural
fortress, with dizzyingly steep slopes cut by narrow, even steeper
gorges. The Asociación Hondureño de Ecología report, *Areas Silvestres de Honduras,* noted that tapir trails were the only trails on
most of the mountains. In the buffer zone of the park are the offices
of AMARAS, a wild bird rehabilitation center that tries to reestablish parrots, macaws, and other birds in the wild.

There's a good day hike into the park from La Ceiba. Take the
Ruta 1 de Mayo city bus (which starts from Parque Bonilla at Ave.
14 de Julio between calles 1 and 4) out to the town of Armenia Bonito, about an hour's ride to the west. From the end of the bus line,
follow a dirt road that leads toward the peaks (which seem to get
larger very rapidly as you walk). The road runs past a soccer field
and some houses, which get poorer as you go southward, then
winds through some shady cacao plantations (note the purplish ca-

cao pods hanging from the trunks). You'll come to a turnoff to the left, but keep straight, and the road leads into rocky pastures, then fords a north-running stream. From there, the way leads past a homestead (watch out for dogs) and more pastures down to the Bonito River, a clear stream dotted with massive red boulders and bordered with big, colorful trees. Pico Bonito and its attendant bluffs and waterfalls rise directly above this spot, and it is one of the most beautiful places I've seen, a kind of epitome of tropical splendor. When I was there, a rainbow arced overhead, a common phenomenon in the wet climate, and large flocks of emerald green parakeets billowed around the trees, the sun glittering on their plumage as it played through the clouds. The scene was like a painting by Frederick Church. The river is full of fish—mollies, cichlids, and gobies. Several kingfisher species fly up and down.

From this spot, the road turns back from the river and ascends past some more pasture into the foothills of the park. There are no more homesteads past here (or weren't in 1992), so the road is easy to follow. Soon you start getting into forest, where you may see parrots, toucans, possibly monkeys. About 5 kilometers from the bus stop, the road dead-ends at a *"campamento"* (campsite) owned by the Centro Universitario Regional del Litoral Atlántico. When I was there in 1992, the house and clearing there were deserted and appeared abandoned (the steps to the porch had rotted away), but there may have been some facilities added since. From the campamento a short trail runs to what is evidently a branch of the Bonito River, but which is quite different from the riverbank place lower down. The forest here is so heavy as to be permanently dark, and the river is deep and turbulent, crashing over massive boulders. You may be able to stay overnight at the campamento: check with COHDEFOR, which has an office outside of La Ceiba in the Barrio Buenos Aires (phone: 42-0800).

Another foothill walk is at Eco-Zona Río María east of La Ceiba on the road to Trujillo. A signed path leads off the road about 9 kilometers east of La Ceiba, just before the Balneario los Chorros, a swimming place with a refreshment stand nearby. There are many beautiful waterfalls on the Río Zacate. About an hour up the trail is a spectacular waterfall about 30 meters high. There is a small tourist area at the first fall.

Whitewater rafting on the Cangrejal River that descends from Pico Bonito is increasingly popular. Ríos Honduras (in affiliation with the Rocky Mountain Outdoor Center in Howard, Colorado) offers frequent trips on the Cangrejal from November to February. Contact Caribbean Travel Agency, Ave. San Isidro, Edificio Hermanas Kawas in La Ceiba (phone: 43-1360; fax: 43-1360), or Pepe Herrera, executive director of Fundación Cuero y Salado (see below). The river has many Class V rapids; the entire first half hour of the trip is said to be continual rapids.

Cuero y Salado Wildlife Refuge

This 13,225-hectare refuge is located between the Cuero and Salado rivers on the coast about 35 kilometers west of La Ceiba. The refuge is mainly mangrove swamp in the estuaries of the two rivers, although the mangroves are so big (as much as 30 meters tall) that it looks like rain forest. A recent census of the refuge found twenty to thirty manatees, which was more than was found in a country-wide survey in the 1970s. The manatees live mainly on the ocean side of the reserve, where a barrier beach provides a lot of lagoon habitat. The refuge was established because the manatee population was thought to be stable and reproducing. There's subsistence fishing for robalo (snook), sabalete, and guapote, but fishermen are required to use lines instead of nets to prevent accidental manatee drownings. Crocodiles and otters survive in the waterways, and the foundation was planning to reintroduce caimans in 1992. Collared peccary, white-tailed deer, paca, two-toed sloth, and possibly a few tapirs and jaguars live in the mangrove forest, along with howler and white-faced capuchin monkeys. In 1992, there were twelve howler troops of five to seven individuals each in the refuge.

The Cuero y Salado Foundation (FUCSA) has managed the refuge since 1987. You should coordinate a visit through their La Ceiba office, which is also a good place for information on the area in general. Their office is in Edificio Reyes, Calle San Isidro next to Carrion's Dept. Store (phone: 43-2971/0329; fax: 43-1391/0204). (In 1992 it was at Calle 1 just east of Ave. Atlántida near the beach.) You can pay the roughly $10 refuge entrance fee there, and can arrange for a guide and possibly for transportation to the refuge (when I was there they arranged for me to tag along with a local

Peace Corps volunteer who was visiting). The guide costs about $20, and you'll need one because the only way to get around in the refuge is by boat. Transportation to and from the refuge is also a little involved. You take a bus to the Standard Fruit town of La Unión, about an hour and a half from the La Ceiba bus station (buses leave every two hours, although if you are making a day trip to the refuge and want to get an early start you may want to take a taxi to La Unión before the first bus leaves). In La Unión, you get on a flatbed railway car (a leftover from Standard Fruit, which originally owned the land—the fare is about $8) and travel 9 kilometers past pastures and wetlands to refuge administrative and visitor center. There is an overnight guest house which sleeps four and provides meals: you can arrange to stay (book in advance) for about $5 a night. Getting back to La Ceiba may involve some waiting for the railcar and bus; or you can walk back to the highway along the railroad and across pineapple fields, and get a bus or hitchhike. (If these arrangements seem too involved, you can get one of the travel agencies in La Ceiba to make them for you: when I was there the FUCSA people didn't speak much English.) Agencies are Hondutours, Calle 9, Ave. 14 de Julio (phone: 43-0457); Lafitte, calles 5 and 6, Ave. San Isidro (phone: 43-0115); La Ceiba Ecotours, Hotel París (phone: 43-2391).

The refuge is well worth the trouble of getting there. The railcar ride leads past big flocks of herons, egrets, and other waterbirds, and there's often something interesting going on at headquarters (when I was there a TV crew was filming, and the humane society was releasing two flocks of parrots confiscated from smugglers). A boat trip through the rivers and canals of the refuge proper definitely is one of the best introductions to a high-quality mangrove habitat in Central America. If you go with one of the foundation's guides, you will see and learn a great deal. We saw monkeys, bat falcons, boat-billed herons, tiger herons, anhingas, sungrebes, crocodiles, and iguanas. Basilisk lizards leapt out of trees and ran away across the water. The guide told us, among other things, what howler monkeys mainly eat in the refuge (mangrove leaves and the leaves, flowers, and fruit of a small tree called zapaton), and about Garífuna history and language (he was a Garífuna).

Diver videotaping a school of yellowtail snappers. Photo by Julie Robinson.

The Bay Islands

The three Bay Islands north of La Ceiba are an underwater continuation of the Sierra de Omoa which looms west of San Pedro Sula. The islands were connected to the mainland during the Miocene and Pliocene epochs, but only the closest island, Utila, is now part of the continental shelf. The others are separated from it by a deep trench. The islands have (or had) some fascinating endemic species, some of which may be relics of mainland connection. At least twenty bird species or subspecies are known only from the islands, and four reptiles are known to be endemic, including a coral snake on Roatán (the only poisonous snake on the islands). There's an endemic agouti on Roatán, and until historic times there were peccaries. Deer still survive on Roatán.

The Bay Islands are best known for their underwater habitats. There are three small islands (Morat, Santa Elena, and Barbareta) as well as the three large ones, and sixty-five cays. The clear, warm waters around them support some of the biggest and best coral reefs in the world. There are many underwater caves, and the islands' fame as a diving spot is growing rapidly. There's also some mangrove swamp and eel grass flats. Fishing, lobstering, shrimping, and other marine pursuits are the main activities of the island's population. It is noteworthy (and unusual) that English is the first language of many of the islanders.

The Paya people were the original inhabitants of the islands. They left numerous archaeological remains, and were present when Columbus arrived. Spanish slaving and disease reduced their numbers, and after 1640 Spanish authorities tried to exile the Paya to the mainland to stop them from supplying food to pirates, who used the islands as ports. As many as 5,000 buccaneers may have frequented the vicinity when Henry Morgan had his headquarters on Roatán in the early seventeenth century. The Spanish destroyed Port Royal and drove the pirates away in 1782, leaving the islands depopulated again, but in 1797, British authorities on the island of St. Vincent exiled some 4,000 rebellious Garífuna to Roatán. In the nineteenth century, most of the Garífuna moved to the mainland (they still have a village at Punta Gorda on Roatán), and British and Afro-Caribbean settlers from the Caymans and other islands immigrated to the Bay Islands. They continue to make up the majority of the population, although many ladinos have moved to the islands in recent years. The islands have been Honduran territory since Britain ceded them in 1859, but many islanders still relate as much to the Anglo world as to the Hispanic, calling mainland Hondurans "Spaniards."

Utila

Utila is the smallest island, 13 by 5 kilometers, and the least expensive to visit. It lacks the scenic, travel-poster panache of the other two islands, but it has plenty of interesting qualities. Most of the island's west end is low and wet, ranging from freshwater marsh in the interior to salt marsh and mangrove on the edges. The east end is hilly, a mixture of farmland and woodland, and there are small caves. Sandflies and mosquitoes can be bothersome from September to January. The best beaches for swimming are on some small cays off the southwest coast, about a 40-minute boat ride from Utila town (East Harbor), but there is access to reefs within walking distance of town.

An iguanalike creature called the "*garrobo*" can be seen lounging about the airstrip. When I asked a Honduran biologist if it were one of the endemic reptiles, he said he wasn't sure, adding that a lot of work needs to be done on Honduran fauna. A land tortoise shell was found in the swamps thirty years ago, although tortoises don't live there now. Freshwater turtles live in the swamps, and there may still be crocodiles. In 1992, a Turtle Harbor National Park was proposed to protect a transect from the interior freshwater swamps to the coral reef north of Utila.

You can fly to Utila from La Ceiba on Isleña or Sosa for about $20 round-trip. It's advisable to get a return reservation since you'll be given precedence if the airport gets closed by a storm and the island begins to fill up with people ready to leave. "Northeasters" can last several days. Flights run most days of the week. The dirt airstrip is within walking distance of Utila town; taxis cost $2 for 300 meters. You also may be able to get a boat from La Ceiba for about $5 one-way. The 32-kilometer trip takes about three hours. Departures are unpredictable, however.

The Utila Lodge is the best hotel, usually booked through the U.S. (phone: 904-588-4131) with eight clean modern rooms overlooking the harbor: fairly expensive. Trudy's, east of the center of town a few minutes from the airport, is a very pleasant place, in a big old house overlooking the bay. You can get a room with bath for about $12, or without for less. Trudy's old-fashioned island food is rather like American cooking, and quite good, especially if Trudy herself cooks (she's semiretired). She's a real islander, and has interesting stories of the old days, when islanders could almost starve during long storms because no food could get in. Grant's has cabins for four at $15. Cross Creek Houses has various accommodations for around $5 (rooms are free if you take scuba courses offered there). Blue Bayou, about a half-hour's walk west of town on the other side of the bay from the airport, has good snorkeling off its beach, but may be closed in off-season. Selly's restaurant up the hill behind the Bucket of Blood Bar is good. The Manhattan Restaurant on the main road through town, Orma's overlooking the harbor, and the Comedor el Teleño on the hill are good, inexpensive places to eat or snack.

It's easy to rent snorkeling gear along the road to the airport. The closest snorkeling spot to town is at the southwest end of the airport. There's a little beach by a grove of small trees which you can swim from. Close to shore the water is shallow, with mangroves, dead coral, and turtle grass flats. You can see quite a lot of interesting fish—wrasse, grunts, butterflyfish, barracudas—in the shallows, but watch out for getting stung by soft corals. If you swim offshore westward for about 500 meters, or walk out across the dead coral flats, you can reach deeper water where huge hard corals loom out of the blue. (Watch out for sharp coral, fishermen in boats, and other possible hazards—you're on your own.)

For about $30, you can hire a boatman to take you out to the cays south of the island, leave you there for a day of snorkeling and swimming, and pick you up in the evening. It may be possible to stay overnight at Water Cay but you'll need to bring food, water, and other necessities. Watch out for sunburn and sandflies on the cays.

It's possible to rent scuba gear and take scuba lessons. An introductory course leading to PADI (Professional Aqualung and Diving Instruction) certification costs about $200. Contact Bay Islands Divers in Tegucigalpa for more information (phone: 22-7576). The owner of Cross Creek, Ronald Janssen, gives diving instruction with licensed instructors, rents scuba and snorkeling equipment, and offers boat trips (phone: 45-3134). Other operators are Troy's Dive Shop and the Utila Dive Center. Scuba trips to the reefs cost around $35 per person.

A walk to Pumpkin Hill on the island's northeast edge is a good morning or afternoon hike. The cross-island track branches off from the main road in the center of town. In winter, the woodlands of fig, gumbo-limbo, and pochote are full of North American migratory warblers. As you climb, you move away from the coral rock that rings the island and come to grainy metamorphic rock, the tops of the drowned mountains. Blue land crabs live in holes all along the way. On the other side, you come to a small sandy beach with a small bar-cabana (closed when I was there). West from there, an unclear path runs along the shore, and eventually goes inland through dense scrub to a small freshwater cave, a fissure slanting down about 3 meters to standing water so clear it looks dry at first. There are also caves on Pumpkin Hill itself, which is east of the beach. (Chiggers are numerous in grass and brush.)

Roatán

This is the largest Bay Island, 50 kilometers long, although only a few kilometers wide. It's a classic "island paradise" with a line of hardwood- and pine-forested hills rising above white sand beaches ringed with coral reefs. About 100 kilometers of reefs surround the island. A Marine Park has been established at Sandy Bay on the island's west end, and there's an 810-hectare Watershed and Wildlife Protection Area at Port Royal on the roadless east end. For more information on these, contact the Bay Islands Conservation Association, Edificio Cooper, Calle Principal, Coxen Hole (phone: 45-1424). The Honduran Tourism Institute (IHT) has an office in Coxen Hole, by the park. Also at Sandy Bay are the Carambola Botanical Gardens, with guided tours, nature trails, and breeding parrot and iguana populations. They're open 7–5 daily (phone: 45-1117).

Isleña flies to Roatán from La Ceiba several times a day for around $30 round-trip. They and Lacsa also have flights from Tegucigalpa and La Ceiba. Since the airport at Coxen Hole takes jets, you also can fly direct from the U.S. on Taca from Miami. Sosa has flights from La Ceiba to Roatán Mon.–Sat., which then continue on to Guanaja. The airport is a 20-minute walk (taxi $1.50) outside the capital of Coxen Hole, but most of the tourism destinations are in other towns. Boats occasionally travel between Roatán and Puerto Cortés or La Ceiba for about $5 one-way. You can't fly from Utila to Roatán, but you may be able to find (or charter) a boat.

Roatán has roads along most of its length: paved between West End and French Harbor, unpaved east to Punta Gorda. There is car rental at the airport for about $25 a day. Minibuses to towns east and west leave hourly or half-hourly from the Calle Principal at Coxen Hole. Scooter or bicycle rental are also possibilities.

Accommodations on Roatán generally are more expensive than

on the mainland or Utila, with a number of very fine resorts, but there also are budget places. Moving from west to east along the island, the areas with accommodations are:

WEST END: The Lost Paradise Inn has rooms and beachside cabins and a good restaurant in the $50 range (phone: 45-1306; fax: 45-1388). Sunrise Resort is comparable, and offers diving packages (phone: 45-1265). Seagrape Plantations is more mid-price, with cabins and restaurant (phone: 45-1428). In the $10–20 range are Half-Moon Bay Cabins (phone: 45-1080), Roberts-Hill Hotel, and Seaside Cottages. You can get rooms for less at Jimmy Miller's, Mario's, and others. Foster and Vivian's Restaurant on the beach has good seafood, and also rents inexpensive beach cabins and runs daily glass-bottom boat trips to the reefs. West Bay, a ten-minute boat ride away, has an excellent beach and snorkeling. Other good restaurants are the Sea View, Luna's Bay Cafe, and The Bite.

SANDY BAY: Anthony's Key Resort has wooden cabins on a wooded hillside overlooking a small bay. It's expensive, around $100 a day with board, but oriented to environmental values. The resort owns a cay with a small wildlife reserve and has a museum and natural history laboratory and lecture hall. There's a launch and diving facilities (phone: 45-1003; fax: 45-1140). The Bamboo Inn has nice rooms in the $10–20 range, with a restaurant next door. Beth's Inn on the hill above is less.

COXEN HOLE: Cay View Hotel on Calle Principal has rooms for $20–30 with bath and A/C, less without. Coral has nice rooms for about $10; Peace Corps volunteers stay here. The Burger Hut opposite the Coral has good, inexpensive meals.

BRICK BAY: Island Garden House is a guest house in the $50–70 range with snorkeling, sailing, and diving (phone: 45-1585; fax: 45-1588). Romeo's Resort Dive and Yacht Club is in the $20–30 range (phone: 45-1127; fax: 45-1594).

FRENCH HARBOR: Fantasy Island is a large luxury resort on a small cay, in the $80–120 range, with three-day packages (phone:

45-1128; fax: 45-1268). French Harbor Yacht Club is $40–60 with good food (phone: 45-1478; fax: 45-1459). Britos has rooms with fan for about $10. Romeo's Restaurant has good seafood.

OAK RIDGE: The Reef House Resort is a quiet diving resort on a cay across the harbor from town, with various packages in the over-$100 range (phone: 45-2142; in U.S. 512-681-2888; 1-800-328-8897; fax: 512-341-7942). San José Hotel has rooms with bath for about $10.

PORT ROYAL (an hour by boat east from Oak Ridge): Roatán Lodge is a luxury diving resort, with scuba and snorkeling expeditions.

DIVING: Lessons and equipment are supplied by: Tyll Sass (phone: 45-1314) and Roatán Divers (phone: 45-1255) at West End; John Davis and Off the Wall Yacht Club at French Harbor. Diving lessons and equipment are also available at many resorts.

Guanaja

Also known as Bonacca and the Island of Pines, this 18-by-6-kilometer island is largely a national forest reserve (established in 1960), and the extensive cays and reefs around it are a marine park. It was Columbus's first landfall on his 1502 voyage: he was impressed by the tall pine trees, but disappointed when the Paya inhabitants proved so ignorant of the gold and pearls he showed them that they offered to *buy* them from *him*. (Plundering a large dugout full of cotton, copper axes, and other trade goods cheered him up.) The island remains roadless (Guanaja town is offshore on a cay), but several trails lead into the hilly, forested interior, which has streams and waterfalls. Sandflies are fierce, especially in the rainy season: coconut oil is supposed to discourage them.

Isleña has daily flights from La Ceiba (except Sundays) for about $40 return. The airstrip is on the main island: a boat runs to Guanaja town for $1. There are boats from La Ceiba and Puerto Cortés. To travel to and around the island from Guanaja town you need to hire boats, which is expensive.

Guanaja is the most expensive island to visit. The Bayman Bay Club on the main island (phone: 45-4179) and the Posada del Sol on a cay (phone: 45-4186) are dive resorts in the $150–250 range. The Club Guanaja Este is somewhat cheaper and features hiking and horseback riding as well as diving (P.O. Box 40541, Cincinnati, OH 40541). In Guanaja town, the Hotel Alexander has rooms in the $30–50 range overlooking the water. The Hotel Miller and Hotel Rosario are somewhat less. Hotels can arrange trips for beaches, snorkeling, and diving. The Nest and the Harbor Light are good, reasonable restaurants. Glenda's is good for sandwiches.

Tela

Staying in this beachside resort town 100 kilometers west of La Ceiba is like going back in time fifty years. The pace of life is easy, and if you climb to a roof or other vantage point at dawn or sunset, you can see sizable flocks of big Amazon parrots going overhead toward roosts or feeding grounds. The pace will speed up, however, partly because the area is slated for more tourism development. There also are plans to increase protection of natural habitats nearby, so maybe the parrot flocks will remain. The protected areas include a botanical garden, a wildlife refuge, and a national park and marine reserve.

Traliasa runs direct buses between Tela and La Ceiba and Tegucigalpa daily, stopping at Hotel los Arcos. Cati and Tupsa have buses every 30 minutes to Progresso, where you change to go to San Pedro Sula. The nearest airport with regular flights is San Pedro Sula (most planes to Tegucigalpa also stop there).

Villas Telamar on the beach west of downtown has rooms, apartments or bungalows at moderately expensive rates, with pool and golf club (phone: 48-2916; fax: 48-2984). On the beach in town is Nuevo Puerto Rico, with small rooms at $10–20 and a good restaurant (phone: 48-2413). Marazul, Ave. 5, Calle 11, is a budget place near the beach. Downtown, the Presidente on the central plaza has good rooms for $20–30 (phone: 48-2841; fax: 48-2992). Hotel Tela, aves. 3 and 4, Calle 9, is like being fifty years in the past, with rundown but airy and comfortable rooms for $5–10 (phone: 48-2150). Bertha's near the bus terminal, Ave. 9, Calle 8, is new, and has rooms for around $5.

Luces del Norte is a good seafood and breakfast restaurant on Ave. 2, Calle 11 near the beach. Also on the beach are Cesar's and Sherwood's. Los Angeles, Ave. 2 and Calle 9, has good Chinese food.

Lancetilla Botanical Garden

This garden was founded by United Fruit in 1926 as a research station for tropical horticulture. The national forestry school, ES-NACIFOR, now manages it. It's well maintained, and has labeled specimens of tropical trees and other plants from every continent as well as native ones. There are inexpensive dormitory accommodations, often full on weekends or when student groups are there, but otherwise available, and you can buy meals. The garden also includes a large expanse of forested land maintained as a biological reserve, so there's a good deal of wildlife around. The reserve watershed provides water for much of Tela. Guided tours are available. It's open Tues.– Fri. 7:30–3:30, Sat.–Sun. 8:30–4, admission $.20.

It's an hour's walk to the garden from downtown Tela, a half hour to the highway west toward El Progreso and the garden entry road (clearly marked) and a half hour through forest to the garden itself. I heard tinamous and a laughing falcon on this walk. Over two hundred bird species have been identified. A clear stream runs through the garden, frequented by basilisks and huge marine toads, and good for watching the cichlids, tetras, and 8-inch-long freshwater shrimp that live therein (the shrimp hide under rocks and try to catch fish with their sticklike claws). You can also take the employees' bus from downtown at 7 A.M. or a local bus to the entrance.

Punta Izopo Wildlife Refuge

Established in 1992, this refuge includes the cape at the east end of Tela Bay and the nearby mouth of the Lean River. You can get there via the Garífuna village of El Triunfo, a $.40 bus ride from Tela. Or you can walk along the beach from Tela to La Ensanada, where a road cuts overland to El Triunfo. The refuge has no facilities as yet: for more information, contact the visitor center at aves. 2 and 3, Calle 9 in Tela, or the NGO Prolansate (phone: 48-2035).

Punta Sal National Park

This park includes the Punta Sal peninsula on the west end of Tela
Bay, wetlands and forest in the Ulua River estuary, and offshore
reefs. There's a large tidal lagoon, the Laguna de los Micos, and
wonderful little coves on the far side of Punta Sal. Birding is excellent around the lagoons. Huge flooded forests in the park are almost inaccessible, but rich in wildlife. To get there, you can take a
local bus or boat to the village of Tornabe, from which it's about
12 kilometers on a hard sand road to the village of Miami. The
point is another 10 kilometers along the beach. Another possibility
is to hire a boat to take you to the park area and then walk back.
For more information, contact the visitor center in Tela at aves. 2
and 3, Calle 9.

The Mosquitia and Olancho

The Patuca River and its tributaries drain most of eastern Honduras, beginning in the wide plains and mountains of Olancho and
running east to the rain forests, savannas, and wetlands of the Mosquitia. Olancho has been settled since the sixteenth century, but is
still sparsely populated, with some fine cloud forest in two national
parks, La Muralla and Sierra de Agalta. The Mosquitia remains
wilderness, without roads to the outside world, and is the major
reservoir of endangered wildlife in the country, with a large manatee population in its coastal lagoons, and a breeding population
of harpy eagles, the biggest New World eagle and the top of the rain
forest canopy food chain. The Río Plátano Biosphere Reserve protects the watershed of the river of that name west of the Patuca, and
there are plans to include it with projected nature and indigenous
reserves in a 2-million-hectare protected complex named Plapawans (after the three main rivers, Plátano, Patuca, and Wans Coco).
In 1992, Honduras signed an agreement with Nicaragua creating
a 2.8-million-hectare international protected area, La Solidaridad,
including Plapawans and Nicaragua's Bosawas reserve. The Tawahka Sumu people, about eight hundred of whom live along the
lower Patuca, are trying to establish an indigenous reserve in the
area.

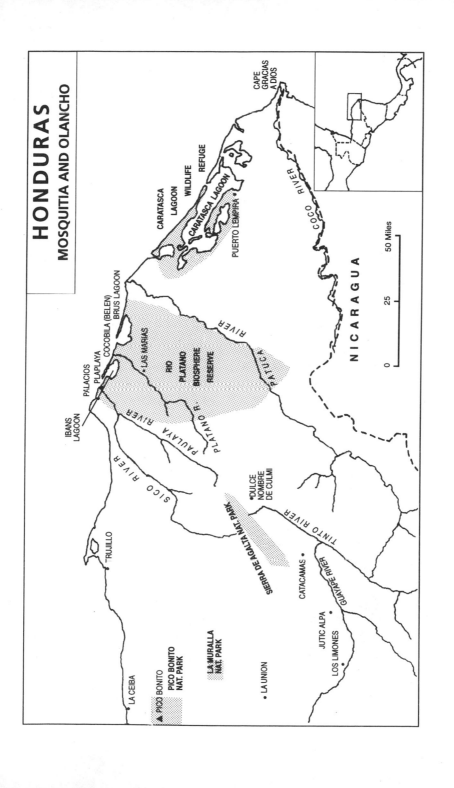

HONDURAS
MOSQUITIA AND OLANCHO

CAPE GRACIAS A DIOS

CARATASCA LAGOON WILDLIFE REFUGE

CARATASCA LAGOON

PUERTO LEMPIRA

COCO RIVER

NICARAGUA

50 Miles

25

0

COCOBILA (BELEN)
BRUS LAGOON

PALACIOS

PLAPLAYA

LAS MARIAS

RIO PLATANO BIOSPHERE RESERVE

PATUCA RIVER

IBANS LAGOON

PAULAYA RIVER

PLATANO R.

SICO RIVER

DULCE NOMBRE DE CULMI

SIERRA DE AGALTA NAT. PARK

TINTO RIVER

TRUJILLO

CATACAMAS

GUAYAPE RIVER

JUTICALPA

LA MURALLA NAT. PARK

LA UNION

LOS LIMONES

LA CEIBA

PICO BONITO

▲ PICO BONITO NAT. PARK

Farmers from the impoverished lands of southern Honduras have been moving into the Mosquitia's west edge for several decades. The area along the Nicaraguan border was one of the main theaters of the 1980s Contra War, and extensive minefields, as well as roving guerrilla bands, remain on both sides of the border.

There are two ways to get to eastern Honduras. One is to fly from La Ceiba to the towns along the Mosquitia coast; the other is to drive the road that runs from Tegucigalpa to Olancho's capital at Juticalpa and then on to Trujillo on the coast east of La Ceiba. The first provides access to the Río Plátano's mouth and to the area around the huge Catarasca Lagoon to the east. The second provides access first to Sierra de Agalta and, eventually, to the Plátano's headwaters beyond the frontier town of Dulce Nombre de Culmí at the Mosquitia's northwest margin.

The Río Plátano Biosphere Reserve

This roughly 500,000-hectare area, the watershed of the Plátano River, was one of the first established under UNESCO's biosphere reserve program, which aims to integrate wildlands protection with human use. A number of Miskito villages occupy the coastal part of the reserve. The Miskitos divide their time between fishing and other commercial occupations on the coast and tending farm plots which they own inland along the river (land ownership is matrilineal). Farther upstream are a few Pech and Tawahka villages. They mainly live by shifting cultivation combined with fishing and hunting. Above the navigable part of the river is largely undisturbed rain forest, but colonizers have been clearing land in the highlands of the river's headwaters. There are Pech villages in the highlands as well, but they are being marginalized and assimilated by ladino culture.

In 1544, the archbishop of Honduras, Cristóbal de Pedraza, climbed to a peak east of Trujillo and saw "very great populations" in the plains of the Tinto and Sico rivers near the eastern border of the present Plátano reserve. Local people told him there were cities there whose inhabitants ate from golden plates. Almost nothing was heard of such "populations" in ensuing centuries, but recently evidence has been found that suggests that they may have existed at the time of the Spanish Conquest. A 1985 expedition into the forest just west of the Plátano found at least eighty archaeological sites, including some with two hundred structures, some of which were 15 meters high and 100 meters long. In 1987, another expedition explored an area southwest of the Plátano reserve, Las Crucitas, and found equally impressive sites with architectural styles, construction methods, and artifacts suggesting they were related to and contemporary with the sites nearer the coast. One observer noted that cacao trees were abnormally abundant in surrounding forest, suggesting that the area was being used as a vast "cacao plantation" by the cosmopolitan Meso-American empires. Such use may have lasted from about a thousand years ago until the Spanish Conquest.

It's possible to travel to the Miskito village at the mouth of the Plátano (Barro del Plátano) and hire a guide with a motorboat to take you up the river's navigable stretch to the Pech village of Las Marías. If you find the right guide, you might be able to hire boatmen to pole you four more days upriver through the pristine forest to the mouth of the Río Cuyamel. You'll have to carry your own food and shelter, or negotiate for meals and lodging with local people (Honduran Miskitos don't speak much English, but most know Spanish). The trip can only be made from January to May, in the dry season.

The quickest way to start is to fly from La Ceiba to Palacios, a town (with basic hotel and comedor) on the coast just west of the reserve. When I went in 1992, the flight cost about $25 round-trip. From there you can hire a motorized canoe, or "*tuk-tuk*," to take you across the Río Tinto estuary and Ibans Lagoon to the hamlet of Cocobila on the barrier beach between the lagoon and the ocean. I saw jabiru storks during this ride, which cost $15 and took a couple of hours. (There may be a regular tuk-tuk for about $4.) There was a MOPAWI office with a radio at Cocobila, also a refrigerator with "*gaseosas*" (soft drinks), which I drank every chance I got. (There's an airstrip at Cocobila, also called Belén, but there are fewer flights than to Palacios.) From Cocobila, a trail runs east through the savanna for a few kilometers and emerges on the beach at a place called Kuri, where there is a COHDEFOR office and reserve headquarters, which was closed during my trip. If it's open, they may be able to offer you lodging and help you find a guide (but don't count on this). From there, it's an hour or so's walk on the beach to Barro del Plátano, which is just across the river.

I was looking for a guide named Allen Riven, who was recommended and whose family lived in a community just west of the river from Barro del Plátano. I'd been told he could take me on a five-day trip to the mouth of the Río Cuyamel, but his boat was broken. The ferryman to Barro del Plátano, a very friendly, black-skinned individual named Gonzalo, with a large scar on his neck, arranged for a local Miskito trader and his assistant to take me as far as Las Marías in their Boston whaler for $58 round-trip. It's a one-day trip upriver, but we left in the afternoon so we had to stay overnight at somebody's (I was never sure whose) house on the river. There are many snags in the river, so it's a tricky passage. Big toucan and parrot flocks cross the river, and upstream where the terrain got hilly there are strange, brightly colored sediments on the banks. Las Marías is very different from the teeming Miskito towns on the coast, with widely scattered palm-thatched houses that seemed almost deserted when I was there.

To get back to Palacios, I had to hitch a boat ride with a health worker at Cocobila to the Garífuna town of Plaplaya halfway between Ibans Lagoon and the Río Tinto. There the local airline agent (who was watching a Rambo movie on his satellite set) arranged a tuk-tuk ride to Palacios so I could get the morning plane. Insects weren't a problem on the trip (somewhat to my chagrin, since I'd packed a net), but malaria and dengue are present.

The other way to travel on the Plátano is to raft downstream from the headwaters northeast of Dulce Nombre de Culmí. This is an expedition of at least two weeks, and requires good whitewater equipment and experienced guides. There are dangerous stretches, particularly a place called El Subterraneo, where the river dives under a huge rock, and there is a kilometer-long stretch of obstacles that takes a day to traverse. Chances of seeing increasingly rare animals such as macaws and eagles are good. A highly prized fish, the cuyamel or bobo, still thrives in the river here (it's threatened in settled areas) and is supposed to be delicious. It's a kind of mullet, and feeds by scraping algae from rocks.

Such an expedition, or any other into the Mosquitia's rain forest, is obviously a major undertaking. Unless you want to plan and equip it yourself, your options are either to tag along on somebody else's expedition or to hire a tour agency. The Peace Corps, either through its Tegucigalpa office or local volunteers, would be a good source of information on the "expedition grapevine," as might Ríos Honduras, which organizes trips on the Río Cangrejal near La Ceiba (see above). La Moskitia Ecoaventuras, P.O. Box 3577, Tegucigalpa, offers raft trips down the Plátano as well as custom trips to anywhere in the Mosquitia (phone/fax: 37-9398). Two other tour agencies run Mosquitia expeditions from Trujillo, three hours by bus east of La Ceiba. Turtle Tours is at Hotel Village Brinkley (phone: 44-4444; fax: 44-4200). Cambio C.A. at Barrio el Centro near the main plaza, Apdo. Postal 2, Trujillo, Colon (phone: 44-4044; fax: 44-4055) has professionally guided trips for about $100 a day. Operators speak English and German. There are two new lodges in the biosphere reserve, one in Palacios and one on Isla Cañon in Brus Lagoon. Both are mainly for sportfishing, but will accommodate others. Contact tour operators for more information.

La Muralla National Park

This 150-square-kilometer park is perhaps the best place in Honduras to see quetzals, which have a sizable population in its cloud forest. The spectacular birds are best seen in the March–May breeding season. There are three main peaks in the refuge: 1,981-meter La Muralla, 1,985-meter Los Higuerales, and Las Parras, at 2,064 meters. The refuge is a 4-hour drive from Tegucigalpa on the road to Juticalpa. Just west of the village of Los Limónes, at a crossing of the Guayape River, an all-weather unpaved road runs north to La Unión. The refuge is 17 kilometers north of La Unión on the road to El Dictamo. The trip can be made in a rental car, or you can take hourly Empresa Aurora buses to Juticalpa from Tegucigalpa, leaving from near 615 Calle 8 and Ave. Morazán, and hitchhike or take a local bus to La Unión, where there is a small hotel.

The park has a visitor center with natural history exhibits. Quetzals and toucans can be seen from the center. Several nature trails lead into the forest from the center, and there is a camping area along one trail. Mammals of the park include brocket deer and white-faced capuchin and howler monkeys. COHDEFOR also has a campamento called "Carta" 45 minutes' drive from the refuge where you can stay overnight for a few dollars. Another natural attraction in the area is the waterfall at Mucupina, 3 or 4 hours' walk southeast of the park. The small towns in the area have retained a more traditional lifestyle than in less remote areas, farming with oxen and painting their adobe houses with folk art.

Sierra de Agalta National Park

For some reason the colonists who are moving east into the Mosquitia have bypassed this isolated range, which has the biggest cloud forest of Olancho. Because it is so far to the east, it has different flora and fauna than most other Honduran cloud forests. Wildlife includes tapirs, monkeys, and brocket deer as well as quetzals, peccaries, and pumas. The roughly 60,000-hectare park includes the highest point in eastern Honduras, a 2,590-meter peak on the Monte de Babilonia. The climb to "La Picucha" is highly recommended by photographer Vince Murphy: "It goes through pine and oak forest, then through a beautiful rain forest, and then through a very distinct and mysterious cloud forest. Farther up there is a moss forest and a sort of dwarf vegetation on top. It has spectacular views, and a very interesting natural history. There are three-wattled bellbirds."

The Sierra de Agalta lies north of Catacamas and Dulce Nombre de Culmí on the Olancho road past Juticalpa. Buses from Tegucigalpa to Juticalpa (see above) also continue to Catacamas, where you can get a bus to Dulce Nombre de Culmí (both have basic hotels and comedores). The park has no headquarters yet, although one is under development and there are trails leading up some of the peaks. Contact the Peace Corps or COHDEFOR for more information. There's a possibility that this park will be enlarged to make a transect north to the coast and east to the Río Plátano reserve.

Western Honduras

This rugged region of extinct volcanic mountains and deep-cut river gorges contains two of the most important glimpses into Central America's past. The magnificent Mayan ruins at Copán near the Guatemalan border are well known. Less famous are the Miocene fossil beds near the ancient, remote town of Gracias. First excavated in the 1930s, these beds yielded the bones of fauna that were entirely North American (there were horses, dogs, rhinos, deer, and elephants, but no ground sloths or other South American species), providing the first actual proof that the two continents did not come into contact until about five to three million years ago. Traveling to western Honduras is generally like heading back in time. Population and commerce have moved east and north, leaving towns like Gracias and La Esperanza not much different from what they were when paleontologists explored the area half a century ago. Because of this remoteness, the forests of the region's two large national parks, Celaque and Trifinio, are under less pressure than those farther east.

Celaque National Park

This 27,000-hectare park contains the highest point in Honduras, 2,849-meter Mt. Celaque, which began as a volcano millions of years ago when gomphotheres (primitive mastodons) and osteoboruses (strange, bone-eating wild dogs) roamed the savannas that then covered the land. Today many different kinds of forest grow in the park, from tropical dry forest and evergreen gallery forest in the valleys, to oak and liquidambar forest in the foothills, to cloud forest above 1,800 meters, to fir forest on the peaks. All but one of Honduras's pine species grow at various elevations, and the park has the southernmost native population of a cypress species, *Cupressus lusitanica*. There are endemic species of trees and salamanders, and a new frog species was discovered here in 1975. Wildlife ranges from white-face capuchin monkeys, brocket deer, and jaguars at lower elevations to pumas, cottontail rabbits, and weasels at higher. "Celaque" is believed to be a Lenca word for "watershed": eleven rivers have their headwaters in the park. Northern bird species such as ravens, Steller's jays, and acorn woodpeckers live alongside emerald toucanets, parakeets, and quetzals.

The best access to the park is from Gracias, which is an interesting town. It was founded in 1536, and for a short time was the administrative center of Central America when the Audiencia de los Confines was located there in 1544. There are several colonial churches and a restored fort. The cobbled streets and quiet squares probably haven't changed much from colonial days. You can get to Gracias from Tegucigalpa on two routes, both of which take a couple of days (a long-planned paved road from Siguatepeque to Santa Rosa de Copán via Gracias remains uncompleted).

The longer, but more comfortable, route is to go via Santa Rosa de Copán, a pleasant little city on the main road to the north. Direct buses leave Tegucigalpa daily on the Sultana line from Comayagüela, or you can go to San Pedro Sula and get hourly buses on Empresas Torito or Transportes Copánecos. In Santa Rosa de Copán, the Hotel Elvir, Ave. 2 and Calle Real Centenario, has good rooms and restaurant in the $15 range. Hotels Copán, Ave. 3 and Calle 4, and Erik, 362 Calle 1, are less. El Pollo Dorado restaurant, two blocks north of the Hotel Elvir, has "*baleadas*," a burritolike food typical of Honduras. Buses to Gracias leave from the main square six times a day, beginning at 7:30.

The shorter but more "iffy" route is via La Esperanza, a beautiful but somewhat remote mountain town on a good dirt road southwest of Siguatepeque (a main town between Tegucigalpa and San Pedro Sula). Direct buses on the Empresa Joelito line leave from 834 Calle 4, Comayagüela, at 6 A.M. The trip takes 8 hours. La Esperanza is in a green high valley of oak and pine, the Lenca country: it gets quite chilly at night. There are several inexpensive but comfortable hotels, including Hotel Solis for about $10 and Hotel Mina for less, both near the market. The road from La Esperanza to Gracias is not good, with steep stretches and washed-out river crossings. Buses run, but not often, and not particularly safely. It's an interesting trip, however, over high ridges and through strange eroded canyons. I left La Esperanza hitchhiking in the early morning, got about halfway to Gracias in two rides (for which I paid), then got a very crowded bus the rest of the way.

Gracias is an inexpensive place to stay—in fact, it's impossible to spend much. It's at fairly low elevation, 765 meters, so you won't miss a hot shower much. There are public hot springs an hour's walk outside of town: ask for Balneario las Aguas Termales. The Hotel Erik on the street where buses stop (phone: 98-4066) has rooms with cold shower for less than $5. Iris, opposite the church of San Sebastián three blocks south of the plaza, is a little more. When I was there, an unnamed comedor a few blocks south of the plaza had good baleadas.

A COHDEFOR office near the plaza in town can provide information about the park. There probably will be a Peace Corps volunteer you can talk to as well. A road goes to the park from the southwest side of town, branching off from the main road by a church. It's 8 kilometers to park headquarters, most of it driveable by a non-4wd. There are sleeping and cooking facilities at headquarters which you can arrange to use with COHDEFOR (if you just walk up there without making arrangements, the center is likely to be closed). From there a good trail goes to the summit, a steep 4- to 6-hour climb. There are campsites with water along the way. Some large farm clearings exist in the cloud forest halfway up the mountain, but these are growing back, with alder the main pioneer species. Views from the higher slopes are breathtaking. There are plans to extend the trail across the park to the town of Belén Gualcho to the west.

The Miocene fossils at Gracias were dug from the banks of nearby streams, and suggest that the area was very different when the animals lived—a swampy plain surrounding active volcanoes. There is no museum or other facility on the fossil beds (when I was there, nobody even remembered the paleontological expeditions—in the 1960s as well as the 1930s), but fossils are still common in the vicinity. Don Antonio Miranda, the teacher at a nearby school, has a collection.

Trifinio–Montecristo National Park

This is an international park, including mountains in El Salvador and Guatemala as well. The Honduran part is quite remote, beyond the border town of Nueva Ocotepeque. Buses make the 3-hour trip from Santa Rosa de Copán every morning at 6 and 9. The Hotel Sandoval and the Hotel y Comedor Congolon are two places to stay. There is a natural history museum in the Governor's Office of the Parque Central, open 8–4 Mon.–Fri. The COHDEFOR office is opposite the Texaco Station two blocks from the Hotel Congolon. Access to the park is easier from Metapán in El Salvador, but there are good trails on the Honduras side, and there is supposed to be more wildlife than in El Salvador. Easier to visit (right on the Santa Rosa–Ocotepeque road) is the much smaller Guisayote Reserve, with trails from which quetzals have been seen.

Copán

This site near the Guatemalan border was a major Maya city from about 1,700 to 1,200 years ago. Its ruins were first explored archaeologically by John Lloyd Stephens in 1839, and excavated and restored by the Carnegie Institute in the 1930s. The abundance of inscriptions on the stelae and other stone structures has caused archaeologists to call Copán "the Paris of Maya culture." The Hieroglyphic Stairway at the south end of the Great Plaza, which records the history of the ruling dynasty, is the longest such inscription known. The ruins include a ball court, temples, tombs, and a residential complex. Excavations are still under way. The city was abandoned around the same time as other Maya cities of the Guatemalan Petén. The extent of Copán's urbanization, and signs of poor health in human remains found among the ruins, suggest that the city may have collapsed in part because it exceeded the carrying capacity of the surrounding ecosystem.

A small remnant of tropical forest with some huge old trees still surrounds the site. A nature trail ("*sendero natural*") departs from near the entrance to the ruins. In his classic *Incidents of Travel in Central America*, John Lloyd Stephens wrote: "The only sounds that disturbed the quiet of this buried city were the noises of the monkeys. . . . They moved over our heads in long and swift processions, forty or fifty at a time . . . and with a noise like a current of wind, passed on into the depths of the forest . . . like wandering spirits of the departed race guarding the ruins of their former habitations." Today, unfortunately, the monkey troops also have departed from this area. Recent studies suggest that the Copán Valley is getting as deforested now as it was when the Maya city was abandoned.

You can get to Copán from San Pedro Sula by taking regular Copanecos, Impala, or Torito buses to the town of La Entrada and then getting hourly buses on to Copán, or by taking direct Etumi buses at 10:30 A.M. and 2 P.M. Direct buses also leave at 11 from Calle 7 and Ave. 6 sur. There are plenty of accommodations at the town of Copán Ruinas, 1 kilometer from the ruins. The Marina Hotel on the plaza has a pool, sauna, and restaurant, with rooms ranging from $20–50 (phone: 98-3070 or 39-0956 in Tegus). The Maya and Popul Nah, also on the plaza, have clean rooms with bath in the $10–20 range. Los Gemelos and Brisas de Copán have rooms for about $5. Comedor Izabel and Comedor Llama del Bosque are good, inexpensive restaurants near the plaza. Restaurante El Sesteo, opposite from Brisas de Copán, and Tunkul Bar are also good. Tunkul offers trips to nearby Maya sites and caves.

A path leads along the road from town to the ruins, which are open from 8 to 4 daily, admission $6, good for two days. There's a cafeteria, shop, and tourist office at the entrance, and guided tours are available. The admission fee also pays for a visit to the archaeological museum on the plaza in town (same hours), where artifacts found in the ruins are housed. A good time to walk the nature trail is right after the ruins close.

There is also a new regional archaeological museum on the main road west of La Entrada. A nearby Maya site is open for visitation.

CHAPTER EIGHT

El Salvador

E L SALVADOR IS A country of contrasts and contradictions. It is the smallest Central American nation, with 21,040 square kilometers in area, but has one of the largest populations in the region, over 5.4 million in 1992. Its population density is similar to India's. Traditionally the most progressive and enterprising of Central American nations, El Salvador took advantage of fertile volcanic soils to become a major exporter of coffee and other crops, but its social and political institutions did not evolve to support its growth. It has suffered some of the worst poverty and social upheavals of the region in the twentieth century, although the end of its recent civil war has raised hopes of a more peaceful and stable future.

El Salvador's landscape is one of the richest and most beautiful in Central America, with lines of volcanic cones rising over lakes, valleys, and a long Pacific shoreline of scenic bluffs and bays. Its indigenous people called it Cuscatlan, "land of the jewel." Rapid economic and population growth have degraded its ecosystems, however. Soil erosion has affected 50 percent of farmlands, and crop yields have declined. Coastal siltation has reduced shrimp and fish catches. Pollution by pesticides and sewage is a serious problem. Native vegetation covers only 7 percent of the land, and primary forests cover only 3 percent. Large and rare wildlife—macaws, tapirs, jaguars, etc.—is long gone, and even the more common animals such as monkeys, coatis, and armadillos are largely extirpated. Iguanas, for example, are reduced to .01 percent of their original population, according to the natural history museum in San Salvador.

Yet El Salvador still has a lot to offer the visitor. About 20,000 hectares of parks and reserves recently have been set aside, including dry forest, cloud forest, semideciduous montane forest, mangrove forest, lakes, and estuarine wetlands. Environmental awareness is increasing. The capital, San Salvador, has a surprisingly good natural history museum and zoo, and one of the finest botanical gardens I've seen anywhere. It's too early to write off wildlands in El Salvador, and if Salvadorans can prove as enterprising in protecting their environment as they have proved in exploiting it, things may get better. Certainly, if you want to encourage conservation in your role as ecotourist, this is the place to do it.

The Shaking Valley

El Salvador is mostly within the Pacific volcanic zone, so it has frequent earthquakes and much volcanic activity. The highland valley that lies between the two lines of volcanoes paralleling the country's length is known as "El Valle de las Hamacas," which translates roughly as "the rocking valley" (or valley of the swings—"*hamaca*" also means hammock). El Salvador has 180 volcanoes, more than any other Central American country except Guatemala. Volcán Santa Ana in the northwest part of the country is the highest (2,365 meters). Near it is Volcán Izalco, a 1,870-meter cinder cone which was level farmland until it appeared in 1770, and which kept erupting continuously until 1957. The lakes of Coatepeque and Ilopango occupy extinct craters: the Ilopango crater is thought to have resulted from an explosion about 1,800 years ago that covered much of northern and central El Salvador with ash and sent local people fleeing into Guatemala and Honduras. Earthquakes have often damaged San Salvador.

Basilisk lizard (*Basilisus vittatus*). Photo by Carolyn Miller.

El Salvador also has an alluvial coastal plain along its 320-mile shoreline. Volcanic sand deposited by rivers forms extensive beaches and offshore spits, behind which mangrove forests have developed. The shifting nature of the sands has precluded the development of coral reefs, except in a few places such as Punta Remedios near Acajutla, where corals grow on shell banks. On El Salvador's eastern and northern borders, the active volcanic zone ends in the volcanic plateaus of Honduras and Guatemala, where there is also some older granitic rock. These are the highest points in the country, reaching an altitude of 2,730 meters at Cerro el Pital on the Honduran border.

The valleys of eastern El Salvador have yielded some of the best fossils from Central America. The remains of horses, camels, and early mastodons and dogs from the Torola River valley date from the Miocene epoch, before the land bridge formed. Fossils from the Valle del Sisimico near Volcán San Vicente are from the later Pleistocene epoch, and include bones of South American animals such as ground sloths as well as of North American animals. Some particularly fine fossils were formed when a volcanic eruption covered a lake bottom with ash, preserving leaves, fish, and insects in detail. The fossils are on display at San Salvador's natural history museum (see below).

Since it doesn't border on the Caribbean, El Salvador lacks low-land rain forest. There is a marked dry season from November to April, except above 1,800 meters in the cloud forest zone. The original forest cover was very diverse, however, ranging from savanna and dry forest on coastal lowlands, to semideciduous montane forest on high valleys and volcanic slopes, to cloud forest and conifer forest at higher elevations. Some impressive forest remains, particularly the montane forest at El Imposible, which has a number of endemic trees, and the cloud forest at Montecristo. Even in San Salvador, there's a gorgeous forest remnant on a slope above the La Laguna Botanical Garden. Animal diversity in these forests also was high, with 465 bird species recorded from the country.

Despite its earthquakes and eruptions, El Salvador is one of the most livable areas in Central America for humans. Volcanic soil is high in mineral nutrients, bringing abundant and nutritious crops; temperatures in the high interior valleys aren't too warm; and the dry season limits pests and disease. Caves in the Torola River valley near the town of Corinto contain wall paintings said to be 10,000 years old. Abundant archaeological remains throughout the country show that settled farm populations have lived here for at least 3,000 years. Early artifacts suggest the influence of the Olmec culture of southern Mexico. Later ones, from the Classic Period of 1,700 to 1,000 years ago, show a cosmopolitan civilization in which elements of the Teotihuacán and Toltec cultures from central Mexico, the Maya from the Guatemalan highlands, and the Lenca from Honduras were integrated with local traits. Sites include the "Jewel of Ceren," a Maya village that was buried in an ashfall 1,400 years ago and that has yielded surprisingly detailed information about ancient Maya daily life. "They lived better than we had pictured them," wrote excavator Payson Sheets. "We realize now that their domestic architecture was much more sophisticated than we thought. . . . Even their poorest houses were better than much of the rural houses in El Salvador today."

Beginning about 800 years ago, a group called the Pipils came to dominate El Salvador's cultural mosaic. They spoke Nahuatl, a Uto-Aztecan language from central Mexico, and presumably originated there, but little seems to have been recorded about them. The Pipils resisted the Spanish for a number of years after Pedro de Alvarado first invaded El Salvador in 1524, but finally succumbed in 1539. A relatively small number of Spaniards divided the country into large landholdings where they forced the indigenous population to work growing cacao, tobacco, and indigo for export. Spaniards married into indigenous elites, so El Salvador developed as a racially homogeneous colony, but the great inequality between the landed oligarchy and the landless majority remained a source of conflict.

The Coffee Republic

Agricultural fertility made El Salvador a prosperous colony. John Lloyd Stephens called it "the richest in Central America . . . producing tobacco, the best indigo, and the richest balsam in the world." (Balsam is a medicinal resin made from the sap of a native tree, *Myroxolon balsamun*.) Because of this affluence, Salvadoran ruling society became liberal in the sense that it approved ideas of republican self-government and economic progress current in the early nineteenth century. It was the first Central American colony to rise against Spain, when José Matías Delgado organized an unsuccessful revolt in 1811, and it played a major part in the complicated political maneuverings that followed the successful break with Spain in 1821.

Affluence increased after the development of the coffee trade in midcentury. With rich volcanic uplands easily accessible to ports, El Salvador became the fourth greatest coffee exporter in Latin America, and the foremost in Central America. By the early twentieth century, coffee comprised 95 percent of its exports. As export agriculture expanded, however, small farmers were increasingly pushed off the land. As early as 1833, campesinos under an indigenous leader named Anastasio Aquino rebelled in an attempt to reestablish communal land rights. When coffee prices crashed during the 1930s Depression, the situation became desperate. In 1932, Agustín Farabundo Martí, a socialist, led a revolt that was put down so violently that it is known as *"la matanza,"* the massacre. Pipils and other indigenous groups were singled out, and their language and culture suppressed. General Maximiliano Hernández Martínez emerged as military dictator, and the army remained in control until the 1980s.

El Salvador began to lead Central America in industrial production in the 1960s, particularly in textiles. This resulted in the growth of a labor movement, which also came into conflict with the ruling class. Increasingly violent repression erupted into civil war in 1980, with a guerrilla army, the Farabundo Martí Liberation Front (FMLN) controlling much of the north and east of the country. Although the FMLN and the government signed a peace accord in 1992, political tensions between leftist groups and the right-wing National Republican Alliance (ARENA) have remained high, and the economy is in bad condition, with high unemployment and two-thirds of the population living in extreme poverty.

The Tarnished Jewel

The effects of population growth and export agriculture on El Salvador's landscape had become evident by the time American biologist William Beebe visited in 1936. Beebe wrote that "every speck of level or reasonably oblique ground was covered with coffee or maize." He saw little wildlife except in the national museum, where "several hundred abominably made bird skins hung by their feet. Some, beneath the dust, were recognizable as caciques and others as tanagers and herons; many were literally skins with all the feathers in piles on the floor. . . . A few mastodon bones, molars, and vertebrae were also covered with feathers which dropped from the birds overhead. . . . The collection as a whole was the work of another president who had also been shot or stabbed . . ." By this time, floods from deforested watersheds had joined earthquakes and eruptions as hazards: floods had destroyed much of San Salvador two years before Beebe's visit. After World War II, heavy pesticide use and industrial growth introduced Salvadorans to another environmental danger, with one to two thousand a year dying from chemical poisoning. Pesticides and siltation killed fish, shrimp, and the mangrove forests in which they breed.

The Salvadoran government took some steps to protect remaining wildlands in the 1970s. To alleviate flooding, the natural resources agency established forest reserves, and in 1974 created a national parks and wildlife unit to manage flora and fauna. In 1982, the unit was upgraded to the Parks and Wildlife Service. The civil war interrupted conservation work for most of the 1980s, however. "*Guardaparques*" (rangers) found themselves cut off from the government, and army and guerilla units invaded parks. Bombing and resultant fires destroyed much forest as well as farmland, and at least one forest reserve, the Cerro Nejapa, lost its original forest cover.

With the cessation of hostilities, there has been a resurgence of conservation activity. The Parks and Wildlife Service has identified a number of areas for protection, and hopes to add more in areas formerly made inaccessible by the war. It has also identified the six areas with the greatest ecotourism potential at present: Montecristo, El Imposible, Barra de Santiago, Los Andes, Laguna El Jocotal, and Deininger. The Parks and Wildlife Service is located in CENREN, the Department of Natural Resources complex in Canton El Matazano, Soyapango, east of downtown San Salvador, a $4.50 cab ride from downtown San Salvador (phone: 77-0622, 27-0484; fax: 77-0490). The Instituto Salvadoreño de Turismo (IST) manages several national parks and a network of "*turicentros*" or recreational sites, around the country (see below for details). Nongovernmental organizations (NGOs) manage some protected areas under supervision of the Parks and Wildlife Service. The main NGO in El Salvador is SalvaNatura, which since 1989 has been active in natural areas protection, biodiversity conservation, pollution prevention, and environmental education. SalvaNatura manages the El Imposible reserve, and hopes to manage at least one more protected area in the future. It is at No. 422, Ave. 77 norte, Colonia Escalón (phone: 98-4001; fax: 23-3620, 98-0348). The U.S. Peace Corps is active in conservation (phone: 98-3330, 98-3337).

Pressures on wildland from fire, poaching, woodcutting, grazing, and other activities remain intense, and management agencies have adopted restrictive policies to try to deal with them. In 1994, these policies also affected visitors—walking from the entrance to the public use area in Montecristo National Park was prohibited, for example. Ecotourism facilities are developing rapidly, however, and opportunities for access to wildlands will increase. You should still check with the Parks and Wildlife Service before visiting a protected area.

San Salvador

This metropolis of 1.5 million is a microcosm of El Salvador's strengths and weaknesses. Its physical setting in a 600-meter-high valley ringed by volcanoes is beautiful and healthy, but earthquakes have repeatedly destroyed the city, and air pollution is a problem in its enclosed basin. Although the city was first founded in 1525 (in a nearby location), no colonial architecture remains because it has been leveled so often. Many public buildings damaged by the 1986 earthquake have yet to be repaired, and the city's center of plazas and cultural institutions has been more or less abandoned by the ruling class, which has retreated to an insulated world of shopping centers and "*colonias*" in the suburbs. Lively but chaotic street markets have taken over the downtown, and ramshackle squatter colonies occur wherever a bit of spare land presents itself.

Downtown San Salvador is laid out in a fairly rational grid pattern, with avenidas running north and south and calles east and west. The main artery is the Calle Rubén Darío, which turns into the Alameda Franklin D. Roosevelt and then into the Paseo Escalón as it heads west into the exclusive Colonia Escalón. Avenidas north of Calle Arce are labeled "*norte*," those south are labeled "*sur*." Calles east of Avenida Cuscutlán are labeled "*oriente*," those west of it are labeled "*poniente*," abbreviated as "Pon." There are some pleasant, if crowded, downtown parks, and some beautiful and uncrowded ones in the outskirts. The vast suburbs are a warren of colonias and "*urbanizaciones*" connected by winding "*autopistas*." Bus service is excellent if you know where you're going. If you don't, there's usually a taxi around to take you back to familiar ground. Average in-town fares are $2–3.

Once you get used to the crowding (the main plazas and markets are literally packed with people), San Salvador is an enjoyable and interesting city to visit. There are plenty of good places to eat and stay (although fast food franchises were too pervasive for my taste), and Salvadorans are very friendly and accommodating. The spirit of enterprise may get a little out of hand at times—I've been short-changed in San Salvador more than in other cities—but the friend-liness and helpfulness outweigh this. More serious problems emerge after dark, when the downtown becomes unsafe for pedes-trians, and the suburbs retire behind iron bars and armed guards. Things are much safer than in the 1980s, however, when guerrillas routinely blew up electric plants and occasionally invaded the city.

Transportation

In 1994, El Salvador was the only Central American country re-quiring visas for holders of U.S. passports. Visas weren't required for most European and Latin American nationals. Getting a visa required presenting to an El Salvadoran consulate a passport valid for three months beyond entry date, proof of employment, a letter of clearance from local police, a return ticket, and two passport photos. There was no charge, and visas were good for up to ninety days. Procedures may have changed since then: check with a con-sulate or travel agent. Baggage is often searched, and there's a $12 airport tax. Restrictions on travel to northern and eastern parts of the country have been lifted. Salvadoran law prohibits visitors from participating in Salvadoran politics, which can be cause for revo-cation of visas and deportation.

INTERNATIONAL AIRLINES: American flies to San Salvador via Miami (800-433-7300); Taca, the Salvadoran national airline, flies via San Francisco, Los Angeles, Houston, New Orleans, and Miami (800-535-8780); United flies via San Francisco and Miami (800-222-8333); Aviateca flies via Los Angeles and Miami (800-327-9832); Lacsa flies via Los Angeles (800-225-2272); and Con-tinental (800-525-0280) flies via Houston.

DOMESTIC FLIGHTS: There are no regular internal airlines, but small planes can be hired to fly from the old airport at Ilopango, 13 kilometers from San Salvador. Planes fly to San Miguel, La Unión, and Usulután. Contact TAES, Taxis Aéreos El Salvador (phone: 27-1020; fax: 23-3898).

BUSES, TAXIS: The new Comalapa International Airport is 44 kilometers from San Salvador near Costa del Sol Beach. Acaya Minibus shuttles passengers to and from the airport, leaving from Calle 3 Pon. and Ave. 19 Norte at 6, 7, 12, and 3 in town, and from the right of the door as you go out of the terminal when the van fills up (phone: 71-4937 in town; 39-9721 at airport). Fee is $2 one-way. Taxis at the airport door may try to charge up to $40, but if you go to the side and bargain you can go to downtown San Salvador for $15. There are also buses outside the airport toll station, but they run only to a station at the edge of town (from which you could easily get a taxi, however). There is a money exchange window just inside the airport security barrier which gave me a good rate. Just outside the security barrier is an Instituto Salvadoreño de Turismo booth which I found of mixed value: the attendant was friendly and watched my bags while I changed money, but told me I'd have to pay $40 for a taxi.

ROADS: Salvadoran roads are in fairly good shape, considering that the country was at war throughout the 1980s. Most are unpaved except for major highways and around San Salvador. Bus service is good. International buses to Tegucigalpa and Guatemala City run from the Puerto Bus Terminal, Ave. San Pablo and end of Ave. San Antonio Abad at the west end of San Salvador (city bus 29). Domestic buses go from two terminals, depending on whether their destination is west or east of San Salvador: the Terminal de Occidente (west) is off the Boulevard Venezuela (city bus 4, 27, or 43); the Terminal de Oriente (east) is at the end of the Ave. Peralta (city bus 7, 29, 33, or 34). Most city buses start from the main plaza downtown. Taxis are yellow and unmetered. Ask the fare to your destination before you get in, and you can probably bargain.

CAR RENTAL: Most major companies have San Salvador offices: Hertz (phone: 39-9481), Budget (phone: 39-9186), and Avis (phone: 23-7268) have airport offices. Motorists may be targets for bribery requests by police or for armed robbery, since the war greatly increased the number of weapons in the country. High population density requires special care to avoid running over domestic animals or people. Drivers are advised to keep well clear of armed services vehicles. As elsewhere, damage from unpaved roads and widespread theft can greatly increase your expenses if you're not very careful.

TRAINS: There are a few passenger services, but nothing of interest to visitors.

U.S. Embassy

Boulevard Santa Elena, Urbanizacion Santa Elena, APO AA 34023, San Salvador (phone: 98-1666, 78-4444; fax: 98-2336, 78-6011).

Health Advisory

Intestinal disorders are widespread because of poor water supplies. There are mixed reports about San Salvador tap water, but it would probably be best to play it safe and drink only bottled or treated water. Cholera is active. Malaria is highly active below 1,000 meters in rural areas, particularly in the east. Dengue has been reported, in San Salvador as well as rural areas.

HEALTH FACILITIES: In San Salvador, International Association for Medical Assistance to Travelers (IAMAT) Center, 21 Calle Pon. 1605 (phone: 25-8325); Clinicas Medicas (phone: 25-0277).

Hotels

The Camino Real near the south end of the Boulevard de los Héroes is very expensive ($100 range) but well located near inexpensive guest houses: its restaurant is good for meetings and breakfasts (phone: 79-3888; fax: 23-5660). The Hotel Alameda on the Alameda Roosevelt at Ave. 43 Sur is very conveniently located for buses, and is good, in the $60 range, with a pleasant restaurant (phone: 79-0299; fax: 79-3011). Casa de Huéspedes Austria, just off the Plaza Beethoven at 3834 Calle 1a Pon., has big airy rooms with baths and a quiet, homey atmosphere in the $20–40 range, with breakfast included (phone: 24-0791). Novo Apartotel at 4617 61 Ave. Norte is comparable (phone: 79-0099). Casa de Huéspedes Florida at 115 Pasaje de los Almendros (turn off to the right two blocks past Hotel Camino Real on Blvd. de los Héroes) has clean rooms with bath (cold water) for $10–20. Owner speaks English (phone: 26-1858). (A bit noisy—rent a fan for a few dollars extra and it masks noise as well as cooling room.) American Guest House, 953 Calle 1a Pon. and Ave. 17 N. (phone: 71-0224), and Family Guest House, nearby at 925 Calle 1a Pon. (phone: 22-1202) are comparable. Hotel Panamerican, 113 Ave. 8 Sur, is in the $7 range (phone: 22-2959). Pension Rex, 213 Ave. 10 N. has rooms in the $5 range.

Restaurants

The Zona Rosa on the Boulevard del Hipodromo has the best and most expensive restaurants, including Marcelino's, Mediteranee, and Paradise. The Paseo Escalón around Plaza Beethoven has many mid-price restaurants: Betos has good seafood pasta and friendly service (one waiter practiced his English on me) (phone: 24-3038); La Carnitas de Don Carlos on Plaza Beethoven has Mexican food, nice patio; others are Siete Mares and La Mar for seafood, Diligencia (Ave. 83) and El Bodegon (Ave. 77) for steaks, Asia for Chinese, and Rancho Alegre. The street behind the Hotel Camino Real and the shopping center across the Blvd. de los Héroes from it have many inexpensive restaurants, including branches of Betos (Hola Betos), Rancho Alegre, and Asia. On weekends, mariachis play in this area. Shaw's has good coffee and desserts in both the above areas. Downtown, small cafes serve good "*plato del dia*" lunches: Café Teatro in the National Theater, Ave. 2 and Calle 2; Café Don Alberto, Ave. 15 Sur and Calle Arce; Actoteatro, on Calle 1 Pon. between aves. 15 and 13 N. La Zanahoria, 1144 Calle Arce, has vegetarian food. A 10- to 15-percent tip is customary.

A Salvadoran specialty is the "*pupusería*," small restaurants or stands that sell "*pupusas*," tortillas that are filled with cheese,

meat, or beans before they are cooked, then eaten with pickled vegetables. You can find these almost anywhere, like hot dog stands.
(Street stand sanitation may be questionable.)

Communications

The main post office is at the Centro de Gobierno, Ave. 13 N. and
Calle 15 Pon. (the Centro also contains the immigration office
where visas are renewed). There are several branches, including at
Metrocentro, the shopping center across from the Hotel Camino
Real, and Centro Comercial Gigante in Colonia Escalón. They're
open weekdays 7:30–5; Sat. 7:30–noon.

The state telecommunications company, ANTEL, has offices in
the above locations, and provides phone and telex services.

Money Exchange

The Salvadoran currency unit is the colón, with 100 centavos to the
colón. The 1994 exchange rate was $8.71 colones to the U.S. dollar.
Banks generally change dollars and traveler's checks, though they
may ask to see the receipts for checks. Casas de cambio, as common
as banks, give better exchange rates, about as good as illegal street
markets. There's a good casa de cambio at the Centro de Gobierno.
American Express, Visa, and MasterCard are widely accepted;
Diner's Club less so. The American Express office is at El Salvador
Travel Service, Centro Comercial, La Mascota (phone: 23-0177).

Tourist Information

The Instituto Salvadoreño de Turismo office is at 619 Calle Rubén
Darío at Ave. 9 Sur. The staff speak English, and are very friendly
and helpful (phone: 22-8000). They have information handouts on
natural areas and archaeological sites (particularly areas managed
by the instituto, including Cerro Verde National Park), maps of the
country, and they can help you make reservations with hotels or
tour agencies. They also run Sunday bus tours to points of interest
outside San Salvador. Hours are weekdays 8–5, Sat. 8–noon.
(Their airport bureau is open 8–4:30, except Christmas and New
Year's.)

Maps

Good city ($3) and country ($2) maps are available at the Instituto Geográfico Nacional, 79 Ave. Juan Bertis, Ciudad Delgado. Esso and Texaco sell road maps at their service stations, and you can buy a road map at the Budget Rent-a-Car office, 220 Ave. 85 Sur, or at their airport office. J.P.K. Maps publishes a good, small country and city map in English: ask at bookstores or hotel newsstands.

Museums and Zoos

El Salvador's present natural history museum is a vast improvement over the one William Beebe saw in 1936. It's located in the leafy, quiet Parque Saburo Hirao (named after a Japanese textile magnate) at the end of Calle Los Viveros near the zoo south of downtown. No. 2 "Modelo" buses leaving from Ave. 1 Sur near Calle Arce go there—look for the "Museo de Historia Natural" sign. The museum is in a mansion surrounded by gardens (there are plans to move to a bigger building) and contains a fine fossil exhibit, especially the detailed fossils of laurel, ceiba, oak, and other kinds of leaves, and of small fish and frogs from an ancient lake under San Vicente volcano. There's also a fossil beach exhibit, and paintings of prehistoric habitats. Other exhibits include one on birds of Parque Saburo and several on endangered species and habitats. The museum is active in conservation and environmental education. Hours are 9:30–4:30, Wed.–Sun.

The entrance to the Parque Zoológico is on the Calle Modelo, a short distance north of the turnoff for the natural history museum. The zoo is large and lavish by Central American standards (though somewhat rundown), with island habitats for white-faced capuchin and spider monkeys in a small lake. The spider monkeys are a gray color unusual in Central America: there are only a few of these left in the wild in eastern El Salvador. Several other native species—coyotes, coatis, foxes—have been given spacious enclosures, while cats, Old World monkeys, and bears are in iron cages. There's a reptile house, also an aviary across a small stream, which unfortunately is polluted and appears a poisonous green color. A shantytown is visible behind the bird cages, but there are also wild motmots and parakeets. Hours are 9:30–4:30, Wed.–Sun.

The Jardín Botánico la Laguna (also called Jardín de los Planes) is an enchanted place, not least because it's so hard to find, tucked away in a deep crater otherwise occupied by huge factories. The No. 42 bus from downtown is supposed to pass near it, but I found myself wandering in distant suburbs and finally got a cab, which took a sudden hard right when headed north on the Blvd. Cuscatlán and dived down the cul-de-sac street into the crater. We wandered through the factories a while, and finally found the garden entrance, passing through which was like entering another world. Clay-colored robins and magpie jays were everywhere, there is a large, beautifully landscaped and tended collection of native trees and other plants, and the natural forest on the crater rim above the garden is tall, lush, and vibrant with insect and bird calls. There are exhibits on El Imposible and Montecristo. Hours are 9–6, Tues.–Sun.

The Museo Nacional David J. Guzman on the Ave. de la Revolución just off the Pan American Highway has good archaeological exhibits, but has been closed for renovation. Check with the tourist bureau for reopening time. Bus No. 34 goes there from downtown.

Bookstores and Libraries

La Revista at 235 Ave. Hippodromo, Zona Rosa, has English magazines and secondhand books, as do Shaw's cafes. Cervantes, 114 Ave. 9 Sur and on Paseo Escalón, and Bautista, 124 Calle 10 Pon., are good Spanish bookstores.

Excursions Around San Salvador

There's quite a lot of open space on the steep volcanoes ringing the city, but public areas are heavily used, and are not considered very safe. Littering was common in 1993, with otherwise lovely woodlands literally smothered in garbage in some places. (Solid waste disposal is a SalvaNatura priority, so this may improve.) There are gorgeous views, and plenty of interesting vegetation and birdlife. Butterflies can be abundant.

A visit to Parque Balboa and Cerro Chulo on the heights south of town is good for a morning or afternoon. Take hourly No. 12 "Mil Cumbres" buses from the east of the Mercado Central. The bus passes Parque Balboa then climbs to Cerro Chulo, where the Puerta del Diablo, a massive rock formation, provides spectacular views, with swallows and vultures soaring overhead. You can get off there, then walk back down about a kilometer to the park, which has paths and food stands (there have been reports of muggings in the area, but I had no trouble).

A longer trip is to the crater of San Salvador volcano west of the city. You take a No. 101 bus from Ave. 3 Norte and Calle Rubén Darío to Santa Tecla (also known as Nueva el Salvador). From there, No. 103 buses go hourly to within a kilometer from the crater (called Boquerón). The last bus back to town leaves at 3 P.M., so get an early start. A path leads around the forested crater, a two-hour walk, but the going may be rough in places. A small crater within the big one is the result of San Salvador's latest eruption, in 1917. Past Santa Tecla on the highway to Santa Ana is Turicentro los Chorros, a popular swimming resort of waterfalls and pools, accessible by No. 79 bus from Ave. 11 Sur and Calle Rubén Darío.

The important archaeological sites of San Andrés and the Jewel of Ceren (La Joya de Ceren) are located between Santa Tecla and Lago de Coatepeque, 30–40 kilometers from San Salvador. Either would be a good long day trip by bus, or you could see both with a car. San Andrés is also called La Campaña de San Andrés because its principal ruin is bell-shaped. First excavated in 1940 and again in 1977, the 2-kilometer site includes fifteen ceremonial structures dating from about 1,200 years ago. The site shows Maya, Pipil, and Aztec influences. There are small pyramids, terraces, and two large plazas. Artifacts housed in a small museum include a large flint piece that may have belonged to a high-ranking Maya, as well as metates and pottery. The site is just north of the Pan American Highway. There's a sign at 33 kilometers just past the Río Sucio. Any bus going west from the Terminal del Occidente (Ave. Venezuela and Calle 49 Sur) will stop there.

Just before San Andrés, a gravel road leads north from the highway to the village of San Juan Opico. The Jewel of Ceren is located a few miles along this road. It is a Maya farm settlement that was buried by 5 meters of ash during an explosion of Laguna Caldera about 1,400 years ago. As at Pompeii, the ash preserved a unique record of daily life. "No other site in the New World has domestic architecture so well preserved," said archaeologist Paul Amaroli. A bulldozer accidentally opened the site in 1976, and "local people who observed the bulldozing reported seeing a number of bodies on the floor of the house, clustered around a few polychrome pottery vessels." Excavations in 1979 uncovered a farmhouse with a fired clay floor, clay walls, and thatched roof as well as an area for making polychrome pottery. In 1989, renewed excavations found domestic details like a flock of ducks in a courtyard, a digging stick leaning against a doorway, and a book, or codex, in a wall niche beside three painted pots and an oyster shell. Outside the structures, remains of Maya cornfields with soil conservation ridges were found. Excavations are continuing, and there are plans to restore the site with facsimiles of the artifacts in place. You may need permission to visit the site: check with the tourism institute office, which has English handouts on the site. The No. 108 bus from the Terminal del Occidente goes to San Juan Opico.

The Pacific Volcanic Zone

Everything in this landscape has been erupted from volcanoes—not just the towering cones, but the hills, which are strata of ash and lava uplifted by faulting, and the valleys, which are filled with volcanic soil washed downhill by streams. It is a very young landscape, formed within the last few million years as subduction of the Cocos Plate under the Caribbean Plate caused the volcanic activity. Much of what is now El Salvador probably lay under the ocean before the Pliocene epoch, which began about 5 million years ago.

Since volcanic rock and ash break down into soil quickly, most of the landscape was originally covered with deep, rich soil. Except where recent eruptions had destroyed it, forest grew almost everywhere—dry deciduous forest on lowlands, semideciduous forest on hills and stream courses, evergreen rain and cloud forest on volcanoes and high ridges. This forest probably was quite resilient to indigenous agriculture, growing back when cornfields were left fallow. Forest also was a major part of indigenous economies. Even with the coffee boom of the nineteenth century, which covered virtually every hill and mountain with coffee plantations, much wood-

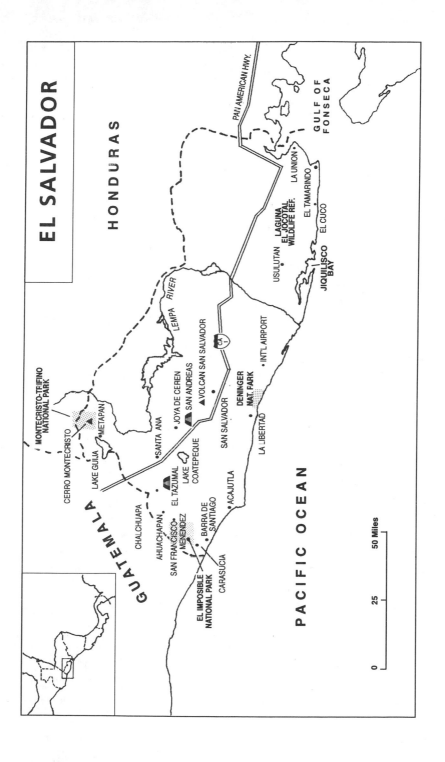

EL SALVADOR

HONDURAS

GUATEMALA

PACIFIC OCEAN

GULF OF FONSECA

PAN AMERICAN HWY.

MONTECRISTO-TRIFINO NATIONAL PARK

CERRO MONTECRISTO

MONTECRISTO

METAPAN

Lake Guija

LEMPA RIVER

JOYA DE CEREN

SAN ANDREAS

SANTA ANA

VOLCAN SAN SALVADOR

DENINGER NAT PARK

SAN SALVADOR

LA LIBERTAD

INTL AIRPORT

CHALCHUAPA

AHUACHAPAN

EL TAZUMAL

LAKE COATEPEQUE

SAN FRANCISCO MENENDEZ

BARRA DE SANTIAGO

ACAJUTLA

CARASUCIA

EL IMPOSIBLE NATIONAL PARK

USULUTAN

LAGUNA EL JOCOTAL WILDLIFE REF.

EL TAMARINDO

LA UNION

EL CUCO

JIQUILISCO BAY

0   25   50 Miles

land remained because coffee was planted in the traditional way, under a canopy of large trees to protect the coffee shrubs from drying out. Much of El Salvador's coffee is still grown in this way, which conserves soil and allows some biodiversity to coexist. Most of the country's woodlands are severely modified from their natural state, however, with a scarcity or absence of game, valuable timber trees, and showy birds such as quetzals and macaws. It is said that El Imposible is the only place in El Salvador where one can stand on a hilltop and see nothing but natural forest.

Cerro Verde National Park

This is more of a recreational than a natural area park, but it has some fine scenery and hiking on Izalco and Santa Ana volcanoes. The tourism institute manages it. Cerro Verde is a 2,023-meter extinct volcanic cone just east of the two more active volcanoes, and trails lead from the parking lot 14 kilometers into the park to the summits of both. A campground and rental cottages are located at the parking lot. Free permission to camp can be obtained from the Departamento de Bienestar, Ministerio de Trabajo, in San Bartolo just outside San Salvador. The paved road continues to the summit, where the twenty-room Hotel de la Montaña is located. It's in the $20–30 range, with a good restaurant. Reservations are recommended, especially on weekends (phone: 71-2434; fax: 22-1208), or you can make them through the San Salvador tourism office. Weekdays are best for visits. The hotel was begun in the early 1960s, when Izalco was still erupting occasionally, and provides a fine view of its crater, but Izalco has not erupted since 1966, just before the hotel was finished. The park is about 70 kilometers from San Salvador, with access roads either off the Pan American Highway and along Lago de Coatepeque from the north, or off the Sonsonate Highway from the south. By bus, you need to go to Santa Ana (see below) and take the No. 248 bus from the terminal, which leaves twice a day.

It takes about two hours to walk from the Cerro Verde parking lot to the top of Izalco. Except for its quiescence, it probably is much as when John Lloyd Stephens visited it in 1839 and found "its sides brown and barren, and all around for miles the earth covered with lava." Stephens met a local clergyman who had watched it grow from "a small orifice . . . puffing out . . . pebbles" to the 3,000-foot cone Stephens described: "The crater had three orifices, one of which was inactive; another emitted constantly a rich blue smoke; and after a report, deep in the huge throat of the third appeared a light blue vapor and then a mass of thick black smoke, whirling and struggling out in enormous wreaths, and rising in a dark, majestic column, lighted for a moment by a sheet of flame."

Volcán de Santa Ana, the summit of which is also about two hours' walk from the Cerro Verde parking lot, is still active, with four concentric craters and a lake in the center. (Crater fumes can cause eye and throat irritation.) Unlike barren Izalco, Santa Ana has some mature forest on its slopes. Around 127 bird species, 17 of them hummingbirds, have been counted in the vicinity. Santa Ana will be included in the Los Volcanes National Park complex slated for tourism by the Parks Service. Features include endemic herbaceous vegetation, a community of heath family plants on the first platform of the Santa Ana crater, and the community of agaves, bromeliads, and cloud forest trees on the slopes.

You can also climb Santa Ana Volcano from Los Andes National Park on the other side from Cerro Verde. A trail from the park headquarters leads to the summit in about an hour and a half, leading through dwarf cloud forest. At the summit, a trail to the left leads to a good view of Lake Coatepeque. The park is managed by the Parks and Wildlife Service, and you need to check with them before visiting. The park can be reached by taking a bus from Santa Ana (see below) to the small town of Los Naranjos, from which a dirt road leads to the park entrance—a couple hours' walk through coffee plantations.

Another attraction in the area is the volcanic Lake Coatepeque, where there are a couple of inexpensive hotels: the Hotel Torremolinos and the Hotel del Lago. Both have boats that can take you to Teopan Island, which has trails and forest (the island is private property). The lake is accessible from the Pan American Highway by turning west on the overpass at the town of El Congo.

The town of Santa Ana is a good headquarters for trips to Cerro Verde and other nearby attractions. It is large enough to have good accommodations, but small enough to walk around, with an attractive central square. To get there from San Salvador, take bus No. 201 from the Terminal del Occidente at Blvd. Venezuela and Ave. 49 Sur (you can get there from downtown on city buses 4, 27, and 34). The brand-new Hotel Sahara at Ave. 10 Sur and Calle 3 Pon. has comfortable rooms around a courtyard for $16–27 without air-conditioning and $22–76 with a/c, and a good restaurant (phone: 40-8865). It also has seminar rooms, tea rooms, and a terraza with panoramic views. The Hotel La Libertad near the cathedral at Calle 4 Oriente and Ave. 1 Norte has pleasant, clean rooms in the $10–20 range (it was full when I tried). The Hotel Nuevo Roosevelt near the Sahara at Ave. 8 Sur and Calle 5 Pon. has windowless but clean rooms with cold-water bath and fan for $8. Restaurants are less plentiful than hotels: Las Canoas near the cathedral; Kiyomi at Ave. 4 Sur between calles 3 and 5.

El Tazumal

This impressive ruin is part of a 6-square-kilometer complex of structures around the town of Chalchuapa west of Santa Ana. The area shows signs of occupation going back at least 3,200 years and demonstrates the mobility and diversity of pre-Columbian cultures. Gold ornaments found in the ruins indicate that trade was carried on as far south as Panama. The main structure at El Tazumal is 23 meters high and looms impressively above the cemetery of present-day Chalchuapa. Excavations beginning in 1942 found two different construction complexes within the structure: one from the Classic Period of 1,700 to 1,000 years ago, which shows the architectural influence of the Teotihuacán culture and the Maya highlands, and one from the early Post-Classic Period of 1,000 to 800 years ago, which is influenced by Toltec architecture. A large ball court abutted the main structure but has been covered by the cemetery. There is a museum at the site, with an impressively cosmopolitan artifact collection: little Pre-Classic clay dolls with an Olmec cast, Classic Maya pottery, Lenca pottery with angular, feathered figures that might be Navajo. "*Tazumal*" is a Quiché Maya word meaning "the pyramid where the sacrificial victims were burnt."

The Tazumal ruins are in a small but leafy park; admission is free, open Tues.–Sun. 9–12 and 1–5:30. The No. 236 bus from the Santa Ana terminal goes there in twenty minutes. When I was there in late afternoon, the trees were full of warblers and tanagers, and large emerald green lizards ran about the fencerows. A basilisk lizard that must have been a meter long with its tail scurried up a tree.

Several other ruined structures remain in the area. El Trapiche to the north of Tazumal is a tall, wedding-cake structure, of which there were originally eighteen. A model in the museum shows the other sites.

El Imposible

This 5,000-hectare area west of Ahuachapán has the least disturbed forest in the volcanic zone. It is extremely rugged, with deep gorges and steep ridges ranging from 350 to 1,400 meters in elevation, and is composed of uplifted and eroded deposits of volcanic conglomerates and lavas. The name refers to the difficulty of access. Although much of the area was planted with coffee in the past, and about half of the forest is second-growth, flora and fauna remain highly diverse. A biodiversity study conducted by SalvaNatura on the 35,600-hectare watershed of which the forest is a part noted over four hundred tree species and over three hundred bird species.

Two of the trees—"seven red shirts" (*Guapira witsbergi*) and wild amaranth (*Parathesis congesta*)—are recently discovered and known only from the area. It contains El Salvador's last remaining population of great curassow (*Crax rubra*, known as *"pajuil"* in Spanish), a turkey-sized bird, males of which are jet black with an ornately curled crest and a bright yellow knob above the beak. Other birds include four parakeet and parrot species, three trogon species, two toucan species, three motmot species, and seven cuckoo species. Opossums, armadillos, pacas, foxes, ringtails, coatis, and jaguarundis remain common, while anteaters, porcupines, tairas, kinkajous, pumas, margays, collared peccaries, and white-tailed deer still occur. Freshwater fish include convict cichlids, tetras, mollies, and the strange "four-eyed fish" (*Anableps dowi*), the eyes of which are adapted to see both in and out of water. Called *"cuatro ojos"* in Spanish, four-eyed fish rest in the shallows with just their eyes protruding from the water, watching what goes on above and below simultaneously. They're common in local streams and estuaries.

Other organisms such as amphibians, reptiles, and insects haven't been inventoried, but are also believed to be diverse, with many rare species. (Big blue morpho butterflies and heliconians were abundant when I was there.) El Imposible is a rare remnant of forest that once grew all along the Pacific coast, but that has been reduced to a few patches, and there is much more to learn about it. The SalvaNatura study found three zones in the "*bosque de montana*" that grows from 300 to 1,450 meters: a high zone with oaks and other species characteristic of cloud forest and some endemic trees; a middle zone with many endemic trees, those growing on steep, rocky slopes largely deciduous or semideciduous, those on deeper soils largely evergreen; and a lower zone with characteristics similar to the mixed forest and gallery forest of the adjacent coastal plain.

The SalvaNatura study also found that the "quality, quantity, and availability" of El Imposible's natural resources were clearly diminishing under pressure from local communities. For example, a poll of local woodworkers found all valuable wood species declining. Forest fires in 1986 and 1988 caused considerable damage. Given the critical situation, SalvaNatura is anxious that tourism not become simply another pressure on the area. The park is not open to the general public because of lack of facilities at present, but you can get a special permit to visit from SalvaNatura, 422 Ave. 77 Norte, Colonia Escalón, San Salvador (phone: 98-4001). You will need to be accompanied by a park ranger or guide in all areas of the park. Guides should be tipped; depending on the length of the guided hike, 25 to 50 colones per day is recommended by SalvaNatura.

The park has two main access points. The easiest is via the town of San Francisco Mendenez, accessible from San Salvador by taking a bus from the Terminal del Occidente (see above) to the town of Sonsonate southwest of Cerro Verde, and then by taking a twice-daily bus to San Francisco Mendenez. From there you follow the main road a short walk to the park entrance, where you can check in with the park rangers. A nursery for endangered tree species has been developed at park headquarters. Camping is permitted at "La Fincona," 2 hours' walk into the park. You'll need to bring camping equipment, food, and water. A trail leads from La Fincona to the Río Mixtepe, and there are interesting cave formations along the way. Sr. Vidal Campos is a recommended guide for this area.

Visiting the park via the Ahuachapio entrance will require 3 to 4 days unless you have a 4wd vehicle, but there is more primary forest and wildlife. Bus access from San Salvador is the same, except that you get off the bus from Sonsonate at the Ahuachapio Bridge before you get to San Francisco Mendenez. Ask the bus driver to let you off at the bridge. From there, a very steep and rough road leads 13.5 kilometers to the park entrance just past the village of San Miguelito. You can camp at an old wooden hacienda nearby: there are latrines, an outdoor shower, and drinking water. Sr. Miguel Chinchilla lives at the hacienda and can arrange for a ranger or guide to take you through the park. A short walk away is the mirador at El Mulo, which provides a breathtaking view of the park interior. About an hour and a half away is Cerro el Leon with a 360-degree view of the park and the mangroves of Barra de Santiago on the coast. You can also hike to the Guayapa River, where there are deep pools at a place called Los Enganches. If you're adventurous, you can arrange to walk across the park, from San Benito to the quiet colonial town of Tacuba on the north side. This will require at least 4 to 5 hours of walking, but leads to the least disturbed, highest forest area at Cerro Campana. From Tacuba, you can get a bus back to San Salvador via Ahuachapán and Santa Ana. You'll need to arrange this in advance with SalvaNatura.

Barra de Santiago

This 2,000-hectare area of estuary, mangrove forest, and coastal marsh also is part of the 36,650-hectare watershed in the Salva-Natura biodiversity study (see above). All the watershed's streams drain into the lagoon behind the barrier beach at Barra de Santiago. Red, white, and black mangroves grow around the lagoon, and along the tidal waterways that lead inland from it. This habitat is extremely rich in aquatic life, with 114 estuarine and marine fish species listed in the report, and abundant crustaceans and mollusks. It is thus an important feeding and roosting place for resident and migratory waterbirds, including rarities such as roseate spoonbills, wood storks, and Muscovy ducks. One hundred and sixty bird species have been recorded for the area. Many land birds live in the mangrove forest as well, including the only colony of white-fronted Amazon parrots known in El Salvador. Populations have rebounded since 1980, when protection was augmented and pollution from adjacent cotton plantations reduced, although some species, including anhingas and cormorants, have not recovered former numbers. "El Colegio de los Aves" is an important breeding colony. Crocodiles, sea turtles, and iguanas also are present.

Twenty mammal species have been reported in the area, but they're generally uncommon, partly because Barra de Santiago's woodlands are cut off from those of El Imposible by a wide deforested strip. There is a remnant of the coastal plain forest that once connected them to the north of Barra de Santiago, but it too is isolated. Proposed restoration of a wooded corridor connecting them would probably augment biodiversity in the area.

As with El Imposible, Barra de Santiago's resources are under pressure from pollution, woodcutting, poaching, and other factors, and facilities for tourism didn't exist as of late 1993. Check with SalvaNatura (see above) for present status.

Deininger

This is a sizable wooded, hilly area between the coastal highway about 10 kilometers east of the major beach resort of La Libertad and the village of Panchimalco south of San Salvador. It's under the jurisdiction of the Instituto Salvadoreño de Turismo but was without facilities as of 1993. Check with their San Salvador office, Ave. 9 and Calle Rubén Darío (phone: 22-8000).

Laguna El Jocotal

This was the only managed wildland in eastern El Salvador in 1993, although some rare species held on in the east longer than in the west because it was more remote. Macaws are supposed to have been present into the 1930s, and spider monkeys persisted at least into the 1980s. Laguna El Jocotal is a shallow freshwater lake ringed with marsh vegetation about 10 kilometers east of Usulután on the highway to La Unión. The lake is about a kilometer south of the highway, past a small village. Fifty-six waterbird species have been recorded, including Muscovy ducks and two species of tree (or whistling) ducks. The Parks and Wildlife Service manages the area: a warden is in residence. Check with the San Salvador parks office (phone: 77-0622, 27-0484; fax: 77-0490) to arrange a visit.

Usulután is a good-sized market and administrative center. Take bus No. 302 from the Terminal de Oriente at the end of the Ave. Peralta east of San Salvador. The Hotel and Restaurant España on Usulután's main square (phone: 62-0378) is moderately priced, and there are cheaper places, too. South of Usulután are the Bay of Jiquilisco and the estuary of the Río Lempa, El Salvador's major river. This was a combat zone during the war, but was historically a major wildlife area. Farther east, toward La Unión on the Gulf of Fonseca, there are beach resorts at El Cuco and El Tamarindo.

The Northern Highlands

The plateau that covers southwest Honduras rises like a rampart along El Salvador's northern border. Most of the peaks are volcanic, their rocks having originated when eruptions were still occurring several million years ago, and there are also much older granitic rocks that have been exposed by the uplifting of the plateau. Because they are older, these northern rocks are less fertile than those of the active volcanic zone (erosion has leached out some of the mineral nutrients). Vegetation resembles that on the Honduran side, with remnant dry forest in valleys, ocote pine and temperate hardwoods such as oak and liquidambar on slopes up to 1,800 meters, and dense cloud forest above that. Remnant populations of jaguar, tapir, quetzal, brocket deer, and monkeys may persist in remote areas, but the area was the major combat zone of the civil war, so it hasn't been explored much recently. Areas away from roads may be mined, particularly around and eastward from Chalatenango.

Parque Nacional Montecristo

This park in extreme northwest El Salvador is part of the international Trifinio Park which includes adjacent parts of Honduras and Guatemala. The extent of the Salvadoran park is unclear, but it includes Cerros Montecristo, Brujo, and Miramundo and adjacent highlands. The peak of Cerro Montecristo is where the three borders intersect, so it's called Trifinio. It's 2,418 meters above sea level. The heart of the Salvadoran park is a 825-hectare cloud forest that persists above 2,100 meters (it originally occurred down to 1,800 meters, but has been cleared up to 2,100). This is a high-quality, primary forest, with gigantic old oaks, magnolias, laurels, and pinabete pines covered in moss, orchids, bromeliads, and other epiphytes towering over an understory of tree ferns, fuchsias, agaves, and hundreds of other species. Seventy percent of orchid species recorded from El Salvador occur here. With 2,000 millimeters of annual precipitation, it is almost always wet and misty, and chilly, here. Of the forest, 190 hectares are in state ownership.

The nature of resident wildlife also is unclear. An Instituto Salvadoreño de Turismo (IST) handout lists jaguar and brocket deer, but a ranger I talked to said they were long extinct in the area. The ranger said white-tailed deer and puma were present, as well as monkeys, although most were across the borders in Honduras and Guatemala. He said monkeys have been seen around the public use area at Planes de Montecristo, and that flocks of up to fifty emerald toucanets can be seen in some parts of the park. Quetzals are known to survive here, along with other threatened species such as blue-throated motmots, cinnamon flower-piercers, and bumble-bee-sized, wine-throated hummingbirds. Much of the park below 2,100 meters has been cut and burned for timber and pastures, or planted to coffee. Many areas have been reforested with commercial stands of pine and cypress, which helps to control erosion, but supports little wildlife.

The park rises majestically above Metapán, a pleasantly cool and breezy small city a few hours' bus ride north of Santa Ana on the No. 235 bus from the main Santa Ana station. There is a good new hotel in Metapán, located near the bus station at the start of the road to the park. It's the four-story Hotel San José, which has rooms with air-conditioning, balcony, and television for $22, and rooms without (but with bath) for $12. There's a good restaurant, and you can sit on the patio in the evening and watch the large numbers of bats and vultures that frequent the vicinity (the bats live in house eaves and the vultures roost at the slaughterhouse). There are plenty of small restaurants and pupuserias in town, which is friendly (many people have relatives in the U.S.), also a less expensive hospedaje, the Gallo de Oro. There are two interesting baroque cathedrals, with silver altarpieces from local mines, among the oldest buildings in El Salvador.

Access to the park from Metapán was a little problematic when I was there. There was no public transport, but it's only 5 kilometers to the park entrance, an interesting (if uphill) walk past friendly hamlets and farmlands with flocks of magpie jays. Once at the entrance, I had to wait to hitch a ride, because walking to the public use area at Planes de Montecristo 17 kilometers up the mountain was prohibited. I was lucky: some meteorologists soon arrived and took me to the top along with a Los Angeles couple and a ranger. Partway to Planes de Montecristo is park headquarters, Casco Viejo, which was once an ironworking forge. Planes de Montecristo has camping areas which can accommodate up to 325 (and which is full every weekend, I heard), also a very nice orchid garden developed by local people, with two hundred species, including the spectacular white nun. There were interesting flocks of big, brilliant blue bushy-crested jays feeding on some kind of grub in the cypress plantations. Before you get to headquarters, the road branches left and climbs to a private finca near the summit. After the road enters the primary cloud forest, a signed trail climbs to Trifinio, from which views must be spectacular on the rare occasions that it's not enveloped in fog. If you don't want to take serendipity in getting around the park, you may want to rent a 4wd vehicle in San Salvador, which would cost about $60 a day. Or you might find someone in Metapán to take you up, although I couldn't.

Permission from the Parks and Wildlife Service at CENREN in Canton El Matazano, Soyapango (phone: 77-0622) was required for park entrance as of late 1993, and the park was closed from February to May, apparently for wildlife breeding season. The regulations may change, however. The park administration was still recovering from the war, when the park was a zone of guerrilla activity. Visitors to the cloud forest must be accompanied by a ranger or guide.

On the way to Metapán from Santa Ana, the road passes the San Diego dry forest area, which may become a park in the future. A Peace Corps volunteer was working on this in 1993. Also along this road are interesting lakes, the Lago de Guija and Lago de Metapán. The Lago de Guija is half in Guatemala. There are archaeological sites on Azacualpa Island and the Igualtepec Peninsula on Lake Guija, and a number of lesser sites along the shoreline. There are no tourist facilities, however.

CHAPTER NINE

Nicaragua

NICARAGUA IS IN MANY ways at the heart of Central America. It is the largest country in size, with 141,000 square kilometers, and has always been a cultural leader in the region. It was second only to Guatemala as a colony. For centuries it rivaled Panama as a "path between the seas" because of its unique geography. Yet Nicaragua's distinctions have often led to misfortune. Its canal potential attracted opportunists from around the world, without ultimate benefits for Nicaraguans. Its very size has led to social and political conflicts. Nicaragua's centrality dictates that its problems generally are felt throughout the rest of Central America, as when its recent civil war threatened to draw its neighbors into conflict as well.

Nicaragua's environment is also crucial to the rest of the region. With its great lakes and volcanoes, vast shorelines, pine-forested highlands, and rain forests, it perhaps has more potential for wildlands conservation than any other Central American country. Yet poverty and political turmoil have so far worked against this potential's realization, and time is running out. Nicaragua's population, between 4 and 5 million, is still relatively small, but it is growing faster than any other Western Hemisphere nation's. If Nicaragua fails to protect its rain forest, the last truly extensive, complete samples of the forest that once grew unbroken from Yucatán to Darién will be lost.

Despite the conflicts of past decades (and partly because of them—the war retarded rain forest colonization), Nicaragua has taken steps to protect its ecosystems. It has a wildlands conservation system with a few national parks, and an impressive array of reserves that await development. Many of these reserves are presently hard to visit (some were impossible as of 1994 because of lingering conflict), but tourism is expanding. Reserves such as the Miskito Cays, Indio-Maíz, and Bosawas contain some of the most important ecosystems not only in Central America, but in the Western Hemisphere. Despite their problems, most Nicaraguans welcome visitors: people kept asking me when I was coming back.

Land of the Sweet Seas

Nicaragua contains three major geographic regions. A southward extension of the Tertiary era volcanic ranges and plateaus that cover southwest Honduras occupies the northern and central part of the country. The Cordillera Isabelia that looms northeast from Matagalpa is the tallest of these, reaching 1,990 meters at Cerro Saslaya. The mountains become lower and narrower southward, and end at the Cordillera Chontaleña east of Lake Nicaragua. These highlands are mostly made up of lava flows interspersed with beds of volcanic ash deposited during the Miocene and Pliocene epochs. East of the mountains is a vast Caribbean coastal plain underlain by thousands of meters of alluvial sediments. Soils tend to be heavily leached and lateritic, with low fertility despite heavy rain forest cover in some areas. Pine savannas and wetlands occupy much of the northeast coast, called the Miskito coast. The southern Caribbean coast has broad-leaved rain forest and extensive raphia palm swamps. Coastal lagoons and offshore coral reefs support abundant marine life.

West of the volcanic ranges and plateaus is the Nicaraguan Depression, a 50-kilometer-wide lowland that stretches from the mouth of the San Juan River on the Costa Rican border to the Gulf of Fonseca on the Honduran border. A line of active or recently active volcanoes, part of the Pacific volcanic chain that extends south from El Salvador, occupies the cénter of this region, from 807-meter Volcán Cosigüina on the Gulf of Fonseca to 1,326-meter Volcán Madera in Lake Nicaragua. The depression, which averages about 30 meters above sea level, marks the boundary between the old lands of northern Central America and the newer ones to the south. Today's large freshwater lakes, Nicaragua and Managua, appeared following land subsidence caused by faulting activity in fairly recent times. The native Nahuatl-speaking people called Lake Nicaragua "Cocibolca," the Sweet Sea. The abundance of recent volcanic activity has left highly fertile soil on the floor of the depression.

Each region has a characteristic climate. Rainfall is abundant and almost year-round on the Caribbean coast, particularly in the San Juan River basin, where as much as 6 meters may fall annually. Humidity is high, but temperatures generally aren't uncomfortably warm. In the highlands, climates vary according to altitude and exposure, with east-facing ridges getting much higher precipitation than valleys. The western margins of the highlands, and the Nicaraguan Depression, have a marked dry season from November to April, and the dryness is accentuated by strong winds that blow in January and February. Temperatures on the floor of the depression can be blisteringly hot, although humidity is relatively low during the dry season.

Human cultures developed in accordance with landscape and climate. There is dramatic early evidence of human occupation in the "Huellas de Acahualinca" in Managua, the footprints of a band of people who hurried across a mudflat during a volcanic ashfall an estimated six thousand years ago. We can guess from the footprints that they were a nomadic band of hunter-gatherers, but it's impossible to tell what their language or other cultural attributes might have been.

It's likely that the Chibchan-speaking, manioc-growing peoples who occupied the Caribbean slope when Columbus arrived had been there a long time, judging from archaeological finds. Nineteenth-century naturalist Thomas Belt noted "many evidences of a large Indian population having lived" in the region between Lake Nicaragua and the Caribbean. The Sumu and Rama people who still inhabit the area probably are their direct cultural descendants. The Lenca and Chontal people who occupied the Nicaraguan highlands before European arrival also seem to have been long-established inhabitants, although less is known about their language and cultural affinities than about the Chibchan-speakers.

The rich lowland of the Nicaraguan Depression was a dense mosaic of peoples, many of whom originated in the north, judging from the prevalence of the Uto-Aztecan Nahuatl language. Spanish naturalist Gonzalo de Oviedo y Valdés remarked in the early sixteenth century that "they speak the same language in the province of Nicaragua as they do in New Spain [Mexico]." A few decades later, Italian adventurer Girolamo Benzoni wrote: "The habits of these people are nearly all like those of the Mexicans; they eat human flesh, and they wear cloaks, and waistcoats without sleeves." Their society also resembled those of the Pacific coast of El Salvador and Guatemala, with intensive cultivation of maize, cacao, and other crops. Ceremonial centers were not as large and elaborate as those to the north, but remains of statuary, ceramics, and ceremonial burials are abundant.

Mahomet's Paradise

Columbus sailed quickly past Nicaragua's east coast in 1502, perhaps hurrying to make up time after his difficult passage around Cape Gracias a Dios. The first European to reach the heavily populated west was Gil González Dávila, who led an expedition from Panama in 1519. A cacique named Nicarao greeted Dávila at Lake Nicaragua, gave him gold worth 15,000 castellanos, and allowed himself and nine thousand subjects to be baptized (although not without first asking Dávila some tough theological questions, such as why God had made darkness and cold, when light and warmth were so much more pleasant). Dávila reciprocated with "a silk costume, a red cape, and some geegaws." This perhaps led the indigenes to have second thoughts, because the next cacique Dávila encountered, named Diriangen, attacked him with three or four thousand warriors. Dávila returned to Panama with 112,524 castellanos worth of gold, however. "The country of Nicaragua is not very large, but fertile and delightful," wrote Benzoni. "It produces a great deal of honey and wax, balsam, cotton, and many fruits of the country. . . . From the great abundance that reigned in the province when the Spaniards first subjugated it, they called it Mahomet's Paradise." Benzoni also noted "an incredible multitude of parrots."

In 1524, the governor of Panama, Pedro Arias de Ávila, sent Francisco Hernández de Córdoba to settle Nicaragua, which led to the founding of León and Granada, the main colonial cities. Ávila, known as "Pedrarias," may have been the cruelest conquistador of all ("a man who found his pleasure in the spectacle of Indians being torn to pieces by dogs specially trained for the purpose," according to historian Ricardo Guardia), and much of Nicaragua's native population was deported to slavery in the West Indies or later to Peru. As elsewhere, the Spanish set up large "*encomiendas*" and forced natives to work them. Because of its proximity to the Pacific coast, León became the main administrative center, although it was the poorer of the two colonies. Rivalry between liberal León and conservative Granada has persisted to the present.

Spain never conquered the Caribbean slope, where the Miskito Indians and their English pirate allies held sway and periodically raided up the San Juan River as far as Granada. The Miskitos probably were related to the Sumu people who still live inland from the coast. The Miskitos intermarried with whites and runaway slaves to some degree, and contact with Western ways changed their culture and language. They expanded aggressively in the 1600s and 1700s, raiding as far south as Panama. From 1687 to 1894, Britain supported a Miskito kingdom in the region. Pirates also raided the west coast, as pirate John Dampier recorded in his *Voyages*. They found the west coast "surpassing most places for health and pleasure in America" because of the well-drained soil and breezy savannas, which didn't stop them from burning León in 1685 when the city failed to pay a ransom of 300,000 gold pieces.

A Divided Republic

Independence from Spain in 1821 and the breakup of the short-lived Central American federation in the late 1830s intensified Nicaragua's internal conflicts. The León faction sought an egalitarian republic on the French model, while Granada clung to the aristo-cratic and ecclesiastical model of the Spanish Empire. Ten years af-ter nationhood, Nicaragua became a focus of international interest with the discovery of gold in California. Cornelius Vanderbilt es-tablished a steamship and stagecoach route via the San Juan River that rivaled the Panamanian crossing, and John Lloyd Stephens ex-plored canal possibilities, writing that it would furnish Nicara-guans "with a motive and a reward for industry, and inspire them with a taste for making money."

Stephens went to build a railroad in Panama, however, and in-stead of a "motive and reward for industry," Nicaragua got Wil-liam Walker. The liberal faction invited Walker, a Tennessee doctor and lawyer turned "*filibustero*" (Spanish for "freebooter") to help them against the conservatives, and he arrived in 1855 with fifty-five men and promptly captured Granada by commandeering one of Vanderbilt's steamships. Walker declared himself president, but Nicaraguans turned against him when he suspended laws against slavery in preparation for annexing their country to the U.S. They drove him out in 1857 with the help of Vanderbilt and neighbor states. (Walker made two more attempts to conquer Central Amer-ica before he was executed in Honduras in 1860.)

A canal became an issue again after the failure of the French attempt in Panama. There was a strong pro–Nicaraguan canal fac-tion in the U.S. Congress before the pro–Panama canal faction out-maneuvered them (by, among other things, sending congressmen a Nicaraguan postage stamp of a volcano—an indication of geolog-ical instability—on the eve of a crucial vote). After liberal President José Zelaya offered Germany and Japan canal concessions, U.S.–owned banana companies helped finance a rebellion to overthrow him. The U.S. government sent marines to occupy Nicaragua for much of the time between 1909 and 1933, and thus maintained a controlling influence over Nicaraguan politics and economics. Na-tionalist guerrillas led by Augusto Sandino resisted the occupation from 1926 until the marines left following the election of liberal President Juan Sacasa in 1933.

Before they left, the marines trained the Nicaraguan National Guard which came under the command of Anastasio Somoza, a

Nicaraguan who had worked in the U.S. (as a used car salesman in Philadelphia). Somoza had Sandino assassinated in 1934, and assumed the presidency in 1937, maintaining dictatorial powers until his own assassination in 1956. His sons Luis and Anastasio continued the dictatorship. The Somozas brought some stability and economic development, rebuilding Managua after an earthquake and fire in the 1930s, but at the cost of corruption and harsh repression. They completely alienated the public by seizing international relief funds after a 1972 earthquake flattened Managua and killed 11,000 people. In 1979, the Sandinista National Liberation Front (FSLN), a revolutionary group formed eighteen years before, led a coalition to overthrow them.

The FSLN assumed control of Nicaragua and began to move it toward the left, which alienated some of its former allies and alarmed the U.S. government. The Sandinistas made significant improvements in public health, literacy, and other social welfare areas, although some Nicaraguans, such as the ethnic minorities of the Caribbean, saw them as repressive. The Sandinistas could not maintain economic stability in the face of a U.S.–led trade embargo and war with the Contras, a guerrilla force of former National Guardsmen and former FSLN allies. Inflation in 1988 reached 30,000 percent. After the Contra War ended in 1989, the FSLN lost the 1990 election to the National Opposition Union (UNO), a coalition of fourteen parties. Nicaraguans hoped for an economic recovery, but it has been slow to come, partly because promised U.S. aid was held up by the issue of continued control of the army and police by the FSLN, which retained much public support.

An Ecological Frontier

Nicaragua attracted early scientific attention with its spectacular natural features—sweet seas, 500-kilometer-long depression, volcanoes. In 1874 it became the subject of a seminal classic of tropical biology, Thomas Belt's *A Naturalist in Nicaragua*, which Charles Darwin called "the best of all natural history journals that have ever been published." Belt was an English mining engineer who lived in Nicaragua from 1868 to 1872 and made many pioneering observations (although his "social Darwinist" ethnology—he thought Central America's destiny was to be colonized and annexed by the U.S.—has not held up as well as his biology). He discovered that leafcutter ants use the leaves they carry into huge underground nests as a culture medium for the fungi they eat, and that the ants that live on bullhorn acacia protect the shrubs from browsers and feed on nectar and special protein-rich structures the plants produce. "Though I had dived into the recesses of these mountains again and again, and knew that they were covered with beautiful vegetation and full of animal life," he wrote, "yet the sight of that leaden-colored barrier of cloud resting on the forest tops . . . ever raised in my mind vague sensations of the unknown and unfathomable."

Much remains unfathomable about Nicaragua. Because of its political turmoil, its rain forests have not been studied as thoroughly as those of other countries. A curious thing about Nicaragua is that it apparently has fewer species than Costa Rica, Guatemala, or Panama, even though it is larger. Biologists have speculated that this might be because Nicaragua has less high-altitude terrain than Costa Rica and Guatemala, or because it is farther from highly diverse South American rain forest than Costa Rica and Panama. It may also be simply because it has not been studied as thoroughly as the other countries. For example, Nicaragua is known to have three monkey species—howlers, spiders, and capuchins—but local people I talked to near the little-explored Indio-Maíz reserve said there were large "black monkeys" that live in the mountains and smaller "yellow monkeys" that live in the lowlands. A ranger showed me one of the "yellow monkeys," which was a spider monkey, but with different coloration than the red spider monkeys common on the Caribbean coast.

Nicaragua's first nature reserve was created in 1958 at Volcán Cosigüina, whose 1835 eruption was the greatest recent volcanic explosion in Central American history. Like most reserves in the late fifties, it was only on paper. The Somoza government was more inclined to environmental exploitation than protection, as with the sea turtle industry it developed on the Caribbean coast in the 1960s. In the mid 1970s, however, Nicaragua began to establish a small park system with the development of Masaya National Park near Managua and Chacocente Wildlife Refuge, a turtle nesting beach on the Pacific coast. The government created a large number of new reserves in 1983, including the volcanoes and mangrove forests in the trough lowlands, where population growth and export agriculture have caused much environmental degradation. The Sandinista government also eased some of the colonization pressure on eastern rain forest by its policy of redistributing land in the fertile west. The government didn't implement effective protection and management policies for wildlands, however, and Volcán Masaya National Park suffered considerable damage and deterioration in the mid 1980s.

Colonization pressure rebounded in the 1990s as large landholdings in the west reverted to former owners, and demobilized soldiers sought land. Pressure for clear-cut logging in rain forests has also increased, with foreign companies competing for concessions. The government decreed a number of large new reserves in 1991, particularly in the Caribbean region, and began measures to restore and protect the existing system, although economic problems have made this difficult. Parks and reserves are administered under the Service of Natural Areas and Wildlife of the Ministerio Nicaragüense de Recursos Naturales y del Ambiente (MARENA). Their headquarters is at P.O. Box 5123, Edificio 3, Kilometer 12, Carretera Norte in Managua, a few kilometers past the international airport (phone: 3-1278, 3-1110; fax: 63-1273). MARENA is interested in encouraging ecotourism. The Bosawas, Miskito Cays, and Si-a-Paz (including Indio-Maíz reserve) areas are administered by separate offices within the main headquarters. The Nature Conservancy is assisting the Bosawas project. The Miskito Cays Protected Area has an office in Puerto Cabezas (see below) and is being assisted by the Caribbean Conservation Corporation, with funding from U.S. AID in collaboration with the World Wildlife Fund.

Managua

There once was a large Indian town on the shore of Lake Managua (the Nahuatl name of which is "Xolotlan"), but it dwindled to a village after the Conquest. The present city of Managua began to take shape after independence from Spain, and in 1858 it was named the capital in an attempt to compromise between León and Granada. Unfortunately, the city stands on an unstable substrate (what MARENA Minister Jaime Incer described as "layer upon layer of old volcanic mud flows, ash, cinders and pumice—which is really just hardened volcanic foam"), and lies within a zone of frequent faulting activity. Earthquakes have destroyed the city twice in this century, and it has never really recovered from the latest, in 1972, which left little of the original center except the Palacio Nacional and the cracked, empty shell of the cathedral.

Government rebuilding plans have so far lacked funding, so Managua has remained a kind of ghost city, unlike any other Central American capital. There's no grid pattern of numbered streets and avenues in the center because what was the center is now an expanse of grass dotted with ruins and occasional buildings that survived or were rebuilt. The Avenida Bolívar runs north and south through the middle of this expanse: at its north end is the lakeshore and a cluster of official buildings including the national theater, the ruined cathedral, the National Palace, and the post office. Most of a 1939 monument to Central America's greatest poet, Rubén Darío, still stands, with a marble statue of the poet surrounded by nymphs and dolphins. Nearby is the tomb of FSLN founder Carlos Fonseca. The Ave. Bolívar runs south for about a kilometer through tree-lined open spaces, including a new arboretum, and ends in a cluster of upmarket restaurants and offices crowned by the luxurious, pyramidal Hotel Intercontinental, which is overlooked by a giant cutout of Augusto Sandino on the small volcanic crater of Tiscapa to the south.

West of Ave. Bolívar is an area of restaurants, small hotels, and restaurants that is known as Barrio Martha Quezada, or "gringolandia," because low-budget tourists stay there (most of them in 1993 weren't North Americans but northern Europeans). To the northwest of gringolandia looms the futuristic baseball stadium; to the south, at the intersection of Ave. Monumental and Pista Benjamin Zeledón, is the Plaza España, a commercial center with restaurants, open-air cafes, banks, and airline offices.

The rest of Managua, which contains about a fourth of Nicaragua's population, spreads out in a bewildering welter of barrios interspersed with large outdoor markets and connected by crowded avenues. Managuans use landmarks instead of addresses for directions, and refer to north as "*al lago*," to south as "*al sur*," to east as "*arriba*," and to west as "*abajo*." Buses are usually packed, and except for a few obvious routes (from the airport to Mercado Roberto Huembes, or along the lake), they are not easy for visitors to use. The Inturismo office near Hotel Intercontinental has route maps. Taxis are abundant, if somewhat ramshackle, and you could go most places in town for less than $2 in late 1993, if you could tell the driver how to get there.

Considering the mugging opportunities presented by vacant lots, squatter settlements, makeshift street lighting, and power outages, I was surprised that there wasn't more street crime. It is said to have increased in recent years, but, to me, Managuans seemed more interested in selling things on the street, from Chiclets to car seats, than robbing tourists. The heat is a major deterrent to strolling around even the relatively small distances of the Ave. Bolívar, however. I found myself scurrying between patches of shade. Power outages and downed phone lines were very common.

Transportation

A passport valid for the next six months, an onward or return ticket, and (possibly) proof of sufficient funds ($500) are the requirements for entry. Visas aren't required for most American and European nationalities (including the U.S. and U.K.), and visitors can stay up to 90 days. There is a $5 entry tax, and a $12 airport exit tax, which must be paid in dollars. Be sure to keep the slip with your date of entry; it's flimsy and easy to lose.

INTERNATIONAL AIRLINES: American Airlines (800-433-7300), Nica Airlines (Nicaragua's national airline, 800-831-4396), and Central American Airlines (305-599-0070) fly to Managua via Miami. Lacsa (800-225-2272) and Aviateca (800-327-9832) fly via Miami and Los Angeles. Continental (800-525-0280) flies via Fort Lauderdale, and Taca flies via San Francisco.

DOMESTIC FLIGHTS: Nica and La Costeña airlines have small plane flights to Bluefields and Puerto Cabezas on the Caribbean coast. Flights leave from a small terminal to the right of the international terminal at the main airport in Managua. Baggage and document checks are likely to be stringent.

Sandino International Airport is about 12 kilometers east of downtown Managua on the Carretera Norte. Buses run frequently on the highway, which is right across from the terminal entrance, but are usually very crowded. (Most go to Mercado Roberto Huembes, from which you can get a cab downtown for about $2.) Cabs from the terminal entrance are $15–20, but you can get one for about $5 if you walk out to the highway and flag one down (from the far side, in front of the Hotel Las Mercedes). Get to the airport *at least two hours in advance* of your return flight: there's much crowding, and formalities are slow.

ROADS: The roads between the main cities of the western lowlands and adjacent highlands are in remarkably good shape, considering the turbulent recent past and present heavy use. Other roads are unpaved, and may be impassable in the rainy season, but they have improved considerably in the past few years. Bus service also has improved, particularly to outlying areas such as the north side of Lake Nicaragua, although routes between main cities are still extremely crowded. Watch out for shortchanging by conductors on crowded routes. Pickpocketing and other crime is supposed to be a problem, although I didn't encounter any. Nicaragua's bus service is fast catching up with Central America's in general.

Buses to the north and south of Managua (Estelí, Matagalpa, Masaya, Granada, etc.) leave from Mercado Roberto Huembes, Pista de la Solidaridad (city bus 109 from near the Hotel Intercontinental). Buses to the Pacific coast and west (León, Corinto) leave from Mercado Israel Lewites on Pista de la Resistencia on the southwest of downtown (city bus 118 from near the Intercontinental). Buses to the east (Rama, Juigalpa, San Carlos) leave from Mercado Ivan Montenegro on Pista José Benavides east of downtown. Ticabus has daily service to San José (at 7 A.M.) and also goes to

San Salvador and Guatemala City; their terminal is at Cine Dorado two blocks west of the Hotel Intercontinental (phone: 2-2094). Reserve in advance; all border documentation must be completed before ticket is issued.

Taxis are inexpensive and easy to find in central Managua, although they get scarcer in outlying barrios. They often take more than one fare at a time. They're unmetered, but fares were pretty consistent—up to 10 córdobas in the city center, 20–30 to the airport. Always ask first, anyway. Phone-dispatched cabs are safer than street cabs, but about four times as expensive. The taxi situation is similar in other cities.

CAR RENTAL: Hertz, Avis, and Budget rentals are available in Managua and at the airport. Non-Nicaraguan licenses are valid for 30 days. Credit cards are accepted. The U.S. State Department advises that travel by road between Nicaragua and Honduras is potentially hazardous, particularly after dark. Because of land mines in certain rural areas, it may be dangerous to venture off main roads. Incidents involving armed bandits continue.

BOATS: Large ferryboats are the main way of carrying passengers and freight around Lake Nicaragua, and are quite inexpensive, although they tend to be crowded and can pitch about surprisingly when the lake is windy or stormy. Their safety record seems good, however. They usually run at night to avoid the staggering heat and glare on the lake in midday, picking up passengers in late afternoon and landing them in early morning. On the San Juan River, smaller launches run regularly between San Carlos and El Castillo, usually leaving in the morning (see below for details). Boats run from Rama to Bluefields on the Río Escondido and from Bluefields to the Corn Islands offshore or to communities along the coast. Ferry service on the Gulf of Fonseca between La Unión, El Salvador, and Potosí, Nicaragua, has resumed, but travelers have reported harassment at the border crossing. Hiring boats is the main way to get to nature reserves in the Mosquitia, and is much more expensive than scheduled service.

U.S. Embassy

Apartado A-169, Kilometer 4.5 Carretara Sur, Managua, Nicaragua 34021 (phone: 666-6010, 666-013, 666-026-27, 666-032-34; fax: 666-046 or [USIS] 666-032-34).

Health Advisory

The usual intestinal parasites are present, particularly in the countryside. There are mixed reports on tap water in cities, but it would probably be wise to stick to bottled or treated water. Cholera is present. Malaria is active in both the western and eastern lowlands, especially during the rainy season, and also occurs in Managua. Medical care and supplies are limited.

CLINIC IN MANAGUA: Clínica Tiscapa, Dr. Guillermo Marenco Torres, director (phone: 71-300, 71-457, 71-420, 75-193).

Hotels

The Hotel Intercontinental is very expensive, but has a reasonable outdoor restaurant, and nonresidents can use the pool and sauna for $3 (phone: 2-23-532; in U.S. 1-800-327-1200). The Las Mercedes is right across the highway from the airport, in the $70–90 range, with good restaurants and a garden atmosphere (phone: 2-3211/9; fax: 23-1713). The Casa de Fiedler, Colonia Residencial Pereira, 2a Calle Sur-Oeste No. 13020-22 (CST 2 c. al Sur y 1½ c. abajo—just west of gringolandia) is excellent in the $20–40 range, with a/c rooms with or without bath in a big family home that survived the 1972 earthquake, with many indigenous artifacts on display. Staff are friendly, manager speaks English; good breakfasts, including poached eggs! (phone: 66-66-22). The Hotel Managua in Villa Venezuela, 150 meters south of the streetlight on Sabana Grande at Mercado Ivan Montenegro, has new rooms with fan and/or a/c and private bath for $18–20 single, a very good deal, although its location may be inconvenient (don't walk after dark). The restaurant is all right, if you don't mind instant coffee and cooks giggling at you from the kitchen (phone: 9-7760). In gringolandia, one block from the Ticabus Station, Hospedaje Quintana has rooms with fan for $12; Casa de Huéspedes Santos has basic rooms for $7, and Hospedaje Mesa a block away is comparable. Hospedaje Carlos west of Cine Dorado has $5 rooms. Other inexpensive places abound in this area.

Restaurants

For Nicaraguan *"comida típica,"* La Plancha in Barrio Altamira, and Rincón Criollo, across the street from Plaza Julio Martínez, are good and inexpensive. (Típica food specializes in gigantic slabs of broiled beef or pork, or fried lake *"guapotes,"* garnished with equally hearty portions of rice, french fries, patacones, beans, tortillas, and seasoned with a selection of chili sauces.) For something lighter (and pricier), La Marseillaise, entrada principal, Colonia Los Robles, has a lovely setting with original paintings of Nicaraguan country scenes, and good meat with somewhat French sauces. My favorite restaurant in Managua was Bavaria Haus, two blocks "al lago" (north) of the Plaza España on Ave. Monumental, which has air-conditioning, an appetizing delicatessen ambiance, and good sandwiches, soups, potato salad, homemade beer, breads, and sausages, etc.—at $7–10 an entrée (phone: 25 915). (Nicaragua has a sizable German immigrant community that arrived in the 1890s.) For lunches and snacks, La Panadería de Plaza España on Ave. Monumental across from the plaza is good for things like lasagna and *"platos del día."* Gringolandia has many inexpensive restaurants and comedores. Dos Anclas, three blocks toward the Hotel Intercontinental on the same street as Casa de Fiedler, has good shrimp dishes and pleasant outdoor tables. Others are Comedor Sara, Cipitio, and El Bambu. Magica Roma, a half-block west of the Intercontinental, has good, expensive Italian food (entrées from $10) and glacial air-conditioning: bring a sweater.

Communications

The main post office is three blocks west of the cathedral and is open weekdays from 7 to 4, Saturdays in the morning. It featured an interesting children's art exhibit when I was there, and sells beautiful stamps.

The post office is in the same building as Telcor, which provides post, telephone, and telecommunication services in towns throughout Nicaragua. There are Telcor offices in Managua's main markets also. Service was not exactly brisk at the one I tried.

Money Exchange

Nicaragua's currency is the gold córdoba, which is divided into 100 centavos. In 1994, the exchange rate was 6.50 gold córdobas to the U.S. dollar.

Buro Internacional de Cambio and Multicambio change U.S. cash and traveler's checks: both have offices near the Plaza España. Some banks also will change traveler's checks. There are illegal moneychangers at Plaza España, Mercado Huembes, and outside the Hotel Intercontinental. Increasing numbers of restaurants and hotels will accept credit cards and traveler's checks, but ask first. Changing money will be harder outside Managua.

Tourist Information

The Ministry of Tourism (MITUR) office two blocks east of the Hotel Intercontinental, Apdo. Postal 122 (phone: 22-498; fax: 25-314), has an information booth via a side door. They provide standard information on travel, accommodations, etc., but their information on access to wildlands was less up-to-date than that available from the park service at the MARENA office on Carretera Norte. Ministry of Tourism offices in other towns were more reliable and helpful, although their knowledge of wildlands may also be limited.

The Nicaraguan Chamber of Tourism publishes a guidebook. Their office is next door to the MITUR office in Managua.

Maps

Good maps are rare because of the war, when much of the country was off-limits to travelers. A number of maps are available at bookstores, supermarkets, and gas stations, but all contain misinformation. MITUR publishes a Mapa Turístico with a country map showing nature reserves and a city map of Managua. Price estimates on this vary: I paid $5 for a copy in the small town of San

Carlos. I didn't see it for sale in Managua. A park service employee I showed it to had never seen it, and said some of the information was wrong.

Museums and Zoos

The Museo Nacional has exhibits on natural history and archaeology. It's located in a pleasant garden compound overlooking the lake a block north of the Pista Pedro Joaquín Chamorro and east of the railway station. Hours are 9–5 weekdays; admission for tourists is $1.50. There's a small refreshment stand on the other side of a large mansion that houses an art school, with nice views of the lake. The natural history section has mounted displays of land and water wildlife, including specimens of freshwater sharks and sawfish. There's an interesting display of a possibly 10-million-year-old whale skeleton found 11 kilometers inland in the coastal plain south of Managua; its species is unknown. The archaeological section has artifacts ranging from hand axes and hide scrapers of the big game–hunting Stone Age cultures to ceramics, statues, and metates from the past 2,000 years. Many come from the islands of Ometepe and Zapatera in Lake Nicaragua. The earliest ceramics show a South American influence, while the latest resemble Aztec ware.

Las Huellas de Acahualinca preserves the footprints of a band of hunter-gatherers who hurried across a mudflat during a volcanic ashfall an estimated 6,000 years ago. The site is located about 2 kilometers west of the cathedral. You cross a canal, and then follow the first road to a white building just before the lake. Hours are 8–3 daily; admission is $1.75 for tourists. The footprints, about 4 meters below present ground level, were first discovered in the 1870s, then excavated in the 1940s and 1980s. They are housed in situ under sheds, and look as though they were made yesterday. Half a dozen individuals of various ages made the tracks. Some were carrying loads, judging from the depth of the tracks. Deer and possibly cat tracks cross the human tracks. The site also yielded 2,000-year-old pottery fragments, which are also on display.

There is a Museo de Arte de Las Américas across from the main post office, but it never seemed to be open during my visit. The same was true of a Museo de la Revolución at Mercado Huembes. A museum on the Sandinista literacy campaign is located near Parque Las Palmas west of gringolandia, open Tues.– Sun.

Bookstores and Libraries

There is a library of environmental material at the MARENA headquarters on Carretara Norte. Casa Ben Linder near Estatua Monseñor Lezcano has a lending library and book exchange.

There are Spanish bookstores in Centro Commercial Managua on the Pista de la Solidaridad south of Mercado Huembes. The Intercontinental has some English periodicals and books.

Excursions Around Managua

Lake Managua is polluted, mainly by a refinery and factories west of town (the refinery recently was closed). Swimming is supposed to cause skin ailments, although boys fish with throw nets in the water off the lakeside promenade downtown. The smaller Laguna de Xiloa, a crater lake 16 kilometers from town just off the road to León, has facilities for swimming and boating. Buses run to the lake on weekends from Parque Piedrecitas, Kilometer 6, Carretara Sur, although the lake is supposed to be much less crowded on weekdays.

Masaya National Park

Nicaragua's premier national park, Volcán Masaya, is only a forty-five-minute ride from Managua. Although not very big (5,100 hectares), Masaya contains enough fascinating natural phenomena to occupy a visitor for many days. Its center is a five-cratered volcano, one of which, Crater Santiago, is the only crater in Central America where you can actually look down and see molten lava. This volcano had an extraordinary hold on the imaginations of pre-Columbian people, who called it "Popocatapete," the burning mountain, and on the Spanish, who called it "*la boca del infierno*"—according to Pedrarias, "a giant mouth of fire that never stops raging." The lava so obsessed a monk named Blas de Castillo that in 1538 he had himself lowered into the then-active crater (called Nindiri) and scooped some up, thinking it was molten gold.

The volcano has changed continually since then. Nindiri sent lava flowing over the countryside in 1670 and 1772, and then went dormant. In 1839, John Lloyd Stephens saw "none of the fearful marks of a volcanic eruption, nothing to terrify, or suggest an idea of an inferno. . . . It seemed an immense conical green basin . . . a scene of singular and quiet beauty." (He added, "At home this volcano would be a fortune; with a good hotel on top . . . and a glass of iced lemonade at the bottom.") In 1852 the present active crater, Santiago, began forming, and had caused so much trouble with eruptions and poison gases by 1924 that two Germans tried to cap it, without success. The Nicaraguan air force tried bombing the volcano into quiescence in 1953, also without success. The level of lava in the crater rises and falls. In 1965, it surged up and filled adjacent Nindiri with gray lava pavement. In 1975, "a pool of molten lava was sloshing to and fro . . . and surged like surf against the walls of the shaft," according to Time/Life writer Don Moser. In 1993, it merely glowed and made loud breathing noises.

A constellation of volcanic features surrounds the craters. Lava tube caves full of bats lead hundreds of meters into the earth. They really seem like tunnels to the underworld: skeletons from apparent pre-Columbian sacrifices have been found in them. Lava flows are covered with different stages of revegetation, from desertlike scrub to tall forest. Flowers are profuse in the early dry season, including a pink orchid that seems to grow on every tree trunk. A trail leads down into the forest of extinct crater San Fernando just east of the active Santiago. Other trails lead to the Laguna de Masaya, a large lake surrounded by lava cliffs, and to other small craters and fumaroles. Wildlife tends to be scarce and timid, perhaps because of lack of protection during the 1980s, but birds are abundant, including magpie jays, parrots, motmots, trogons, tityras, and many others. Green parakeets are famous for nesting and roosting on the walls of the active crater: nobody knows how they tolerate the sulfuric fumes, which quickly cause eye and lung irritation in humans. The laguna is a good place to watch cichlids in the shallows; the water teems with fish (although it's supposed to be too polluted for people to swim in).

The park entrance is 23 kilometers from Managua on the Masaya Highway. Buses leave every twenty minutes from the Mercado Huembes: ask the conductor to let you off at Parque Nacional Masaya. The entrance is well marked, just past a wide lava flow. An admissions booth has map pamphlets and information about visiting the lava caves and fumaroles. The park is open 8–4:30 daily except Mondays (you can't enter the park after hours, but you can remain until after sunset). A 6-kilometer paved road leads to the craters. You can probably hitch a ride if you wait a while (although there's not that much traffic), but if you arrive before the midday heat, it also makes an interesting hike (bring water and a hat). A kilometer past the entrance, the Sendero de los Coyotes forks to the south—it leads through forest and lava flows to the laguna. Next you come to the visitor center, which has an excellent museum on the park's and Nicaragua's natural history, and a small botanical garden. It was undergoing renovation (but still open) when I was there, and the restaurant was closed. There's a picnic area and refreshment stand. A few hundred meters past the center is Cerro el Comalito, a small cone with fumaroles. Picnic areas here were vandalized in the mid 1980s and dismantled by the park staff in 1988, but a self-guided nature trail is being renovated.

Another 2 kilometers toward the crater an unpaved road forks to the north. This leads past some small craters, and loops back along the south edge of the park then up to the main craters, a distance of about 10 kilometers. The main craters are at the end of a fairly gentle slope. The highest point is at the Cruz de Bobadilla north of Crater Santiago. The conquistadors originally erected a cross here to exorcise the devil. You get a good view of Nindiri Crater from here, but to see into the Santiago's lava well, you have to continue to the south side, where the paved road ends. If you have a car, stay until twilight, when the parakeets are coming to roost, and you can see how the lava glows dramatically. From a rest platform halfway around the crater, a trail leads east around and into Crater San Fernando.

To return to Managua, you can flag any passing bus. The highway margin just outside the park entrance is narrow, so it's safer to walk down to where it widens.

The Highlands

Although not very high compared to Guatemala's or Costa Rica's, Nicaragua's highlands have remained relatively remote except at their western edges. This is partly because the region has always served as a point of resistance for groups expelled from the rich lowlands, first the Chorotegas and other indigenous groups, later the anti-Walker faction in the 1850s, then Sandino and the anti-Somozistas, then the anti-Sandinista Contras. Most of the highlands was still heavily forested in Thomas Belt's time, and he was struck by the contrast between the pine forest north of Matagalpa and the broadleaf forest to the south. "All that I thought characteristic of tropical forest had disappeared, and the whistling of the wind through the pine tops, which I had not heard for many years, carried me back in imagination amongst the Canadian forests. . . . Clumps of evergreen oaks were the only other trees." Germans and other Europeans began colonizing the area in the late nineteenth century, establishing coffee plantations and ranches, and growth was rapid in the 1950s and '60s, but the area was a war zone for most of next two decades.

A number of forest reserves were decreed in the area in 1990 and 1991, including wet or mesic tropical forest as well as cloud forest and pine forest. So far, they are more or less "paper parks," without infrastructure or facilities. These include Bosawas at the northern end of the Cordillera Isabelia, an area so large it is in a category all its own: "National Resource Reserve." Under a 1992 agreement with Honduras, Bosawas is to be included in a 2.8-million-hectare "La Solidaridad" international reserve with adjacent areas in the Honduran Mosquitia. (Bosawas is an acronym for the area's three main natural features, the Bocay River, Saslaya Peak, and Waspuk River.)

Encompassing 730,000 hectares, Bosawas has a 15,000-hectare national park tucked into its southern end. Decreed in 1971, the park protects Nicaragua's highest peak, Cerro Saslaya, but is without access or facilities. Only about 40 percent of Bosawas has even been studied, and that wasn't until 1992, when the German government helped to fund a survey in the lower, eastern part. The

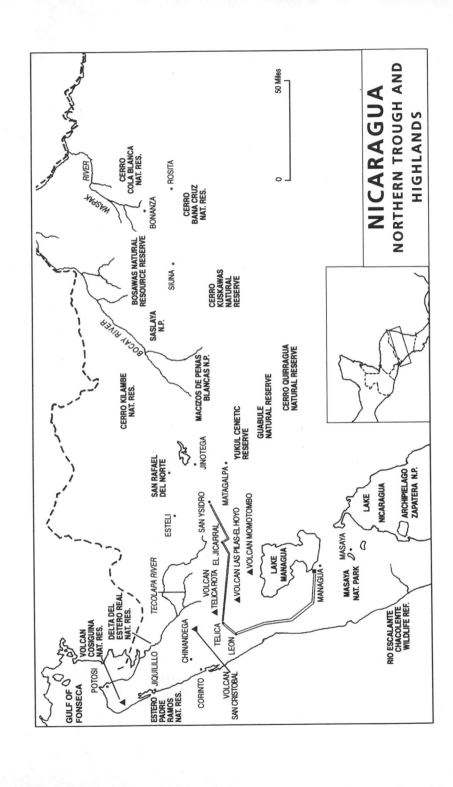

NICARAGUA
NORTHERN TROUGH AND HIGHLANDS

50 Miles

0

GULF OF FONSECA

VOLCAN COSIGUINA NAT. RES.

DELTA DEL ESTERO REAL NAT. RES.

POTOSI

ESTERO PADRE RAMOS NAT. RES.

JIQUILILLO

VOLCAN SAN CRISTOBAL

CORINTO

CHINANDEGA

TECOLAPA RIVER

ESTELI

SAN RAFAEL DEL NORTE

CERRO KILAMBE NAT. RES.

BOCAY RIVER

WASPAK RIVER

CERRO COLA BLANCA NAT. RES.

• ROSITA

BONANZA

CERRO BANA CRUZ NAT. RES.

BOSAWAS NATURAL RESOURCE RESERVE

SIUNA •

CERRO KUSKAWAS NATURAL RESERVE

SASLAVA N.P.

MACIZOS DE PENAS BLANCAS N.P.

YUKUL CENETIC RESERVE

JINOTEGA

MATAGALPA •

SAN YSIDRO

EL JICARRAL

VOLCAN TELICA ROTA

VOLCAN LAS PILAS-EL HOYO

VOLCAN MOMOTOMBO

TELICA

LEON

LAKE MANAGUA

MANAGUA •

MASAYA NAT. PARK

MASAYA •

GUABULE NATURAL RESERVE

CERRO QUIRRAGUA NATURAL RESERVE

LAKE NICARAGUA

ARCHIPELAGO ZAPATERA N.P.

RIO ESCALANTE CHACOLENTE WILDLIFE REF.

study found two climate zones in the area, with precipitation ranging from 2,000 to 5,500 mm yearly, and vegetation ranging from
tropical to subtropical. The Tertiary volcanic rocks have outcrop-
pings of Cretaceous plutonic rocks bearing heavy metals, which
has led to gold mining around the Las Minas area just east of the
reserve. (The mines are accessible via a dry-season, 4wd road between Matagalpa and Puerto Cabezas.) Water pollution is a problem around the mines.

The 1992 German study estimated that there are 3,000 plant
species in the 2,000-square-kilometer study area—50 percent of
them trees or bushes. It noted the presence of many endangered animal species, and added that there is considerable commercial
hunting, with small spotted cat pelts selling for $20–50 and (live)
parrots for $20–30. (Nicaragua exported 2,500 parrots and 8,500
crocodilian skins legally in 1991.) According to the study, about
15,000 indigenous Sumu (who call themselves "Mayangna") live
in and around Bosawas by shifting agriculture, hunting, and gathering. The Nature Conservancy employed an anthropologist to
work on the matter of Sumu land rights in Bosawas in 1993.

In 1993, the western part of Bosawas along the Honduran border was still inhabited by armed bands of "re-Contras" (Contras
who kept opposing the government after the 1990 election of Vio-
leta Barrios de Chamorro). Another hazard in the area is the presence of an estimated 100,000 land mines laid on both sides of the
Honduran border during the 1980s.

The only nature-related tourism facility in the entire highland region in 1993 was the Hotel Selva Negra in the mountains between
Matagalpa and Jinotega. The hotel owners have set aside a private
forest preserve of about 100 hectares on the ridge above the hotel.
A loop trail around the preserve takes 2–3 hours to walk. The forest
is largely primary cloud forest, with huge, epiphyte-covered oaks,
laurels, strangler figs, and palos de leche. Trogons, quail doves, and
other birds are abundant. Enough forest remains on the surrounding hills that howler and capuchin monkeys, deer, ocelots, and even
pumas and quetzals may be seen.

The hotel has a variety of accommodations, from dormitories to
cabins, in the $20–50 range per night for singles. The restaurant

and bar look out on a small lake. The owners are of German descent, so the establishment has a (slightly kitschy) Bavarian ambience, including the food. A $3 entrance fee can be applied to meals at the restaurant. It's very popular, so reservations are recommended, although this may not be easy to do because of difficulties with phone lines. There is a phone in Matagalpa: 61-3883, and a fax: 61-2554. Or you could try the owners' mother in Managua: 265-8342. The hotel is easy to reach. Buses to Matagalpa leave Mercado Huembes every twenty minutes—an interesting ride up the windy escarpment between the trough and highlands—and you can quickly change for a Jinotega bus at the Matagalpa station. About 12 kilometers up the steep road from Matagalpa, on a ridgetop, there's a sign for Selva Negra next to a tank left over from the war. From there it's a couple of kilometers through coffee plantations to the hotel.

It's also possible to stay in Matagalpa and make a day trip to Selva Negra to eat lunch and hike the trail. The Hotel Ideal on the other side of town from the bus station (a few blocks from the parque central) has good rooms for $8–15. (When I was there, running water was available only from 6–7 A.M. and 5–6 P.M.) The Hotel Bermudez and Hospedaje Plaza near the bus station are cheaper. Matagalpa is a picturesque if slightly gloomy town. There's a Carlos Fonseca Museum near the secondary plaza, and a small zoo north of town.

The Nicaraguan Depression

Volcán Masaya is just one of dozens of natural wonders in this extraordinary 500-kilometer-long fissure through the heart of Central America. You can get a sense of its grandeur from the top of Cruz de Bobadilla: volcanoes stretch away in both directions, some with their tops enveloped in smoke. Because the region is heavily populated, it's easy to travel in. None of the other volcanoes or other natural features are yet developed like Masaya for visitors, however, so penetrating their wildlands takes time and effort. Unfortunately, except at the east end of Lake Nicaragua and the San Juan River, and other less accessible spots, wildlife has suffered from over-hunting and habitat loss, and is not very easy to see.

Volcán Cosigüina and the Estero Real

Traveling to the peninsula that forms the northwest end of the depression is like going back to the turn of the century. Except for a few mechanized export farms (largely overgrown with wild marigolds when I was there in 1993), people live in houses of palm thatch and poles. This area, where in 1835 Volcán Cosigüina blasted an estimated 9 cubic kilometers of rock and ash into the atmosphere, remains the wildest part of the region north of Lake Nicaragua, with three reserves: 12,420-hectare Volcán Cosigüina, 8,800-hectare Estero Padre Ramos, and 55,000-hectare Delta del Estero Real.

John Lloyd Stephens described Cosigüina's explosion as "the most awful in the history of volcanic eruptions, the noise of which startled the people of Guatemala four hundred miles off. . . . The face of nature was changed, the cone of the volcano was gone. . . . One river was completely choked up, and another formed, running in an opposite direction. . . . Wild beasts, howling, left their caves in the mountains, and ounces, leopards and snakes fled for shelter to the abodes of men." An observer 60 miles away said the ashfall's darkness was so great candles were barely visible even indoors. Some 3,000 meters high before the explosion, it was reduced to 870 meters. Today, Cosigüina is a low, broken shape on the horizon, thickly overgrown with semideciduous forest. Nicaragua's national tree, a white-flowered species called madroño (*Calycophyllum candidissimum*), is common on the hillsides. There's a crater lake at the summit. No visitor facilities exist, but it is possible to hike up the mountain from the fishing port of Potosí on the Gulf of Fonseca. The trail is overgrown and unmarked; hiring a guide would be worth it. It's about 12 kilometers to the lake, a good morning's walk. Several buses a day go to Potosí from the town of Chinandega, a slow, dusty ride. There are no hotels in Potosí, but there are comedores, and you may be able to find overnight accommodation if you ask around.

The Delta del Estero Real reserve is the largest and wildest mangrove forest remaining on the Gulf of Fonseca, and on the entire Pacific coast of Central America north of Panama. There have been confirmed jaguar sightings recently, and coyotes and smaller cats

Mangrove forest, eastern Nicaragua. Photo by Charles Luthin/Lighthawk.

are common, as are crocodiles and iguanas. Thousands of pelicans, egrets, herons, wood storks, ibis, and roseate spoonbills live in the area. William Beebe described parakeets flying to roost in 1936: "I saw a faint mist of dots moving high over the mangroves. . . . I watched until my eyes ached, for I had never seen so many feathered creatures at once. I was rewarded, for at last one dark mass veered and swung downward, and as they went, the rays of the setting sun painted them for a moment with pure emerald, and a thousand green meteors vanished below the mangrove horizon." (Beebe also described "hundreds of small, sad-faced monkeys and parrots" crated for shipment to New York in the nearby port of Corinto.)

Sea turtles and dolphins live in the Gulf of Fonseca, and it's a major breeding ground for shrimp and fish. The estuary extends from above the confluence of the Aquespalapa and Tecolapa rivers down to the Gulf and includes many winding tidal channels bordered with four mangrove species. Mangrove forest covers about 28 percent of the area; the rest is transition forest and savannas. The mangroves have been heavily exploited for lumber; also the wood is used to make banana stakes because it is rot-resistant. There also has been pesticide pollution from surrounding cotton fields, a problem throughout the Nicaraguan Depression in past decades, although cotton acreage has decreased in recent years. There are no visitor facilities, and the area is inaccessible by land. You could hire a fisherman in Potosí to take you into the estuary.

The smaller Estero Padre Ramos on the Pacific side of the peninsula is easier to reach, although less diverse, consisting almost entirely of the highly salt-tolerant red mangrove, and even they are stunted. Estuarine marsh is limited because only small streams drain into the area. It's a lively habitat anyway, full of the snapping sounds of *"conchas negras,"* big scalloplike mollusks, and of scuttling crabs. An American redstart was hopping among the mangrove stilt roots when I was there. The reserve extends northward from Jiquilillo, a beach resort 42 kilometers from Chinandega off the road to Potosí. The side road leads a couple of kilometers through pastureland, then along the beach until it dead-ends at the estero, where there is a nameless motel and an *"embarcadero"* (wharf). You can hire a boat to take you through the reserve: there's an island in the middle which could be visited, or you could have the boat take you around the peninsula to Potosí. The beach road is in bad repair because a tsunami or *"maremoto"* hit the resort in 1992, sweeping away most of the asphalt and some of the houses. The land is subsiding, and old foundations stand far out on the beach. (If driving to this region, 4wd is advisable north of Chinandega.)

Four volcanic complexes stretch southeast from Cosigüina to Lake Managua, and all are reserves. North to south, they are: 17,950-hectare San Cristóbal, 9,088-hectare Telica-Rota, 7,422-hectare Pilas–El Hoyo, and 8,500-hectare Momotombo. All are active in varying degrees. San Cristóbal wears a cap of smoke that resembles snow from a distance. Cerro Negro, near Telica-Rota, erupted in 1992, burying León in ash and sand. The National Light and Power Company is using Momotombo's heat to generate electricity. All the volcanoes have pockets of dry deciduous forest where not denuded by eruptions, and San Cristóbal, the highest, has groves of ocote pine on its upper gullies, near the southernmost natural occurrence of pines in the Americas. Wildlife on all has suffered from lack of protection. A local landowner was reported to have bragged of having personally killed the last cats and guans on one volcano. There are no facilities on any of the reserves, but there is some road access. A road to Estelí forks northeast from the road to Chinandega about 10 kilometers north of León, and crosses the Telica-Rota complex. Buses run from León to Estelí on this road. There is also a road leading to a community near the foot of Volcán San Cristóbal.

The city of León is a good starting point for trips to the above areas. It's a real colonial city, built in 1610 after the original town, León Viejo on the lake, was destroyed. It has Central America's largest cathedral, an extraordinary white structure that billows above the roofs like something out of the Arabian Nights. Rubén Darío's tomb is there, and his house, now a museum open Tues.–Sat., is a few blocks west. León's cobbled and tiled streets are a relief after frenetic Managua. Half-hourly buses run from Mercado Israel Lewites in Managua to the new market northeast of León's downtown. Most hotels are near the railway station: Hotel Europa, two blocks south, $10–20 with or without bath and a/c; Hospedaje Primavera, 5 blocks north, $5 with shower. Hotel America, comparable to Europa, is two blocks east of the cathedral. Restaurants are numerous, including Cueva del León and Casa Popular de Cultura north of the central park by the cathedral, La Casa Vieja a few blocks north of Rubén Darío's house, and Lacmiel, near a former National Guard jail which was destroyed during the Sandinista revolution and is now maintained as a garden. A Supercambio office a block from the cathedral will change traveler's checks.

Río Escalante–Chacocente Wildlife Refuge

Established in 1983, this 4,800-hectare area on the coast south of Managua is one of two national wildlife refuges decreed as of 1993. It protects a major nesting beach of olive ridley sea turtles. In good nesting years, thousands of these relatively small turtles (as compared to other sea turtles) come out of the Pacific to lay their eggs. Ridleys may nest during any month, but most come to Chacocente between June and December, particularly from August to October.

Ridley nestings are perhaps the most spectacular of sea turtle nestings because of the sheer number of turtles that can be on the beach at once, even in the daytime. There are photos of Central American Pacific beaches with nesting ridleys every few meters (although this is a rare sight). Leatherback turtles, which can reach a length of 2 meters, nest on the beach in smaller numbers in December and January. A few hawksbill and Pacific green turtles also may nest. The hills above the shore support a remnant of the dry deciduous forest that once covered most of the Pacific coast.

There is a MARENA ranger station at the refuge, but it is not easy to get to. About 20 kilometers south of the small town of Nandaime on the Pan American Highway between Managua and Rivas, a rough dirt road leads to the village of Las Salinas. A high-clearance or 4wd vehicle is needed on this road. From Las Salinas, a road follows the coast north to the fishing cooperative of El Astillero, and the refuge headquarters is 8 kilometers past that. It would be possible, but strenuous, to visit the refuge on a day trip, but it would be more relaxing to camp overnight. Contact MARENA headquarters in Managua (see above) about current conditions at the refuge before making your visit.

Lake Nicaragua

This 148-by-55-kilometer lake is the largest body of fresh water between Lake Superior and Lake Titicaca in Peru. It is mostly no more than 8 meters deep, but there are places where it exceeds 50 meters. Its indigenous name was Cocibolca, or "sweet sea," and it does seem more like a sea than a lake, especially when you're tossing around in the middle of it with only the tops of distant volcanoes in sight. There are no true tides, but levels may fluctuate considerably when winds are blowing, and they blow often. Another reason it seems marine is that so many of its fish are also seagoing. Lake Nicaragua is the only freshwater lake in the world inhabited by sharks. The sharks, belonging to a common marine species, the bull shark, reach lengths up to 2 meters and have been known to eat swimmers in the lake. Other marine species such as sawfish and tarpon also live in the lake. Biologists once thought that a gradual change from inland sea to lake may have forced the fish to make an

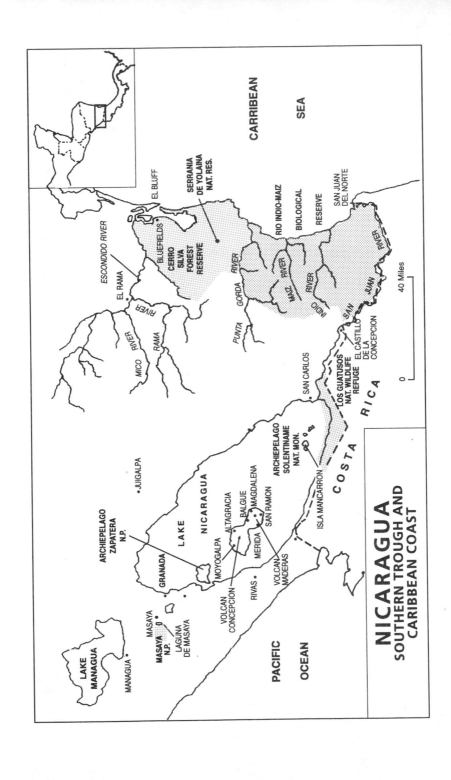

NICARAGUA
SOUTHERN TROUGH AND
CARIBBEAN COAST

unusual shift to fresh water, until they learned that there are no marine sediments under the lake, which formed by fault subsidence after the trough became dry land. They later discovered that sharks, tarpon, and sawfish all pass back and forth between lake and ocean by swimming up and down the San Juan River. "*Robalo*" (snook) and "*roncador*" (grunts or croakers) also move between fresh and salt water, and are caught in the lake at the San Juan River mouth.

On the other hand, most of the lake's thirty-four fish species are basically freshwater. A number of endemic freshwater organisms have evolved in the lakes, including twelve fish, two reptiles, and four mollusks. There are twelve cichlid species, and biologist Archie Carr has noted "a tendency for some of the perfectly distinct and evidently only distantly related species there to show two of the same bizarre variations—a grotesque high hump on the forehead and a color phase of golden red." This tendency has not been explained, although it may have something to do with sexual selection in the turbid lake water. (Wind quickly stirs up the sediments on the shallow lake bottom.) Most freshwater species belong to South American groups, including a small relative of the Amazon's electric eel (a fish which for some reason is named in Spanish "*madre de barbudo*," or "mother of catfish"). One spectacular North American related species, the gar ("*gaspar*" in Spanish), is common where the lake flows into the San Juan River, and is important commercially. Gars have changed little since the Paleozoic era, some 180 million years ago. The Nicaraguan species grows to 1.5 meters long.

When Thomas Belt crossed the lake in 1867, the banks were "everywhere clothed with dark, gloomy-looking forests." Freshwater sharks were common: "Sometimes, when in shallow water, we saw a pointed billow rapidly moving away from the boat, produced by a large fish below, and I was told it was a shark." Most of the lakeshore has been deforested since then, and heavy fishing pressure in recent decades has greatly reduced the populations of sharks, sawfish, and tarpon that move up the San Juan into the lake, although they are still present.

The lake still teems with fish, and is unpolluted enough to swim in, at least. There are hundreds of islands, ranging in size from

30,000-hectare Ometepe, whose two volcanoes preside over the lake with an almost ominous grandeur, to the tiny lava Isletas off the coast of Granada. The islands are important to wildlife, providing safe nesting and roosting space to the thousands of cormorants and other waterbirds that live on the lake. Lakeside wetlands are also important for fish and birds, particularly at the lake's southeast edge, where the San Juan River drains out of the lake.

Granada is the lake's main port, and there you can get boats across the lake or to the islands. Although it sits at the foot of Volcán Mombacho, the city has suffered more from human destructiveness than from eruptions or earthquakes. Its wealth from trade and cacao and sugarcane farming attracted the depredations of, among others, Sir Francis Drake in the sixteenth century, and Henry Morgan in the seventeenth. William Walker's men burned and plundered various parts of the city at both the beginning and end of his 1855–57 sojourn. The city retains a pleasant colonial atmosphere, and is cooled by lake breezes. Buses leave Managua from Mercado Huembes every twenty minutes. The Granada bus station is about a kilometer west of the central plaza, which in turn is about a kilometer west of the lakeshore.

The cathedral, post office, civic buildings, and expensive Alhambra Hotel ($25–50 range, with a good restaurant and comfortable rooms) are located on the Parque Central. On Calle la Calzada, the road from the center to the lake, are the Hotel Granada in the $30–50 range with a pool, the Hospedaje Cabrera in the $10–20 range, most rooms without bath, and the Pensión Vargas, basic. Hotels may fill up by 9 P.M. Restaurants include Drive-in El Ancla by Hotel Granada, Coffee Shop and China Nica near Hospedaje Cabrera, and Asia south of the Parque Central. At the end of Calle la Calzada is the Plaza España, which looks on the lake. To the south of the plaza is a tourist complex with a beach, restaurants, and boat trips and rentals.

Careli Tours, with an office in the Alhambra Hotel (phone: 3835; fax: 2035), has a variety of scheduled and custom tours on the lake and the San Juan River (more standard, upmarket tourism than ecotourism as of 1993). Their Nicaragua office is P.O. Box C-134, Calle Principal Los Robles (phone: 78-2572; fax: 78-2574). English spoken.

Archipiélago Zapatera National Park

This 5,227-hectare park south of Granada centers on Isla Zapatera, the second largest lake island. The island is famous for its archaeological finds, many of which are on display at the National Museum in Managua. There's also a small museum in Granada housing twenty-eight large statues from the island. Dated from 1,200 to 800 years ago, the statues combine anthropomorphic and animal forms, particularly jaguars and crocodiles. Located next door to the Church of San Francisco a couple of blocks north of the Parque Central, the museum is open 8–12 and 2:30–5. The island apparently was used as a cemetery, and contained many burials. These included ceramic urns shaped like moccasins (from which the island gets its name—"*zapatera*" means "shoemaking") which contained skulls and artifacts. The National Museum has some of these puzzling objects. Artifacts from the island show the influence of both Chibchan and Nahuatl cultures.

The island is composed of andesitic volcanic rock and has very rugged terrain, with many cliffs and bays. Cormorant colonies use the cliffs on islets for nesting and roosting. The diverse terrain fosters semideciduous to dry forest. Egret and oropendula colonies nest in the trees. (Oropendulas are large relatives of orioles and build long, sacklike hanging nests.)

The park is an hour by motorboat from Granada. No scheduled service goes there, but boat rentals and tours are common. The Rincon Criollo Restaurant in Granada's tourist complex has boat rentals for about $20 an hour. Other rentals range from $50 an hour for motor launches to $10 an hour for rowboats. On weekends, tour boats go around the islands for inexpensive fares. You can also rent boats in Puerto de Asese a few kilometers south of the tourist complex. If you want to go ashore on the island for any length of time, you should check with the park service office at MARENA headquarters in Managua.

Isla de Ometepe

This island is formed by two volcanoes, Concepción and Maderas, which are connected by a neck of lava erupted by the still-active Concepción. Although not exceptionally high (Concepción is 1,610 meters, Maderas 1,340 meters), they look gigantic above the

lake, their tops often hidden in clouds. In 1983, a 2,200-hectare reserve was decreed on the peak of Concepción, and a 4,100-hectare
reserve on that of Maderas. Both peaks have cloud forest on the
higher elevations, which is very interesting considering their complete isolation from other cloud forest areas. Trees include *Den-
dropanax, Clusia,* and other typical cloud forest genera. Middle
elevations support rain forest, while dry forest grows on lower
slopes. The forest on Concepción is degraded and fragmented by
volcanic activity and farm clearing, that on Maderas is less so except on its lower slopes, and is very dense and rocky higher up.
Maderas has several permanent rivers, and a 3.5-hectare, 250-
meter-deep crater lake at 1,175 meters. There is a spectacular waterfall at 530 meters above the village of San Ramon on the southwest flank. Monkeys and parrots live in forested areas.

There are no maintained trails or other MARENA facilities. To
climb either volcano, it would be advisable to hire a guide, and/or
notify the police of Altagracia or Moyagalpa (the main towns) of
your intention and ask them for information on routes.

Like Isla Zapatera, Ometepe is famous for its many indigenous
artifacts. Several large statues similar to the ones in Granada line
the main square in Altagracia, portraying figures with animal heads
or strange, twisted figures, all carved in volcanic stone. Enigmatic
petroglyphs cover rock formations in the forest.

Large boats plying between Granada and San Carlos at the
mouth of the San Juan River stop daily at Ometepe. They leave Granada's main dock in the mid-afternoon of Mondays and Thursdays,
and get to a dock near Altagracia at around 8 P.M., where trucks
wait to take passengers into either Altagracia or Moyagalpa. Altagracia is the pleasanter of the two towns, and the closest to volcano forest areas. The Hotel Castillo is a popular tourist spot
because the owner and his son know a lot about the area: they offer
tours to petroglyphs for $5, and can help find hiking guides. Ac-
commodations are spartan, with tiny rooms and one cold shower,
but at $3.50 a night it's very inexpensive, and there's a convivial
bar-restaurant. The Hospedaje Central a block farther down the
main street has more comfortable rooms with bath for $6 a night.
Buses run from the plaza in Altagracia to Balgue and Mérida on
Maderas, and all the way around Concepción to Moyagalpa. There

are some white sand beaches on the shore, although the lake is often rough and turbid from the wind. The best-known petroglyphs are in the forest above a place called Magdalena past where the bus stops at Balgue.

You can also get to and from the island via the port of San Jorge near Rivas. Several boats a day leave San Jorge around noon and in late afternoon, stay overnight in Moyagalpa (loading bananas), and return early next morning. There are a number of hotels and restaurants around the Moyagalpa dock: the new Hotel Ometepelt has comfortable rooms with bath for $7, but may be full: others are cheaper and more basic. Pensión Aly farther up the main street is quieter than the dockside dives.

San Carlos

The market and fishing town of San Carlos on the north bank of the San Juan River where it flows out of the lake is the jumping-off point for the exceptional wildlands to the southeast, and also for the Solentiname Islands, a famous cultural as well as natural destination. Boats from Granada arrive Tuesday and Friday mornings at around 3:30, and passengers remain on board until dawn. The boats leave to return to Granada Tuesday and Friday afternoons. A more direct route from Managua is by buses that leave from the Mercado Ivan Montenegro early on Mondays and Thursdays (possibly other days, too), and arrive in San Carlos around 2 P.M. via an unpaved but (in late 1993) fairly smooth road. The bus left at 6:45 when I went, by which time a good crowd had gathered, and there was a rush to get on, but everybody got a seat. It was a new bus. The Hotel Managua (see above) is a short walk from the Mercado Ivan Montenegro.

San Carlos has a very friendly, comfortable new small hotel, Cabinas Leyko, 150 meters west of the plaza on the same street as the police station. Singles are $9, doubles are $18; rooms are screened, with fans and baths. You can order meals. The Casa de Protocolo on the east side of the plaza is somewhat cheaper (and reportedly "horrible"), and there are several cheap places in the market area on the waterfront. There's a very good open-air restaurant, El Mirador, on the ruins of the fortress that overlooks the town, and numerous comedores in the marketplace. The Ministry of Tourism

(MITUR) is planning major tourism developments in the area and has an office on one of the streets off the plaza toward the river.

Big flocks of parrots and parakeets fly over morning and evening. It's interesting to go down to the market in the early morning when the fishermen come in (if you don't mind watching fish being chopped up with machetes). I saw dozens of big gars, a meter-long tarpon, and piles of robalo, roncador, and sabalete. You might see a shark or a sawfish.

Los Guatusos National Wildlife Refuge

This 43,750-hectare refuge, decreed in 1990, occupies the southeast end of the lake and extends to the Costa Rican border. It encompasses about half of what is considered the most biologically productive part of the lake, the swampy areas between the rivers San Juan and Sapoa. Gars can be seen breeding in the rivers here in huge numbers during their spawning season, their eggs covering the aquatic vegetation. Planktonic and bottom-dwelling invertebrates are abundant, providing a rich food supply for fish, freshwater shrimp, waterbirds, and larger animals. Wildlife populations in the refuge have been little studied, but 270 bird species have been counted in the Caño Negro Wildlife Refuge on the Costa Rican side of the border. Particularly common are anhingas, roseate spoonbills, white ibis, wood storks, cormorants, and black-bellied tree ducks. Crocodiles, caimans, jaguars, and deer are present.

There are ranger stations, campsites, and trails within the refuge. Visitors are required to check in at ranger stations and carry entry permits at all times. The refuge is accessible from San Carlos via "*collectivo*" boats to local communities that run on Tuesdays and Fridays. You also may be able to rent a boat. Ask at the MITUR office off the main square in San Carlos for current information on tours to the refuge. Boat rentals to the refuge also are available on the Solentiname Islands just to the north.

Archipiélago Solentiname National Monument

Decreed in 1990, this national monument encompasses a group of islands in the lake west of San Carlos. Ernesto Cardenal, a priest, poet, and Sandinista cabinet minister, made the islands famous as a center of poetry and art in the 1970s. The "Solentiname School" of landscape painting, fantastic and "naive," is influential. The islands also have archaeological significance, with petroglyphs and stone carvings. Most of the forest that once covered the islands has been cleared for farming, but there is still original forest on Cerro Santa Ana of Isla Mancarrón, the largest island, and one of the smaller islands, Zanate. Howler monkeys, whitetail deer, agoutis, and armadillos that now live on the islands were brought there by the inhabitants, according to Park Service documents.

Boats run from San Carlos to the islands on Tuesdays and Fridays, and probably other days as well. Check with the San Carlos MITUR office for times. The Albergue Solentiname on Isla Elvis Chavarria has rooms for about $20 a night single, with a restaurant. The Hotel Donald Guevara on Isla Mancarrón has rooms for $25 single, and a restaurant (phone: 113-75537).

Si-a-Paz

Si-a-Paz is a binational project for sustainable development on the biosphere reserve model, encompassing 12,700 square kilometers of southeast Nicaragua and northeast Costa Rica. It's the largest protected coast in Central America. In Nicaragua, this area is divided into a rural development zone in the watersheds of the rivers draining into the southeast margin of Lake Nicaragua, a buffer zone north from the upper San Juan River, and a biological reserve in the watersheds of the Indio and Maíz rivers between the Costa Rican border and the Punta Gorda River. Controlled hunting is allowed north of the Indio River: to the south is a "reserva absoluta."

The main access to the area is via the San Juan River. Boats run downriver from San Carlos to the town of El Castillo de la Concepción on Tuesday and Friday mornings (leaving around 10) and return on Mondays and Thursdays (leaving around 6). The boats serve small settlements along the river, and stop frequently. Some carry livestock as well as people. Little original forest remains along the river from San Carlos to El Castillo, although there are extensive marshes near the lake, where you can see Muscovy ducks standing on tree limbs, and the occasional crocodile slipping into the water. Cattle egret roosts in riverside trees are spectacular sights.

El Castillo is located at the first of three rapids that the river descends before it reaches the sea. The rapids aren't particularly steep, but are impressively large and noisy. Big fish, probably tarpon, can often be seen jumping. El Castillo is a picturesque town crowded along the steep riverbank below the Spanish fort for which it is named. The fort was built in 1673 to prevent pirate incursions up the river (San Carlos and Granada had been sacked in 1670). The fort's attackers in the next two centuries included British Admiral Horatio Nelson, who led a 1780 attempt to cut the Spanish Empire in two by conquering Nicaragua. Nelson blew up the fort, but eventually retreated back downriver with ten of the two hundred men he'd set out with. The fort fell into ruin in the nineteenth century, but has been restored recently, and now contains a museum with artifacts found on the site and exhibits on Spanish fortifications of Central America. The fort is still an impressive structure, and provides striking views of the countryside and river from its top. Hours are Wed.– Sun. 10–12 and 3–5, admission $1.50.

There's an attractive and comfortable new hotel right above the dock, the Albergue El Castillo, which is $15 single a night. It has a nice restaurant and bar, and a long shady veranda with hammocks and rocking chairs, a good place to relax, particularly on weekdays. On weekends, the hotel may fill up with energetic and vociferous Costa Rican sport fishermen (phone: 055-4635). Because of a limited water supply, there are no private baths, but space is ample in the communal lavatories. The cheaper Hospedaje Aurora is on the water below the Albergue. There are a number of comedores along the waterfront, serving freshwater shrimp ("*camarones*") which live in the river, and which are almost lobster-sized. Stories of sharks and sawfish are common. Almost every house in town has a sawfish "saw" on the wall, often with a painting on it.

Río Indio–Maíz Biological Reserve

This 295,000-hectare reserve contains the least altered rain forest in Nicaragua, and encompasses the north bank of the San Juan from just below El Castillo to the sea. It was decreed in 1990. The area is underlain by recent river and lake sediments, with eroded

Tertiary volcanoes forming hills along the riverbank. Rainfall is higher than anywhere else in Nicaragua (up to 6,200 mm a year) and soils are heavily leached and acidic. You'd never know this from the vegetation, however: an estimated five thousand plant species grow here, and the trees are as big as I've seen anywhere in the tropics. There are extensive swamps of yolillo (raphia) palm as well as rain forest, also some mangroves near the coast. The area has been little studied, but it is believed that the entire spectrum of native wildlife survives, including scarlet and great green macaws, harpy eagles, giant anteaters, white-lipped peccaries, brocket deer, and manatees. A square mile of the reserve may contain more invertebrate species than the continent of Europe. El Castillo is full of romantic tales about the reserve—pre-Columbian ruins, unknown animals. They may be true for all anyone knows.

No regular boat service goes downriver from El Castillo (as of late 1993), but it's easy to hire a boat, and you can go as far as you want to pay for. I paid $25 for a morning ascending the Río Bartola at the east side of the reserve. The transition from the rangelands around El Castillo to the pristine forest in the reserve was striking: Brahma cattle paths on one side; deer and peccary trails on the other. The huge ceibas and barrigons along the Bartola were shedding their leaves as we floated along, giving an exceptional sense of agelessness and serenity. There is a ranger station at the Bartola's mouth on the San Juan, and the ranger showed me up a very rough trail that leads a short way into the forest. He said jaguars and tapir were abundant farther in, but it "took a lot" to see them. (If he thought so, I could believe it. He was one of the more rugged individuals I've encountered.) There's a hotel on the riverbank across the Bartola from the ranger station, the Refugio Bartola, a rustic affair with eight rooms for $15 nightly single. Their Managua address is Apdo. 2715 (fax: 29-7924). They have a restaurant, although I heard they have some trouble with food supply. Occasional cargo boats go all the way downriver to San Juan del Norte (formerly Greytown), but there were no tourism facilities there as of 1993; there probably will be soon. The town is being rebuilt after destruction during the war. Careli Tours (see

Granada section) offers upmarket "on request" tours on the San Juan and Indio rivers, including week-long luxury cruises on the *Rain Goddess* with air-conditioning, hot water, and even a cellular phone.

The Southern Caribbean Coast

There are two large forestry reserves, Wawashang and Cerro Silva, around Bluefields, Nicaragua's main Caribbean port. A 40,000-hectare natural reserve, Serrania de Yolaina, is located in the southern part of Cerro Silva near the border with the Indio-Maíz reserve. Although there are no tourism facilities in the reserves, the area is fairly well populated so there is almost daily inexpensive boat service between Bluefields and the many villages around Pearl Lagoon to the north. It's also possible to travel up the Kurinwás and Río Grande de Matagalpa rivers to pioneer towns inland. (You'll need to carry food on any such trips or try to buy it from local people, who may not have enough to sell.) The Bluefields area is still recovering from the damage of Hurricane Joan in 1988, which flattened much local forest and destroyed much of the town and port.

La Costeña and Nica fly to Bluefields for about $90 round-trip. You also can get there by taking a bus at Mercado Ivan Montenegro in Managua, which goes to the town of El Rama on the Río Escondido, from which there is boat service to Bluefields. Buses leave Managua at night on Mon., Wed., Fri., and Sat. to connect with boats that leave in the early morning on the alternate days. (Exact departure times and dates tend to vary—you'll need to ask around. You can also take regular morning buses from Managua and stay overnight in Rama to get the boat next day.) Accommodations in Bluefields may be crowded or full. The Hotel South Atlantic near the plaza is in the $30–60 range, with a good restaurant. The Caribbean, also in the center of town, is about $20. There are a number of budget hotels (Hollywood, Marda Maus, El Dorado, Cueto) in the southeast part of town near the water. Also in this area is the Costa Sur, in the $30 range. As with Puerto Cabezas, baggage and document checks may be rigorous when going to the Bluefields area.

Corn Islands

The Corn Islands about 50 kilometers offshore from Bluefields are a popular vacation spot for fishing, surfing, and snorkeling, with clear water and white coral beaches. Cargo boats to Big Corn Island leave in the early morning from a dock just north of Bluefields; passenger fare is a few dollars. La Costeña flies from Managua for $120 round-trip, although flights may not run because the airstrip is occasionally in disrepair. There are several inexpensive hospedajes. English is widely spoken, and dollars may be accepted, but credit cards and traveler's checks probably won't be.

The Miskito Coast

The Caribbean slope contains half of Nicaragua's land, but about 10 percent of its population. Until 1894 it was a Miskito kingdom, with a hereditary king crowned in Bluefields. Even after 1894, its population of Miskitos, Sumus, Ramas, Garífuna, and immigrants from the West Indies (called Creoles) retained an independent attitude. Sandinista attempts to increase government control led to armed resistance, and in 1987 the area was granted a degree of self-government, divided into RAAN (Región Autónoma Costa Atlántica Norte) and RAAS (Región Autónoma Costa Atlántica Sur). Although English and Miskito are still widely spoken, the area is becoming steadily more "Nicaraguan" as communications increase and immigration from the west continues (ladinos now predominate in the population).

Along rivers and the Caribbean coast there are huge areas of swamp and marsh interspersed with lakes. To the north are large expanses of Caribbean pine savanna, where seasonal fires maintain open bunch grasslands dotted with pines and interspersed with gallery forest along streams. A scattering of pine forest reserves have been established to protect the genetic base of future forestry operations. Although about twenty reserves for wetlands and rain forest as well as pine forest were decreed here in 1991, they don't begin to encompass the enormous amount of wilderness (even including the vast Bosawas and Indio-Maíz reserves). As with the highlands,

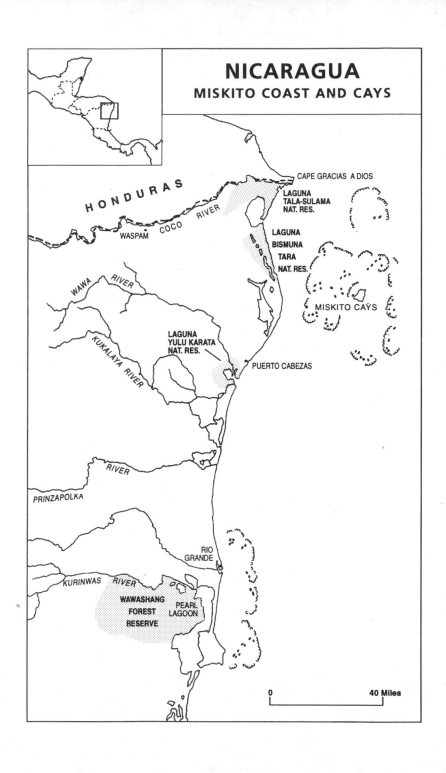

NICARAGUA
MISKITO COAST AND CAYS

HONDURAS

CAPE GRACIAS A DIOS

LAGUNA
TALA-SULAMA
NAT. RES.

COCO RIVER

WASPAM

LAGUNA
BISMUNA
TARA
NAT. RES.

WAWA RIVER

MISKITO CAYS

KUKALAYA RIVER

LAGUNA
YULU KARATA
NAT. RES.

PUERTO CABEZAS

RIVER

PRINZAPOLKA

RIO
GRANDE

KURINWAS RIVER

WAWASHANG
FOREST
RESERVE

PEARL
LAGOON

0   40 Miles

reserves are without easy access or facilities as yet. The only access to the Miskito coast is via boat, plane, or a single 4wd, dry-season road from Matagalpa to Puerto Cabezas.

Aerial surveys of the Miskito coast in 1992 by biologist Thomas Carr (son of naturalist Archie Carr II) yielded some surprising results which show how little explored the area has been. There were frequent manatee sightings, indicating "a substantial and previously undocumented population." There were even more frequent sightings of the South American river dolphin (*Sotalia fluviatilis*), a freshwater species seldom before found in Central America.

The Miskito Cays

This 50,000-hectare archipelago of eighty-five coral and mangrove islets northeast of Puerto Cabezas, decreed a biological reserve in 1991, is vital to the present economy of the entire Caribbean coast because it is the main habitat for lobster, shrimp, and green turtles. Archie Carr has written of the green turtle's importance. "All early activity in the New World tropics—exploration, colonization, buccaneering, and even the maneuverings of naval squadrons—were in some way or degree dependent on turtles. . . . It was almost unique in being a marine herbivore—an air-breathing vertebrate which grazed submarine beds of seed plants as the bison grazed the plains and which, like them congregated in tremendous bands." Although turtle populations are much reduced today, they are still very important to the subsistence economies of people like the Miskitos and Garífuna.

Green turtles come from all over the Caribbean to fatten on the turtle grass beds of Miskito Cay shallows before moving south to breed at places like Tortuguero. The size of this congregation of turtles is indicated by the figures of the turtle industry which the Somoza government ran at Puerto Cabezas beginning in 1969. (Green turtles are prized for their meat and for "*calipee*"—cartilage, which is the main ingredient of turtle soup.) Between 10,000 and 20,000 green turtles a year were exported from the area. Turtle populations were unable to support this level of exploitation, and declined sharply before the industry was terminated in 1977. The industry also disrupted traditional Miskito subsistence use of turtles for food.

The cays are important as breeding grounds for spiny lobster and shrimp, the primary commercial fisheries in the area now. This resource also is suffering from overexploitation. In the past, Miskito divers could find plenty of lobsters in shallow offshore waters. More recently, they've been forced to dive in increasingly deep water, using substandard scuba gear with inadequate training. Many have died or have been permanently paralyzed from "the bends."

Puerto Cabezas is a typical Caribbean coast town, which has ridden various boom-and-bust cycles of exploitation. U.S. banana companies developed the area earlier in this century, but have disappeared along with the Somoza turtle industry. It was a major military post during the Contra War (although no actual fighting occurred here) and various ordnance (some of it live) is still scattered around. The shrimp and lobster industries presently dominate, with many battered boats parked along the pier, piled with the canoes from which lobster divers dive. Twenty divers, twenty boys to paddle the canoes, and a crew spend two weeks at a time on the boats to bring back a cargo for the international "surf'n'-turf" market.

Coral reefs are numerous in the cays, but as of 1994 there was no regular way for travelers to visit them. From May to January, offshore winds make the sea tricky for small boats. Hiring boats is expensive. The Miskito Cays Project has an office at the south end of town which may be able to give advice about visiting the cays. The Caribbean Conservation Corporation has been assisting the project since 1990. There's also an MARENA office next door. Even if you don't get out to the cays, there are many interesting things to see and do around Puerto Cabezas. The pine savanna is easy to hike on, and there's a beautiful beach and lagoon a few kilometers north of town, with many winding, mangrove-lined creeks leading inland. A road that goes north out of town to the village of Tuapi has a side spur that leads to the beach. Just before the road reaches the beach, there's a freshwater swimming hole called "Pozo Verde" in a small creek. You can also reach the beach by walking through the savanna from Puerto Cabezas, but the terrain is confusing, with many wooded creekbeds interrupting the open areas. (Tall grasses which grow on creek bottoms can cause skin irritations.) Crested caracaras lurk along the beach to prey on shorebirds: we saw one eating a willet.

About 10 kilometers south of town is the Laguna Yulu Karatá Reserve, a 25,300-hectare area of mangroves. To the north is Laguna de Pahara, a 10,200-hectare area with wading bird rookeries. Both areas provide habitat for manatees, crocodiles, and other coastal wildlife. Still farther north is a large complex of laguna reserves (Tala Sulamas, Bismuna Raya, and Cabo Viejo) near the Honduran border at Cape Gracias a Dios. It's possible to hire boats to take you into such wetland areas, but it's expensive, about $100 a day. There are many Miskito villages in the area, with people living in the traditional subsistence way. Buses run northeast from Puerto Cabezas to the town of Waspám on the Coco River, the border with Honduras.

La Costeña airline has daily flights to Puerto Cabezas from Sandino Airport in Managua, leaving around 8 A.M. It's about $116 round-trip (phone: 631-228 and 631-281). Nica also has flights. Baggage and document checks are thorough, and immigration officials at Puerto Cabezas may be suspicious of travelers. The 560-kilometer road from Matagalpa via the mining towns of Siuna and Rosita east of Bosawas takes two to three days in a 4wd when it is passable in the dry season. Trucks make this trip commercially, and it might be possible to get a ride on one.

The El Cortijo Hotel on Puerto Cabezas's main street is comfortable and homey, with a friendly live-in owner who can provide good meals on request. It's about $20 a night single, not including breakfast and dinner. Also in town is the Hotel Cayos Miskitos, about $10 a night. On the bluff overlooking the sea near the town stadium is the Hotel Malecón, $10 a night with shared bath and a pleasant outdoor restaurant and bar. The Atlantico is the best restaurant in town, located on the west side from the Hotel Cortijo. El Chino Dragon near the Hotel Cortijo, and Pizzeria Mercedita near the docks are also good.

CHAPTER TEN

Costa Rica

COSTA RICA MIGHT BE called the Cinderella of Central America. Despite its promising name (which means "rich coast") it was the most obscure and impoverished Spanish colony in the region, far from trade routes and political centers. Yet after independence, Costa Rican farmers and merchants were the first in Central America to take advantage of the U.S. and Europe's growing demand for coffee, bananas, and other tropical products. Despite many political upheavals in the nineteenth and early twentieth centuries, Costa Rica eventually developed a stable democracy with high levels of health and literacy. This achievement has had its costs, however. High economic and population growth rates resulted in high rates of deforestation, soil erosion, and pollution. Recently, Costa Rica's tradition of encouraging foreign investment has inflated land prices beyond the buying power of many farmers, threatening the traditional family farm.

Costa Rica also has been the first Central American nation to respond substantively to environmental problems. A destination for naturalists in the nineteenth century, it passed early conservation laws and created some national parks in the 1950s. These measures failed for lack of funds, but by the 1960s Costa Rican conservationists saw the potential for protecting nature with the help of parks, public education, and tourism. In 1970 they began to create a national park system which has since become one of the best in the world, with over 20 percent of the land protected in a natural state (although only 13 percent receives the full protection of national park status). Costa Rica has pioneered the concept of parks as repositories of the nation's biotic diversity and ecological quality as well as its scenic and recreational treasures. Visitors can see an extraordinary variety of habitats in the several dozen parks and wildlife refuges.

Again, success has led to problems. Popularity has caused high visitation and pressures for inappropriate commercial development around some parks. This has combined with other pressures such as poaching, squatters, and illegal logging and mining to make Costa Rica's wildlands less than secure. Nevertheless, these parks continue to offer some of the world's best opportunities to enjoy tropical nature. Conservation-oriented visitors may want to exercise a little extra consideration. Try to stay off the beaten track, and think about visiting at times other than the main tourist season. (This guide doesn't include some of the most heavily visited areas, such as Monteverde, Carara, Cabo Blanco, Manuel Antonio, and Cahuita.)

Crossroads of Continents

Costa Rica is where northern and southern Central America meet. The forests of the Osa Peninsula near its southwest border have been compared quite favorably to the richest Amazonian rain forest, while those of Guanacaste Province near the northwest border are the last significant remnant in Central America of the dry deciduous forests that once covered the Pacific coast south from Mexico. Costa Rica is also one of the most diverse parts of a highly diverse region, with the highest mountains south of Guatemala, and numbers of bird and tree species second only to Panama's. It is 50,100 square kilometers in size, about the same as New Jersey.

Costa Rica's mountains form a series of ranges, or "cordilleras," along its entire length, trending from the northwest to the southeast. The Guanacaste and Tilarán cordilleras to the north have several active volcanoes, notably 1,916-meter Rincón de la Vieja in Guanacaste Province, and 1,633-meter Arenal in Alajuela Prov-

Cloud forest, Costa Rica. Photo by Kevin Schafer.

ince. Arenal exploded in 1968, killing 78 people. The Cordillera Central which surrounds the central valley (or Valle Central) also has active volcanoes. Poás, 2,708 meters high, has an enormous crater and a long history of eruptions, some of which have sent spouts of water from lakes in the crater 200 meters in the air. Volcán Irazú, 3,432 meters tall, almost destroyed the first colony at Cartago when it exploded in 1723. Despite the destruction they cause, the volcanoes are also responsible for Costa Rica's prosperity, since nutrient-rich volcanic soil is very fertile. The Cordillera Central volcanoes are farmed almost to their summits. The southernmost mountains, the Cordillera de Talamanca, are not actively volcanic, and are composed largely of much older igneous rocks. Chirripó Peak, 3,819 meters high, is Costa Rica's highest, and there are others almost as high in Talamanca.

Most of the rest of Costa Rica is hilly, so population first concentrated in the few flat areas, mainly the Valle Central and the Tempisque Basin area of the Nicoya Peninsula. The Valle del General in the southwest and the "*llanuras*" (or plains) of the northeast Caribbean area were colonized later, but soils there aren't as good as the other areas' volcanic soils. The Caribbean coast is swampy and low-lying except in the south, where the Talamanca foothills extend to the coast. The Pacific coast is hilly and rocky except for river estuaries. The northern half of the Pacific coast has a marked dry season, so much of it is dry forest or savanna; the southern half's dry season is shorter, so the vegetation is much lusher. Two large peninsulas extend into the Pacific: the Nicoya in the north and the Osa in the south. Costa Rican territory includes a number of Pacific islands: the largest is 2,400-hectare Isla del Coco, which is 500 kilometers offshore. A national park, the island is like the Galápagos in having many unique species that have evolved in isolation.

Costa Rica has long been known as a "cultural crossroads" between the pre-Columbian peoples of north and south. Ice Age spearheads of both the northern Clovis and southern Magellan types have been found. The earliest farming may have come from South America, since it seems to have relied mainly on root and tree crops similar to those of Colombia. About 3,000 years ago, a

maize-centered culture from the north, manifested by elaborate artifacts using a great deal of jade, brought an increase in population
and social stratification. Large settlements developed in alluvial
plains. About 1,500 years ago, northern influence declined, as evidenced by a replacement of jade ornaments with gold and other
changes. This was about the time that the great classic civilizations
of Teotihuacán and the lowland Maya began to collapse. South
American imagery in pottery and statuary suggest either a migration of Chibchan-speaking people from Colombia and Panama, or
increased trade and other contacts. The ruins of Guayabo National
Monument near the city of Turrialba in southeast central Costa
Rica are representative of this period. Their cobblestone causeways, bridges, mounds, and terraces and stone statuary are quite
unlike Guatemalan or Mexican artifacts. Large floodplain settlements were replaced by smaller, more scattered ones, suggesting increased intergroup conflict.

The Spanish found no single indigenous group dominant in
Costa Rica. Probably the most numerous and affluent were the
Chorotegas, who lived in the dry forest zone of the Nicoya Peninsula and Guanacaste in northwest Costa Rica. Their culture resembled that of Nicaragua and El Salvador, with large settlements
surrounding central plazas and temples, and intensive farming of
cotton, cacao, and tobacco as well as maize and beans. Also numerous were various peoples of the Caribbean coast and Valle Central with cultural ties to the Chibchan-speaking peoples farther
south. They lived in scattered chiefdoms connected by stone causeways and suspension bridges. The Guayabo ruins, which were inhabited until about 1400, may have been built in part by these
people. In the southwest lived Chibchan-speaking peoples such as
the Cotos, Quepos, and Borucas (who now have a reserve there),
who probably were the makers of mysterious granite spheres, some
very large, which have been found throughout that area. A little-
known but evidently very ancient people called the Corobicí inhabited the northeast, and there also were several colonies of recently arrived Nahuas or Aztecs on the Caribbean coast.

Early Spanish explorations received friendly welcomes from
natives, although some groups were very warlike. Columbus was

impressed with the large wooden buildings, metalworking techniques, and abundant wildlife he saw during his voyage along the coast in 1503. His brother called the Costa Rican Indians "the most intelligent." Friendliness disappeared as Spanish greed and brutality became evident. Indians inflicted some stunning defeats on various conquistador expeditions, such as that of Diego Gutiérrez in 1544, when most of the Spanish including the leader were killed in a battle with red-painted warriors. "The Indians threw stones with such force," wrote a survivor, the ubiquitous Italian adventurer Girolamo Benzoni, that his helmet looked "as if a smith had hammered it all over." Starvation was an even greater obstacle to Spanish conquest because Nicoya was the only intensively farmed region.

The first successful colony didn't come until 1563, when Juan Vásquez de Coronado founded Cartago in the Valle Central. By that time, most native people had either died from disease and mistreatment or had withdrawn to inaccessible areas. Without a large native work force, Costa Rica's growth depended more on European immigration, mostly from southern Spain, than did other colonies. It also depended more on cooperation among its members. Large landowners and ecclesiastics had to run shops to make ends meet. Threatened by earthquakes and volcanic eruptions, isolated from trade routes, the colony remained a minor part of the Spanish Empire, and of subsequent attempts to found a Central American Federation. Costa Rica didn't know that it was independent of Spain until a month after independence was declared in Guatemala.

From Banana Republic to Stable Democracy

The suitability of Costa Rica's volcanic soils and climate to coffee cultivation changed its history after 1830. The government encouraged farmers to grow coffee and sell their crop to large landowners who processed the beans and exported them. In 1840, John Lloyd Stephens described "the rich coffee plantations of San José . . . laid out into squares of two hundred feet, enclosed by living fences of trees bearing flowers. . . . It was not, like the rest of Central America, retrograding and going to ruin, but smiling as the reward of industry. Seven years before the whole plain was an open waste."

With the development of a road to the Pacific port of Puntarenas in mid-century, Costa Rica became a major coffee supplier to Europe. This brought European immigration and intellectual ties, giving Costa Rican society a liberal cast. Costa Ricans were immune to the charms of the "liberal" William Walker, however, and were largely responsible for the defeat of his attempt to turn Nicaragua into a U.S. colony in the 1850s. Under coffee magnate President Juan Rafael Mora in 1856, a citizen army first repelled an attempt by Walker's filibusters to invade Guanacaste Province (a hacienda in today's Santa Rosa National Park where the decisive battle took place has become the Costa Rican equivalent of Lexington and Concord) and then invaded Walker's Nicaraguan headquarters, which led to his expulsion in 1857.

Bananas became another source of revenue in the late nineteenth century, although more disruptively than coffee. Foreign entrepreneurs pushed the construction of a railroad inland from the Caribbean coast (using Italian, Chinese, and West Indian labor), then made large profits growing bananas for export on tracts they had acquired along the railroad. Big companies such as United Fruit became major political powers, and exercised semifeudal influence over workers and local communities. The companies' power declined after the 1930s because of labor organizing and environmental problems. The banana industry has been on an upsurge in the past decade, with a corresponding resurgence of social and environmental problems (including heavy pesticide pollution and ongoing deforestation).

The stable democracy for which Costa Rica has become known in recent decades did not arrive easily. General enfranchisement did not come until 1889, and even then excluded women and blacks. The first half of the twentieth century saw a number of political upheavals as liberals, conservatives, communists, foreign companies, and the church jockeyed for position, sometimes in unlikely combinations. In the early 1940s, a coalition that included the church, the army, and the Communist party instituted a number of social reforms including social security, land reform, and labor rights. Another alliance that included upper-class landowners, urban businessmen, and young intellectuals resented the power of the ruling coalition and its leader, Rafael Calderón Guardia, however. After a questionable election in 1948, this alliance, led by a young coffee grower named José "Don Pepe" Figueres, overthrew the Calderón government. Figueres kept the social reforms, but abolished the army, and temporarily outlawed the Communist party.

The 1948 "revolution" set the stage for Costa Rica's present stability and high standards of literacy, health, education, and housing. Revenues spent elsewhere on arms could be applied to public welfare. Costa Rica has not been without its problems. Government attempts to modernize the economy by taking out large international loans to subsidize dams, industry, and factory farming almost led to disaster in the 1980s, when oil prices soared and coffee and banana prices dropped. Costa Rica remains burdened with a debt on which it must pay a third of its annual budget in interest. The nation has tried to respond to this situation by diversifying its economy away from energy-intensive, large-scale industrial and agricultural production toward smaller-scale industries more appropriate to its geography. Tourism has been a success, recently surpassing coffee and bananas as an earner of foreign currency, and there is hope for sustainable forestry and other innovative natural resource uses. The country's growing population (now about 3 million) and fiscal problems pose challenges to future stability.

A Naturalist's Paradise

Despite its poverty, Costa Rica attracted early naturalists. Girolamo Benzoni in 1538 was impressed by its "huge abundance of peccaries, jaguars, and pumas," and in 1562, Juan Yanez de Castro described it as a "fertile land . . . of good and sweet water and air, sky and soil, with a climate as much cool as warm, with different kinds of oaks and other trees like those of Spain." In the nineteenth century, European immigrants such as the Swiss botanist Henri Pittier stimulated local interest in natural history. More recently, biologists have taken advantage of Costa Rica's peace and stability to conduct some of the most important work on tropical ecology, such as Daniel Janzen's studies of dry forest biology and Alexander Skutch's observations of tropical bird life histories.

There's still much work for biologists. Many of Costa Rica's over 830 bird species, 1,200 orchid species, and other conspicuous organisms are still very little known, and most species of insects and other inconspicuous organisms are still unknown. Costa Rica may have as many as 9,000 moth species. There are more species of one moth family, the large, colorful Saturniidae, in Costa Rica's parks than in all of Mexico and the U.S. combined.

Naturalists and biologists, both Costa Rican and foreign, helped the government to create the national park system in 1970. Starting with only three parks and five employees, the system expanded rapidly through the 1970s with the support of President Daniel Oduber (1972–76), a Guanacaste rancher. "We are a developing nation," said Oduber, "nevertheless we consider vital the preservation and protection of the natural environment." The government invested large sums in land acquisition and park development, and the Costa Rican public became enthusiastic users of the parks. Government support declined during the fiscal crisis of the 1980s, but Costa Rica was able to continue development of its park system with the help of nongovernmental organizations (NGOs), international conservation agencies, and innovative funding techniques such as the debt-for-nature swap. National parks also have been augmented, particularly in recent years, by the creation of a growing number of private nature preserves, often within the buffer zones of parks.

The parks have been effective in protecting forests and wildlife. Animal populations and vegetation in parks are usually in good shape, and opportunities for seeing wildlife are correspondingly good. Outside park boundaries, Costa Rica's fast-growing population (which doubled between 1950 and 1970) and economic needs have drastically altered the country's ecosystems. A system of forest reserves has been less successful than parks in protecting forest. Three-quarters forested in 1950, Costa Rica now retains less than a quarter of its land in a forested state. Since tropical hardwoods have great commercial value, failure to conserve them represents an enormous loss to the country's economic future. Deforestation has led to siltation of rivers and shores and declines in farm productivity. Although Costa Rica passed laws protecting rare animals such as macaws and harpy eagles in the 1970s, loss of habitat continues to threaten their survival.

Costa Rica's wildland conservation system is one of the most active and complex in the world today, with dozens of government and private organizations. The National Park Service, a division of the Ministry of Natural Resources, Energy, and Mines (MIRE-NEM), administers the parks. Its headquarters are in the MIRE-NEM building at Calle 25, aves. 8 and 10, Apartado 10104, 100 San José (near the Ministry of Justice) (phone: 257-0922). For information on visiting the parks, there is also an office at the Parque Bolívar Zoo, Ave. 11 and calles 7 and 9, open 8–11:30 A.M. and 12:30–3:30 P.M. Tues.–Fri. (phone: 233-5673, 233-5284). They sell maps and brochures. Costa Rica also has a wildlife refuge system which is administered by the National Wildlife Directorate (phone: 233-8112, 221-9533).

Most parks can be entered without a permit. The entrance fee recently was raised to $15 per day for foreign visitors (as a way of supplementing scarce park operations budgets), with a surcharge for camping. Some parks have developed campsites. It's also possible to get accommodations and even food at park headquarters and ranger stations in some cases, but you'll need to arrange this beforehand. For general information, and to find out about making reservations or getting permits to restricted units, phone: 257-0922; fax: 223-6963. For technical information on park ecology and conservation, you can phone the Conservation Data Center (236-7690) at the National Biodiversity Institute, an organization which catalogues the scientific and economic values of native organisms.

Numerous NGOs support the parks or other conservation endeavors. The National Parks Foundation (Apdo. 1008, 1002 San José; phone: 220-1744, 232-0008) promotes park protection and management. Fundación Neotrópica (Apdo. 236, 1002 San José; phone: 253-2130) works to integrate parks with surrounding communities, and also publishes books and posters on parks and wildlife. The Organization for Tropical Studies (Apdo. 676, San José; phone: 240-6696, 240-5533), an association of U.S. universities and the University of Costa Rica, administers several biological reserves. The Tropical Science Center (Apdo. 8-3870, 1000 San José; phone: 253-3308) does ecological research for government and industry and also administers the Monteverde Cloud Forest Reserve. The Caribbean Conservation Corporation (Apdo. 246-2050, San Pedro; phone: 224-9215) is concerned with protection of sea turtles and other marine life throughout Central America. ASCONA (Apdo. 8-3790, 1000 San José; phone: 222-2296, 222-2288) promotes environmental protection throughout the country. Arbofilia (Apdo. 512, 1100 Tibas; phone: 235-5470) works with campesinos to promote reforestation with native trees (tours of their projects are available). Most NGOs welcome contributions of money and, in some cases, of volunteer time.

San José

At about 1,100 meters in elevation in the Valle Central, San José has a breezy, temperate climate. Nights are cool, and mornings often overcast. During the rainy season from May to November, afternoon downpours come as regular as clockwork. It must have been a peaceful town before the automobile invaded its narrow streets. Noise and air pollution currently can be quite uncomfortable in the city center, although this thins out in the outskirts. San José is in the process of flowing together with the other Valle Central cities of Cartago, Heredia, and Alajuela to become a metropolis, although there is still open space in the form of deep ravines and farmlands. Almost two-thirds of the nation's population lives in the Valle Central.

Downtown San José is laid out in a grid pattern on both sides of the Avenida Central. Avenidas run west-east, while calles run north-south. Most street addresses don't have numbers, but are identified by the intersection nearest them and by landmarks. At the west edge of town, the Avenida Central becomes the Paseo Colón, a wide boulevard that terminates in a large park, La Sabana. The highway north from there leads to Juan Santamaría International Airport (named for Costa Rica's national hero, a young soldier who died fighting Walker's filibusters). Several new luxury hotels are located along the airport highway, while medium-priced hotels are near the Paseo Colón and Avenida Central, and cheap ones around the older, east edge of town and near the Central Market on the west side. Because of earthquakes and the city's relative newness (it was founded in 1737), there is not much colonial architecture, but the east end has some charming nineteenth-century buildings in what might be called the "banana republic style."

San José is a boisterous city, especially for motorists or unwary pedestrians, but it's largely friendly. I walked or took crowded buses across it daily for several months, and never had any trouble, but vigilance is required. Street crime has increased in the 1990s, and gangs (called "*chapulines*") operate in upscale areas as well as slums. Travelers should beware of pickpockets during the day, and of muggers in the tourist bar area around the Parque Morazán at night. The north part of town around the outdoor markets and bus stations has a lot of cheap bars and other low life patrolled by pairs of "civil guards." There are scenes right out of Goya or Velázquez.

Transportation

Travelers with U.S., U.K., Canadian, German, and Japanese passports are allowed a 90-day stay without visa; those with Australian and New Zealand passports are allowed 30 days without visa. The law requires travelers to have their passports at all times (illegal immigration is a problem), but a photocopy carried in wallet or purse will be enough for most situations. Travelers also need a return ticket to be allowed entrance. Because Costa Rica is so popular, flights are often overbooked, so reconfirm your return flight at least 2 days before your departure date, and *get to the airport 2 hours early.* There's a $7 airport tax at departure.

INTERNATIONAL AIRLINES: American has flights via Miami and Dallas/Fort Worth (800-433-7300); United has flights via Miami, Mexico City, and Guatemala City; Continental has flights via Houston (800-525-0280); Lacsa, Costa Rica's national airline, has daily direct flights from Miami, and flights from Los Angeles, New Orleans, and New York with various stops en route (800-225-

2272); Aviateca has flights from Chicago and Miami via Guatemala City (800-327-9832); Aero Costa Rica has flights from Miami and Orlando.

DOMESTIC FLIGHTS: SANSA, a government-subsidized airline, flies from a domestic terminal at Juan Santamaría Airport. Office on Calle 24 north of Paseo Colón (phone: 233-0397, 233-3258; fax: 255-2176). Flights to most lowland towns are inexpensive but heavily booked and somewhat unreliable. Buy tickets well in advance.

Travelair, a more expensive private line, flies from Tobias Bolaños Intl. Airport in the suburb of Pavas (phone: 232-7883; fax: 220-0413). Small planes are also available for charter from this airport, at about $200–400 per hour.

There's a bus stand right outside Juan Santamaría Airport, and buses run often, but also are crowded and make stops on the way into town. Buses labeled Alajuela on the Paseo Colón will take you to the airport. If you have much luggage, a taxi may be best. Taxis are metered but drivers don't always use them, so it's best to ask for an estimate of the fare: one-way to the airport is about $16 from downtown.

ROADS: Main highways are in good to poor condition. Mountain stretches such as Braulio Carrillo and Cerro de la Muerte may have landslides and many potholes. Most roads to smaller towns outside the Meseta Central are gravel, and may involve potholes, stream crossings, and other difficulties. Similarly, buses on main routes are usually new and comfortable, but they get older and more rickety (and sometimes more crowded) the farther you get from the highways. Costa Rica's bus system is very good on the whole: you can go just about anywhere in the country for less than $10, although it may involve some waiting. Most buses from San José to other parts of the country leave from the "Coca Cola" station, Calle 16 and aves. 1 and 3 (beware of pickpockets), but there are many other terminals. The Tourism Institute (ICT) has a list of bus stops at their Plaza de la Cultura office.

CAR RENTAL: San José has all the major car agencies, but they may be booked well in advance during the high season. Budget, Calle 30 and Paseo Colón and also at the Juan Santamaría Airport (223-3284). Avis, Sabana Norte (232-992). National, Calle 36, Ave. 7 (233-4044). Hertz, Calle 38, Paseo Colón (241-0097). Fees are somewhat higher than those in the U.S., and there's more chance of extra costs from accidents, breakdowns, theft, or other mishaps, given the road conditions—and thieves' attraction to rental plates. If caught speeding, you may have your license plate confiscated. Costa Rica is not free of "*la mordida*" (literally, "the bite"): traffic cops may present you with tickets for supposed offenses and give you a choice between appearing in their remote town at some impossible time or paying them on the spot. You can take the ticket, and give it to your rental agency, which will see that your "fine" at least goes to the proper authorities. You'll still have to pay, but it will help to discourage the practice. Or you could get the officer's ID number and license plate and report him to the Ministry of Transport.

TRAIN: The "Jungle Train" that ran between San José and Limón on the Caribbean coast was a popular tourist attraction, but it has been discontinued because of track deterioration. It is still possible to take a narrow-gauge train ride in the Caribbean lowlands on part of the original track. Several tour operators offer day trips, some combined with bus rides through Braulio Carrillo National Park.

U.S. Embassy

The embassy and consulate are located in the suburb of Pavas west of San José, across from the Centro Comercial (phone: 220-3939). Ruta 14 buses from Ave. 1 and Calle 18 in San José run by the embassy.

Health Advisory

Costa Rica has among the highest standards of public health in Latin America, and works aggressively to minimize disease. Tap water is drinkable in major towns. In the countryside, particularly in the lowlands, water should be boiled or treated. Reintroduced into the country by refugees in the 1980s, malaria is declining. Chloroquine prophylaxis is recommended in the lowlands, particularly in the banana plantation region of the Caribbean coast, where 90 percent of cases occur. Cholera and dengue fever have occurred recently, but chances of getting them are slight and facilities for diagnosis and treatment are numerous.

Hotels

San José has undergone a hotel boom in recent years, particularly in smaller hotels. This makes rooms easier to find, but quality may be uneven, and some places probably will go out of business as supply outstrips demand. There's a 10 percent sales tax and 3.3 percent hotel tax on Costa Rican hotels.

The following are some of the older, established hotels: Gran Hotel Costa Rica, Calle 3, aves. Central and 2 (phone: 221-4000; fax: 221-3501). Central location, good outdoor cafe. Try to get a room over central courtyard: $70–80. Hotel Irazú, on airport road at La Uruca next to San José 2000 shopping center (phone: 232-4811; fax: 232-3159). Shuttle bus to downtown, pool, tennis, sauna, restaurant and coffee shop, tour agencies: $60–110. Ambassador, calles 26 and 28 on the Paseo Colón (phone: 221-8155; fax: 255-3396). Paseo Colón location is quieter than downtown, except for rooms directly in front. Cable TV, small refrigerator: $50–80. Ara Macao, south of Pizza Hut in Barrio California near the National Museum (phone/fax: 233-2742). A bed and breakfast with sunny upstairs rooms: $50–60. Galilea, calles 11 and 13 near Plaza de la Democracia (fax: 223-1689). Clean, comfortable rooms in noisy but safe area: $20–30. Bienvenido, Calle 10, aves. 1 and 3 (phone: 221-1872). Located near tumultuous Central Market, but clean and friendly, with private baths: $12–20. Boruca, Calle 14, aves. 1 and 3 (phone: 223-0016). Windowless rooms, shared baths, clean: $3–7.

Some specialty hotels and inns: Rosa del Paseo, P.O. Box 287-1007, Centro Colón (phone: 257-3213; fax: 223-2776): $60–70. Casa Verde Victorian Hotel, Barrio Amon (an upscale neighborhood near downtown), P.O. Box 357-1007, Centro Colón (phone: 233-1812; fax: 223-0969): $55–65. Hotel Don Carlos, Barrio Amon (phone: 221-6707; fax: 244-0828): $40–60. Le Bergerac, Los Yoses (near the University of Costa Rica south of downtown), P.O. Box 1107-1002 P.E. (phone: 234-7850; fax: 225-9103). Hotel Bougainvillea, Santo Domingo (northern outskirts of San José), P.O. Box 69-2120 (phone: 240-8822; fax: 240-8484).

Restaurants

Restaurants also have responded to the tourism boom, with great variety, and unpredictability. Some of my favorite 1990 places had disappeared by 1994.

Hotel Amstel has a good, moderately priced, centrally located restaurant, open daily. Calle 7, aves. 1 and 3 (phone: 222-4622). Balcón de Europa has good Italian food, closed Saturday. It's at Calle 9, aves. 1 and Central (phone: 221-4841). In the Paseo Colón area, Machu Picchu has recommended Peruvian food. It's open for lunch and dinner except Sundays: Calle 32, aves. 1 and 3 (phone: 222-7384). Also in Paseo Colón is La Bastille at Calle 22 (phone: 255-4994), with good French food. For lunches or afternoon coffee breaks, Azafrán in the Los Yoses district out toward the University of Costa Rica has very good sandwiches, pasta, and desserts. Hours are 10–6 daily (phone: 225-5230). The National Theater at the Plaza de la Cultura has a nice cafe. Another good lunch place that's also open for breakfast is Soda La Casita, which has Costa Rican home cooking—*"casados," "gallo pinto," "empanadas," "olla de carne"* (a meat soup with big pieces of squash, yucca, plantain, or potato). It's at calles Central and 1, Ave. 1, open weekdays. For vegetarian and health food, Soda y Restaurante Vegetariana Vishnu, Ave. 1, calles 1 and 3 (phone: 221-3549), is good and moderately priced. The Central Market at calles 6 and 8 and aves. 5 and 7 has many inexpensive (and possibly not too clean) food stalls, although it's very crowded at mealtimes. (All restaurant bills include a 10 percent service charge as well as 10 percent tax. Tips above that will be appreciated anyway.)

Communications

The main post office is at aves. 1–3 and Calle 2. Sending or receiving parcels will involve paperwork and, possibly, theft. "Courier" companies may be safer.

You can phone direct to the U.S. from hotel phones or pay phones. There are public phones, telex, and fax facilities at Radiográfica SA, Ave. 5, Calle 1 and Ave. 2, Calle 1, both offices open 7 A.M.–10 P.M. seven days.

Money Exchange

The colón is the unit of currency, subdivided into 100 centimos. In mid 1994, the exchange rate was 15.4 colones for one U.S. dollar. Banks change dollars and traveler's checks for a commission; many hotels and restaurants accept traveler's checks or credit cards. There is a legal street market for dollars. American Express has an office on the fourth floor, Edificio Alde, Ave. 1, Calle 1, open Mon.– Fri. 8–5.

Tourist Information

The information center of the Costa Rican Tourism Institute (ICT) is in the Plaza de la Cultura on the Ave. Central, calles 3 and 5. The center is under the plaza, down some steps from Calle 5, next to the Gold Museum. Open 9–5 weekdays and 9–1 Saturdays (phone: 222-1090). They have free maps, tour information, and can answer questions in English.

The local English newspaper, the *Tico Times,* Apdo. 4632, San José (phone: 222-8952), is an excellent source of information, especially on current environmental and political issues. It's widely available, published Fridays. *Costa Rica Today,* Calle 25, aves. 5 and 6 (phone: 296-3911), is another English weekly specializing in tourism, published Thursdays.

Maps

The Tourism Institute (ICT) publishes a road map with the locations of most protected natural areas. It's available at their office in the Plaza de la Cultura. Topographical maps (mapas cartográficos) are available at the Instituto Geográfico Nacional, calles Central and 1, Ave. 20, and at librerías Lehmann and Universal (see bookstores). There's also a nature atlas guidebook available at bookstores.

Museums and Zoos

San José's best museums are about archaeology. The National Museum, Calle 17, aves. Central and 2, is dramatically situated in Bellavista Fortress above the new Parque Nacional. The fortress was once army headquarters and its walls are pocked with bullet holes. Inside the museum is a pleasant courtyard and garden and excellent exhibits on Costa Rican archaeology, anthropology, and history, including a room devoted to Nobel Laureate Oscar Arias's peacemaking activities. The prehistoric and pre-Columbian section has been remodeled, based on new archaeological evidence, and is highly informative. Hours 9–5 except Monday, admission $.25 (phone: 257-1433). The Jade Museum (Calle 9, Ave. 7 on the 11th floor, hours 9–3 weekdays) and the Pre-Columbian Gold Museum (Calle 5, aves. Central and 2 in the basement, hours 10–5 except Monday) have very impressive artifact collections.

The Natural History Museum is located in Colegio La Salle in Sabana Sur, diagonal from the southwest corner of Sabana Park at the west end of the Paseo Colón. Hours 7:30–3 weekdays except Monday, 8–12 Saturdays, admission $.25 (phone: 232-1306). There are dioramas and cases of mounted specimens, not very professional or well preserved, but some of the specimens are impressive, like a 20-foot crocodile from Guanacaste Province.

There is a small but extensive Entomology Museum in the Fine Arts Department building of the University of Costa Rica in San Pedro east of town: take a San Pedro bus on Ave. 2 to get there. Hours are variable: usually open in the afternoon (phone: 225-5555, 253-5323, ext. 318).

Two art museums give an idea of Costa Ricans' evolving relationship with their landscapes. The Costa Rican Art Museum at Sabana Park at the end of the Paseo Colón has historical nineteenth- and twentieth-century work and changing shows of contemporary local artists. Hours 10–5 except Monday, admission $.50, free Sunday (phone: 222-7155). The National Contemporary Art Gallery has shows of working artists. Ave. 15, calles 3 and 5. Hours 10–1, 1:45–5, except Sunday.

The National Zoo is in Parque Bolívar, entrance at Ave. 11, calles 7 and 9 (phone: 233-6701). The park is in a wooded ravine that would be altogether charming if not for the polluted and smelly Río Torres that runs through it. There are wild birds such as motmots and parakeets as well as caged macaws, parrots, toucans, etc. When I was there, the macaw cage had a hole through which the macaws would crawl and sit with wild parakeets on the outside. There was also a porcupine which shared a cage with a boa constrictor: the two liked to sleep curled up together. A lion was notorious for urinating on unwary visitors. Some of the cages are depressingly small: the zoo administration would like to improve it if funds ever become available. The Park Service Information Office is in the back of the zoo past the monkey cages (see above for details). The zoo is open 8:30–3:30 Tues.–Fri., and 9–4 weekends, admission $.30.

The Serpentarium is a small private zoo of reptiles and amphibians, mainly of Costa Rican species (phone: 255-4210). The animals seem well cared for, and the staff are friendly and helpful. This is a good way to learn about creatures you may see in the wild (or to see creatures you may not *want* to see in the wild, like terciopelos and other vipers). There are also photo exhibits, and a small gift shop. Avenida 1, calles 9 and 11, hours 10–7 daily, admission $1.50.

Bookstores and Libraries

The Bookshop, Calle 1 and Ave. 1, has books, periodicals, and cards in English, including books on natural history and parks.

Lehmann's, Ave. Central, calles 1 and 3, has some books in English, Costa Rican maps, and some interesting natural history books in Spanish.

Librería Universal, calles Central and 1, Ave. Central, has office and art supplies as well as books.

The National Library (Biblioteca Nacional) faces the Parque Nacional on Ave. 7 and Calle 15. A periodical room is upstairs.

The Centro Cultural Norteamericano, 25 meters west, 150 meters north from the Automercado in Los Yoses, has a library with books in English.

Excursions Around San José

You can see a lot of birds in a few hours' walk around the parks of the older, east side of San José, particularly on a Sunday morning before the traffic gets heavy. After an outdoor breakfast at the cafe of the Gran Hotel Costa Rica in the Plaza de la Cultura, walk down Ave. 2 to the Plaza de la Democracia, then past the National Museum to the Parque Nacional, with its massive statue of Central America driving out William Walker. From there turn west on Ave. 3 and walk a long block to the Parque España, which has many beautiful old trees where birds like to congregate. Farther west is the Parque Morazán, and then north on Calle 7 is Parque Bolívar and the zoo.

Very little remains of the mixture of evergreen and deciduous tropical forest that once covered the Valle Central. The best remnant is located at El Rodeo across the road from the Universidad de la Paz outside Ciudad Colón, a small town an hour's bus ride from San José. You can get a Ciudad Colón bus every hour or so on the Paseo Colón, but if you take the bus you will have to get a taxi in Ciudad Colón, walk for a couple of hours, or hitchhike to reach the forest. Just follow the main street of Ciudad Colón straight on to the paved road to the university. The walk is an interesting one through coffee plantations and wooded ravines, with some big mahogany and guapinol trees by the road. I saw masked tityras and a striped cuckoo along the way, and small brown basilisk lizards frequented a stream bottom about twenty minutes from Ciudad Colón. When you reach the Universidad de la Paz, it would be polite to ask permission to walk on the trails in the forest across the road, since it is private property, but if nobody is around to ask, they probably won't mind. The university owns much of the forest: check at its headquarters for information on trails and access. The forest lies across a steep pasture, and has some huge trees, white-faced monkeys, and coatis. On the other side, a trail runs along a steep escarpment where you can see miles of mountain country.

There are many guided tours of tourist attractions. Finca de las

Mariposas, a butterfly farm in Guacimo de Alajuela, has tours of the gardens where butterflies are reared, including a video of butterfly life cycles. P.O. Box 2132-4050, Alajuela (phone/fax: 438-0115).

The Central Volcanic Cordillera

The great volcanoes that loom north and east of the Valle Central may seem ancient, but they've arisen within the past few million years. They're still rising, venting lava, steam, and gas in pulses. There was much activity around the turn of the century, much again in the 1950s and '60s, and much again in the late '80s and early '90s. The mountains also are eroding rapidly in the torrential rains they receive from the Caribbean year-round. Streams such as the Río Sucio run bright orange with sulfuric mud they carry from the craters.

The volcanoes are studies in contrasts, between the bare desolation of the active craters and the lush forest that quickly invades once activity pauses. There's also great contrast between the Valle Central side of the cordillera, where farming has cleared the forest nearly to the summits, and the Caribbean side, where forest is largely undisturbed. The Caribbean side forest is so undisturbed, in fact, that it is difficult even to hike there without carefully maintained trails.

The volcano forests may look uniformly green and lush, but above about 2,000 meters, temperate species begin to replace the guapinol and Indio desnudo of the Valle Central. (On the Caribbean side the lowland forest is wetter, with different species.) Birch-like alders, called "*jaules*" in Spanish, are very common around the pastures and strawberry fields, and growing as "living fenceposts" along roads is a little white-flowered tree, *Drimys winteri,* which is considered one of the most primitive angiosperms, perhaps little changed from ancestors of 100 million years ago. It's called "*quiebra muelas*" or "*muelo*" in Spanish, and the pungent bark is used to treat toothache and stomach trouble. Around the summits grows a low, "elfin forest" in which plants are adapted to the stress of high altitude. Gnarled "*clusias*" have succulent, leathery leaves, and bayberry and blueberry have small, waxy ones. There are also

COSTA RICA
CENTRAL VOLCANIC CORDILLERA
AND NORTHEAST LOWLANDS

CARIBBEAN

SEA

NICARAGUA

BARRA DEL COLORADO

❼

LLANURA DE TORTUGUERO

TORTUGUERO

PUERTO VIEJO
DE SARAPIQUI

*CHIRRIPO
RIVER*

❺

❻

LAS HORGUETAS

*REVENTAZON
RIVER*

PARISMINA

❸

GUAPILES

VOLCAN
POAS ▲

❹

GUACIMO

VOLCAN
▲ BARVA

SAN PEDRO
DE POAS •

• SACRAMENTO

SIQUIRRES

PUERTO LIMON

• BARVA

❷

ALAJUELA •

• HEREDIA

VOLCAN
▲ IRAZU

❶

MOIN •

CIUDAD COLON •

• SAN JOSE

CARTAGO •

TURRIALBA •

PARAISO •

PACAYAS

❽

*PACUARE
RIVER*

PACIFIC

OCEAN

1. GUAYABO NATIONAL MONUMENT
2. IRAZU NATIONAL PARK
3. POAS NATIONAL PARK
4. BRAULIO CARRILLO NAT. PARK
5. LA SELVA BIOLOGICAL STATION
6. TORTUGUERO NATIONAL PARK
7. BARRA DEL COLORADO
   NATIONAL WILDLIFE REFUGE
8. TAPANTI NATIONAL PARK

many lowland tropical genera that have species in the cold mountain forest, such as *Miconia*.

National parks were decreed in the central volcanoes as early as 1939 as a measure to ensure the Valle Central's water supply, but effective protection didn't begin until the creation of the Park Service in 1970. By that time most of the wildlife of the Valle Central side had been hunted off, and it has been slow to recover on smaller parks such as Poás and Irazú because they are isolated. Wildlife remains abundant on the Caribbean side.

Poás National Park

Poás Volcano was long the destination of a mass pilgrimage from San José on the Saint's Day of March 19. This may have been related to the volcano's tendency to drench the city in volcanic ash every few decades. The most spectacular recent eruption occurred in 1910, when the cone ejected an 8,000-meter cloud that distributed an estimated 640,000 tons of ash on surrounding areas. In 1989, the volcano produced a kilometer-high ash plume. The present crater is 1.5 kilometers across and 300 meters deep, when you can see it. It's often obscured by mists or gases.

The 5,600-hectare park, created in 1970, is one of the most developed and accessible in the country, despite the powder keg it sits on. Acid sulfur gases from the crater have caused some premature deterioration of the visitor center and sporadic interruption of its services. At last report, the center contained a gift shop run by Fundación Neotrópica and a small snack bar as well as interpretive exhibits. The volcano may have decreed otherwise since then, however.

One asphalt trail leads to the crater past small meadows where sooty robins hop about: a parallel trail through misty forest leaves from the parking lot's upper terrace. Another trail goes to beautiful wooded Botos Lake in an inactive crater, from which there is no sign of the nearby geological turbulence. Watch the trees for the Poás squirrel, a small russet subspecies that lives nowhere else. Quetzals are sometimes seen here. You'll probably hear the haunting song of the black-faced solitaire, or "*jilguero*," and see troops of bush tanagers moving through the blueberry scrub. On one visit, I saw what might have been puma scat right above the active crater.

Poás is an easy day's excursion from San José. If you have a car, go early in the morning, before the mists rise and cut off the view, which can encompass both oceans. Hours are 8–2:30 daily except Monday, but you can get there earlier or stay longer. There's no camping. The park is 60 kilometers north of Alajuela via San Pedro de Poás. You can take regular buses to Alajuela and San Pedro de Poás, and then hire a taxi to the park (about $20 round-trip). Alajuela buses leave San José from Ave. 2, Calle 12 every few minutes. Buses from Alajuela to San Pedro de Poás leave from the same station about every hour. On Sundays you can get a bus direct to the park at 8:30 in Alajuela from Calle 12, aves. 2 and 4, for about $3 round-trip. This tends to be crowded. Many tour agencies offer Poás trips for $20–40.

Braulio Carrillo National Park

When developers proposed to build a San José–to–Limón highway in the 1970s, ecologists demonstrated that if an army of colonists cut the forest along the road, soil erosion and floods would make the road unmaintainable. This park, presently 45,900 hectares, was created in 1978 as a compromise between growth and preservation. With elevations ranging from 2,906 meters at the top of Barva Volcano to 50 meters in the Caribbean lowlands, the park has extraordinary biodiversity, including six thousand plant species and five hundred bird species. In 1986, the park was enlarged to encompass a foothill corridor extending to La Selva Biological Station, greatly enhancing its diversity, since many wildlife species migrate to different altitudes at different times of year. The bare-necked umbrellabird (which is named for males' ability to erect their head feathers into umbrella-shaped displays during mating rituals) is an uncommon species that depends on such migrations. Although only twenty minutes from San José, the park's forests have never been completely explored. A 1983 expedition into the lowland corridor found twenty-eight plant species previously unknown to science.

It's easy to see the park while driving across it on the highway (which goes north to Guápiles before turning east to Limón). The vast stretch of unbroken forest is impressive after the heavily populated Valle Central. An hourly bus to Guápiles leaves from Calle 12 and aves. 7 and 9, and costs about a dollar. It will let you off at stops within the park. Actually getting into the forest is harder. About 2 kilometers before the Zurqui Tunnel (which is near the San José side entrance to the park) is a ranger station where you can get information and pay the entrance fee. There is an alarmingly steep and rocky picnic area past the station, but it has a reputation for robberies.

The only well-marked trail from the highway is the La Botella trail, located 17 kilometers past the tunnel and 2.5 kilometers before the Quebrada Gonzales station on the park's Guápiles side. The trailhead and a parking area are to the left of the road as you go toward Guápiles. You can walk for about two hours through primary forest down to the Río Patria. When I was there, howler monkeys were roaring back at the diesels on the highway, a lesser anteater (or "*tamandua*") was nosing about, and snowcap hummingbirds little larger than bumblebees were squabbling over flowers. The trail is very rocky and slippery, and there are terciopelos and other poisonous snakes, so wear appropriate footgear, and rain gear.

Another access is a trail that leads up 2,900-meter Barva Volcano at the southwest edge of the park. You reach the trail on a day trip from San José via Heredia, Barva, San José de la Montaña, and Paso Llano. A 6 A.M. bus to Paso Llano leaves from the central market in Heredia. From Paso Llano, it's an 8-kilometer hike up a steep dirt road to the ranger station and park entrance. There are some good specimens of Costa Rica's mountain oaks in pastures along the road, huge trees with massive plates of gray bark. Within the park, the forest is low and dense, with huge-leaved *Gunnera* or "poor-man's umbrella" growing along the trail. The summit and a crater lake are a few more kilometers along the trail, a misty pool floored with black gravel and surrounded by elfin forest, a magical place. There is supposedly a trail from here across the park to La

Selva, but it should only be attempted by experienced cross-country walkers. In 1989, three hikers who simply started out to walk around the crater lake on Barva got lost for eleven days. When I was there (during the rainy season), mist reduced visibility to near zero at times, and a chilly, wind-driven rain fell constantly. There is a campsite near the ranger station. A modest *"albergue"* (shelter) with horse rental and restaurant is located near the park entrance on the right. Two upscale hotels, the Cypresal and Pórtico, are near San José de la Montaña.

La Selva Biological Station

Probably the best way to experience Braulio Carrillo's diverse wild-life is to visit La Selva in the lowlands at its northern extremity. Well protected by the Organization for Tropical Studies since the 1960s, the 1,500-hectare reserve has very confiding wild inhabitants. Sloths, kinkajous, and anteaters can be seen many evenings in trees above a bridge over the Sarapiquí River, and peccary, three monkey species, coatis, and agoutis are often seen from trails. I saw otter and tayra (a giant tropical weasel) there, and others saw ocelot and paca. The trail system is excellent, encompassing some 50 kilometers, and there is a large arboretum with many tree species labeled if you want to tackle the monumental task of tropical tree identification. La Selva is somewhat unusual for the tropics in that a single tree species predominates in its forest (although there are hundreds of other species). The predominant species is *"gavilán"* (*Pentaclethra macroloba*), a feathery-leaved member of the legume family. A very similar species lives in West Africa, suggesting that neither species has changed much in the 100 million years since Africa and South America diverged.

Access to La Selva is mainly limited to scientific researchers, and it's always very full during the dry season. When there is room for tourists, it costs about $88 a day for accommodations, which include three cafeteria meals. You can also make day visits from San José, which costs about $25 including lunch and a bus ride from the OTS (Organization for Tropical Studies) office in San José, Apartado 676, 2050 San Pedro, San José (phone: 240-6696; fax:

240-6783). Enthusiastic young naturalists from the nearby community of Puerto Viejo act as guides on day trips. The guides have taken a course in tropical biology.

There are two other small private reserves near La Selva. El Gavilán is a former cattle ranch of 180 hectares, mostly still forested. The owners offer horse tours of the forest, and boat trips on the Sarapiquí and other rivers, including the San Juan on the Nicaraguan border. Rooms are $20–30 a night with private or shared bath, breakfast included, in a former hacienda building with attractive grounds. Bus transport from San José is available (phone: 234-9507, 223-7479; fax: 253-6556). Selva Verde Lodge is about 7 kilometers west of Puerto Viejo on the road to San José on a 200-hectare former farm near the Sarapiquí. It has trails on a private rain forest reserve. There are several buildings, with accommodations ranging from $46–73 per night. A dining room serves buffet-style meals. Selva Verde, Chilamate, Puerto Viejo de Sarapiquí, Costa Rica (phone: 766-6077 or 271-6459). You can also make reservations through Holbrook Travel, 3540 NW 13th St., Gainesville, FL 32609 (phone: 800-451-7111). Transport from San José is available at $15 each, with at least four people.

Rara Avis

Located on the east side of Braulio Carrillo about 10 kilometers south of La Selva, this was one of the first of many private nature reserves of recent decades. It was formerly a prison colony (called "*el plástico*" because prisoners slept under sheets of plastic). The penal colony building was renovated to serve as one of the reserve's two lodges. El Plastico is basic, with bunks and communal showers, $45 per day including meals; the Waterfall Lodge has rooms with private showers, $75 per day with meals. There are discounts for students, researchers, and visitors making extended stays. The reserve is 15 kilometers up a dirt track from Las Horquetas on the road between the Guápiles Highway and Puerto Viejo. Reservations to the lodges include tractor transport up the track. Contact Apartado 8105, 1000 San José (phone/fax: 253-0844). The 1,335-hectare reserve has hiking trails and other recreational amenities, as well as experimental programs on economic use of rain forest flora and fauna, including harvesting of aerial roots for furniture and basket wicker, and raising of pacas for meat.

The Rain Forest Aerial Tram

Biologist Donald Perry carried out some pioneering explorations of the rain forest canopy at La Selva and Rara Avis in the 1980s. Perry's new project, an aerial tram that takes visitors for 2 miles through the canopy of a rain forest just north of Braulio Carrillo N.P. off the San Jose–Limón Road, opened to the public in 1994. Phone: 257-5961 or 225-8869; fax: 257-6053. Visitor accommodations, trails, and a nature center and restaurant are planned.

Irazú National Park

English novelist Anthony Trollope visited Irazú Volcano in 1859, and described its active crater matter-of-factly as "a wide opening which could possibly hold a 600-acre farm." The volcano has strewn the equivalent of much more than a single farm across Costa Rica in subsequent eruptions. From 1963 to 1965, it periodically ejected steam, boulders, and clouds of ash that covered an estimated 2,000–3,000 square kilometers, falling as far away as the Nicoya Peninsula. The volcano has been mainly dormant since then, except for some tremors in 1991, but the crater still resembles a giant shellhole. At 3,432 meters, it's Costa Rica's highest active volcano.

Irazú was first declared a national park in 1955, and was managed by the Costa Rican Tourism Institute until the Park Service took over in 1976. Its 2,308 hectares include the four craters and two small lakes at the summit and *páramo*, elfin forest, and cloud forest on the upper slopes. There's relatively little wildlife. A paved road goes to the summit, where there is a parking lot. A 1-kilometer trail leads to the craters from there.

Access from San José is via Cartago, with a turnoff to the left about halfway along the road from Cartago to the town of Pacayas. It's an easy day trip by car, through picturesque farmland. Buses to the park run Wednesdays, weekends, and holidays at 8 A.M. from

Ave. 2 across from the Gran Hotel Costa Rica. Fare is $3.00 (phone: 551-5795, 272-0651). Other days you could take the bus to Cartago (leaving frequently from Calle 13, aves. 2 and 4) and hire a cab from there (about $30). About halfway from Cartago to the park, a paved road to the left leads to the Prusia Recreation Area, which adjoins Irazú. Although it's mainly planted forest, the area is more sheltered than the park, and camping is allowed.

About 6 kilometers east of Cartago on the road to Paraíso is Lankester Gardens, an orchid collection managed by the University of Costa Rica (phone: 551-9877). The country is one of the global hot spots of orchid diversity, with 1,100 known species, 88 percent of which are epiphytic, growing on trees or rocks instead of the ground. A dark pink orchid, *Cattleya skinneri,* is the national flower. The bus driver will let you off nearby. Hours are 9:30–3:30 daily. Early spring is the best time to see the orchids in flower.

Guayabo National Monument

This unusual ruined settlement may have included about 15 hectares of central towns and surrounding hamlets during its heyday from about 1,200 to 700 years ago. The site may have been occupied for as long as 3,000 years. It apparently was abandoned about 600 years ago, for unknown reasons. First excavated in 1822, the site yielded intricately carved stelae and tablelike ceremonial stones now on display at the National Museum. At the site, you can see circular stone mounds, stone-paved causeways, a still-working aqueduct system with an intact bridge, and various petroglyphs which may have had religious or astronomical significance, although almost nothing is known for certain about the people who lived here. There are a few similar sites on Costa Rica's Caribbean slope, but this is the best one.

The National Monument encompasses 218 hectares in the Guayabo River Canyon among the foothills of Turrialba Volcano. The ruins were included in the park system in 1973. In 1980 a sample of the area's premontane rain forest was added, an addition comprising 90 percent of the monument. Many birds live among the ruins, including Montezuma's oropendolas—big, colorful relatives of grackles and orioles that form colonies of hanging, sacklike nests in the trees and make a variety of squeaking and gurgling sounds. Among other species, armadillos, jaguarundis, and agoutis have been seen in the forest. The monument is open 8–4 every day, although the ruins may be closed on weekdays if excavations are under way. There is an interpretive staff to introduce visitors to the ruins.

The monument is north of the town of Turrialba, which was the halfway point on the only road from San José to Limón before the Guápiles Highway was built. Buses from San José to Turrialba leave from Calle 13, Ave. 6 every hour. A Santa Teresita bus leaving from Turrialba's main bus stop at 10:30 A.M. and 1:30 P.M. can let you off about 4 kilometers from the ruins. A taxi from Turrialba will cost about $12. The road is paved except for the last 4 kilometers to the monument. You can make a day trip by taking the morning bus and then catching the afternoon bus back. You can also camp (but be prepared—it rains a lot), or stay at the Hotel la Calzada located a few hundred meters before the entrance. It's a small country inn with shared bathrooms and an open-air restaurant, $7–12. Advance reservations are recommended (phone: 556-0465).

Whitewater Rivers

Turrialba has become a center for rafting and kayaking on the beautiful rivers that descend toward the Caribbean nearby, the Reventazón and the Pacuare. These rivers actually head in the Talamanca Cordillera to the south, but most rafting occurs where they flow northeast toward the Central Cordillera foothills. They offer some exciting rafting as well as a chance to see some relatively undisturbed riverside forest. The Reventazón has Class III rapids, while the more remote Pacuare has some hair-raising Class IV whitewater. The Pacuare passes through a deep, heavily forested gorge where local Indians still hunt, and where you can see increasingly rare wildlife such as sun bitterns, heron-sized birds that get their name from the surprising sunburst of orange and yellow feathers they display when they open their wings to fly. At the bottom of the Pacuare Gorge is an awe-inspiring place called Dos Montañas where the river has cut through a massive block of stone that towers hundreds of feet above it, with cliffs festooned with epiphytic plants. The Pacuare was declared Costa Rica's first wild and scenic river in 1986. Sadly, there are plans to dam it at Dos Montañas, an agonizing situation for Costa Rican conservationists because hydroelectric power from such dams is the country's main domestic energy source (there is one geothermal plant, and more are planned).

Several San José tour agencies offer river trips. Trips can go year-round, although June to October has the liveliest water. Costa Rica Expeditions is experienced and well organized: Apdo. 6941, San José (phone: 222-0333, 257-0766). Other agencies that offer trips are Ríos Trópicales (phone: 233-6455); Aventuras Naturales (phone: 225-3939); and Costa Sol Rafting (phone: 233-6664; fax: 233-6881). Trips range from one to three days and cost $100–300 per person, depending on group size. Agencies can provide information about river conservation. Transportation to the river is included in trips. If you want to stay in Turrialba, the Hotel Wagelia has rooms with private bath for about $30–40, with a good restaurant and attractively landscaped grounds (phone: 556-1596). They are on Ave. 4 on the edge of town where the road to San José begins. They also offer river trips. The Hotel Interamericano on Ave. 1 near the railway station is $7–12 for rooms with shared bath (phone: 556-0142).

Turrialba is named for the 3,328-meter volcano to the north, which seemed a "*torre alba*," a white tower, to Spanish settlers because of the smoke plumes it ejected.

A few kilometers from Turrialba on the road to Limón is CATIE, the main agricultural and natural resource training center in Central America.

Tortuguero

Costa Rica's northeast coast is one of its two remaining lowland rain forest wildernesses. The "Llanura de Tortuguero" stretches inland for dozens of swampy miles in the alluvial basins of the Tortuguero, Suerte, and Chirripó rivers, and provides habitat for most native species. Sizable populations of tapirs and white-lipped peccaries find ample food among the raphia palm groves that cover much of the region. Jaguar also thrive in this swampy environment. Big crocodiles and caimans survive in the rivers, along with gars, one of the few North American fish families that has succeeded in extending its range this far south.

The Tortuguero region's wilderness acts as an indispensable buffer to its most precious biological resource, the 30 kilometers of sea turtle nesting beach that is the Caribbean's major breeding ground for these endangered animals. Four of the world's eight sea turtle species breed on the beach: greens, hawksbills, leatherbacks, and loggerheads. The green turtles (*Chelonia mydas*) are the most numerous, and, depending on conditions, anywhere from a few hundred to a few thousand female greens may visit the beach to bury their clutches of leathery white eggs during the mating season, from July to early October. Individual females may come ashore multiple times to lay eggs, and lay around a hundred eggs during each nesting. The baby turtles hatch about two months later: less than 1 percent survive to reach adulthood. Green turtles are herbivores, spending most of their time feeding on underwater pastures of turtle grass. The Miskito Cays along the Nicaraguan coast are a major feeding ground for Tortuguero's greens. Others go as far south as Colombia.

Lesser numbers of hawksbills also visit the beach from May to October. Smaller than greens, they eat mostly sponges and other sessile animals, as well as algae. Loggerheads also have nested at Tortuguero in May–October but they're quite rare. The biggest turtles, the 2-meter-long leatherbacks, nest from April until August, and several hundred may come ashore during this period, concentrating at the southern end of the park.

Other coastal wildlife benefits from the wilderness. Coveted for their meat, manatees have been hunted out from southern Costa Rica. They still survive along the Tortuguero coast, although they're seldom seen. Populations of game fish such as tarpon and snook are still large, and the area is popular with sport fishermen.

Tortuguero is swampy because of its level alluvial terrain (the only hill on the coast is 119-meter Cerro Tortuguero, a volcano that didn't get very far before becoming extinct) and its high rainfall, up to 6,000 mm a year. They say there are two seasons at Tortuguero, the rainy season and the monsoon. Sudden downpours can occur anytime, although there's less rain from February to April and August to October.

Tortuguero National Park

Dutch explorers recorded green turtles nesting at Tortuguero in 1539, and turtle numbers remained high into the early twentieth century. Green turtle eggs and meat are highly edible, however, and by the 1950s, populations were in steep decline from overexploitation. At that time, naturalist Archie Carr, who was trying to unravel the turtles' mysterious migratory habits, became concerned about the decline and joined with other conservationists to create the Caribbean Conservation Corporation in 1959. Scientists sponsored by CCC have been studying the Tortuguero turtles ever since, and have discovered, among other things, that none of the female turtles tagged there have shown up at other breeding grounds. The Conservation Corporation maintains a newly rebuilt research station on the beach side of the inland waterway 1 kilometer north of Tortuguero town. See Archie Carr's books, *The Windward Road* and *So Excellent a Fishe,* for accounts of his lifelong study of the turtles.

The CCC lobbied the Costa Rican government to protect the beaches, and in 1963 a reserve was established, although it offered only limited protection. Protection became more effective after the area was decreed a national park in 1970; wardens were stationed on the beach and regular armed patrols were stepped up. In 1975 the park was enlarged: it now encompasses 18,946 hectares. There are plans to enlarge it further and link it with Barra del Colorado Wildlife Refuge to the north. Park headquarters is located near the little town of Tortuguero just north of the park boundary between the ocean and the inland waterway. The headquarters has exhibits and there is a small campsite with drinking water and latrines. There is also an information kiosk in the center of Tortuguero town.

The park remains inaccessible by road, which is probably good for the turtles and manatees. At least, many local people, conservationists, and tour operators think so. You can get there by boat on the inland waterway that runs north from the town of Moín outside Limón, or by plane from San José. Buses to Limón leave San José at Ave. 3, calles 19 and 21, hourly. Moín buses leave Limón frequently from the same part of the town where the San José buses stop. You can probably negotiate a trip on a boat going to Tortuguero, but it may not be easy or cheap to do so, and the trip may take a while, possibly days. Riverboat *Francesca* charges about $50 return for a leisurely trip in a canopied boat (phone: 226-0986). TravelAir has daily flights from San José to Tortuguero (phone: 327-883). Another possibility is to take a TravelAir or SANSA flight to Barra del Colorado and hire a boat from there. It would be advisable to make a reservation at a hotel before you arrive, because the area is very popular.

Most visitors go to Tortuguero on tours, since this solves the travel and accommodation insecurities. The deluxe way to go is to fly in on one of Costa Rica Expedition's planes and stay at their Tortuga Lodge on the inland waterway 2 kilometers north of Tortuguero town. The lodge is on 50 hectares of rain forest, a good location to enjoy beach and forest. It has hot water (a rarity in lowland resorts), private baths, good food, and attractive grounds. It's $60–70 a night, with various package tours—about $250 for one night by plane, less by bus and boat (phone: 257-0766, 222-0333). The Mawamba Lodge a kilometer closer to town is comparable (phone: 223-2421). Inexpensive hotels include Sabina's in town, one of the earliest places, $7–40 a night, and Tatane on the waterway north, $7–12. There are a wide variety of package tours that include bus from San José, boat from Moín, and lodging. I went that way in 1987, and saw a lot of wildlife on the boat trip. Cotur (phone: 233-0155, 233-6579) and Mitur (phone: 255-2031, 255-2262), both based in San José, are other possibilities, each costing about $200 for a two-night package.

Tortuguero is not a place for swimming because of sharks and tricky surf on the ocean side, and caimans and crocodiles on the river side. Forest hiking is also limited because of the area's swampiness, although there are trails at park headquarters, Tortuga Lodge, and Cerro Tortuguero (the view from Cerro Tortuguero of rain forest stretching unbroken to the Sierpe Hills is quite inspiring). You can walk on the beach, of course. The best way of getting around on the land side is to rent a *"cayuca,"* a dugout canoe, on the dock at Tortuguero town, presently about $1 an hour. I seemed to be regarded as eccentric when I did this in 1987, but it's caught on. I found cayucas not that easy to maneuver, especially in the currents of the Río Tortuguero's mouth, and with their tendency to leak, but they are a good way to get close to the environment. For a little more, you can hire a guide to go with you.

Another good way to get close to the forest is to take a guided night motorboat trip, offered by most resorts. This gets you farther inland, where there's a better possibility of seeing crocodiles, tapir, or other nocturnal creatures. One likely sighting is the boat-billed heron, a black and white bird with a strangely enlarged bill and huge eyes, which haunts the waterways. You may hear the manlike cries of potoos or "poor me ones," strange night birds that spend the day resting in attitudes that make them resemble dead branches.

Local people act as guides when turtles are nesting. You can buy tickets for tours at the park information kiosk in town. Tours are at night, when the turtles usually come ashore. The guides will show you how to watch and even photograph the turtles without disturbing their nesting behavior. (Turtles may fail to nest if disturbed.)

Resorts also provide guide service for saltwater and freshwater fishing.

Barra del Colorado National Wildlife Refuge

Like Tortuguero N.P., this 92,000-hectare refuge is a swampy alluvial plain covered with palm swamps and dotted with a few volcanic hillocks. Fewer turtles nest along the beach, but forest wildlife populations are similar to Tortuguero's, including howler, spider, and white-faced capuchin monkeys and great green macaws. The region has over three hundred bird species. Unfortunately, there has been illegal logging, road building, and colonization in the western part of the refuge in recent years.

The town of Barra del Colorado on the mouth of the Río Colorado in the northeast of the refuge is the only settlement. It is accessible by SANSA (phone: 229-9414) and TravelAir (phone: 232-7883) flights, or by boat, either north from Tortuguero town or down the San Juan River. A scheduled boat leaves in the late morning from Puerto Viejo on the Sarapiquí River and goes downstream as far as the San Juan, and you might be able to find somebody to take you on from there, or to take you all the way from Puerto Viejo. There's a nature resort, Oro Verde Station, about 40 kilometers downstream from Puerto Viejo on the Sarapiquí that provides tours down the San Juan. They offer a three-day package from San José including transportation for about $200 (phone: 233-6613; fax: 223-7479).

Barra del Colorado is a fishing town, and there are a number of fishing resorts that also accommodate other (nonfishing) travelers. The Río Colorado Lodge has private baths and hot water for $60–80 per person with meals. They have boats with radios and sonar (phone: 232-4063; also 800-243-9777 in the U.S.). Isla de Pesca (223-4560) and Casamar (433-8834) have similar rates and facilities. Tarponland (710-6917) near the airstrip is cheaper, with cold water and shared or private baths, $20–30.

Guanacaste

Costa Rica's northwest plays a special part in the national consciousness. Culturally and ecologically, it resembles Nicaragua more than the Meseta Central, and was part of Nicaragua until independence from Spain. Its political allegiance then remained unclear until it joined Costa Rica by referendum in 1858. Valle Central Costa Ricans, or "Joséfinos," tend to regard it as romantic and exotic because of its indigenous past and wild "savanna." Its name embodies both these elements: *"guanacaste"* is an indigenous word meaning "ear tree" and referring to a common dry forest and savanna tree species (*Enterolobium cyclocarpum*) whose leguminous fruits resemble human ears. The guanacaste is now the national tree. William Beebe described the savanna as "an enchanted forest or rather park of lofty trees where bands of spider monkeys swung by their tails. . . . The grass, the meandering streams, the enormous wide-spreading trees might have all been in an English park. . . . But a pair of loud-voiced macaws and the swooping

flight of trogons, together with fresh tracks of tapirs, refocused our latitude."

Guanacaste includes one of the most fertile parts of the country, and one of the least fertile. The lower Tempisque Valley and Nicoya Peninsula were intensively farmed by the Chorotegas and in this century have again become major farming centers. On the other hand, the volcanoes, lava plains, and canyons north of the provincial capital of Liberia apparently have always been wildlands. Spanish explorers found them relatively uninhabited and, except for large ranching haciendas, they've remained so. Water is seasonally scarce (most rivers shrink drastically in the dry season), and part of the area is underlain by a very infertile bedrock called peridotite.

Guanacaste's parks contain the largest remaining expanse of dry deciduous forest in Central America, which makes the region very significant ecologically. About 60 percent of tropical forest world-

wide was originally of the dry deciduous type, but because dry forest is very vulnerable to burning and other human impacts, little
remains (about 2 percent of the original expanse in Central America, and only .08 percent is protected). Dry forest plants and animals are thus much more threatened than those of rain forest, and
Guanacaste's parks are major refuges for them.

Most trees in this forest shed their leaves in the November–May
dry season, although they don't necessarily become dormant as in
northern deciduous forest. Many flower or fruit, and the forest can
be spectacularly colorful at this time. Many tropical rain forest animals live just as well in dry forest, but there are specialized species
too. The white-throated magpie jay, a pale blue, long-tailed jay
with an exotic head plume, occurs only in the northwest in Costa
Rica.

Guanacaste also contains a number of other habitats, from mangroves and evergreen gallery forest to rain forest and cloud forest
on volcanoes. Its emptiness and openness make it one of the best
places in Central America for long hikes, although the heat in midday can be extraordinary. Its coast also has significant turtle nesting beaches and seabird rookeries.

Santa Rosa National Park

This 49,515-hectare park was established in 1971. Before that
much of it was a hacienda belonging to Nicaraguan dictator Anastasio Somoza. It was also the site of three battles stemming from
invasions from Nicaragua—the most famous one of which was
when Walker's filibusters were repelled in 1856, and others in 1919
and 1955. A restored ranch house in the park's center, called the
Casona, was the site of the 1856 battle. Somoza bought the hacienda in the 1930s; Costa Rica paid him $349,000 after expro-
priating it in 1966.

Santa Rosa is the nucleus of the dry forest refuge, and its forest
and wildlife are doing well after three decades of protection. Trees
have reclaimed many former pastures. Since the mid 1980s, the
Park Service has also had a program to restore some areas to forest
by planting trees or using controlled livestock grazing to spread
seed (many species, including guanacastes, probably coevolved

with prehistoric horses, mastodons, and other megafauna and have fruits adapted to being eaten). This program also tries to employ the skills of local *"guanacastecos,"* who have a long tradition of ranching and woodcraft, in managing land and animals.

Santa Rosa is one of the best places in Central America to see wildlife, particularly in the dry season when visibility is good and animals concentrate around streams. An early morning walk on the nature trail that begins at the Casona may provide good looks at howler, spider, and capuchin monkeys, large coati troops, peccary, deer, and great curassow (a spectacular turkey-sized bird) along a stream. (Watch out for stinging acacia ants, don't scare animals away from drinking by talking, and don't go off-trail—there are rattlesnakes in the dry forest.)

Another good place to watch quietly for animals is a small pond or laguna about a kilometer northwest of park headquarters. The road there branches off to the right from the road to Playa Naranjo. If you stay on a little wooded rise above this pond at dusk, you may see coyotes or other predators come to monitor the rabbit and deer populations. Five cat species live in the park—jaguars, jaguarundis, ocelots, margays, and pumas.

A good day hike is to walk down to Playa Naranjo on a jeep road that leads over the level volcanic plateau, then drops steeply into the dry forested Cañon del Tigre and the green gallery forest along the Río Caldera, and then to mangrove and mesquite swamp behind the beach. At the ocean, follow the beach north to the river's mouth, which is fordable, then around a salty, crocodile-inhabited lagoon to a track that loops back to the same road you walked in on. It's a good six-hour walk round-trip: carry plenty of water and leave early to avoid the midday heat, when you'd be wise to rest for a few hours in the gallery forest. From this road, there's also a well-marked footpath northwest to Playa Nancite, which is a major nesting beach for Pacific ridley turtles in September and October. In good years, thousands of these relatively small sea turtles may be on the beach at one time. A park researcher told me he saw a jaguar eating one. Leatherback turtles also nest from October to March. You can camp without permission at Naranjo; there is water at the Argelia and Estero Real sites. Naranjo is popular with 4wdequipped vacationers. It's a couple of hours' walk from the Playa Naranjo road to Playa Nancite. (You'll get very thirsty on these hikes, but resist the temptation to drink from streams because there probably are amoebas. I cooled off by getting *into* a stream.) Camping at Nancite is only by permission, and access is restricted during turtle nesting season.

Another, even drier, day hike is into the peridotite country of the Santa Elena Peninsula north of park headquarters. You follow the road that forks north from the Playa Naranjo road just outside of headquarters. Instead of turning right to the pond mentioned above, you stay on the road northwest. After a few kilometers, the country changes markedly from the tall jaragua grass and dry forest copses of the volcanic plateau to a gnarled country of low bunch grass and little nancite and curatella trees. The black and red rock underfoot is peridotite, which is brought up from the earth's mantle during the plate subduction process. Little agave plants that grow in the grass are endemic to the area. Again, carry plenty of water, and watch where you're going: roads and trails aren't marked and you could easily get lost.

Santa Rosa has a well-developed campsite with toilets and showers near park headquarters. The park entrance is on the Pan American Highway 37 kilometers north of Liberia. You can take the bus from San José to Liberia, leaving from Calle 2, aves. 3 and 5, then get a bus to La Cruz near the Nicaraguan border and ask the driver to let you off at the park. It's 7 kilometers from the entrance to headquarters, so arrive in the cool of the morning or evening. Headquarters phone: 695-5598. You can eat at the park comedor for about $11 a day if you arrange it in advance: otherwise bring your own food.

Liberia is a large, pleasant town with a number of hotels and restaurants. The Hotel Las Espuelas (phone: 666-0144) just south of town on the highway is the best, at $60–90 a night. Hotel El Sitio has similar facilities for $56–84 (666-1211). The hotels located at the main intersection are about $30–50, with good rooms and service. Hotel Boyeros (666-0722); Hotel Bramadero (666-0371). The Hotel La Siesta ($20–30; 666-0678) and Hotel Oriental ($7–12; 666-0085) are a few blocks into town. Reservations are advised during the dry season. The Casa de Cultura three blocks south of the church is open Tues.–Sat. 9–6, Sun. 9–1, with tourist information and exhibits.

Guanacaste National Park

This park was established in 1989 to ensure the survival of the dry forest ecosystem by extending protection to the lands east of Santa Rosa N.P. The 32,512-hectare park extends from the Pan American Highway to include the Orosí and Cacao volcanoes of the cordillera, thus providing a beach-to-mountain altitudinal transect for wildlife migration. Many species spend part of their life cycles in the dry forest, and part in the evergreen forest of the volcanoes. Much of the land was ranched until the early 1980s: it is now being managed to encourage forest regrowth. The evergreen rain forest and cloud forest on the volcanoes is largely primary, and is unusual in that little forest remains at this elevation (1,000 to 2,000 meters) in Central America generally. Most has been cut for farms or towns. Rare and little-known species live in it. In recent years the Park Service and the Institute of Biodiversity have been training local people to collect and identify plants, insects, and other organisms as part of an overall survey of Costa Rica's biotic resources.

Several research stations have been established at Guanacaste National Park, and may offer basic accommodations and food to visitors for a fee. This can be arranged with the park administration at the Santa Rosa headquarters (phone: 695-5598) or in San José. The station on Volcán Cacao provides a breathtaking view of the entire park as far as the Pacific, and has trails into the rain forest and cloud forest where monkeys, toucans, guans, and various trogon species are common. It's an 11-kilometer walk or horseback ride beyond the town of Quebrada Grande to get there, and nights are chilly.

Rincón de la Vieja National Park

Rincón de la Vieja is an active volcano (1,895 meters) north of Liberia. It has nine craters at the summit, two of them active, and a 3-hectare lake. The last significant activity was from 1966 to 1970, but there was a mudflow as recently as 1990. At the foot of the mountain's south slope are two areas, Las Pailas and Las Hornillas, where the volcano vents steam and gases in the form of boiling mudpots, hot springs, sulfur lakes, and geysers. Surrounded by dry forest, these are fascinating but tricky places (there's a danger of falling into one of the pits and getting burned).

Established in 1974, the 14,083-hectare park encompasses the volcano and nearby peaks and the mixture of dry and evergreen forest on the slopes down to 600 meters. An almost pure stand of leathery-leaved *Clusia* trees covers the upper slopes below the bare, windswept craters. Tapir tracks are often seen around the summit lake, Laguna Jilgueros. The park also includes one of the largest populations of the national flower, *Cattleya skinneri*. Some thirty-two stream systems begin on the volcano slopes, making it very important for the irrigated farming of the Tempisque Valley.

The park isn't heavily visited because it's a little hard to reach. The Santa María Ranger Station is 25 kilometers northeast of Liberia via the village of San Jorge. The road may require 4wd depending on the season and state of repair. You can arrange lodging and meals at the station through the Santa Rosa headquarters. From the station, a trail leads 3 kilometers west to some hot springs, and then another 3 to Las Pailas and Las Hornillas. There is a campsite and a ranger shack nearby, and good swimming in a river. From there the steep, not-very-well-marked trail to the summit begins. It's an all-day climb up and back, fog can reduce visibility to zero at times, and rain and wind can be very cold, so it would be advisable to go with a guide or someone familiar with the area.

There are rustic accommodations near the park. The Albergue Rincón del Turista near the entrance has cabins with cold water and outhouses for $7–12, meals included, and rents horses and guide service. You can make arrangements through the Casa de Cultura in Liberia (phone: 666-1606). The Albergue Rincón de la Vieja is located on a private road not too far from Las Hornillas, $30–50 per night with shared or private bath, meals included (phone: 223-5502, 233-4578; fax: 223-5502). It also has horses and guides.

The Hacienda Lodge Guachipelín, with a view of the volcano, is 18 kilometers from the Pan American Highway on the road to Curubande (phone: 441-6545; fax: 442-1910). Rincón de la Vieja Mountain Lodge is nearby (phone/fax: 695-5553).

Palo Verde National Park

This complex of marshes and dry forested hills occupies the foot of the Tempisque River Valley where it empties into the Gulf of Nicoya. It is one of the last places on the Pacific coast where scarlet macaws and jabiru storks still breed, and its marshes are vital habitat for thousands of migratory and resident waterbirds, including ibis, wood storks, anhingas, and roseate spoonbills. Although the area has many of the same species as Santa Rosa N.P., the atmosphere is quite different because of the vast expanses of marsh and limestone hills. The area is named after the palo verde tree, *Parkinsonia aculeata,* which also grows in North America's deserts. Like other dryland trees, the species can photosynthesize through its green bark.

Palo Verde National Park's roughly 16,804 hectares are augmented to the northwest by 2,279-hectare Lomas Barbudal Biological Reserve. There is some doubt as to whether this will be sufficient to support rare species indefinitely, however. Fires set by hunters or ranchers during the dry season continue to threaten the forest.

Access to the area is easiest during the dry season, since much of it is flooded during the rains. To get to the main park headquarters, turn south off the Pan American Highway at the town of Bagaces and go 35 kilometers on dirt roads. Headquarters is in a spacious old hacienda on the edge of the marshes 8 kilometers into the park. Wildlife is abundant and easily seen in the relatively open country, especially in the dry season. When I was there, a deer had taken up residence in an old barn. A trail leads up to a spring in the forest, where you can see animals coming to drink (watch out for Africanized bees—there have been fatalities in the area). There is a campsite with toilets and showers available if you make arrangements with the Park Service in advance, and you may be able to arrange for meals and transportation, and possibly to accompany rangers on patrols to a bird refuge in the Tempisque River. The phone is 671-1062, or you could stop at the regional office in Bagaces, which is on the Pan American Highway at the turnoff for the park. There's also a shorter, less-traveled road from Cañas via Bebedero that leads to the park.

Tour agencies offer boat trips to the park: Guanacaste Tours (phone: 666-0306); Transporte Palo Verde in Cañas (phone: 669-1091); CATA Tours, P.O. Box 10173-1000, San José (phone: 296-2133, fax: 296-2730, or phone/fax: 669-1026 in Guanacaste). The Organization of Tropical Studies (OTS) has a research station in the Catalina Section where travelers can stay at $35 a day (if it's not full of researchers and students). Check with their San José office: 236-6696. Rancho Humo is a new resort on the Tempisque River just west of the park, with a luxury hotel, rustic lodge, and boat trips. Apdo. 322-1077 Centro Colón, San José (phone: 255-2463; fax: 255-3573). The Centro Ecológico La Pacífica on the highway 4 kilometers north of Cañas has comfortable cabinas, pool, and restaurant for around $65 a night. It's on the Coribicí River, with good birding on the grounds (669-0050). A nearby agency, Safaris Coribicí, offers river tours, as does CATA Tours (see above). There's a nice riverside restaurant, Rincón Coribicí, just past La Pacífica.

Lomas Barbudal Biological Reserve

This reserve was established in 1986 to protect the high-quality dry forest on its limestone hills, and also as a refuge for the very diverse tropical bees and wasps which inhabit it (as pollinators, these insects are indispensable to the forest). It has scarlet macaws and other locally rare species. A 1994 wildfire destroyed much vegetation, unfortunately. The reserve is located 6 kilometers down a gravel road that turns west off the Pan American Highway 11 kilometers north of Bagaces. There is a Heritage Center with interpretive displays on the Río Cabuyo in the reserve. An NGO, Friends of Lomas Barbudal (U.S. phone: 510-526-4115; fax: 528-0346; Costa Rican phone: 667-1069), helps to manage the reserve, and also helps support the Nature Conservation Center in Bagaces.

Barra Honda National Park

This 2,295-hectare park near the town of Nicoya has an extensive limestone cave system as well as a sample of the forest that once covered much of the Nicoya Peninsula. An early naturalist thought they were volcanoes because of noises and smells coming from their entrances, but these may have been caused by bat colonies. (Most of the bats seem to have disappeared, perhaps because of pesticides in neighboring farmlands.) The caves are up to 420 meters deep, and explorers have found blind fish, salamanders, and other creatures, and pre-Columbian human remains. The only access to most caves is from above with rappelling gear, so they've remained little disturbed. You can arrange to have park rangers accompany you into them by contacting the Bagaces headquarters (phone: 671-1062) a week in advance. Ríos Tropicales (233-6455) and Turinsa (221-9185) also provide cave tours. Caving is mainly done during dry season, but you can hike the park's two hours of trails all year. The local community offers accommodations at the Las Delicias Ecotourism Project at the park entrance, with three bungalows and meals (668-5580).

The Osa Peninsula

Although only a couple of hundred kilometers from Guanacaste, this spit of land on the southwest coast is another world, almost like a bit of Amazonia rafted up from the south. "The abundant rainfall coupled with a short, three-month dry season seems ideal for tree growth," wrote ecologist Gary Hartshorn, "for these forests are by far the most exuberant in Central America. In fact, the Corcovado forests are just as impressive in height as the best forests I have seen in the Amazon basin or the dipterocarp forests of Malaysia and Indonesia." There probably are at least five hundred tree species on the peninsula, and many South American species reach their northern limit here. The park also contains one of the last sizable populations of the little squirrel monkey remaining in southern Costa Rica and Panama.

About 5,500 mm of rain a year falls on the peaks at the peninsula's center, almost as much as at Tortuguero. The reasons why it

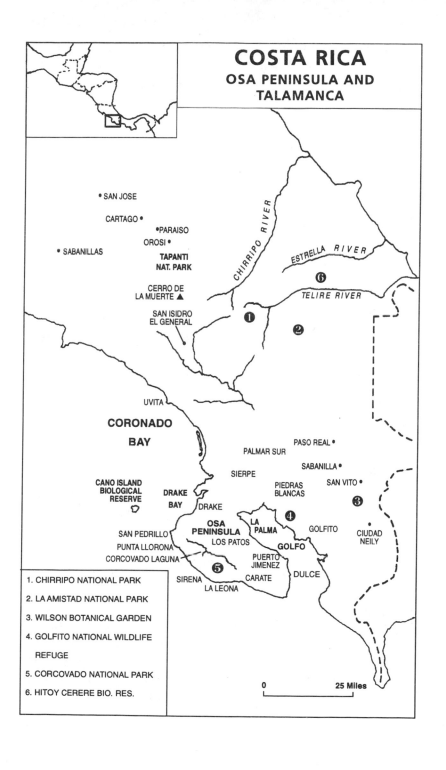

COSTA RICA
OSA PENINSULA AND TALAMANCA

SAN JOSE

CARTAGO

PARAISO

OROSI

SABANILLAS

TAPANTI NAT. PARK

CERRO DE LA MUERTE ▲

SAN ISIDRO EL GENERAL

CHIRRIPO RIVER

ESTRELLA RIVER

TELIRE RIVER

①

②

⑥

UVITA

CORONADO BAY

PASO REAL

PALMAR SUR

SABANILLA

SAN VITO

SIERPE

PIEDRAS BLANCAS

③

CANO ISLAND BIOLOGICAL RESERVE

DRAKE BAY

DRAKE

OSA PENINSULA

LA PALMA

④

GOLFITO

CIUDAD NEILY

SAN PEDRILLO

LOS PATOS

GOLFO

PUNTA LLORONA

CORCOVADO LAGUNA

⑤

PUERTO JIMENEZ

DULCE

SIRENA

CARATE

LA LEONA

1. CHIRRIPO NATIONAL PARK

2. LA AMISTAD NATIONAL PARK

3. WILSON BOTANICAL GARDEN

4. GOLFITO NATIONAL WILDLIFE
   REFUGE

5. CORCOVADO NATIONAL PARK

6. HITOY CERERE BIO. RES.

0   25 Miles

is so wet compared to the Pacific to the north are complicated, but the effects are obvious. Where they have not been logged or cleared, the lowlands are overgrown with raphia palm swamps and huge ceibas (one ceiba is 3 meters in diameter above its buttress roots and 70 meters tall), espavels, and ajillos, and the mountains with heavy cloud forest. Unlike other parts of Costa Rica, the peninsula hasn't been covered by volanic ash eruptions; the mountains are of Cretaceous epoch sedimentary and volcanic rocks, and the lowlands have recent alluvial soil. The area is less fertile than the Meseta Central, despite its botanical exuberance, and doesn't seem to have supported large human populations in the past. It remained almost uninhabited until gold was discovered in the 1930s. In the 1960s, colonization and land speculation threatened to destroy the forest.

Corcovado National Park

This 54,540-hectare park was established in 1975 in response to the imminent threat of deforestation by a "land rush" of squatters on the property of a North American timber company that had acquired much of the area. The Costa Rican government bought the land from the company, and also compensated the squatters and paid to relocate them in other areas. In the early 1980s, several thousand gold miners invaded Corcovado's southern half, and the government had to remove them and help them find livelihoods outside the park. Illegal mining is still a problem.

Despite continuing difficulties, Corcovado's value as a world-class rain forest preserve is undisputed. Conservationist and former MIRENEM Vice-Minister Mario Boza has called it "without a doubt the most important wilderness to be conserved of the country's natural heritage." Although relatively small (many conservationists think it must be enlarged to maintain its diversity), it contains almost all the Osa's native species, and thirteen major ecosystems, from intertidal beach sand and rocks to cloud forest. Travelers return from it with tales of close jaguar sightings (one researcher spent a night with his tent surrounded by a love triangle of roaring, purring jaguars), white-lipped peccary herds, and sizable scarlet macaw flocks. Deforestation in surrounding areas of the peninsula, particularly in the adjacent Osa Forest Reserve, continues to threaten this diversity, however. A Fundación Neotrópica project, BOSCOSA, has been working with local campesinos to develop ways of land use that will be less destructive than the traditional burning of the forest to create pasture or cropland.

Corcovado offers excellent opportunities for rain forest hiking and backpacking, with a good system of trails and ranger stations. Insects and flooding are less of a problem in the January-to-April dry season. The quickest way to get there is to charter a plane from San José to the park headquarters at Sirena. Fare is $400 via Saeta (phone: 232-1474). Veasa (232-1010) and Tacsa (783-3294) also have flights. Or you can fly from Golfito across the Golfo Dulce ($110 via Aeronaves de Costa Rica, phone: 735-0278). There are accommodations at Sirena, and you can arrange for meals. Any park visits should be arranged in advance with the Park Service, either in San José or at the administration office in the town of Puerto Jiménez on the Osa south of the park. The office is next to the Banco Nacional (phone: 735-5036).

Puerto Jiménez is the main jumping-off place for entering the park from the ground. Buses to Puerto Jiménez from San Isidro de El General south of San José run at 5:30 A.M. and noon. (Just outside the town of Rincón on the northeast side of the Osa, the BOS-COSA forestry project offers inexpensive visitor accommodations: contact Fundación Neotrópica, Calle 20 and aves. 3 and 5, San José.) You can fly to Puerto Jiménez from Golfito daily at 6 A.M. and 2 P.M. for about $8 (Aeronaves de Costa Rica). A small cafe, La Carolina, is an unofficial tourist information center (fax: 735-5073). Cabinas Manglares (near the airport, $7–12) and Cabinas Marcelina offer lodging. From Puerto Jiménez, there are two ways to the park. You can take a bus to La Palma at 5:30 A.M. and then walk 12 kilometers from La Palma to the park's entrance and ranger station at Los Patos. From there, a 20-kilometer trail runs down from the hills and across the Corcovado plain to La Sirena station. There are many river crossings. At Sirena there are nature trails and you can swim in the rivers if you watch out for crocodiles. Ocean swimming is discouraged because of sharks.

You can also reach Sirena by getting a 4wd vehicle from Puerto

Jiménez around the tip of the peninsula to Carate. There are several eco-resorts along the way. Tierra de Milagros is vegetarian, with very simple facilities, located 20 kilometers south of Puerto Jiménez, $20–30 (fax: 735-5073). Bosque del Cabo is on the coast at the tip of the peninsula; private cabins with baths, $50–60 including meals (phone: 222-4547; fax: 735-5703). In the same area is Lapa Rios Lodge, with 14 luxury bungalows on a 400-hectare private reserve (phone/fax: 735-5130). The Corcovado Tent Camp run by Costa Rica Expeditions is on the beach at the park's south border; $30–40 including meals (phone: 257-0766; fax: 257-1665). You can hire a vehicle (up to $60) or find a truck going that way for less. From Carate it's an hour's walk on the beach to La Leona Station in the park. The beach will be impassable at high tide. From La Leona it's 15 kilometers' beach walking to Sirena. Watch out for sand flies and sunburn.

The uplands of the northern part of the park above Punta Llorona have some of the best forest—huge trees soaring unbranched for many meters. A 1-hectare plot there contained 108 tree species. The largest tree, belonging to a species known only from southwest Costa Rica (*Vantanea barbourii*), was 65 meters high and 2 meters in diameter. You can walk along the beach north from Sirena at low tide to reach this area. It's about 15 kilometers to Punta Llorona, and you have to cross three rivers. The first is the Sirena, about a kilometer past Sirena Station, and it is the deepest. A few hundred yards after you cross the third river, the Llorona, the sand beach ends at a big cliff, and the trail heads into the forest. (Just around the cliff is a spectacular waterfall reachable at low tide.) In 1975, one of the founders of Costa Rica's national park system, a Nicoya Peninsula farmer named Olof Wessberg, was murdered at Llorona while exploring the area's park potential. A San José man, whom Wessberg had met en route to the Osa and hired as a guide, was convicted of the crime, but the motive remains unclear.

From Llorona, the trail continues through the forest for 7 kilometers, following ridges and dropping into ravines. Wildlife may be harder to see in the heavy forest than in the level land at the park's center. The trail then returns to the shore for 5 kilometers to the San Pedrillo Ranger Station. A trail goes on from there to the

Drake Bay area outside the park (Sir Francis Drake is said to have anchored here in 1579).

A number of eco-resorts have been developed at Drake Bay. Marenco Biological Station is the oldest and closest to the park, about 5 kilometers. It has 700 hectares of rain forest and a beach and attactively landscaped compound of thatched cabanas from which you can see macaws and king vultures. It's $60–80 a night, meals included, with package tours including transportation from San José and guided trips to the park and to Isla del Caño, a biological reserve that has excellent snorkeling or scuba diving as well as archaeological importance (it may have been an indigenous cemetery). Make arrangements through Marenco's San José office: Apdo. 4025, 1000 San José (phone: 221-1594; fax: 255-1340). Aguila de Osa Inn is an upmarket resort with deep-sea fishing (phone: 296-2190; fax: 232-7722). Others include Drake Bay Wilderness Camp, $50–60 with meals (phone: 771-2436); La Paloma Lodge, $50–60 with meals (phone: 239-0954); Casa Mirador, $12–20 with meals (phone: 227-6914); and Cabinas Cecilia, $12–20 with meals (phone: 771-2336).

Talamanca

The Talamanca Range covering most of southern Costa Rica has the tallest mountains in southern Central America and (extending into Panama) the largest area of mountain wilderness. It is much older than the volcanic cordilleras to the north, with a core of granitic rocks that began to rise about 30 million years ago. It may have been an island between South America and northern Central America for millions of years, as is suggested by a large number of endemic organisms that live there. Of some five hundred bird species in the area, forty-nine are endemic, occurring only in Talamanca or in the Costa Rican volcanic cordilleras and western Panama. They include the volcano junco, large-footed finch, silvery-throated jay, flame-throated warbler, and about a dozen hummingbird species.

In 1982, UNESCO declared a 600,000-hectare La Amistad Biosphere Reserve which includes most of Talamanca. The reserve contains two national parks, two biological reserves, a wildlife refuge, a forest reserve, and five indigenous reserves. The Spanish never conquered Talamanca, and native groups, including the Bri-Bri and Cabecar, remain very independent and tradition-minded. It is hoped that the indigenous reserves will help to buffer the parks, while the parks will serve as a reservoir of wildlife and other resources for the reserves, since game remains important in the indigenous diet and culture. The reserve also is important in protecting the water and hydroelectric power resources of the area.

Tapantí National Park

This 5,113-hectare area is a day trip from San José in the deep Orosí Gorge at the north end of Talamanca. Drive or take a bus to Cartago (buses leave from aves. Central and 2, Calle 13). From the Cartago central square, take an Orosí–Río Macho bus through the town of Orosí to where there's a bridge over the Río Grande de Orosí and an electric plant. This is as far as the bus goes. When I was there, I asked the local general store and pub proprieter, Don Elias, how to get to Tapantí, and he closed up shop and took me round-trip for a fee that seemed reasonable. (He told me his pub, the Bar Marina, had been called that for 80 years.) The staff (it was then a wildlife refuge) was very friendly and helpful, and offered me coffee and cookies after my hike. A beautiful, alder-bordered stream full of diorite boulders runs along the road through the refuge. The gorge walls are impressively steep, high, and heavily forested. Otters and tayras are common. There is good rainbow trout fishing in season.

Hitoy Cerere Biological Reserve

This 9,154-hectare reserve on the very wet Caribbean edge of Talamanca is surrounded by indigenous reserves. You can get there by taking a Valle de la Estrella bus from Limón to the end of the line at Finca Seis, several hours' ride. Despite its pretty name, the Valle de la Estrella is under heavy banana cultivation. (It's been said that North Americans might stop eating bananas if they knew the amount of pesticides it takes to grow them.) From there it's 10 kilometers farther to the reserve. Four-wheel-drive taxis will take you to within a kilometer of the reserve for about $5. There are no camping facilities. Someone I talked to saw an ocelot here. It's a good side trip if you're staying at Cahuita on the coast.

Cerro de la Muerte

This area at the north tip of the Talamancas is very scenic, and easy to reach from San José. A number of resorts offer hiking, fishing, birding, etc. Cabinas Chacón outside the town of San Gerardo de Dota has quetzals on its property and rates in the $30 range: P.O. Box 482, Cartago (phone: 771-1732). Genesis II on the Pan American Highway 58 kilometers from San José has a small reserve and rooms for birders (phone: 225-0271). El Trogón is a new lodge: P.O. Box 10980, 1000 San José (phone: 222-5463; fax: 255-4039). As with other parts of the high Talamancas, be prepared for low temperatures, fog, and altitude stress.

Chirripó National Park

Southern Central America's highest peak, 3,819-meter Cerro Chirripó, is the centerpiece of this 50,150-hectare park, established in 1975. The presence of cirques, lakes, U-shaped valleys, and moraines above 3,500 meters around the peak indicate that the area was glaciated during the Ice Age, until about 25,000 years ago. Trees don't grow on the glaciated area, although it is not above tree-line altitude for Costa Rica's latitude. Thin soils and fires probably account for the treelessness. Large fires have burned through the area at least once a decade since the 1950s.

A scrub vegetation similar to that of the Andes, called "*páramo*," dominates above 3,300 meters. Dwarf bamboos are perhaps the most common plants. Shrubby forms of genera that usually are herbaceous at lower altitudes, such as ragwort (*Senecio*) and St. John's wort (*Hypericum*) also predominate. Most páramo plants are of South American origin, probably having migrated north from the Colombian Andes in the Ice Age. There also are many northern plants such as lupine and paintbrush. Mixed with the scrub are areas of bare diorite and grassy stretches growing on lateritic or sandy soil. The Savanna of the Lions, a grassy valley within the upper forest area (3,100 meters), gets its name either from the frequency of puma sightings or the resemblance of its tawny, windblown grasses to lions' pelts. The Valley of the Rabbits is named for its cottontails, the same genus as in North America.

Most of the park is above 2,000 meters, and from this altitude to the páramo zone, huge evergreen oaks are the predominant trees. There are at least five oak species, including the endemic *Quercus costaricencis,* or black oak. Another oak, *Q. oocarpa,* has acorns the size of hen's eggs. It's usually rainy or misty, so the trees are covered with moss and other epiphytes. Other trees include podocarpus, a broad-leaved gymnosperm of South American origin, *Clusia,* and relatives of ginseng and prickly ash. Quetzals are fairly common (apparently indigenes still eat "quetzal soup"), and there are tapirs and brocket deer. A brown, silvery spangled salamander, *Bolitoglossa subpalmata,* is very common under logs. Two lizard species here belong to the same genera as the common alligator and fence lizards of the western U.S.

A well-marked trail leads from the park ranger station at San Gerardo de Rivas to the glaciated area, where there are sleeping huts. From San José, drive or take a bus on the Pan American Highway to San Isidro in the Valle de El General. Buses of several companies leave from Calle 16, aves. 1 and 3, every hour for the three-hour trip. Hotels in San Isidro include the resort-style Hotel del Sur on the highway south of town ($20–30; phone: 771-0233) and the less expensive hotels in town, Iguazu ($12–20; 771-2571) and Amaneli ($7–12; 771-0352). Buses leave from the San Isidro market to San Gerardo de Rivas at 5 A.M. and 2 P.M. It's about an hour. If you want to stay overnight at San Gerardo, there are the Posada del Descanso ($7–12), and Cabinas Marin and Cabinas Chirripó, both about $7.

Register at the ranger station before starting your climb: there's an entrance fee and an overnight fee, and they'll give you a map brochure (although topo maps are recommended if you plan to go off the main trail). They can help find you guides and horses if you want them. It's a very steep, 14-kilometer hike to the overnight huts, and you'll be very short of breath from the altitude unless you've gotten acclimated beforehand. Start as early as possible, and take your time. Bring a full water bottle: the first water source on the trail is more than halfway up. If you don't make it to the huts the first day, there's a cave a few kilometers below them where you can sleep. There are three huts along the trail about an hour and a half before the summit. There's little wood near the huts, so bring a cookstove. You'll also want a good sleeping bag and warm clothes—it freezes at night. On the other side of the peak, there's another hut in the Valley of the Moraines. There are side trails to various other parts of the glaciated zone, but there's no loop to take you back to the ranger station via another trail.

Most backpacking is in the February–April dry season, and it can get quite crowded then, especially around Easter week. You are advised to reserve sleeping hut space with the National Parks San José office well in advance of dry season trips. At other times, you may have the park to yourself, but it may rain all the time (over 7000 mm of rainfall a year in some places), although mornings tend to be clear during much of the rainy season. But this is definitely not a place to be caught out in the rain without adequate gear: the high altitude and wet cold make a very stressful combination. Remember also that you will only have twelve hours of daylight (often with heavy fog), and night in the oak forest is very dark. The last bus back to San Isidro leaves at 3:30 P.M.

La Amistad National Park

Established in 1982, this 193,920-hectare park is Costa Rica's largest, and combined with the similarly sized Amistad N.P. in Panama, comprises one of the Central America's major wilderness areas. About 60 percent of Costa Rica's animals and plants and 8 of its 12 Holdridge System Life Zones are within the park. Stretching from the border of Chirripó N.P. to the Panamanian border, the park is roadless and little explored. The only trails that go any distance into the wilderness are those used by indigenes, who don't welcome strangers. The best way to backpack in the park is to hire indigenous guides. The Park Service may be able to help you with this. I talked with a North American couple who did it successfully, although on one occasion the only guide they could get was a teenager. Unfortunately, halfway along the trail he decided to quit and go home.

If you just want to explore the edge of the park, the Wilson Botanical Garden outside the town of San Vito near the Panamanian border is a good place to do so. They have an extensive collection of tropical plants and a small forest reserve on the Jaba River. They offer lodging in dormitory-style rooms for $40–50 a day or in cabins for $60–80, including meals, or you can make a day visit for $12 including lunch. Make reservations through the Organization of Tropical Studies (OTS) in San José (phone: 240-6696; fax: 240-6783). There are several hotels in the town of San Vito, including the Hotel El Ceibo ($12–20; 773-3025) and Albergue Firenze ($7–12; 773-3206). San Vito is a modern, pleasant town northeast from Ciudad Neily. It can be reached by paved road and a new bridge across the Terraba River from the Pan American Highway, or by partly gravel road from Ciudad Neily. Express buses from San José to San Vito leave from the Tracopa terminal at Ave. 18 and calles 2 and 4 at 2:45 P.M. Regular buses take two hours longer and leave at 6:15, 8:15, and 11:30 A.M.

To get near the park, you need to go to the Las Tablas area north of the town of Las Mellizas, 25 kilometers east of San Vito. A ranger station at Las Tablas has trails, and you can camp, and possibly arrange for guides and horses. Ask at Wilson Garden for current information on buses or taxis. Just outside of Las Mellizas is the Amistad Lodge, with 23 kilometers of well-developed trails on a working coffee finca that includes 780 hectares of primary forest. Contact Tropical Rainbow Tours, P.O. Box 774, 1000 San José (phone: 233-8228; fax: 255-4636).

CHAPTER ELEVEN

Panama

PANAMA IS A VERY unusual country. Biologically and culturally, it is the most "South American" part of Central America.
Because of the Panama Canal, however, it has become the most
"North-Americanized" country in the region, with an economy
heavily involved with international trade and banking, and a government sometimes very heavily influenced by Washington. This
"split personality" can make Panama a confusing place for a visitor, particularly a North American. Around the Canal Zone, at
least, Panama has a more modern infrastructure than other Central
American countries—a bigger, newer airport, more paved roads,
more high-rises—but these are superimposed over social, economic, and environmental problems similar to those faced by its
less affluent neighbors. Great affluence and high prices (relative to
other Central American countries) coexist closely with abysmal
slums.

Panama's split personality also operates in relation to its wildlands. As the "final link" of the land bridge, it has extraordinary
fauna and flora, and its relative prosperity has allowed it to take
some significant steps toward protecting them through governmental and nongovernmental action. A system of national park administrative offices and ranger stations is in place, and Panama's
transportation infrastructure allows fairly easy access to some

parts of wild areas. On the other hand, Panama's tumultuous politics seems to have inhibited integration of the wildlands into the country's society as a whole. Parks have relatively few visitor facilities, and aren't heavily visited by Panamanians or foreign tourists. This is a danger to the parks, since the rule of "use it or lose it" applies, and pressures from loggers, farmers, poachers, and other rival land users are strong. The scarcity of visitors also presents a great opportunity to travelers with a little perseverance, however, since it's quite possible to have a trail or ranger station to yourself for a day or several days. During a 1993 visit, I never met a tourist in a national park. This will change as word about Panama's parks gets around and plans for increased visitor access are implemented, so the present is a very good time for the adventurous traveler.

The Path Between the Seas

Panama's geography can also be confusing for the visitor. As the link between a northern and a southern continent, one expects it to run in those directions, but in fact it runs mainly west to east. Thus there are places in eastern Darién at the Colombian border that actually are farther north than places in western Chiriquí on the Costa Rican border. There also are places where the sun rises over the Pacific or sets over the Atlantic, which can be disorienting to those from North America's straight-up-and-down coasts.

For one of the youngest pieces of dry land on earth, Panama is surprisingly rugged and scenic. Even Darién, which rose above sea level a mere 3.5 million years ago, has a lot of hills and some fairly high peaks. West from the Canal Zone, the country gets progressively steeper, reaching its highest point, 3,475-meter Volcán Baru, near the Costa Rican border. A central mountain chain runs through most of western Panama. In Darién, east of the Canal Zone, the highlands run mainly along the coast, forming a central depression that is drained by the rivers Chepo and Chucunaque (the Chepo has been dammed for hydroelectric power, forming the enormous Bayano Reservoir). Another effect of Panama's bumpy topography is that some 1,600 islands lie within its territory, notably those of the San Blas Archipelago and Bocas del Toro.

Even Panama's lowest-lying land, the Canal Zone (which is 87 meters above sea level at its highest point), is sufficiently rugged that the French attempt to dig a sea level canal across in the 1880s failed miserably. The Americans succeeded only by building a complicated system of locks and dams to lift ships over the divide. Even so, the Americans had a lot of trouble digging through the geologically young and unstable rock formations, which often collapsed, burying men and equipment. "A spellbound public read of cracks opening in the ground," wrote David McCullough in his Canal history, *The Path Between the Seas,* "of heartbreaking landslides, of the bottom of the canal mysteriously rising."

Much of the land in Panama that isn't steep is wet. Some five hundred rivers drain the country, and most level areas of Darién and the Caribbean coast are swampy to some extent. Ruggedness and swampiness have tended to concentrate human population in the valleys and hills of southwest Panama, where there is a marked dry season and less annual rainfall. Archaeological sites in this area (the present provinces of Veraguas, Coclé, Herrera, and Los Santos) date from as long as 7,000 years ago, and indicate cultures that made use of marine resources such as fish and shellfish as well as land-based foods ("Panama" may derive from an indigenous word meaning "plenty of fish," and the shallow waters and extensive mudflats of the Bay of Panama are very good for gathering seafoods). Population increased after agriculture spread south from the volcanic highlands of Costa Rica about 5,000 years ago. By 2,000 years ago, farming had converted the dry deciduous forests and evergreen forests that originally covered the area to grassland and savanna.

Burials excavated in central Panama suggest that pre-Columbian societies there were large and highly organized, with hereditary elites demonstrating their rank and affluence through display and exchange of gold ornaments and other status symbols. Metallurgy had spread north from Peru after about 3,000 years ago. Warfare among these heavily populated groups could be intense. The Spanish chronicler Andagoya wrote of a conflict between two Panamanian chiefs: "Where the battle took place we found a great street entirely paved with the heads of the dead, and at the end of it *a tower of heads* which was such that a man on horseback could not be seen on the other side." (The "tower of heads" suggests cultural influence from Mexico.)

Rodrigo de Bastidas was the first European to see Panama (and Central America) when he sailed along the coast in 1501. One of his companions was Vasco Nuñez de Balboa, who in 1510 returned to Panama as a settler of the town of Santa María la Antigua del Darién. Balboa befriended the local indigenous elite, married a chief's daughter, and heard from them of a fabulously wealthy civilization on another ocean across the mountains. In 1513, Balboa crossed to the Pacific, taking 25 days to do so, killing some six hundred local Quarequas in the process, and returning to the Caribbean with large quantities of pearls and cotton cloth and 40,000 pesos' worth of gold looted from the inhabitants. In 1519 (after executing Balboa on trumped-up treason charges), colonial governor Pedro Arias de Ávila moved the Spanish capital to near the present site of Panama City on the Pacific.

The wealthy civilization Balboa had heard about was the Inca Empire of Peru, and after Francisco Pizarro conquered it in 1532, the *"camino real"* between Panama City and the settlement of Nombre de Dios on the Caribbean side became the main route for the transshipment of the Andean gold and silver to Spain. This made Panama one of the most important places in the New World during the next two centuries, and for a short time (1538–43) it was the main administrative center for colonies from Nicaragua to Cape Horn. This wealth also made Panama a target for pirates, from Sir Francis Drake, who destroyed Nombre de Dios in 1573, to Henry Morgan, who crossed the isthmus to sack Panama City in 1671.

Panama's importance declined in the eighteenth century because of changes in trade patterns. In 1751 Spain took away its status as an independent administrative center, or *"audiencia,"* and merged it with the colony of New Granada in South America. Panama remained a quiet backwater throughout the colonial revolution against Spain in the early nineteenth century (although Simon Bolívar made it the location of his 1826 Congress of American States), and it was a province of Colombia until 1903. As before Columbus, population concentrated in the southwest of the country.

The Canal

Gold and empire made Panama globally important once again after 1849. The fever of thousands of would-be miners to reach the California mother lode by the shortest route was the most dramatic reason for renewal of interest in the trans-isthmian canal first considered by Spain's Charles V in 1524. The Gold Rush spurred construction of the trans-Panama railroad in 1850–55. The desire of burgeoning North American and European commercial empires for a convenient trade link with the Pacific was the main reason for the canal, and first France and then the U.S. went to extraordinary lengths to build it.

As well as costing 22,000 lives, Ferdinand de Lesseps's 1880–89 attempt engulfed the life savings of hundreds of thousands of French families when it went bankrupt. After the U.S. first engineered Panama's 1903 secession from Colombia, it made the new country a virtual protectorate with a treaty that gave the U.S. perpetual sovereignty over the Canal Zone and other extraordinary concessions. (The Panamanian ambassador to the U.S., a former engineer on the French canal named Philippe Bunau-Varilla, and U.S. Secretary of State John Hay signed the treaty without the knowledge of the delegation authorized by the new Panamanian government to negotiate a treaty.) While building the Canal from 1904 to 1914, the U.S. also built a system of towns, schools, and hospitals for U.S. Canal Zone personnel that amounted to a rich North American country within a poor Central American one.

Panama has spent the twentieth century struggling to come to terms with its national origins. In 1936, the Hull-Alfaro Treaty restricted U.S. military intervention in Panamanian affairs outside the Canal Zone and increased Panamanian income from the Canal. It didn't stop public resentment against the Canal Zone, and confrontations were sometimes violent, as in 1964 when 21 Panamanians were killed in demonstrations over the right of Panama to fly its flag over the Zone. The government remained unstable, and in

1968 was overthrown by the Panamanian Guardia Nacional. Guardia General Omar Torrijos emerged as a popular leader, doing much to modernize Panama's infrastructure. In 1977, Torrijos and U.S. President Jimmy Carter signed a treaty (which had been under negotiation for years) providing for the gradual phasing out of U.S. control over the Canal, with Panama to assume full ownership in the year 2000.

Life has not been easy for Panama since the 1977 treaty. Seven years of chaotic and dictatorial rule by Manuel Noriega ended in the U.S. invasion of December 1989, the effects of which remain evident in the burned-out Chorrillo District of Panama City. Political instability is still a problem—Panama has dozens of political parties. Attitudes toward the U.S. are divided, with some Panamanians glad for the measure of stability the 1989 military intervention brought, and others resentful of continued U.S. interference in Panamanian affairs.

A Land of Birds and Butterflies

Panama's historical confusions between wealth and poverty extend to its natural environment. It is an environment with an enormous wealth of tropical biodiversity, probably the highest in Central America. It has more bird, mammal, and amphibian species than any other Central American nation. This wealth derives largely from Panama's proximity to the highly diverse forests of South America. About 40 percent of Panama's land mammals are South American in origin, 27 percent are Central American, and 1 percent are North American. The remaining 32 percent are of indeterminate tropical origin, either Central or South American. One mammal, the vesper rat, appears to have spread from northern Panama to the Colombian border since 1920. Panama also has at least a thousand endemic animal species that occur nowhere else. With a still relatively small population of around 2.5 million on its 75,517 square kilometers, Panama retains a high proportion of forest land. Another natural asset is the highly productive fisheries of the Bay of Panama.

Yet Panama is relatively poor in other natural resources. The conquistadors exhausted its gold quickly, and few other mineral resources have been discovered. Farming remains the main source of livelihood outside the Canal area and Panama City, but only about 30 percent of the land is suitable for crops and pasture. As the best farmlands of the southwest have declined in productivity because of erosion, farmers have migrated to forested areas such as Darién, and deforestation has been occurring at rates of hundreds of thousands of acres a year. Much of the deforested land has poor soil for farming, and produces crops for only a few years after migrant families clear it. The Bay of Panama fisheries also have suffered from overexploitation, with catches declining and some species nearing commercial extinction. The huge mud plumes that shrimp trawlers leave behind them as they drag their nets along the bay bottom, visible from airplanes flying out of Panama City, show how roughly the "abundance of fish" is being used. Pollution and destruction of the coastal mangroves in which shrimp and other commercial species breed also threaten this resource.

Since the building of the Canal, which depended on understanding how to control tropical diseases, Panama has been a center for research on tropical ecosystems. The Smithsonian Tropical Research Institute (STRI) in Panama City (Tupper Center, Roosevelt Ave., Ancón; phone: 27-6022) administers the Barro Colorado Island Research Station and other facilities. In 1985, Panamanian business and academic leaders formed a nongovernmental organization called the Asociación Nacional para la Conservación de la Naturaleza (ANCON), which promotes strengthening of parks programs. Their office is on Calle Alberto Navarro, El Cangrejo, Edificio de ANCON; Apdo. 1387, Panama 1 (phone: 64-8100; fax: 64-1836). ANCON is supported by private Panamanian donors and by international organizations such as The Nature Conservancy, and administers projects to encourage sustainable developments such as reforestation and agroforestry in private lands around parks. Another important nongovernmental conservation organization is the Kuna Indians' Project for the Study and Management of the Wildlands of the Kuna Yala (PEMASKY), which works to protect wildlands within the Kuna Autonomous Region. Phone is 82-3226. Parks and other national nature reserves are administered by INRENARE (Instituto Nacional de Recursos

Naturales Renovables). INRENARE headquarters is presently at the small town of Paraíso along the Canal Road to Gamboa (P.O. Box 2016, Paraíso ANCON; phone: 32-4518, 32-4325), but there are plans to move closer to Panama City.

Panama City

Panama City is the only Central American capital on the coast, which means that it has a warm, lowland climate, but also that it is usually cooled by breezes off the Bay of Panama. The city overlooks a dramatic crescent of seafront adorned with a gigantic statue of Balboa. When the tide is out, exposed rocks and mudflats stretch far into the bay. Unfortunately, the seafront is almost deserted because of pollution and fear of muggers. This fear is pervasive in the city and really seems to limit people's freedom of movement. Streets tend to be either thronged with people or empty. I walked frequently from my hotel in the Calidonia district to the Smithsonian headquarters at Ancón Hill without problems, but there were some threatening areas along the way (most of this area is listed as a high crime area by the U.S. Embassy), and the extremely crowded streets are somewhat distracting. It's a spread-out, modern city, so you'll probably want to take a bus or taxi across it, especially at night.

The three parts of the city travelers are most likely to frequent are strung around the crescent of the bay shore. At the west end is the San Felipe or Casco Viejo district, a peninsula on which are concentrated inexpensive hotels and historical tourist attractions (plazas, cathedrals, the historical museum, the religious art museum). San Felipe and the adjacent El Chorrillo district are also listed as high crime areas by the U.S. Embassy. In the middle, between the Avenida Central and the bay, is the Calidonia district of medium-priced hotels and restaurants which also contains several museums and which abuts on the Ancón Hill area. To the east, over some highway bridges and other obstacles, is a district of banks and luxury hotels and shops centering on the Via España. You can shuttle between the three areas on buses along the Avenida Central.

Transportation

Panama does not require visas for U.S. or Canadian citizens possessing valid passports. A $5 tourist card is good for 30 days, after which you need to obtain a card permitting another 60 days in the country from the Office of Migration and Naturalization in Panama City. Regulations are different for other nationalities: citizens of the U.K. and Germany can stay 90 days without visa or tourist card; citizens of New Zealand, Australia, and Japan need a visa. Airlines provide tourist cards on the in-flight. There is a $20 airport tax, payable when departing.

INTERNATIONAL AIRLINES: COPA (800-359-2672) departs Miami; Taca (800-535-8780) departs Houston; AeroPeru (800-777-7717) departs Mexico City; Continental (800-525-0280) departs Houston; Aviateca (800-327-9832) departs Los Angeles; American (800-433-7300) departs Miami; United (800-241-6522) departs Miami.

INTERNAL FLIGHTS: Small airlines serve most parts of Panama from Paitilla Airport in Panama City. See region descriptions for names and phones.

International flights arrive at Omar Torrijos Airport, at Tocumen about 25 kilometers from downtown Panama City. Buses serve the airport from Plaza Cinco de Mayo. Taking a solo taxi to or from the airport costs about $18, but you can get cooperative taxis from the airport for about half that. Taxi fare from Paitilla Airport to the Calidonia district is about $3–4. Taxis aren't metered, so agree on a fare before you get in.

ROADS: Tica Bus has daily buses on the Pan American Highway between San José, Costa Rica, and Panama City. Their Panama phone is 62-2084; their terminal is at Calle 17 near Hotel Ideal. The San José–Panama City trip takes 18 hours, $25 one-way. There may be a scarcity of tourist cards at the border, and you will need a return bus or plane ticket to be allowed into the country. No return ticket is required if you enter the country in a private vehicle. Local buses run throughout the country: see region descriptions for stations and schedules.

CAR RENTAL: A valid driver's license from the country of residence and an international driving permit are required, and drivers must complete a one-page driving record certification. Drivers 20–25 may be charged an extra $10.00 per day. Renters are advised to buy optimal collision/damage insurance, about $8 per day.

TRAIN: The trans-isthmian railroad was closed because of damage from the 1989 invasion. There are plans to reopen it: check with IPAT, the national tourist office.

U.S. Embassy

Apartado 6959, Panama 5, Republic of Panama; AMEMB Panama, Unit 0945, APO AA 34002 (phone: 507-27-1777; fax: 507-27-1964).

Health Advisory

Yellow fever vaccination isn't required unless you're arriving from an infected area within six days, but it's highly recommended if you plan to visit eastern Panama. Cholera is active within the country but vaccination is not recommended or required by the U.S. Centers for Disease Control. Year-round malaria risk exists in rural areas of northwestern (Bocas del Toro and Veraguas) and eastern (Darién and San Blas) provinces. Urban areas and those adjacent to the Panama Canal are malaria-free. Dengue fever and leishmaniasis are present in rural areas. See chapter 3 for information on disease prevention and treatment.

HOSPITALS AND DOCTORS IN PANAMA CITY: Gorgas Army Hospital (phone: 313-382-5102). Carlos García, M.D. (63-7977/26-1278). Centro Médico Paitilla (63-6060; a private hospital with 180 beds; emergency services available); Clínica San Fernando (61-6666; a private hospital with 150 beds, includes trauma unit).

Hotels

The Hotel Ejecutivo, Calle 52 & Aquilino de la Guardia, P.O. Box 5370, Panama City Post Code 5 (phone: 64-3333; fax: 69-1944), is a tower hotel in the Vía España commercial district, one block from sea. Popular with local businesspeople. Free parking. Small pool. Takes American Express, Visa, MasterCard. Single $75, double $82. Gran Hotel Soloy, Avenue Peru & Calle Apartado 3385, Panama City 4 (phone: 27-1133; fax: 27-0884), is a large hotel in the Calidonia district. Rooftop pool, restaurant, casino. Takes American Express, Visa, MasterCard. Single $35, double $40. Hotel Acapulco, Calle 30 Este between aves. Cuba & Peru, around the corner from Hotel Soloy (phone: 25-3832). Small hotel in Calidonia district, air-conditioned rooms, private baths, restaurant. Single $18, double $20. (Mainly Panamanian clientele. Restaurant is popular with local people, with typical Panamanian food and gaudy but interesting murals of wildland regions.) Hotel Foyo, Calle 6, No. 825 (phone: 62-8023). Small hotel in San Felipe district, near cathedral, $5–7 without private bath, $11 with private bath. Noisy area, mice, some rooms better than others. Other cheap lodgings nearby: Hotel y Restaurant Central on plaza across from cathedral, $7–9 (phone: 62-8044); Hotel Herrera, Calle 9 & Parque Herrera, $4–8 (phone: 28-8994).

Restaurants

The Bar Restaurant Lesseps, Vía España and Calle 46, is in a mansion with Canal-era displays in the foyer (phone: 23-0749). Good, expensive French food. El Pavo Real, Calle 51 Este, Campo Allegre (phone: 69-0504) has good international food, also a comfortable pub. Tinajas on Calle 51 near the Hotel Ejecutivo has Panamanian and international cuisine in a "típico" setting, with floor shows of folk-dancing groups (phone: 63-7890). With more moderate prices, El Trapiche, Vía Argentina, has typical Panamanian dishes like "*empanadas,*" "*ojaldres*" (fritters), and "*carimanola*" (a yucca flour roll filled with meat and eggs, then fried). La Cascada, Ave. Balboa and Calle 25, is open-air with a waterfall and jungle decor, specializing in seafood. Restaurant La Victoria, Ave. Central and Calle 9, is a good inexpensive place. Mireya, calles Ricardo Arango and Ricardo Arias, near Continental Hotel, has good vegetarian food.

Communications

Post office is at Ave. Balboa and El Prado. INTEL office for phone and fax is at aves. Samuel Lewis and Morales. The Panama country telephone code in the U.S. is 507. Panama is in the Eastern Standard Time Zone, but does not observe daylight savings time.

Money Exchange

The balboa was established as Panama's unit of currency in 1903. During Canal construction in 1912, a special agreement between the U.S. and Panamanian governments established that one American dollar would be equivalent to one balboa. The agreement is still in effect (although many Panamanians would like to change it), and dollars are used as paper balboas. Panama does have its own coins, similar in size and denominations to U.S. coins. U.S. coins are also good in Panama.

Cashing traveler's checks isn't as easy as spending dollars. Cashiers in some hotels and restaurants may ask you to "forge" your own signature on your checks—to laboriously copy it from the countersignature to make sure it is identical. They'll even lend you pen and paper to practice with. Traffic in stolen checks evidently is common. Traveler's checks generally are hard to exchange in remote areas such as Darién and Bocas del Toro.

Tourist Information

IPAT, the Instituto Panameño de Turismo, provides free city and country maps and tourist booklets at its information counters at the Atlapa Convention Center, Apdo. 4421, Vía Israel (phone: 26-7000) and at the international airport (phone: 38-4322, ext. 311). They also have current hotel and tour information.

Maps

The Instituto Geográfico Nacional "Tommy Guardia," Via Simón Bolívar, Panama City, has 1:50,000 series of maps excellent for hiking. Other less detailed maps can be purchased on the streets or in a number of bookstores.

Museums

The small Museo de Ciencias Naturales on the Ave. Cuba between calles 29 and 30 has good exhibits on Panamanian geology, paleontology, and natural history, including geological maps and interesting fossils. Mastodon molars from the Pearl Archipelago, presently 70 kilometers offshore, show how much the sea level fell during the last glaciation. Mounted specimens of today's fauna are emaciated-looking, but give an idea of the biotic diversity. Open weekdays 9–4; $.25 admission (phone: 25-0645).

The large Museo Antropológico Reina Torres de Arauz at the Plaza Cinco de Mayo, Ave. Central (across from the Canal Zone bus station), has extensive exhibits on anthropology, archaeology, and pre-Columbian history. It's much more heavily visited than the natural science museum. Hours are erratic; admission $.25 (phone: 62-0415).

The Museo de Historia de Panamá at the Palacio Municipal on the Parque Catedral, Calle 7, San Felipe, has exhibits on history since the Conquest. Open weekdays 8:30–3:30; $.25 admission (phone: 62-8089).

Bookstores and Libraries

The Tropical Sciences Library at STRI's Tupper Center, Roosevelt Ave. Ancón (phone: 62-3151), is open to the public and has one of the most complete specialized libraries in natural sciences in Latin America. Hours: 7–5 Mon.–Fri., 9–4 Sat. STRI also has a small book and gift shop at Tupper Center in the auditorium building across from the library. Gifts include lively "vegetable ivory" (palm nut) carvings by Wounnan artists. The bookstore at the National University, between Ave. Manuel Espinoza and Via Simón Bolívar, has a wide selection.

Excursions Around Panama City

Panama City has a surprising amount of open space which is safe to visit. At least, I never had trouble in frequent walks. To pass an afternoon, you can start at the Smithsonian headquarters, at the Tivoli Building, No. 401 Roosevelt Ave., Ancón, and walk across the east side of Ancón Hill to the former Canal Zone town of Balboa, whose wide avenues are in striking contrast to the thronged downtown. We saw agoutis, parakeet flocks, and many other birds in the hill's woods. Hordes of black vultures ("*zopilotes*" in Spanish) circle the hilltop, riding updrafts. On the other side of the hill (Balboa Heights), you pass the massive Canal Zone administration buildings dedicated to Goethals, the chief engineer. From there you descend a steep staircase to Balboa's main drag (the Prado). At the other end of this, Kuna merchants sell *molas* at a small park (Stevens Circle), and the nearby Tarpon Club (formerly only for Zone residents but now open to all) serves good "*corvina a la plancha*" with a variety of sauces.

For an even more sylvan walk, the 265-hectare Parque Natural Metropolitano (Curundú) contains a forest with a variety of old-growth trees, many of which are labeled, as well as deer, anteaters, sloths, and troops of tiny tamarin monkeys (called "*monos titís*" in Panama). I saw a lineated woodpecker, a yellow-backed oriole, a slaty antshrike, a scarlet-rumped cacique, and a crimson-collared tanager, and heard little tinamous. Freshwater shrimp, turtles, and other creatures live in the Río Curundú. The visitors' entrance is on Avenida Juan Pablo II, and two trails, the winding Nature Trail and the steep Tití Trail, form a loop up to a 150-meter-high "*mirador*" (vantage point) overlooking bay, canal, and city. The city parks department offers free, ranger-led tours on some days; phone 32-5516 for information. Another (temporary) feature is a huge construction crane which Smithsonian scientists have installed to study the ecology of the forest canopy. If you can get somebody to take you up in it, the view is exhilarating. When I was there, the cream-colored flowers of *Luhea* trees had attracted hundreds of chartreuse and black heliconia butterflies.

The ruins of Panamá Viejo, destroyed by Henry Morgan in 1671, are another good place to wander around. Extensive landscaped grounds surround the stone facades of the city's convents, cathedral, and administrative buildings. A still-standing stone bridge marked the beginning of the trans-isthmian trails over which Peruvian gold was carried to the Caribbean and then shipped to

Spain. The ruins are 6.5 kilometers east of the city along the Beach Highway.

If you want to make a day or overnight trip into Panama Bay, Isla Taboga is an hour's ferry ride away from Pier 18 in Balboa. The ferry, run by Argo Tours (phone: 64-3549), costs $5 round-trip and leaves for the island twice a day. Founded in 1515, Taboga is the deepwater port where Pizarro planned the conquest of Peru. The island is heavily visited on weekends. Taboga provides a dramatic demonstration of Panama Bay's high tides—long stretches of sand and rocks disappear entirely when the tide is in. The restaurant at the Hotel Chu in the town of Taboga is a good place from which to watch the phenomenon (phone: 50-2035). The hotel has small rooms without private bath for $20 single, $30 double. The more expensive Hotel Taboga controls the island's beach, and rents snorkeling equipment (if you can find the attendant). There's a small charge to use the beach, which can be applied to lunch in the hotel cafe. P.O. Taboga Island, Panama City Post Code 4421 (phone: 69-1187; fax: 23-0116). Air-conditioned, with private bath. Swimming pool, disco. Single $45–50, double $55–60. Snorkeling is not outstanding in the bay's ever-shifting waters, but you can see schools of sergeant majors and mullet. There are tide pools on the rocks past the Hotel Taboga—the rocks are very slippery.

Taboga is also the site of a brown pelican rookery which is a national wildlife refuge. INRENARE has a visitor center near the dock. The refuge can be seen by walking over the island's wooded spine to a radar installation (there are also abandoned gun emplacements left over from World War II, now inhabited by bats) and looking down over steep, wooded cliffs where the pelicans have their nests. It seems surprising that such big, ungainly looking birds should nest in jungle trees, but they do. The downy white chicks are on the nests in April and May. Migrating whales may be seen out in the bay from January to March from this vantage point.

The Canal Wildlands

Canal construction must have had profound effects on local ecosystems, but no one was studying them at the time. Various exotic

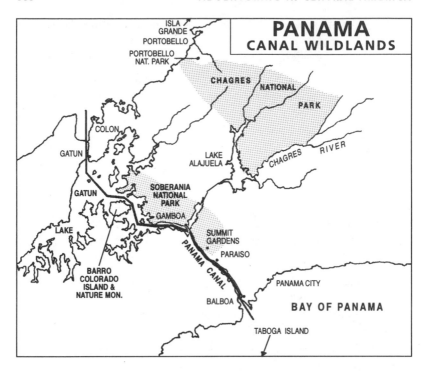

marine creatures have since moved into the Canal, including crabs from Iraq. Caribbean mangrove oysters, gobies, and blennies have moved into a lagoon near the Miraflores Lock on the Canal's Pacific side. Effects have not been as great as if a sea-level canal had been dug, since most marine creatures can't get through the fresh water in Lake Gatún and the Canal locks. If various plans to build a sea-level canal go through, this could become an ecological problem. Highly venomous sea snakes and a coral-eating starfish are among Pacific organisms that might reach the Caribbean through a sea-level canal.

At least in recent years, the Canal has tended to encourage ecological stability, for a very simple reason. The Canal depends on a large and dependable supply of clean water, and if that supply is interrupted by the floods and siltation caused by deforestation, the Canal will be destroyed. This became clear after 1977, when farmers began to move into areas that had been kept forested by the

Canal Zone administration. An estimated 35 percent of the Canal watershed has been deforested. The deforestation also threatens the water supplies of Panama City and of Colón on the Canal's Caribbean end.

Panama has responded by establishing two national parks: 22,104-hectare Soberanía N.P. (Spanish for "sovereignty") just east of the Canal, and 129,000-hectare Chagres N.P. in the watershed of the Chagres River, the ultimate source of the Canal's water. Canal wildlands also include the Barro Colorado Nature Monument, which was created in 1977 to protect Barro Colorado Island in Lake Gatún and the adjacent forested peninsulas. The Smithsonian administers the nature monument for biological field studies. These Canal wildlands are unusual in preserving large, nearly intact rain forest ecosystems close to a large, modern metropolitan area. Fifteen-square-kilometer Barro Colorado Island alone has more plant species than Europe, and even after the decades of studies there, a completely unknown tree species was discovered in 1981.

In 1962, engineering work along the Canal's Gaillard Cut uncovered some significant fossils from the Miocene epoch before the Panamanian Isthmus became dry land. These fossils, called the Cucaracha Fauna, are similar to fossils found throughout North America, and include remains of extinct horses and rhinos as well as of strange creatures like protoceratids (deerlike mammals with bizarre horns) and oreodonts. An abundance of turtle and crocodile bones and coprolites (fossil feces) suggests that the area where these mammals lived was a swamp (possibly near what was then the southernmost extension of land). Most of the mammal bones found were fragments of young animals: they may have been crocodiles' prey. The fossils are now in the collection of the Smithsonian Institution in Washington, D.C.

Despite its turbulent past, the Canal today is a rather quiet, even sylvan place. The locks and dams must have been awesome in 1914, but today they seem small and even quaint compared to the truly massive dams and strip mines of the late twentieth century. The narrow waterway has become an avenue between the oceans for seabirds such as pelicans and cormorants as well as ocean liners.

Several tour companies offer boat day trips from Balboa up the Canal as far as the Gaillard Cut and back. Eco Tours Panama, 7 Ricardo Arias, No. 6a, P.O. Box 465 (phone: 63-3077, 63-3087; fax: 63-3089). Chadwick's, located in the YMCA building in Balboa (English spoken; phone: 52-28-6329).

Soberanía National Park

Soberanía is the easiest Canal wildland to reach from Panama City—surprisingly easy, considering how lightly it is visited. Created in 1980, the park is mostly lowland rain forest, with 5 monkey species, jaguars, tapirs, and 349 known bird species, 79 reptile species, and 57 amphibian species. The approximately 1,300 tree species include the strange *"reseco"* (*Tachigalla versicolor*), an acacialike member of the pea family which produces fruit once in its 40- to 50-year lifespan, and then dies. The large, winged seeds find good growing conditions under the gap in the forest canopy caused by the death of the parent tree. The park headquarters is in Gamboa, Casa 0271, phone: 56-6370.

The buses that leave the Plaza Cinco de Mayo Station every hour after 5 A.M. are the cheapest access to the park. (The station is in a U.S. Embassy–declared high crime zone, so be careful of bags and wallets.) The fare to the end of the line at Gamboa is $.65, and you can get out at several park access spots along the way. Buses are crowded and noisy, but reliable and friendly. Most of the people taking the buses are of West Indian origin, whose ancestors came to build the Canal 90 years ago, and who still live and work along it. The bus also offers access to Canal attractions such as Miraflores Locks, which are open to the public free from every day from 9 to 5. You get off at the Miraflores Locks sign and walk for about fifteen minutes to the locks. Another way of getting to the park that may be possible someday is the trans-isthmus railroad, which has a station at Gamboa. The railroad was closed in 1989, but the Panamanian government has plans to reopen it when funding becomes available. It will make a first-class tourist attraction for those wanting a quick and inexpensive look at Soberanía.

The first park-related stop along the Gamboa Highway is Summit Gardens and Zoo, a very popular attraction for Panamanians as well as foreign tourists. It is located just past the Canal-side town of Paraíso, and is open every day from 8 to 6, admission $.25. The park has an information center here, although the gardens are administered by the Panama City Municipality. The gardens were first established in 1923 as a collection of tropical plants from around the world as well as Panama. Many of these plants are labeled along the extensive paths. The small zoo at the entrance has healthy specimens of many of the more spectacular creatures, some of which are hard to see in the wild. One such is the paca (a large rodent, also called "*conejo pintado*"—painted rabbit—and "*tepiscuintle*"), which is nocturnal in the wild, but in this zoo came hopping across its cage toward us, then stopped and urinated smartly in our direction. Soberanía's forest starts right behind the gardens (although there are no trails into it from there), so they are a good place to get a "feel" for the park.

Three kilometers past Summit Gardens is the entrance to the Sendero el Charco, the "pond trail." This is a short, easy trail for which self-guiding brochures may be available at INRENARE and ANCON offices. (The trail was closed for rebuilding when I was there in 1993.)

The most famous access to Soberanía is the Pipeline Road, a legendary birding location for decades. This makes a wonderful all-day hike, if you get an early start. Take the Gamboa bus to the end of the line at downtown Gamboa (a gas station beside the Canal) then follow the Canal-side gravel road for several hundred yards until you see a Soberanía National Park sign. There the Pipeline Road leads off to the right, and continues across the park to dead-end at Lake Gatún, a distance of about 17 kilometers. It would be conceivable to walk it back and forth in a day, but difficult, partly because there are so many things to see along the way, including the possibility of king vultures and other wilderness specialties. You'll probably see coatis and hear howler monkeys, parrots, tinamous, and oropendulas. The quiet streams that cross the road are like aquarium displays if you take a little time to watch them. They contain wild representatives of some of the popular tropical fish groups—suckermouth catfish, blue acara, and "earth-eater" cichlids, tetras, and live-bearers.

You may be approached by Canal guards or park rangers checking for vandalism or poaching. The guards who approached me
were quite friendly once they knew I was a tourist, and one spoke
English. The sign at the entrance to Pipeline Road said permission
from INRENARE was required to use the road, but I didn't have
it. Make sure you return to Gamboa in time to get a late afternoon
or early evening bus back to Panama City. Night buses are infre-
quent, and Gamboa facilities are sparse. Gamboa seems quite safe:
there's a police station there.

A more strenuous trail is El Camino de Cruces, which is the colonial trail over which Morgan reached Panama City in 1671. Some
of the old cobbles are still there, and there are plans for historical
restoration. The trail starts at the road to Lake Alajuela, which
forks off from the Gamboa Road just south of Summit Gardens.
Old cannons mark the trailhead. The trail leads through hilly,
deeply forested country to dead-end at the Chagres River above
Gamboa. Trail maintenance may be limited.

Barro Colorado Nature Monument

Barro Colorado Island was created by the flooding of the Chagres
River to form Lake Gatún, which is the waterway through which
ships pass from the Gatún Locks on the Caribbean side of the Canal
to the Pedro Miguel Locks on the Pacific side. It took the lake from
1910 to 1914 to fill. The 1,564-hectare island, 171 meters above sea
level at its highest point, is the longest-protected natural area in
tropical America, having been set aside for biological research by
the Canal Zone government in 1923. Ornithologist Frank M.
Chapman, who lived on the island in the 1920s and '30s and wrote
about it in *My Tropical Air Castle,* found that jaguars were the only
large animals that seemed to have been eliminated from the island
by flooding, since he was able to photograph puma, tapir, and
white-lipped peccaries. Since then, however, the above species and
many others disappeared from the island, which is too small to
maintain genetically viable populations of wide-ranging or scarce
species.

The Smithsonian assumed responsibility for Barro Colorado in
1946, and has conducted ongoing research projects on the effects
of climate on the forest, and on the dynamics of forest growth and

reproduction. Researchers have identified and mapped some 238,000 woody plants representing 304 species. A self-guided nature trail looping around the island's center tells much of what has been learned (trail booklets were out of print in 1993, but another edition was planned). Because it has been long protected, Barro Colorado has large, relatively confiding populations of monkeys as well as agoutis, coatis, collared peccaries, tinamous, and crested guans. Your chances of seeing wildlife are excellent. But watch the ground too: trails are steep and slippery. Ticks are abundant, so long pants and shirts are recommended.

In 1977, a special agreement annexed to the Torrijos-Carter treaties declared Barro Colorado and the peninsulas and small islands adjacent to it across Lake Gatún as a 5,400-hectare Barro Colorado Nature Monument under STRI's custodianship. According to this designation, the nature monument is to be strictly preserved for scientific purposes.

Access to Barro Colorado Island and environs is limited to protect the scientific research there, so you'll need to make arrangements in advance to visit. Ecotour agencies usually include a Barro Colorado visit as part of Panama trips. You can make your own arrangements to visit the island for a day through the Visitor Services Office, Smithsonian headquarters at Tupper Center, Roosevelt Ave. Ancón (phone: 27-6022 and 27-6014; fax: 62-5942). Mail: P.O. Box 2072, Balboa, Republic of Panama. Day tours run on Tuesdays for individuals or groups of up to five people and on Saturdays for groups of fifteen or more. Tours may be booked up for months in advance, so you should try to make a reservation by mail or phone, but if you show up at the office you may be able to arrange a trip. A $12-per-person fee covers boat transportation to the island and lunch at the station cafeteria. You need to get to Gamboa to catch the boat by 7:25 A.M.: a 6 or 6:15 A.M. bus from the station at Plaza Cinco de Mayo will get you there. The return boat leaves the island at 3:20 P.M. and gets to Gamboa at 4:30.

Chagres National Park

Founded in 1984 to protect the watershed of the Chagres River above the reservoir at Lake Alajuela (formerly Madden Lake), Chagres is the least explored of the Canal wildlands. It contains areas of cloud forest as well as lowland forest. The park is accessible by the Trans-isthmus Road from Panama City to Colón and by the Pan American Highway. On the Trans-isthmus Road, there is an interpretive trail at the Lake Alajuela Dam. On the Pan American Highway, a road to park headquarters at Cerro Azul forks off about 6.8 kilometers from where the highway east from Panama City begins at the Riande Airport Hotel on the way to Tocumen Airport. A two-wheel-drive car will be sufficient for the roughly 12-kilometer road to Cerro Azul, except during heavy rains. There is no bus service. There is a camping area and nature trail at Cerro Azul.

Portobelo

There is also a national park surrounding the ruins of the old city of Portobelo, Panama's main Caribbean port until the English destroyed it in 1739. The ruins, a World Heritage Site, are accessible by hourly buses from Colón, the town on the Canal's Caribbean side. They run from 6:30 A.M. to 6 P.M. You can also get there from Panama City by taking a Colón bus (the station is at the corner of the Avenida Central and Calle 26: buses leave every 20 minutes) and getting off at Sabanitas, where you can catch the bus from Colón to Portobelo. The advantage of doing this is that you don't have to go to Colón, which has a *very* bad reputation for street crime, and not much in the way of attractions. (By all accounts, tourists walking the streets of Colón are not only liable to get mugged, but *likely* to get mugged.) There are no overnight accommodations at the little town among the Portobelo ruins, but there are at Isla Grande, about a half-hour's walk and a short boat ride past Portobelo. Isla Grande also has facilities for snorkeling, scuba diving, and fishing.

Western Panama

Western Panama is in a sense the "real" Panama, the country that existed before the Canal and that continues to exist in small towns and farms. Much of the natural landscape has been changed by the centuries of human occupation, before and after Columbus. Heavily eroded grassland and savanna has replaced most of the dry

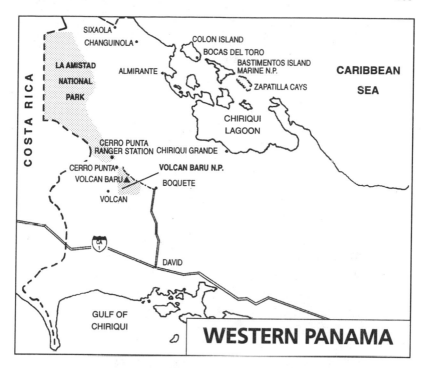

deciduous forest on the Pacific side of the mountains, and coffee
plantations extend far up mountainsides. Large mangrove forests
still cover the estuaries of both coasts, however, and the Caribbean
side is still heavily forested.

Protected wildlands are concentrated in Chiriquí and Bocas del
Toro provinces in the far west. They provide a good sampling of
southern Central America's diverse habitats, from the mangroves
and savannas around Chiriquí's capital of David, to the overwhelmingly lush and damp cloud forest of La Amistad National
Park and the chilly elfin forest of Volcán Barú, to Boca del Toro's
maze of swampy, steamy islands and coral reefs.

Chiriquí

Access to Chiriquí is easy by bus or car to David along the Pan
American Highway. The trip takes about 8 hours from Panama
City. Buses depart from the Interior Bus Station on the Avenida Bal-

boa hourly from 7 A.M. to 1 P.M. and every hour and a half until the last bus at 7 P.M. Fare is $10.60. An express bus costing $15 leaves at midnight. You can also fly to David on Aeroperlas (phone: 63-5363, flights daily, $50 one-way) or Alas Chiricanas (phone: 64-6448, flights daily, $50 one-way). All domestic flights leave from Paitilla Airport in Panama City. David's airport is about 5 kilometers outside of town, and there is no bus service. Taxi fare is $2.00. You can arrange with a travel agent to have a rental car waiting for you at the airport. I rented a reliable one from Budget (phone: 75-5597, 75-1667). If you rent a car, don't leave valuables in it when you leave it to hike or birdwatch.

David is a pleasantly small and easygoing town after the gigantism of Panama City. There is an INRENARE office near where the road from the airport comes into town which has information about parks, if you speak Spanish. There's also an IPAT tourist information office (phone: 75-4120) open weekdays above the FinoFino Department Store in the central plaza.

Hotels

Hotel Nacional, Calle Central, Apartado 37-B, David (phone: 75-2221). A pleasant, older hotel in downtown David, rooms with private bath, phone and air-conditioning. Restaurant, bar, casino. Single $15, double $20. (It was full when we were there.) Hotel Fiesta, Pan American Highway, Apartado 62, David (phone: 75-5454, 75-5456). A motel-style place on the highway just outside David, rooms with private bath, phone, air-conditioning. Restaurant, swimming pool—spacious. Double $34. Hotel Saval, Calle D Norte between Avenida Cinquenenario and Avenida 1 Este (phone: 75-3453). Rooms with private bath, small restaurant, patio. Single $8 with fan, $10 with air-conditioning.

Volcán Barú National Park

This is one of Panama's first parks, founded in 1976, largely because of lobbying by local people. The 3,475-meter volcano for which the 14,000-hectare park is named is inactive, but the presence of hot springs around it suggests it's not "extinct." There are a number of craters. Old-growth cloud forest survives above about

2,100 meters in the park, and the volcano's upper slopes are covered with a mixture of elfin forest and scrubby páramo, a habitat similar to that of the Andes and other South American mountains. Some unusual birds live in this semialpine habitat, including the volcano junco, large-footed finch, and long-tailed silky flycatcher, a yellow and gray relative of the phainopepla of North American deserts. The volcano's lower slopes have been largely converted to coffee plantations or other agriculture, but it's very scenic, and many birds, including quetzals, survive in patches of forest. I found three-wattled bellbirds particularly evident in such patches in 1993, although it took me a while to recognize their calls because they sounded less bell-like than ones I'd heard in Costa Rica.

This is the homeland of the Guaymí people, and many archaeological sites exist. Charred remains of corn intermediate between types known from Mexico and Colombia have been found, along with giant, probably ceremonial, corn-grinding stones or "*metates*" carved in the shape of human figures carrying trophy heads. Many Guaymí still live here, recognizable by the women's handsewn dresses, with bright primary colors and interesting abstract patterns. The Guaymí have been trying to get a semiautonomous tribal reserve or "*comarca*" established, so far without success.

The easiest access to Volcán Barú is from the town of Boquete east of the park. Boquete is an hour's drive from David on a good paved road. Buses leave David every half hour from 6:15 A.M. to 9 P.M. from a station at Avenida Cincuentenario north of the central plaza. Boquete is at just over 1,000 meters in altitude, and has a cool, windy climate. It's a favored vacation spot, so there are a number of good hotels and restaurants. The Hotel Panamonte north of the center of town is a mecca for birders. Its owners, the Collins family, who farm land in the vicinity, can help show you where to see quetzals. (Mail: Entrega General, Boquete, Chiriquí; phone: 70-1327; fax: 70-1324.) The Panamonte is $40 per night for two, with excellent food and beautiful grounds, very quiet and comfortable. Greta Garbo stayed there. The Hotel Fundadores is similar (phone: 70-1298). There are a number of less expensive hotels, including the Pensión Marielos at Avenida A Este and Calle 6 Sur, which has rooms with bath at $10–15 and without at $6–10 (phone: 70-1380). The Coffee Bean Restaurant (phone: 70-1624) at the entrance to town has good food, and also runs tours of the area, including trips to hot springs as well as 4wd excursions into the park.

A jeep road runs from Boquete to the summit of Volcán Barú. The road is paved at first, turning west from the main Boquete road just past the center of town. The paved road continues for about 7.5 kilometers, then forks. Take the left fork, which soon turns into a steep, rough gravel track continuing 14 kilometers to the summit. Given the distance and altitude, this is not an easy day hike. It's possible to camp on the volcano (with permission from INRENARE, see office address above), but high winds, rain, and cold temperatures require that you be well equipped. The trail can be climbed with 4wd, should you want to rent one or hire somebody in Boquete to take you up. Another possibility is to rent horses to ride up the volcano or carry camping gear.

Volcán Barú is also accessible from the west via the towns of Volcán and Cerro Punta, which are reached by driving 25 kilometers west of David on the Pan American Highway to the town of Concepción, then turning north. Buses to both leave from David (same station as Boquete) every half hour from 7 A.M. to 6 P.M. Located in a narrow valley within sight of the peak, Volcán reminded me of a western town in North America because of the way the houses and businesses were strung out along the main road instead of clustered defensively at the center, as with most Latin American towns. The Hotel Dos Ríos just north of town has quiet grounds with a little stream running through and many birds. A black phoebe was nesting in the eaves when we were there. It's $30 a night for two, with a passable restaurant (phone: 71-4271). The Motel California in town has cabins for two for $20 (phone: 71-4272). In Cerro Punta, the Hotel Cerro Punta is medium-priced, but is often full-up with tour groups (phone: 71-2020). Pension Primavera is another hotel nearby. A large luxury resort is located at Bambito between Volcán and Cerro Punta. Bambito Hotel, Volcán, c/o Apdo. 8-055 (phone: 71-4265). Pools, sauna, tennis, fishing, whitewater rafting, horseback riding; takes American Express, MasterCard, Visa. Single $75, double $85.

To reach the park, continue through Cerro Punta to where the road passes a dairy farm, then descends, crosses a small bridge and forks in three directions. Stay on the paved road for about 3.5 kilometers: the park begins where the paving stops. According to Robert Ridgely and John Gwynne's *A Guide to the Birds of Panama,* a house near the park border belongs to the Fernández family, one of whom may be available for hire as a guide. Ridgely and Gwynne list quetzals, black guans, Andean pygmy owls, prong-billed barbets, and silvery throated jays among the local birds. You could ask the Fernández family about a trail that runs from the vicinity over the east side of the volcano and then down the canyon of the Río Caldera to Boquete. The canyon is impressive, with high cliffs of fluted basalt. It is supposed to be a day's walk, but the trail evidently is not well marked. Hiring a guide to take you would probably be worth it. The trail is used by tour groups, so it *is* there.

La Amistad National Park

This 207,000-hectare park was founded in 1988 as the counterpart of Costa Rica's La Amistad N.P.—"*amistad*" means "friendship." Together the parks form what may be Central America's most important wildland, for economic as well as ecological reasons. The watershed the parks protect is vital to hydroelectric energy, which is about the only local energy source Central America has, except geothermal, wind, and solar. Electricity produced from these watersheds is already used on an interconnected grid stretching to Honduras. The parks are also the biggest area of intact highland forest in Central America, and contain many life zones, from lowland rain forest to subalpine wet páramo, and a full range of native species, including many endemics. The mountains are mainly igneous granites and basalts uplifted in the past few million years, but also contain sedimentary rocks from the Eocene epoch, before the land had formed. The presence of many endemic birds and other animals in the La Amistad highlands indicates that the area may have been an island at some time during Central America's formation.

The Panamanian park includes a large area of Bocas del Toro province as well as a small area of Chiriquí. The park is mostly primary wilderness, although surrounding areas are fairly intensively farmed by Guaymís and other people. An indigenous population of Teribes lives along the Teribe River in the northern part of the park.

When you go there, it's easy to understand why La Amistad has remained wild. It is very steep, and although the climate is fairly cool at the park's elevation (largely above 2,000 meters), the vegetation is very much a "green wall"—a dripping, spongy mass of mosses, club mosses, tree ferns, and small palms presided over by oaks, laurels, and magnolias so loaded with epiphytic orchids and bromeliads that you have trouble seeing their leaves and branches. Moving off-trail is more like swimming than walking, and trails disappear within months if not constantly maintained. It is usually raining or foggy.

A good place to see this botanical extravaganza is the Cerro Punta guard station at the edge of the park just above Cerro Punta. Before you get to town, a gravel road heads off to the left past onion fields and a bodega, then crosses a bridge and climbs up toward the foot of a canyon. A church stands at the foot of the canyon, and the road gets rougher and dips into another stream course. You can leave your car at the church, and walk about an hour up the canyon to the park border. The people who live along the road are growing cabbages and potatoes on the almost vertical slopes of the canyon. Cultivation ends abruptly at the park, where in 1993 10-foot-tall alders were growing on what had been a dairy farm owned by one of Noriega's colonels in 1989. After the colonel left hastily during the invasion, the local people came and cleaned out the rather luxurious farm, leaving nothing but the walls. INRENARE and ANCON then rebuilt some of it to serve as a park station. The headquarters building is a comfortable and roomy house. You may be able to arrange with INRENARE in David to stay overnight. You'll need to bring your own food. Short trails, partly built by tour group volunteers, lead into the forest, but the plants constantly try to overgrow them. Swallows and various unknown amphibians breed in the abandoned cow barns. Park personnel are not always in attendance: it would be best to check with the David office before visiting the station. Park personnel told us the area has whitetail deer, puma, rabbits, coati, and opossums and some tapirs, but is too high for monkeys or jaguars.

A good paved road runs west from Volcán along the southern border of the park to the Costa Rican frontier at Río Sereno. It's a lovely road, through rolling pastures and woods, very quiet and bucolic. There's good birding along the Chiriquí and Colorado rivers. The area is lightly populated, with only a few scattered hamlets. We stopped at a little food stand in one for a típico lunch of soup and empanadas. Another park station is located at Cotito along this road, but has no visitor facilities. There is also a station in the Río Teribe area at the north end of the park, but you'd need a boat and guide to get there. Inquire at the main INRENARE office in Paraíso.

Bocas del Toro

This still mainly forested province of coastal mountains and islands has been compared to the Galápagos as a theater of evolution. The large islands of Escudo de Veraguas, Colón, Popa, and Bastimentos were part of the mainland until about ten thousand years ago, when glacial melting caused a rise in sea level. When the rising sea isolated them, the island organisms began to change, and since the process began so recently, biologists see an enormous potential for ongoing evolutionary studies here. One species, a tiny frog named *Dendrobates pumilio,* has evolved particularly dramatically. Related to the frogs South American Indians use to make poison darts (their skins contain toxic alkaloids), the species lives in undergrowth and makes surprisingly loud, cricketlike calls. It's common in Costa Rica, where it is dark red with blue-black legs. In Bocas del Toro, the species is every color of the spectrum, from brilliant orange-red to yellow to green to powder blue, and there's also a black and white variety.

Deforestation in the province has been much slower than in central Panama or Darién, and there's hope that its forest resources will be used in a more sustainable manner than elsewhere. Its swamp forests of "orey" trees are believed to be the most productive in the country, and the year-round rains and warm temperatures provide good growing conditions. The coast is also an important nesting and feeding area for sea turtles.

Access to the province is still quite limited. A paved road runs from the Pan American Highway east of David to the town of Chiriquí Grande on Chiriquí Lagoon. Buses leave from David to make the three-hour trip every hour and a half from 6:30 A.M. It's quite scenic. Chiriquí Grande is an industrial town without great tourist appeal (although the lagoon was the site of Columbus's attempt to found a colony), but it has hotels and restaurants. From there you can get a boat to the town of Bocas del Toro on Isla Colón. A daily ferry leaves at 1:30 P.M. (although service may be reduced at times), or you can rent a motorboat for the one-and-a-half-hour trip to the island. There's also a road from Costa Rica to the port of Almirante in northern Bocas del Toro. Minibuses run from the border to Almirante via the town of Changuinola. The same ferry that serves Bocas del Toro town from Chiriquí Grande originates from Almirante daily at 8 A.M. Bocas del Toro has an airport, with daily flights from David and Panama City. Aeroperlas flies from David for about $20 and from Panama City for about $50. Alas Chiricanas has more expensive flights. You also can buy a continuing ticket from Panama City to David to Bocas and back to Panama City.

Bocas del Toro town is a pleasant place, a little down-at-the-heels (an earthquake in 1991 caused some destruction), but relaxing. Most of the townspeople are West Indians bilingual in English (although you'll hear mostly Spanish spoken). Reefs and beaches lie within sight of town (although the best swimming and snorkeling are at Isla Bastimentos) and the island itself, accessible by a road leading north from town, is very scenic and interesting. The bedrock is limestone, so the landscape has been eroded into many little swampy valleys. A green, polka-dotted version of the *Dendrobates pumilio* froglet is common: you can find them by zeroing in on their cricketlike calls in the underbrush. At the island's center is a small but fascinating cave ("La Gruta") where a stream has cut through a limestone hill. A large bat colony including several species inhabits the cave. (The bats are sensitive about disturbance, and the cave is a religious site for island people, so be circumspect about walking through it. It's also very dark and slippery, and those with respiratory problems shouldn't stay long because there are probably spores of the fungal disease histoplasmosis in the air.) You can get to the cave by walking (about two hours north from town, past the beach and an oil tank farm, then turn left on the trans-island road) or by hiring one of the island's cabs. There's very little traffic, so waiting to hitchhike may be frustrating.

The Botel Tomás (phone: 78-9248, 78-9309; mail: Apartado #5, Bocas del Toro, Republic of Panama) has comfortable rooms and a spacious veranda looking out on reefs and islands. Rooms were about $17 a night for two in 1993. They don't have regular food service, but there's a kitchen, and groups hire cooks from town, and even if you're alone you may be able to buy into this. We ate very well there, conch and fish. Big fishing bats swooped in the veranda and flew around the ceiling fans at night. In the hotel lobby was a terrarium containing blue, green, red, and yellow versions of *D. pumilio*. The Pensión Peck a few doors down has very inexpensive rooms with balconies, about $3 a night. The Bahía Hotel at the other end of town has a restaurant (phone: 78-9211). There's also a restaurant with good Panamanian food a block down the main street from Botel Tomás, and a Chinese restaurant with good chow mein on the next street over.

Isla Bastimentos Marine National Park

This 13,226-hectare park, established in 1988, encompasses parts of Isla Bastimentos (which is just southeast of Isla Colón) as well as keys and reefs surrounding it. Two small islands west of Bastimentos, the Zapatillas keys, are beautiful spots for excursions, shaded with coconut, sangrillo, and cerillo trees, with sparkling beaches and reefs just offshore. Beaches provide nesting space for green, leatherback, and hawksbill turtles, although there are no big *"arribadas"* (arrivals, landings). Many local people rely on sea turtles as a regular source of meat, and sometimes kill them before they lay eggs, so the turtle population is stressed. Hunting pressure also has extirpated manatees and macaws from the area, but crocodiles, caimans, and other wildlife remain common. Different parts

of Isla Bastimentos have different colored *D. pumilio* froglets, and
there are places where you can see half a dozen different color
phases together.

INRENARE has a headquarters in Bocas del Toro halfway
across town from Botel Tomás (phone: 78-9244, 78-8967). AN-
CON also has a station in town, next door to Botel Tomás. Both
can provide information on the park, and possibly suggest ways to
hire a boat to take you out. (The trip takes about 45 minutes.) There
is a ranger station on Zapatilla Key 2, but its use is restricted to
park personnel. There are plans to build a visitor center on one of
the keys.

The Kuna Yala Comarca

The Kuna people probably inhabited Darién when the Spanish arrived. They still have villages in northern Darién. The Kuna say
they came from Cerro Takarkuna, the highest point in Darién. In
the mid nineteenth century, for various reasons, perhaps disease or
conflicts with invading Emberá and Wounnan, many Kuna communities relocated to the San Blas Archipelago off the Darién coast.
There they have succeeded in maintaining considerable cultural
and political integrity. In 1925, they revolted against government
acculturation programs, Catholic missionaries, and colonists, a
successful revolt which led to a 1930 treaty affirming their integrity.
In 1938, the region gained formal status as a *"Comarca,"* a semiautonomous political entity with a general congress that sends representatives to the Panamanian legislature. The Comarca includes
a coastal strip running from the Colombian border to Colón Province east of Portobelo.

Kunas are easily recognizable, in Panama City as well as San
Blas, by the women's colorful dress, decorated with the hand-
stitched appliqué *"molas"* which have become a Panamanian tourist trademark. Men wear Western dress. Tourism is important to
their economy, as are fishing, farm patches on the mainland, coconut plantations on the islands, and cash transfers from Kunas
working in the outside world.

The Kuna are no more willing to be overrun by tourists than they
were by Spaniards or Panamanian colonists, so you can't just go

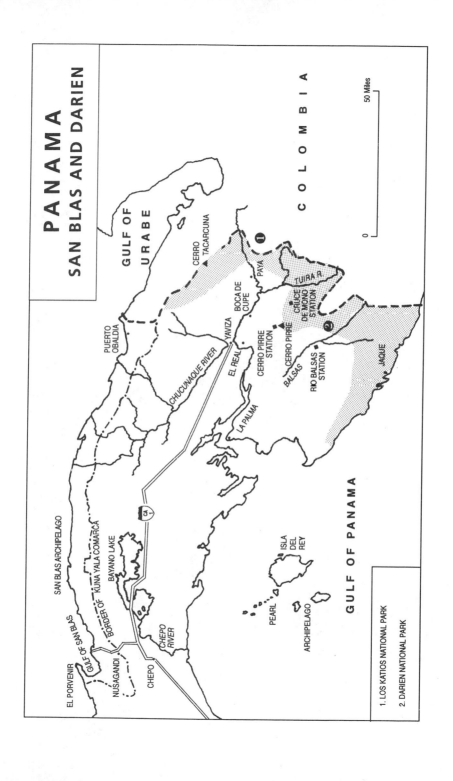

PANAMA
SAN BLAS AND DARIEN

GULF OF URABE

COLOMBIA

50 Miles

0

CERRO TACARCUNA

PAYA

BOCA DE CUPE

TUIRA R.

CRUCE DE MONO STATION

CERRO PIRRE STATION

CERRO PIRRE

BALSAS

RIO BALSAS STATION

JAQUE

YAVIZA

EL REAL

CHUCUNAQUE RIVER

PUERTO OBALDIA

LA PALMA

SAN BLAS ARCHIPELAGO

EL PORVENIR

GULF OF SAN BLAS

BORDER OF KUNA YALA COMARCA

NUSAGANDI

CHEPO

CHEPO RIVER

BAYANO LAKE

ISLA DEL REY

PEARL ARCHIPELAGO

GULF OF PANAMA

1. LOS KATIOS NATIONAL PARK

2. DARIEN NATIONAL PARK

Young Kuna woman, San Blas Islands, Panama. Photo by Kevin Schafer.

wandering about the Comarca. There's even a set price per photo of Kunas: $.25. Although occasional boats go to the islands, the main way to get there is by air from Paitilla Airport in Panama City. Since the islands are very popular (snorkeling, diving, and swimming are excellent) and hotel space is limited, it would be advisable to have a travel agent book your trip in advance. You could do this in the U.S. or in Panama City. Return airfare is about $60. There are several hotels, on separate islands. The Hotel San Blas on Nalunega Island is the simplest, and costs about $25 a day, including three meals and a motor boat and guide to take you about the islands for the day (phone: 62-1606 from Panama City). The Hotel Anai (also spelled Hanay) on WichubHuala Island costs about twice as much, but provides a swimming pool and private baths as well as meals and boat service (phone: 20-6596, 20-0746). Both hotels are accessible from the main airport at Porvenir. The Hotel Las Palmeras is located farther down the coast toward Colombia on Ailigandi Island (phone: 22-3096). The San Blas and Anai hotels also conduct tours for visitors who fly in and out the same day: they cost about half of overnight stays, and include breakfast, lunch, and boat with guide.

Nusagandi

The Kuna have established a 40,000-hectare forest park on the western Comarca mainland to buffer the effects of a road from the Pan American Highway to Cartí on the coast. A Kuna-staffed conservation organization, PEMASKY, administers the project. The park ranges from sea level to 650-meter elevation, and contains several forest life zones, 341 bird species, 61 mammal species, 27 amphibian species, and 19 freshwater fish species. Parrots ("*guaca*" in the Kuna language) and toucans ("*wer wer*" in Kuna) are common. Collared peccary ("*wedar*"), agouti ("*usu*"), and crested guan ("*guama*") can be seen.

The park is accessible to travelers through the headquarters at Nusagandi, which has dormitories, a kitchen and dining room, bathrooms, and labs. A trail system extends into the forest, and guide service is available. Lodging is $15 (not counting suggested tips), and you must bring your own food and drink. It's necessary

to make arrangements in advance to stay at Nusagandi. PE-
MASKY can be contacted by phoning 82-3226 and asking for
Guillermo Archibold (or Gaspar Mendoza at 28-3213), or through
the STRI office at Tupper Center in Ancón (phone: 27-6021). Nusagandi is located on the El Llano–Cartí Road, which branches off
from the Pan American Highway just before the town of El Llano
55 kilometers east of Panama City. You can take a Darién bus at
the Interior Station on Avenida Balboa in Panama City (three
morning departures) and get off at the crossroads, from which it is
a 5- to 6-hour uphill walk to the headquarters. A 4wd vehicle may
be required for the El Llano–Cartí Road in the wet season. If you
continue on the road to Cartí on the coast you may be able to hire
a motorboat to take you to one of the islands, but you will need
permission from Kuna elders to visit any place other than the tourism centers.

Darién

Despite heavy deforestation and colonization in recent decades,
Panama's easternmost province of Darién remains one of Latin
America's greatest wildlands. Darién National Park along the Colombian border is the second largest protected area in Central
America, including 579,000 hectares (1.5 million acres) of mostly
primary forest. This forest is fully as impressive as any that can be
seen in Venezuela or Brazil, with 2-meter-diameter almendro, es-
pavel, and rosa de monte trees forming a subcanopy under the soaring branches of emergent barrigones and cuipos. Established in
1980, Darién has been designated a World Heritage Site and a Biosphere Reserve by UNESCO. Protected forest continues on part of
the Colombian side of the border in Los Katios National Park.

Darién is a line of demarcation for many South American species. Here the black spider monkey of Colombia and Venezuela replaces the red spider monkey of Mexico to central Panama, and the
golden-headed quetzal of the Andes replaces the resplendent quetzal of the Central American cordilleras (the South American species
lacks the Central American's spectacularly long tail plumes). Darién is the only part of Central America where capybaras, giant
South American rodents which resemble miniature hairy hippo-

potamuses, may be seen along rivers. Darién is the only Central American region where four macaw species (the blue-and-yellow, red-and-green, great green, and chestnut-fronted) may be encountered in the same forest.

Darién also has islands of northern organisms in its sea of southern ones. On scattered highlands such as 1,875-meter Cerro Takarkuna and 1,500-meter Cerro Pirre live forests of oaks and magnolias resembling those of western Panama and Costa Rica. There is a subtle difference between the Darién and Chiriquí oaks, however. Those of Darién belong to a South American species which is also scattered through Colombia. This species may have originated when a Central American oak species spread into South America, was cut off from Central America, evolved into a new species in isolation, and then spread north again.

As with other intact wilderness, Darién has largely been protected by its inaccessibility. It's still not easy to get there, and you will either have to spend some money or undergo some risks and hardship (perhaps a bit of both) to do so. Of course, it's nowhere near as difficult nowadays as it was for Lieutenant Isaac Strain and his men in 1854. It took them three months to walk from the Caribbean to the Pacific (largely because they made the mistake of trying to follow the Chucunaque River to the coast—the Chucunaque runs *parallel* to the coast for most of its length). For most of the time, they lived on toads, owls, hawks, vultures, and palm nuts; seven of the men died. Still, in 1972, a British Army expedition equipped with two Land Rovers spent three months traveling the 250-mile gap in the Pan American Highway. It took the help of 27 horses, and U.S. Army helicopters, to complete the trip.

The Pan American Highway currently extends to the town of Yaviza on the mouth of the Chucunaque. The road is only paved as far as Chepo, however, and during the rainy season it is impassable past Canglón. Buses leave from the Interior Bus Station (Piquera de la Ave. B) on Avenida Balboa in Panama City mornings at 6:30, 8:30, 10:30, noon, and 2:30. From January to April buses go to Yaviza, a 10-hour trip with a $14 fare. The rest of the year, an 8-hour trip to Canglón costs $11. The road runs mainly through severely deforested areas, and the town of Yaviza at its terminus is not an encouraging place. (When I told a Darién inhabitant I was thinking of staying overnight there, he responded by drawing his forefinger briskly across his throat.) From Yaviza, a boat and trail route runs through the forest to the Colombian border via the villages of Boca de Cupe, Pucuro, and Paya. This route is a major undertaking since it is not well marked and can take a week or more. There are no hotels or restaurants. It is a route for drug smugglers and illegal aliens, and Colombian guerrillas also operate in the region (when I was in Darién in 1993, they kidnapped three North American missionaries). Considering the difficulties (it also costs about as much as flying to Colombia), this is probably not the best way to experience the Darién wilderness. For detailed descriptions of it, see the general area guides listed in the bibliography, or phone Irving Bennett in Panama City, a specialist in Darién trekking (phone: 23-7035, 64-4148).

Darién National Park

INRENARE maintains several ranger stations in Darién National Park which can accommodate visitors. You need to apply for permission at the Dirección Nacional de Areas Protegidas y Vida Silvestre, Apartado 2016, Paraíso, Corregimiento de Ancón (phone: 32-4325). If you write in Spanish, you may be able to make arrangements in advance, but the surest way to arrange access to the park is to go to the office (in the main INRENARE compound at the town of Paraíso along the Gamboa Road) and apply in person. The people are very friendly, and can probably communicate with you in English if you have no Spanish. It probably will take several days to get the necessary approval, but once you do, you will have the INRENARE people on your side. They can help you to arrange transportation and guides. You will need to bring all your own food. At present there's no entry fee to park facilities, but one may be added soon, probably about $25 for nonnationals. Tour agencies also may begin trips to Darién N.P. soon.

The easiest way to get to the park boundary (and perhaps the cheapest in the long run as well) is to fly from Panama City to the friendly and safe town of El Real, which is about an hour's travel by river from Yaviza. Parsa has thrice-weekly flights to El Real (and

Yaviza) for $67 return, leaving from Paitilla Airport at 6 A.M. (arrive an hour early to be sure of a seat). INRENARE and ANCON both have headquarters in El Real, and there is a hotel (El Nazareno, $7) and restaurant. Travel to ranger stations begins from El Real. Banana boats go to El Real from Panama City on an irregular basis. The trip costs about $12 and takes from a day to three days. Boats leave from the Muelle Fiscal in Panama City, and dock about 5 kilometers downstream from El Real.

Cerro Pirre station (also known as Rancho Frío) is the most often visited. It's located 14 kilometers from El Real, a short distance within the park boundary in the foothills of the Cerro Pirre highlands. Old-growth forest begins right at the park border. The station was originally built to give biologists access to areas with many endemic species (organisms found nowhere else) nearby. In the dry season the path is passable to foot and horse traffic all the way. During the wet season, you may need a boat to get you from El Real to a point in the path about an hour from the station. The path is not well marked, and there's only one village along the way, but INRENARE will provide you with a guide. Horses are also available for rent. Cerro Pirre is in a shady glade with a clear stream running alongside. There are thatch-roofed dormitories for rangers and visitors, and an open-side cooking shed with pots and pans and eating utensils. When I was there, the rangers on duty were an Emberá and a Wounnan. They took me to see the local waterfall and other attractions, and patiently answered questions about flora, fauna, and anthropology. Noisy macaw flocks passed over every morning and evening, and the forest canopy was full of the deep scarlet flowers of rosa de monte. Several trails lead farther into the forest from the station, with clearings for camps at various elevations. STRI botanists have identified over three hundred tree species in the vicinity.

Cruce de Mono station is a day's travel from El Real on the east slope of Cerro Pirre summit. You need to rent a motor launch to take you up the Tuira River for 2–3 hours to the village of Boca de Cupe. (This may cost as much as the plane trip from Panama City.) From there it's at least a 5-hour walk to the station, mostly over flat land, but with some steep hills during the last hour. There are three permanent rangers at the station, usually Kunas or "*darienitas afrohispanos.*" There are trails around the station. The park's research director told me this was her favorite station in Darién N.P.

Balsas station is located southwest of the other stations at the confluence of the Balsas and Tucuti rivers. You need to take a motorboat down the Tuira River from El Real to the mouth of the Balsas, then up the Balsas to the station, a 4-hour trip. The forest along the rivers is largely second growth, and there are many Emberá and "*afrohispano*" communities. The station is the newest one, and the only one with electricity. There are two rangers in attendance.

Another area of the park accessible to visitors is the Cana Valley on the eastern foothills of Cerro Pirre. A gold mine is located there, and visitors must get permission from ANCON, which bought the mine in 1992, as well as from INRENARE. Cana is famed as a birding spot where all four native macaw species, golden-headed quetzals, and many other Darién wilderness species can be seen, but it's not easy to reach. You have to bring your own food and camping gear. There is an airstrip, but you'll need to charter a plane if you want to fly in. There's also a narrow path from Cruce de Mono station which takes at least 5 hours of walking. Tour agencies such as Victor Immanuel run commercial birding trips to Cana.

On Bahía de Piñas near the town of Jaqué on the Pacific coast there is a luxury deep-sea fishing resort, the Tropic Star Lodge, with a package rate of $2,850 a week. The resort has accommodations for about 25 people a day (14 units) during the December–April high season. Package includes charter pickup and return from Panama City and use of a 31-foot twin diesel Bertram boat with captain and mate. Contact c/o Suite 200, 1600 West Colonial Drive, Orlando, FL (phone: 407-843-0124; fax: 407-839-3637). No credit cards. Travel agencies in Panama City also can arrange reservations. The fishing is mainly for marlin. INRENARE has plans to build ranger stations in the area, which is presently not well controlled because of proximity to the Colombian border.

Comarca Emberá Drua

In 1983 the Panamanian government recognized native land rights by establishing the 300,000-hectare Comarca Emberá Drua adjacent to and partly overlapping with Darién National Park. Until the past few decades, the Emberá and Wounnan had a way of life very similar to that of today's remnant Amazonian peoples, wearing loincloths, practicing nomadic slash-and-burn farming, and hunting with blowpipes and poison darts. (In some remote areas, especially in the vast and swampy Colombian Chocó region where they originated, this way of life still prevails.) More recently, they developed a semiagricultural economy centered on raising pigs. Pig farming failed in the 1970s because of disease, however, and the roughly 25,000 Panamanian Emberá and Wounnan have undergone economic problems since. Deforestation and colonization are more of a problem in the Emberá Drua than in the Kuna Yala.

The Emberá are trying to develop tourism as a source of income, and tour agencies offer trips to villages (usually referred to as "Chocó" villages). As yet there are no hotels or resorts, as there are in the Kuna Yala Comarca. Eco-Tours, 7 Ricardo Arias, P.O. Box 465, Panama 9 A, Republic of Panama (phone: 63-3076, 63-3077; fax: 63-3089), offers trips to Darién and other areas.

Selected Sources

General: Travel Guides

Mexico and Central American Handbook. Ben Box, ed. Chicago: Passport Books (new edition every year). The most comprehensive overall travel guide, updated yearly. Information sometimes inaccurate or outdated.

Central America on a Shoestring, 2nd ed. Tom Brosnahan, ed. Berkeley: Lonely Planet Publications, 1994. Mainly for budget travelers. Good maps and well-presented information. Some natural history information is misleading or erroneous.

La Ruta Maya: Guatemala, Belize, and Yucatan. Tom Brosnahan, ed. Berkeley: Lonely Planet Publications, 1994. Much of the same information as in *Central America on a Shoestring.*

Cadogan Guide to Central America. Natascha Norton and Mark Whatmore. Old Saybrook, Conn.: Globe Pequot Press, 1993. Well-written guide for general traveler. Details sometimes skimpy or inaccurate.

General: History and Archaeology

The Rise and Fall of Maya Civilization. J. Eric Thomson. Norman, Okla.: University of Oklahoma Press, 1968. Classic account of Maya archaeology.

The Blood of Kings: Dynasty and Ritual in Maya Art. Linda Schele and Mary Ellen Miller. New York: Braziller, 1986. Recent discoveries and theories in Maya archaeology.

A Forest of Kings: The Untold Story of the Ancient Maya. Linda Schele and David Freidl. New York: William Morrow, 1990. More recent discoveries and theories in Maya archaeology.

History of the Indies. Bartolomé de las Casas; translated and edited by Andree Collard. New York: Harper & Row, 1971. Firsthand account of the Spanish Conquest by a conquistador-turned-advocate of indigenous rights.

History of the New World. Girolamo Benzoni. London: The Hakluyt Society, 1857. Description of Central America in the sixteenth century by an eyewitness.

Travels in the New World. Thomas Gage, edited and with an introduction by J. Eric Thomson. Norman, Okla.: University of Oklahoma Press, 1958. English Catholic priest's confession of rogueries from Guatemala to Costa Rica in the 1600s.

Voyages. William Dampier, edited and with an introduction by John Maesfield. New York: E. P. Dutton, 1906. Memoirs of buccaneering in eighteenth-century Central America by a pirate who was also a gifted writer and naturalist.

Incidents of Travel in Central America, Chiapas, and Yucatan (two vols.). John Lloyd Stephens. New York: Dover, 1969. Classic adventure account of pioneer Maya archaeology discoveries in the 1830s.

General: Nature and Conservation

Central American Jungles. Don Moser. New York: Time-Life Books, 1975. Somewhat outdated but well-written and illustrated survey of Central American wildlands and wildlife.

Book of Bays. William Beebe. New York: Harcourt, Brace, 1942. A naturalist's voyage down the Pacific coast from Mexico to Panama.

The Windward Road: Adventures of a Naturalist on Remote Caribbean Shores. Archie Carr Jr. Gainesville: University of Florida Press, 1979. Reprint of a classic 1956 account of the search for answers to the mysteries of sea turtle life along Central America's east coast.

So Excellent a Fishe (rev. ed.). Archie Carr Jr. Austin: University of Texas Press, 1986. Study of Caribbean sea turtle biology and history.

High Jungles and Low. Archie Carr Jr. Gainesville: University of Florida Press, 1992. Natural history explorations in Honduras and Nicaragua in the 1950s.

A Field Guide to the Mexican Birds. Roger Tory Peterson and Edward L. Chalif. Boston: Houghton Mifflin, 1973. Useful in Guatemala, Belize, and El Salvador, and to some extent in Honduras and Nicaragua. (See below for Costa Rica and Panama bird guides covering southern Central America. See also Peterson's North America guides for information on neotropical migrants.)

Life Histories of Central American Birds. Alexander F. Skutch. Pacific Coast Avifauna nos. 31 and 34. Berkeley, Calif.: Cooper Ornithological Society, 1954 and 1960. Pioneering ornithological studies.

A Neotropical Companion. John C. Kricher. Princeton: Princeton University Press, 1989. Overview of New World tropical ecology, with frequent mention of Central America. Exhaustive bibliography.

In the Rainforest. Catherine Caufield. Chicago: University of Chicago Press, 1984. Global survey of tropical deforestation, contains many references to Central American conservation problems.

Field Guide to the Orchids of Costa Rica and Panama. Robert L. Dressler. Ithaca, N.Y.: Cornell University Press, 1993.

Further Resources, by Country

Guatemala: Travel Guides

Guatemala: A Natural Destination. Richard Mahler. Santa Fe: John Muir Publications, 1993.

Guatemala: History, Nature, and Conservation

Tikal: A Handbook of the Ancient Maya Ruins. William R. Coe. Philadelphia: University of Pennsylvania Press, 1967.

Guatemala: A Country Guide. Tom Barry. Albuquerque, N.M.: Inter-Hemispheric Education Research Center, 1990. Current politics and economics: one of a series (see below).

Bird of Life, Bird of Death. Jonathan E. Maslow. New York: Simon & Schuster, 1986. The quetzal's plight in the context of Guatemala's political and social problems.

Mama Poc: An Ecologist's Account of the Extinction of a Species. Anne LaBastille. New York: W. W. Norton, 1990. Story of the Atitlán giant grebe's extinction during the 1980s.

The Birds of Tikal. Frank B. Smithe. Garden City, N.Y.: Natural History Press, 1966. Well-illustrated field guide to Tikal birds, with natural history notes.

Belize: Travel Guides

Adventuring in Belize. Eric Hoffman. San Francisco: Sierra Club Books, 1994.

Belize: A Natural Destination. Richard Mahler and Steele Wotkyns. Santa Fe: John Muir Publications, 1993.

The New Key to Belize. Stacey Ritz. Berkeley, Calif.: Ulysses Press, 1994.

Adventure Guide to Belize. Harry Pariser. Hunter, N.J., 1991.

Belize: History, Nature, and Conservation

The Maya of Belize: Historical Chapters Since Columbus. J. Eric Thompson. Belize City: Cubola Productions, 1988.

Warlords and Maize Men: A Guide to the Maya Sites of Belize. Byron Foster, ed. Belize City: Cubola Productions, 1989.

The Ancient Maya of Belize: Their Society and Sites. Anabel Ford. Santa Barbara (CORI/MesoAmerican Research Center): University of California, 1994. Brief but authoritative guide to major sites.

Belize: A Country Guide. Tom Barry. Albuquerque, N.M.: Inter-Hemispheric Education Research Center, 1989.

Living Treasure. Ivan T. Sanderson. New York: Viking, 1941. A British zoologist's explorations in the 1930s.

A Belizean Rain Forest: The Community Baboon Sanctuary. Robert H. Horwich and Jonathan Lyon. Gay Mills, Wisc.: Orang-Utan Press, 1990. Account of black howler monkey sanctuary as well as general Belizean natural history.

Jaguar. Alan Rabinowitz. New York: Arbor House, 1986. Adventurous account of jaguar research in the Cockscomb Basin.

One Hundred Birds of Belize. Carolyn M. Miller. Washington, D.C.: International Council for Bird Preservation (in press). Life histories of representative birds.

Honduras: Travel Guides

Honduras and Bay Islands Guide. J. P. Panet, with Leah Hart and Paul Glassman. Washington, D.C.: Open Road Publishing, 1994.

Honduras: History, Nature, and Conservation

Honduras: A Country Guide. Tom Barry. Albuquerque, N.M.: Inter-Hemispheric Education Research Center, 1990.

Explorations and Adventures in Honduras. William V. Wells. New York: Harper and Brothers, 1857. Adventures of a miner and amateur naturalist in the 1850s, mostly in the western highlands and Olancho.

Areas Silvestres en Honduras. Gustavo Adolfo Cruz. Tegucigalpa: Asociación Hondureño de Ecología, 1986. Survey of potential nature reserve sites.

The Bay Islands: Nature and People. Susan K. Jacobson, ed. Bay Islands Conservation Association, 1992. English-Spanish, illustrated guide to Bay Islands history, natural history, and conservation.

Herencia de Nuestro Pasado: La Reserva de la Biosfera Río Plátano. Vince Murphy, ed. Tegucigalpa: Ventanas Tropicales, 1991. Short illustrated collection of articles on Río Plátano Biosphere Reserve, in Spanish.

El Salvador: History, Nature, and Conservation

El Salvador: A Country Guide. Tom Barry. Albuquerque, N.M.: Inter-Hemispheric Education Research Center, 1991.

Biodiversidad y Ecología de la Cuenca de la Barra de Santiago/El Imposible (3 vols.). Francisco Serrano, ed. San Salvador: SalvaNatura, 1993. U.S. AID–financed biodiversity and resource conservation survey.

Nicaragua: Travel Guides

Not Just Another Nicaraguan Travel Guide. Alan Holme, ed. Mango Publications, 1991.

Nicaragua: History, Nature, and Conservation

Nicaragua: A Country Guide. Tom Barry. Albuquerque, N.M.: Inter-Hemispheric Education Research Center, 1989.

The Naturalist in Nicaragua, Thomas Belt. Chicago: University of Chicago Press, 1985. Major early study of tropical ecology and evolution by a British mining engineer in the 1860s and '70s.

Caribbean Edge: The Coming of Modern Times to Isolated People and Wildlife. Bernard Nietschmann. Indianapolis: Bobbs-Merrill, 1979. Entertaining account of the Miskito coast by a geographer who spent many years studying the Miskitos' relationship with their natural environment, especially green turtles.

Costa Rica: Travel Guides

Costa Rican Handbook. Christopher P. Baker. Chico, Calif.: Moon Publications, 1994.

Costa Rica. Rob Rachowiecki. Berkeley, Calif.: Lonely Planet Publications, 1994. Much of the same material as in Lonely Planet's *Central America on a Shoestring.*

The New Key to Costa Rica. Beatrice Blake and Anne Becher. Berkeley, Calif.: Ulysses Press, 1992.

Costa Rica: A Natural Destination. Ree Sheck. Santa Fe: John Muir Publications, 1990.

Adventure Guide to Costa Rica. Harry Pariser. Hunter, N.J., 1991.

Costa Rica: History, Nature, and Conservation

History of the Discovery and Conquest of Costa Rica. Ricardo Fernandez Guardia (Harry Weston Van Dyke, trans.). New York: Crowell, 1913.

Costa Rica: A Country Guide. Tom Barry. Albuquerque, N.M.: Inter-Hemispheric Education Research Center, 1989.

The National Parks of Costa Rica. Mario Boza and Rolando Mendoza. Madrid: INCAFO, 1981. Thorough, profusely illustrated description of national park system.

Costa Rican National Parks. Mario Boza. Madrid: INCAFO, 1986. Abbreviated, Spanish-English park system description.

The Quetzal and the Macaw: The Story of Costa Rica's National Parks. David R. Wallace. San Francisco: Sierra Club Books, 1992. History of park system from 1960s to 1990.

Costa Rican Natural History. Daniel Janzen, ed. Chicago: University of Chicago Press, 1983. Accounts of geology, paleontology, and ecology, and descriptions of more common or significant species.

Sarapiquí Chronicle: A Naturalist in Costa Rica. Allen M. Young. Washington, D.C.: Smithsonian Institution, 1991. Twenty years of ecology studies, mainly of insects, in the rain forests of the La Selva area.

A Guide to the Birds of Costa Rica. F. Gary Stiles and Alexander Skutch. Ithaca, N.Y.: Cornell University Press, 1989.

Life Above the Jungle Floor. Donald Perry. New York: Simon & Schuster, 1986. Popular account of rain forest canopy exploration, including a questionable theory of dinosaur extinctions.

Costa Rica: A Traveler's Literary Companion. Barbara Ras, ed. San Francisco: Whereabouts Press, 1994. A first-rate collection of contemporary Costa Rican writers.

Panama: Travel Guides

Panama Travel Guide. M. Rigole and D. Desjardins. Berkeley, Calif.: Ulysses Press, 1993.

Panama: History, Nature, and Conservation

The Path Between the Seas: The Creation of the Panama Canal. David McCullogh. New York: Simon & Schuster, 1977.

Panama: A Country Guide. Tom Barry. Albuquerque, N.M.: Inter-Hemispheric Education Research Center, 1990.

My Tropical Air Castle: Nature Studies in Panama. Frank M. Chapman. New York: Appleton-Century-Crofts, 1929. Mainly an account of Barro Colorado Island.

A Guide to the Birds of Panama, 2nd ed. Robert S. Ridgely and John A. Gwynne. Princeton: Princeton University Press, 1989.

The Botany and Natural History of Panama. William G. D'Arcy and Mireya D. Correa. St. Louis: Missouri Botanical Garden, 1985. English-

Spanish natural history and ethnology in a large paperback format similar to Janzen's *Costa Rican Natural History*.

The Ecology of a Tropical Forest. E. Leigh. Washington, D.C.: Smithsonian Institution, 1982. About the Smithsonian Tropical Research Institute's work at Barro Colorado.

*A Panama Forest and Shore: Natural History and Amerindian Culture in
Bocas del Toro*. B. L. Gordon. Pacific Grove, Calif.: The Boxwood
Press, 1982.

Some Outdoor Spanish Words and Phrases

las abejas—bees
el aguacate—avocado tree or its fruit
el árbol—tree
el área protegida—protected area
el área silvestre—wilderness area, wild area
el arrecife de coral—coral reef
el ave—bird
las avispas—wasps

la balsa—raft (also balsa tree)
la barra—sandbar, river bar or mouth
la barranca—gorge, ravine
el barro—mud
el bosque—woods, forest
el bosque nuboso—cloud forest
el bosque pluvioso y siempreverde—evergreen rain forest
el bosque seco y deciduo—dry deciduous forest
el búho—owl (or **la lechuza**)

el camarón—shrimp
el campo—field, countryside

el cangrejo—crab
el cañón—gorge
la caoba—mahogany tree
la caverna—cave (or cueva)
la caza—hunting
los cerillos—matches (or fósforos)
el cerro—hill, ridge, peak
la charca—pool (charca de marea—tide pool)
la cima—summit
el colibrí—hummingbird
común—common
la corvina—sea bass
la cuerda—rope, string
la culebra venenosa—poisonous snake

la danta—tapir (or macho de monte)

el encino—oak
la erupción—eruption
escaso(a)—rare
las especies amenazadas (en peligro) de extinción—endangered
   species
la estufa—stove

la fauna silvestre—wildlife
la flor—flower
la fuente termal—hot spring

la garrapata—tick
la gruta—cave
el guapote—large cichlid
el guardabosque—forest ranger
el guardaparque—park ranger

el helecho arborescente—tree fern
el higuerón—fig tree

el incendio—fire (as in forest fire)

el keroseno, canfín—kerosene

la langosta–lobster
el langostino–crayfish, prawn
la lapa–macaw (or la guacamaya)
la leña–firewood
la llanura–plain, flatland
la lluvia–rain
el loro–parrot
la luz–light, flashlight

los manglares–mangroves
el manigordo–ocelot (literally, fat-paw)
la mariposa–butterfly (also warbler)
el matapalo–strangler fig (literally, tree killer)
el mirador–lookout point
la mojarra–medium-sized cichlid
el mono–monkey (or el mico)
la montaña–mountain, jungle
el monte–jungle
el murciélago–bat

la niebla–fog
la nube–cloud

el pájaro–bird
el pántano–wetland, swamp, marsh (or el suampo)
el parque nacional–national park
el pasto–pasture, grass
el pavo silvestre–wild turkey, large wildfowl
el perezoso–tree sloth (literally, the lazy one)
la pesca–fishing
el pescado–cooked fish
el pez–live fish
la piedra–rock
el pino–pine
el pizote–coati
el plátano–plantain tree or its fruit
la playa–beach

la quebrada–stream (also el crique)

la rana—frog
el ratón—mouse
el refugio de fauna silvestre—wildlife refuge
la reserve biológica—biological reserve
la reserva forestal—forest reserve
el riachuelo—small stream
el risco—cliff
el roble—oak

la sabana—savanna
el saco para dormir—sleeping bag (or la bolsa de dormir)
el saíno—collared peccary (also el chancho de monte)
el salto de agua—waterfall
el sapo—toad
la selva—jungle, rain forest
el sendero—trail

el temblor—small earthquake
el tepiscuintle—paca, gibnut (a large rodent) (or el conejo pintado)
el terremoto—big earthquake
los tiburones—sharks
la tienda de campana—tent
la tierra alta—highland
la tierra baja—lowland
la tormenta—storm

el venado—deer
el viento—wind
el volcán—volcano

la yuca—cassava plant or its edible root

el zapote—chicle tree or its edible fruit
el zopilote—vulture (or el gallinazo)

_____

Es ésta la ruta al parque? Is this the way to the park?

Hay un área de acampar en el parque? Is there a camping area in the park?

Es esta área de acampar segura? Is it safe, this camping area?

Hay agua potable en el área de acampar? Is there drinking water in the camping area? **Hay servicios?** Are there toilets? **Hay duchas?** Are there showers? **Hay una estación de guardaparques cerca?** Is there a park ranger station nearby? **Molestan mucho los insectos?** Are the insects bothersome?

Se puede nadar . . . bañarse aquí? Está segura (potable) el agua? Can one swim . . . bathe here? Is the water safe?

Hay hospedajes cerca del parque? Are there places to stay near the park?

Quisiera comprar algunas naranjas . . . bananas (o guineos) . . . tortillas. I'd like to buy some oranges . . . bananas . . . tortillas.

Vende usted refrescos o aguas embotelladas? Do you sell bottled soft drinks or water?

Se puede comprar una comida aquí? Can one buy a meal here?

Dónde comienza el sendero? Where does the trail start?

Estoy buscando el sendero, pero no puedo encontrarlo. I'm looking for the trail, but I can't find it.

Es un sendero difícil? Is it a difficult trail? **Está bien marcado?** Is it well marked?

Buscamos un guía . . . para caminar a través del parque . . . para ver las ruinas . . . para subir . . . bajar el río. We're looking for a guide . . . to walk across the park . . . to look at the ruins . . . to go up . . . down the river.

Quisiera alquilar una canoa (un pipante, una piragua) . . . una lancha para atravesar el lago . . . la laguna. I would like to hire a canoe . . . boat to cross the lake . . . lagoon.

Cuánto cobrará usted para guiarnos? What will you charge to guide us?

Se incluye la comida? el transporte? el alojamiento? Does that include food? transportation? lodging?

Por favor, cuidado! Please, be careful! **Más despacio, por favor.** Slow down, please. **Alto!** Stop!

Estamos perdidos? Are we lost?

Ayúdame! Help me!

Tengo hambre . . . sed . . . miedo. I'm hungry . . . thirsty . . . frightened.

Estoy cansado . . . enfermo . . . sin aliento . . . herido. I'm tired . . . sick . . . out of breath . . . injured.

Tengo frío . . . fiebre. Me siento débil. I am chilled . . . feverish. I feel faint.

Alguien ha robado mi dinero . . . equipo. Someone has stolen my money . . . equipment.

Ella se cayó y se dañó la pierna . . . el pie . . . el tobillo . . . la rodilla . . . la cabeza. She fell and hurt her leg . . . foot . . . ankle . . . knee . . . head. **Está inconsciente.** She's unconscious.

El tiene una picadura de serpiente . . . escorpión . . . araña. He has a snake . . . scorpion . . . spider bite. **Fue un serpiente grande . . . pequeño . . . de tamaño mediano.** It was a big . . . small . . . medium-sized snake. **Fue un cascabel . . . terciopelo . . . coral.** It was a rattlesnake . . . fer-de-lance . . . coral snake. **No pude identificar la culebra.** I couldn't identify the snake.

Muchas gracias por su ayuda. Me siento mejor ahora. Many thanks for your help. I feel better now.

Propiedad privada. Se prohibe entrada sin permiso autorizado. Private property. No entry without authorized permission.

Se prohibe botar basura. No littering.

Perro bravo. Beware of dog.

Disculpe, somos turistas. Se puede caminar en este propiedad para ver el bosque . . . las aves? Excuse me, we're tourists. Could one walk on this property to look at the forest . . . the birds?

Index

Paseo Pantera

T HIS PUBLICATION WAS MADE possible with support from Paseo Pantera, a Regional Natural Resources Management Project conducted by The Wildlife Conservation Society and the Caribbean Conservation Corporation in collaboration with Tropical Research and Development, Inc. Partial funding was provided by the United States Agency for International Development, Guatemala–Central America Programs, Bureau for Latin America and the Caribbean, U.S. Agency for International Development, under the terms of Cooperative Agreement No. 596-0150-A-00-0587-00. The opinions expressed herein are those of the author and do not necessarily reflect the views of the U.S. Agency for International Development.